Strategic Issues
Management

2
edition

Strategic Issues Management

Organizations and Public Policy Challenges

2 edition

Robert L. Heath
University of Houston

Michael J. Palenchar
University of Tennessee

Los Angeles • London • New Delhi • Singapore • Washington DC

For information:

 SAGE Publications, Inc.
2455 Teller Road
Thousand Oaks,
    California 91320
E-mail: order@sagepub.com

SAGE Publications Ltd.
1 Oliver's Yard
55 City Road
London EC1Y 1SP
United Kingdom

SAGE Publications India Pvt. Ltd.
B 1/I 1 Mohan Cooperative
    Industrial Area
Mathura Road, New Delhi 110 044
India

SAGE Publications Asia-Pacific Pte. Ltd.
33 Pekin Street #02-01
Far East Square
Singapore 048763

Printed in the United States of America

Library of Congress Cataloging-in-Publication Data

Heath, Robert L. (Robert Lawrence), 1941–
Strategic issues management : organizations and public policy challenges/Robert L. Heath, Michael J. Palenchar. — 2nd ed.
    p. cm.
Includes bibliographical references and index.
ISBN 978-1-4129-5210-1 (cloth)
ISBN 978-1-4129-5211-8 (pbk.)

    1. Issues management—United States. 2. Industrial management—Social aspects—United States. 3. Strategic planning—United States. 4. Public relations—United States. 5. Industrial policy—United States. I. Palenchar, Michael J. II. Title.

HD59.5.H42 2009
659.2—dc22   2008017669

This book is printed on acid-free paper.

08   09   10   11   12   10   9   8   7   6   5   4   3   2   1

Acquisitions Editor:	Todd R. Armstrong
Editorial Assistant:	Aja Baker
Production Editor:	Astrid Virding
Copy Editor:	Gillian Dickens
Typesetter:	C&M Digitals (P) Ltd
Proofreader:	Dennis W. Webb
Cover Designer:	Candice Harman
Marketing Manager:	Carmel Schrire

Contents

Preface

The topic of strategic issues management (SIM) is one of those hot-button concerns that has attracted a significant amount of attention over the past 4 decades. In the 1970s, SIM received its current name and was touted as an effective and ethical response to corporate critics. This antiwar, highly introspective, and broadly critical time in America demanded that companies become less isolated and more responsive to rapid-fire and hostile charges that touched every part of the U.S. political economy. The 1980s brought a dramatic increase in regulation, followed at times by often inept private-sector efforts to plan and manage in ways based on effective dialogue that fostered mutual interests. Regulation, however badly designed, was implemented because of the rising hostility to the unresponsiveness of industry and the private sector. Some of that continuing indifference is fueling a new push for change that can again convince business that lopsided decision making and unethical marketing will haunt industries, especially those that claim to be barely able to make a profit.

The 1990s saw a cooling. In fact, some even thought that the era of issues had ended. The Reagan years added something to the rhetorical positioning of change, as did the Clinton years. Many organizations returned to business as usual. Large SIM efforts closed. Really smart organizations (government, nonprofit, and business), however, built strategic issues management into their culture. At one level, the issues management movement seemed to suggest that it was no longer a vital player in political and economic discourse and decision making. But closer analysis suggested what many of us had argued for years— SIM is not something pasted onto an organization when needed as a result of a crisis, especially not some short-term public relations or advertising cosmetic for dealing with business critics. It is the essence of smart organizations' organizational cultures.

That trend demonstrates to those of us who have worked in this area for decades that SIM is not really new and not merely a communication function. We have long been interested in the self-promotional efforts of some public relations and even advertising agencies indicating that issues management is a subspecialty. That services-marketing approach would suggest that it is only a communication function and something that can be accomplished, perhaps by a cleverly worded campaign, even though the organization itself makes no corrections or proactive (even reactive) changes in its role in society.

Over the years, issues have often been seen as merely a matter of contest between businesses that seek to avoid constraint in order to maintain an efficient approach to business practices and activists who blindly despise businesses as they might abhor a virulent disease. Experience has demonstrated that such bifurcation dramatically oversimplifies the narrative of change in society. Some businesses and government agencies continue to prefer to be indifferent to the interests and preferences of others. They often believe that steady as she goes is the best motto and that well-turned phrases and deep pockets of political influence are sufficient to protect their planning and management from external influences.

Other organizations realize that conflict can be costly, a real inefficiency to the standard business model. Bad regulation and legislation can harm business and society. So, they are confronted with this communication challenge: Is it best to accommodate critics and seem to change but really not do so? Is it sufficient to issue statements that should assuage critics and reinforce the opinions of current supporters? Is it best to engage in dialogue so that the thoughts and preferences can be known, analyzed, and managed in a more collaborative than dismissive or confrontational way?

As we argue that strategic business planning is one of the pillars of SIM, we advocate that the efforts devoted to understanding the lay of the land and working with other groups and organizations that have aligned interests is vital to the success of organizations, regardless of their type and role in society. In fact, we believe that SIM is inherently able to make organizations more entrepreneurial and less bureaucratic. They are more responsive and give themselves more time to plan and constructively deal with change rather than merely go through the process of dismissal and conflict that often consumes vital resources better spent.

One of the lessons learned over the years is that the best management of any issue is to make appropriate changes in collaboration with groups and organizations that have aligned interests during the issue discussion. This has led to a robust discussion, especially on the part of business, about the nature and benefits of corporate social responsibility. In some ways, that body of literature and consulting practice has split from the larger discussion of SIM. It demonstrates, however, one of the key points that many of us have argued. If through conflict an organization is finally forced to change how it operates as activists and other corporate interests impose change on it, would it not be better to make that change in a more cooperative and constructive manner? Combat can lead to bad policy, hatred, and additional costs and eventual losses by society in the name of making gains. A more constructive approach to corporate responsibility can allow for many thoughts and preferences to collaboratively be brought into the framing of a policy that results from and leads to a more fully functioning society.

In this effort, we have two very broad interests. One is process, often not that far removed from the principles of systems theory and social exchange theory, one of the leading explanations for how relationships start, grow, and even dissolve. Some treatments of SIM and public relations only focus on process. Process, the quality of how various entities work together, is important; certainly, analysis of structures and functions counts. We also assume throughout the book the influence of resource dependency theory, power resource management theory, social construction theory, discourse analysis, and even critical studies. We bring themes together that are based on the three focal point logic of George Herbert Mead (1934; see also Motion & Leitch, 2007) that in order to understand humans, we must address mind (ideation and cognition), self (identity and identification), and society.

We believe, however, that meaning, the formation of meaning through words and the forging of ideas, is crucial to SIM as an organizational and societal effort. Meaning matters. Words count. Ideas drive process, as process helps or hinders efforts to build more sound policy that reflects aligned interests. Communication, especially communication process, may not suffice to reconcile the differences that lead to various periodic and ongoing struggles. So, we are interested in not only how meaning evolves through various voices but also how those voices work together to balance and align interests and seek policy that maximizes societal outcomes.

As we did in the previous edition, we find it useful to quote Renfro (1993), who featured the discipline's management contribution:

> The overriding goal of an issues management function is to enhance the current and long-term performance and standing of the corporation by anticipating change, promoting opportunities, and avoiding or mitigating threats. Attaining this corporate goal, of course, promotes the performance and standing of the corporate leadership, both within and outside the corporations, but this is secondary for issues management. (p. 107)

In such discussions, whether Renfro (1993) used the term *corporate* to refer to all kinds of organizations (business, governmental, and nonprofit, even activist) is immaterial. We use the term broadly, in that encompassing way.

We believe that all kinds of corporate entities, organizations by whatever name, require a sound sense of SIM to maintain effective control of their business planning, to engage positively with other corporate entities that have an interest in some matter, and whose goodwill and support collaboratively bring each organization and society to a better sense of itself and to more harmonious long-term relationships. Thus, we acknowledge the point made by Davis and Thompson (1994): "Management's control within the firm is contingent on rules determined externally by state and federal governments, and the allocation of corporate control thus depends on political struggles among management, capital, and various governmental bodies" (p. 141).

Based on these lines of reasoning, as well as a general confidence in the dialectic among business, government, and collective nonprofit pressures, this book seeks again to advance the cause for a constructive and integrative role to collaborative decision making as the rationale for the political economy and the balance of conflicting and aligned interests. It features four challenges that are vital for comprehensive, effective, and ethical issues management: (1) strategic business planning, based on mission, vision, and budgeting to accomplish these principles; (2) issue surveillance; (3) aggressive efforts to ascertain and achieve corporate responsibility in ways that foster the alignment of stakeholder and stakeseeker interests; and (4) willingness to openly, boldly, and collaboratively contest ideas relevant to the marketplace and public policy arena. Issues management, comprehensively designed and integrated as function and culture, can help organizational leaderships to enact an organization that meets or exceeds the expectations of key publics and builds mutually beneficial relationships.

To that end, we thank the previous generations of students, colleagues, and working professionals from all types of organizations whose influence has been positive if not always well expressed in forming our judgment on this matter. We hope we address the thoughts and concerns of these colleagues appropriately and do so in a way that advances this discipline. Dialogue is sometimes shrill and sometimes quiet and patient. At times, people listen to one another openly and honestly. At other times, they can't listen effectively because they don't want to hear what is being said. They distort often without realizing that flaw. In all of this, the process of statement and counterstatement seems to be the best for internal planning and external advocacy. To speak, however, demands that we also are willing to listen and give regard to others' ideas. Planning without reflection is flawed. Don't count on communicators to make lemonade every time a crop of lemons is harvested. And, as a good friend in the consulting industry once asked, "Are we making this up as we go?"

Acknowledgments

The authors would like to thank the following professors for their review of the proposal and support of this second edition of Strategic Issues Management: Jeong-Nam Kim, Assistant Professor of Communication, Department of Communication, Purdue University; Robert S. Pritchard, Associate Professor of Journalism, Department of Journalism, Ball State University; Risë Jane Samra, Professor of Communication Studies, Barry University; and Matthew W. Seeger, Professor and Chair of the Department of Communication at Wayne State University.

1

A Foundation of Community

Issues Management as an
Organizational and Academic Discipline

Vignette:
British Petroleum—Enlightened Leader or Lightning Rod?

In recent years, the British Petroleum Company (BP) has branded itself as one of the leaders in the petrochemical industry because, according to its branding campaign, it can balance consumer energy needs, quality products and services, environmental stewardship, and profits. It uses the environmentally friendly logo of a stylized flower—or sun—in its branded yellow and green colors. It expanded its operations into alternative energy sources. It is recognized in some circles as being very employee friendly, especially working mother employees.

Nevertheless, several issues related to risks failed, and crisis events had, by 2006, brought BP to be a media and environmentalist target on many issues. At the same time, it was interested in leading efforts to open the Alaskan National Wildlife Reserve (ANWR). Those efforts were severely hampered by the Exxon *Valdez* spill in the 1980s that caused significant negative economic and environmental impact. Even more recent environmental impact events, by BP and other companies, have continued a crisis aura that slows or prevents U.S. Congress's opening of the reserve to oil exploration and production.

Undoubtedly, part of the recent issue attention BP has received began with a March 23, 2005, explosion in its Texas City refinery. Fifteen workers were killed and another 180 were injured (U.S. Chemical Safety and Hazard Investigation Board, 2007). This crisis led to close scrutiny over its safety

(Continued)

1

(Continued)

policies as well as its maintenance and operating procedures. The explosion occurred in what had been an AMOCO refinery that was acquired during BP's merger with that oil company. Investigation centered attention on deferred maintenance schedules as well as training and operations. This industry is one of the potentially least safe, or most dangerous. However, following the release of methyl isocyanate (MIC) in Bhopal, India, at a Union Carbide plant, members of the refining and chemical manufacturing industry bonded to achieve a high safety record that would draw favorable attention rather than make it a regulatory lightning rod. Numerous lawsuits followed, with BP eventually settling. One key case was that brought by Eva Rowe, whose parents were both killed. According to *The Wall Street Journal,*

> After fading from the headlines, the accident had become BP's biggest public-relations headache as the trial approached. In recent days, the U.S. Chemical Safety and Hazard Investigation Board, one of several agencies looking into the blast, partially blamed cost-cutting at BP for the accident, citing internal BP documents. ("BP Settles Claim," 2006, p. A2)

After this crisis event, others occurred that has kept BP on the issue hot seat. It was held responsible for a pipeline leak in the Northern Alaskan Prudhoe Bay oil field, and there were allegations that management had manipulated the U.S. propane market, an allegation that would eventually be fought out in court. Following these mishaps, another article in *The Wall Street Journal* (Cummens, 2006) summarized BP's commitment to improvement in this way:

> The British energy giant said it will increase spending on safety and engineering at its American refineries and Alaskan oil operations, order an independent audit of its trading operations and form an outside advisory panel to help steer the company's American unit. The moves come after a series of accidents and compliance failures in the U.S. BP said it was cooperating with related investigations. (p. A2)

The news story continued in its report of changes BP was undertaking to raise its standard, or achieve its own standard, of corporate social responsibility (CSR).

One fallout from these crises and issues was the early retirement of BP's chief executive officer. He was given great credit over the years for making BP a successful and forward-thinking company. The buck stopped on his desk, however. During the 2006 crises, his retirement was announced to be effective in 2008. That date was changed to July 2007 under the veil, at least, that he was punished for heading a company that could not manage these crises in ways that stopped them from being nagging issues. Such dramatic events suggest how closely strategic issues management (SIM) links to strategic business planning and effective management.

A connection also existed between strategic business planning and CSR. One of the outreach efforts by BP following the Texas City incident was to commission James A. Baker III (former cabinet member of Presidents Reagan and Bush and co-chair of the Iraq Study Group, also called the Baker-Hamilton Commission) to identify problems and suggest ways for BP to operate at a higher safety standard. ABS Consulting performed the technical review. One major conclusion was that the culture of BP led the company to focus more on personnel safety than on plant operating safety: Findings of many inspections were unheeded, the company did not allocate sufficient money to perform needed maintenance, safety equipment was not properly inspected and operable, and safety audits were not thorough. In short, as the company was spending millions on advertising to announce how it was reshaping itself to be a better, more environmentally responsible oil and gas company, application of known safety standards was becoming worse and worse.

Criminal charges can be brought against managers and executives whose policy and operational decisions would endanger their employees. One fallout from the BP case continues to be a working issue. In 2007, U.S. Representatives Gene Green and Al Green introduced federal legislation to extend that protection to contract workers. The employees killed in the Texas City explosion were contract workers.

On June 15, 2007, new BP CEO Tony Hayward said, in the words of a *Houston Chronicle* reporter, that "he is committed to improved safety, a culture in which all concerned voices are heard and making good on promises of improved performance" (Hays, 2007b, pp. A1, A8). He continued by stressing the importance of achieving change, not merely committing to it in principle. On the same day, a business editorialist headlined, "New Boss Knows He Has Plenty to Do to Repair BP's Tattered Image" (Steffy, 2007a, p. A1). The challenge is to bring high standards of corporate responsibility into sound management and operating practices to avert recurrence of harm to industrial workers.

Three days before the press conference Haywood held in Houston at plant facilities, the *Houston Chronicle* reported that the Occupational Safety and Health Administration (OSHA) was stepping up refinery oversight by assigning a massive 300-person taskforce the job of inspecting "refineries across the country over the next two years as part of a stepped-up enforcement program prompted by the BP Texas City Blast and other deadly refinery accidents" (Ivanovich & Clanton, 2007, p. D1). BP's actions before, during, and after had raised the issue of refinery safety. OSHA had to respond lest it become tarnished and demonstrated to be insensitive to the issue of worker safety. These OSHA inspections were programmed to target 81 different facilities, about half of the nation's capacity. A bit more than one month later, OSHA announced that it would fine BP $92,000 for operating "conditions they said were similar to those that preceded the deadly March 2005 blast" (Patel, 2007). "Regulators cited BP for one willful and four serious safety violations" (Patel, 2007, p. A1). This fine followed a $21.3 million fine in September 2006 for 300 willful safety violations. The actions of BP kept the issue of worker safety alive and top of mind within management, regulatory, activist, and legislative circles. In fact, in December 2007, facts of management errors continued to make headlines: "BP Engineer: Facts Hedged to Make Unit Appear Safer" (Hays, 2007a, p. A1).

What does this vignette tell us about SIM? It suggests that how a company operates—the execution of its strategic business plan—can please or offend others, especially employees and regulators. It can meet or violate the expectations others have of how willing and able it is to operate in ways that please or offend others. As a fundamental principle of SIM, forces seek to hold organizations to a certain performance standard. Once it fails to achieve that level, it is subject to criticism. Some of the criticism can be answered through strategic communication, messages that address key issues. However, the BP case also suggests the need for strategic business planning that is sensitive, reflective, and responsive to the public policy arena; a need to monitor issues; and a commitment to know and achieve the level of CSR that is necessary to maintain the legitimacy of the organization. This is the scope of SIM that will be discussed throughout this book.

Chapter Goals

By the time you have completed this chapter, you should be able to define strategic issues management (SIM), understand how it grew out of a unique social and business environment following World War II, and see it as a vital part of the total management planning effort in organizations, as well as justify it as a process that fosters mutually beneficial relationships between organizations and involved publics. Your knowledge of SIM will include its role in planning and the way stakeholders and stakeseekers can affect the planning and operation of an organization, as well as what strengths it brings to the management table. All of this discussion culminates in a brief discussion of the balancing act between responsible advocacy, conflict negotiation, and collaborative decision making. As an ideal, normative process, SIM seeks to balance interests and achieve mutual benefit and support by fostering joint decision making and cooperation rather than opposition for the key organization's planning and operations. Organizations are encouraged to position themselves so they work to balance their interests with those of others. They need effective planning, issue monitoring, appropriate standards of corporate responsibility, and willingness and ability to communicate through advocacy, dialogue, and collaborative decision making. The key to appreciating the value of issues management is to view it as more than a communication function.

SIM is a sturdy discipline that has matured over the years as reflective management has moved to respond to changing threats and opportunities in the economic and public policy arenas in which they operate. Although the precise role and measurable impact of SIM, public affairs, and public relations continue to be problematic in management theory, numerous managers and executives recognize the countless ways SIM adds value to their organizations and society. Academics from an eclectic range of disciplines and savvy issues management and public relations practitioners know that issue debates are a routine aspect of their business function of shaping public- and private-sector policies. Such debates can positively or negatively affect how organizations are managed and the missions that guide effective organizational planning. These debates are more than relationship management, although the quality of relationships can affect how issues are contested and translated into sound business and public policy. For reasons unique to the 21st century, organizational executives have worked with academics to better understand and refine this discipline. SIM's proponents believe it has become essential communication and management theory for the effective running of businesses, nonprofits, nongovernmental organizations (NGOs), and government agencies.

Issues management as an applied discipline is an ancient business and communication practice. For centuries, government leaders as well as business managers have responded to, created, and managed issues as part of their routine activities. Nonprofits, especially NGOs, engage in issue planning and issue debate, which translate into policies that foster and constrain choices by the organizations in each society. Activists raise issues they believe can benefit society. They engage in situationally sensitive planning and communicate through advocacy, conflict negotiation, and collaborative decision making. Every kind of organization can benefit from SIM.

Despite the worries of some, large organizations cannot control how issues arise, are discussed and debated, and ultimately translated into public policy. Without doubt, they participate in the process, but how they participate and the nature of the issues proponents debate determine how those issues are resolved and to whose benefit. The private sector, for many reasons, is the focal point in the development, study, and practice of SIM, but it is not the exclusive purview of business. A case can be made that it arises from the confluence of power resource management and participative democracy.

Historical Evolution:
Defining a Mass Consumption Society

As the foundation for defining issues management, a brief historical overview will help explain SIM's origins, rationale, growth, and place in society (this overview will be expanded in Chapter 2). Here, in simple detail, we note that its origins are those of societal conflict, organization, and risk management. SIM can be found at work in all cultures, societies, and nations. It is inseparable from common law in Western tradition and is the basis for minor and massive changes in political economies around the world.

SIM's iconic role in U.S. history is best embodied in the colonial revolutionaries' claim against the British monarchy: no taxation without representation. It has been at work during the public policy and business battles in the United States since the second half of the 19th century. During the years of industrial growth in America, executives of increasingly large corporations turned strategically to government to seek favorable public policy to define, defend, and champion their business consolidation and mass production practices that helped to spawn the mass consumption society. These "robber barons" fashioned conglomerates almost overnight and often with the desire to dominate entire markets by bringing many small companies together under one organizational umbrella. Business enterprises, such as steel manufacturing and oil companies as well as telephone and electric utilities, struggled to establish state-of-the-art operating standards, including the legitimacy of regulated monopoly. It is not coincidental that SIM and the practice of public relations grew up during this era when executives employed communication specialists to advance their causes.

For the first time in the history of U.S. business, this new kind of boss cloistered themselves in luxurious offices rather than work side by side with laborers. Boards of directors and shareholders came to decide how workers' efforts were directed, and corporate policy was formed and implemented based on industry-wide standards. People's health and safety were often dramatically harmed by manufacturing and marketing practices and working conditions. Efficient processes and huge fortunes, especially for stockholders and senior management, were often the goal rather than excellent business practices, carefully crafted products and services, and wise government oversight of the public interest. Because of their business practices, executives were eventually challenged to respond to outbursts of protest. Activists and investigative reporters argued that business practices were corrupting the market enterprise system and working for the destruction of society.

Turbulent eras continued. The Great Depression of the 1930s challenged government and private-sector organizations to reformulate private-sector practices, and local, state, and federal programs were drafted and implemented to protect the public interest. Following this era of damaged relationships with the general public, World War II allowed corporations and government to link arms to produce a stunning global military and reconstruction victory that served as the hallmark for a period of prosperity. The war effort changed the structure of labor and management relations and led to a new prosperity through research and development efforts fueled by the need for new products and services. This industrial buildup created abundant new synthetic, chemical-based products and other goods that were affordable and available in ways that dramatically changed lifestyles.

Just as all seemed to be going well for industry and large government, the roof fell in. Entering the 1950s, the private sector felt smug. It had helped forge world peace and widespread prosperity. Confident executives were caught off guard by critics condemning a myriad of business activities that in the minds of the executives were profitable, efficient, and realistic. Sparked by antiwar and civil rights protests, penetrating voices, often full of idealism, reexamined the principles of representative democracy and the relationships between companies and labor, consumers, and the environment. Authority was indicted as being irresponsible. Environmentalism, consumerism, and dozens of other "isms" emerged as vocal interests opposed prevailing principles of business and government. Activists once more installed themselves in the political power base of the United States.

Sociopolitical dynamics and changes began in the 1960s, and entire industries and businesses lost much of their public policy clout as the result of four dramatic changes: (a) natural resources, found to be limited and defined as the property of the citizens of the nation, were to be managed in the collective interest; (b) society became sensitive to the increasing heterogeneity of values, attitudes, beliefs, interests, and cultures that destroyed the sense of policy consensus that prevailed at the start of the 1960s; (c) people lost confidence in large institutions, such as government, media, and business, and placed their confidence in activist groups to exert the collective power of individuals; and (d) standards of corporate responsibility and legitimacy changed (Pfeffer, 1981). This fertile ground fed the growth of issues management.

The term *issues management* was coined in the 1970s, but the concept is much older. Other terms, such as *public relations* and *public affairs* in the second half of the 20th century, seemed insufficient to define the scope and purpose of organizational activities needed to participate constructively in this new policy arena. Issues were not new. But the kinds of issues, the depth of attitudes and behaviors demonstrated over them in the United States, and the sophistication of issue advocates prompted public relations, public affairs, and advertising specialists to see it as new communication challenges. The public, in general, and stakeholders, in specific, were angry about safety, asking questions such as the following: How safe are company operations? Can the government keep people safe? What damage is being done to the environment? How can people tolerate racial, age, or gender discrimination in all aspects of public and private life? Such questions were on the lips and typewriters of the 1960s activist groups, media reporters, and government agency heads who pressed for changes in business activities and policies.

This discussion led to the conclusion that SIM is a vital academic discipline, a key element of management for every sort of organization, and more than a matter of skillful communication: *Issues management became a way of thinking, a philosophy of effective management.* Over time, communication specialists realized that SIM entailed more than making one or two "compelling" appeals to the "general public" as a way of defending business policies against critics. Critics and other publics soon tired of the worn claim that an advocated change would cost too much and thereby harm society. Discussion over the scope and purpose of the discipline led people to realize that issue debate was nothing new, even with the increased power and relevance of activists. Although communication was and still is a vital part of what was needed, managers quickly realized that communication alone might not suffice and that strategic planning needed to be more intimately featured in issues management. As well, astute observers realized that much of the debate focused on competing and conflicting standards of how businesses, nonprofits, and government agencies should conduct themselves to achieve objectives that were appropriate in light of the ideological environment that was fluid, a matter of substantial debate. SIM is more than a communication function, certainly more than public relations. It is the rationale and means to make organizations more in harmony and less in dysfunctional conflict with their stakeholders and stakeseekers, those publics and markets that can influence businesses' ability to achieve their missions and visions.

This brief review of the heritage of business and public policy that initiated SIM will be expanded in Chapter 2. The glimpse provided here features the turbulent struggle between public and private interests that has fostered the invention and refinement of SIM. If businesses were free from criticism, they could act as they desire. This freedom prior to the 1960s in the United States, however, is what led businesses to some poor decisions without regard to stakeholder interests.

SIM: Strategic Issues Management Defined

In the broadest sense, SIM is the amalgamation of organizational functions and responsive culture that blends strategic business planning, issue monitoring, best-practice standards of corporate responsibility, and dialogic communication needed to foster a supportive climate between each organization and those people who can affect its success and who are affected by its operations. It centers its attention on the public policy arena but also offers means to contest issues in regard to marketing and brand equity. Taking a bit more societal view—one featuring the logics of power resource management—SIM can be defined as "the management of organizational and community resources through the public policy process to advance organizational interests and rights by striking a mutual balance with those of stakeholders" (Heath, 2006a, p. 79). The marketplace can be equally or even more important to the future of the organization than the public policy arena. For instance, an automobile company that has a corporate mission to be seen as the technological leader in its industry can legitimately be expected to challenge claims by critics that its technology is not as good as it has advertised. The organization needs to defend its reputation by challenging those claims to demonstrate where they are inaccurate, or it must cease making such promotions or improve its management efforts to prove its statements to be true. Similarly, nonprofit organizations such as Planned Parenthood engage in public policy debates on public health issues, as well as debates that center on its role, legitimacy, and societal value.

Issues management is a multifunctional discipline. It "is a leadership process that defines the strategic common ground between a company [or other organization] and its key audiences" (Palese & Crane, 2002, p. 284). It can foster the strategic use of issues analysis to help organizations plan and manage by making strategic adaptations needed to achieve harmony and foster mutual interests within the communities where they operate. It helps organizations survive and even grow. It gives them another tool to maximize the opportunities and lessen the threats that public policy trends and marketplace claims pose to their strategic business planning. It is much more than carefully crafted messages that apologize for business practices as being self-justifying or by placing blame on critics. The role of the communication professional may best be an advocate for discussions, decision, communications, and behaviors that fall in the area of doing the right thing (B. K. Berger & Reber, 2006). The challenge, as well, is to engage in the contest of what constitutes the right or best thing.

Despite the disproportionate attention devoted to SIM in large companies, the principles of issues management can be applied to small businesses and nonprofit organizations as well as governmental agencies and activist groups. All organizations have an interest in public policy trends and outcomes. Small businesses may not be able to engage in issue advertising, but they make rhetorical appeals in the appropriate forums for points of view on issues vital to their well-being. They join ranks through trade associations and coalitions to increase their power.

Legitimacy is a (perhaps *the*) central theme in issues management (Roper, 2002, 2005; Spencer, 2004). Fleisher (2001) observed that publics in general and around the world tend to doubt that corporate interests correspond to theirs. Issues management is a clash for legitimacy (and power), and this struggle is not a recent phenomenon. It is arguably the forge from which issues management emerged in the 1870s and the stone on which it was honed in the 1970s. What Sethi (1977) called the legitimacy gap results from the difference between what specific companies are thought to be doing (what they are actually doing) and how publics expect and prefer them to operate. The gap can result from differences of fact, value, and policy. The width of the gap, conceptualized in Figure 1.1, determines how strongly involved members of the public approve or disapprove of any organization that is expected to be responsive to community interests (Kruckeberg & Starck, 1988).

To address these sorts of questions, this book takes an approach to SIM based on four theoretical perspectives: systems theory, rhetorical theory, social exchange theory, and power resource management theory. Featuring information flow, *systems theory* argues that in a complex manner, each system seeks balance with all other systems; all systems are interdependent. What happens to and is done by one affects other systems. How this balance is achieved requires an understanding of the processes of adjustment, including communication. It requires collective sense making, the co-creation of meaning.

Rhetorical theory provides the rationale for the dialogue and conflict that occur to form collective meaning. It features the paradigm of statement and counterstatement. In the ideal, each statement refines each other statement, leading to co-created meaning that rests on the principles of collaborative decision making. All parties to a controversy are best served by participating in collaborative problem resolution.

How they operate and adjust to one another can be predicted by *social exchange theory*. This theory reasons that norms of cooperation can be known and implemented to achieve agreement and harmony—and legitimacy.

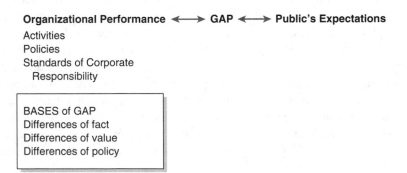

Figure 1.1   Reconciling Organizational Performance and Public's Expectations

Organizations that fail to engage in positive social exchange are likely to be sanctioned as being less legitimate by other organizations.

Power resource management theory views society as a struggle by competing interests to foster and constrain each other by the push and pull of control options—the willingness and ability to shape what others do and the rewards and punishments they earn for their efforts. A realistic view recognizes that companies cannot manipulate issues to their interests for long, if at all. Savvy managers take a larger view of SIM, knowing that in its fullness it can help them monitor issues, sharpen their strategic business plans, improve their operations by implementing higher standards of corporate responsibility, and communicate in ways intended to build and strengthen relationships with key publics.

Those who work to define SIM do so by addressing various questions. According to the Public Relations Society of America (PRSA), issues management is a subfunction of public relations, but the Public Affairs Council (1978) looks at issues management as a program that companies use to improve their involvement in the public policy process. Is issues management merely public relations revisited (Ehling & Hesse, 1983; Fox, 1983)? Is it an executive-level staff function and community-oriented organizational culture that empower public relations by giving it greater involvement in corporate strategic business planning and management (Heath, 1988; Heath & Nelson, 1986; R. A. Nelson & Heath, 1986)? Does it feature "public policy foresight and planning for an organization" (Ewing, 1987, p. 1)?

Is it the organized activity of identifying emerging trends, concerns, or issues likely to affect an organization in the next few years? If so, can it help develop a wider and more positive range of organizational responses toward that future (Coates, Coates, Jarratt, & Heinz, 1986)? Or, as Hainsworth and Meng (1988) asked, does it give "senior management the means to intelligently participate in the public policy process" (p. 28)? Raising and addressing questions of this sort generate a healthy dialogue even if consensus is not easily achieved (Gaunt & Ollenburger, 1995).

How one defines issues management depends on preferences and prejudices. For instance, PRSA's (1987) Special Committee on Terminology defined it as a public relations function: "systematic identification and action regarding public policy matters of concern to an organization" (p. 9). J. E. Grunig and Repper (1992) subordinated issues management to public relations, a function whereby practitioners respond to issues raised by key publics. In similar fashion, Toth (2006) featured public relations as the dominant discipline, whereas public affairs "seems similar to *issues management,* another specialization of public relations focused on public policy issues" (p. 501).

Definitions are most helpful when they specify the actions needed to engage in public policy activities (Hainsworth & Meng, 1988). Lauzen (1994) offered evidence that it is a managerial rather than a technical public relations function. Processes typical of issues management take their rationale from the support they provide in defining and accomplishing the organization's strategic plan. This is not the activity of persons who are outside of the management cadre who otherwise support but do not guide the management function.

Efforts to define issues management must not lose sight of organizations' need to harmonize organizational and stakeholder interests. As Ewing (1987) concluded, "Issues management developed within the business community as an educational task aimed at preserving the proper balance between the legitimate goals and rights of the free enterprise system and those of society" (p. 5). SIM is a foresight discipline that can serve the needs of all organizations that assert their interests through public policy formation, mitigation, and adaptation. Thus, Ewing reasoned, "A corporation exists for the *optimization* of the satisfactions of its stakeholders" (p. 32).

Issues management is a means for linking the standard public relations and public affairs functions and the management function of the organization in ways that foster the organization's efforts to be outer directed and reflective, as well as to have a participative organizational culture. Blending these functions is vital for organizations that seek harmonious relationships in an environment that is complex because of the number of publics and the variety of issues to be considered. SIM can help organizations to be proactive, instead of merely reactionary. Managing the response to these issues for decision making and strategic planning gives public relations personnel access to management (Lauzen & Dozier, 1994). To this end, management scholars are interested in assessing and quantifying the impact of SIM on an organization's performance. To that end, they ask whether it participates constructively in decision making or decision implementation (Fleisher, 2002; Palese & Crane, 2002; Sawaya & Arrington, 1988).

Public relations practitioners who fostered interest in issues management thought they could "expand the role of public relations beyond media relations and product publicity to a senior management problem-solving function critical to the survival of an organization" (Tucker, Broom, & Caywood, 1993, p. 38). In this way, it was designed as "the management process whose goals is to help preserve markets, reduce risk, create opportunities and manage image as an organization asset for the benefit of both an organization and its primary shareholders" (p. 38). To this definition should be added these words: *to the mutual benefit of its key stakeholders and stakeseekers.*

What do we conclude if we draw on the essence of these definitions? Issues management is a multifunctional discipline that includes the identification, monitoring, and analysis of trends in key publics' opinions that can mature into public policy. It involves the staff function that, along with technical and managerial personnel support, can develop an organization or industry stance to be executed through strategic business plans and communication campaigns. No other corporate function more completely stresses the inseparability of ethical

corporate behavior, public judgment of what is legitimate, responsible production and delivery of goods and services, and internal and external attempts
to inform and persuade targeted constituencies to gain their support. It can
penetrate all operations. The underpinning principle of issues management is
not to avoid legislation, regulation, or crisis but to balance the interests of all
segments of the community so that each enjoys the proper amount of reward
or benefit in proportion to the cost of allowing industry free rein to impose its
own operating standards.

The struggle is not exclusively between companies and activists. Changed
operating standards may result when one industry shifts the burden of solving
a problem from itself to another. For instance, over the years, automobile
insurance companies have successfully lobbied for higher standards of car
safety design. If cars are safer, people are less likely to suffer severe and costly
injuries, especially to the head and spine, thereby reducing the cost to the
insurance companies and shifting it to the automobile manufacturers. In addition to concern for cost and profit, society is better if drivers and passengers
suffer fewer traumas in accidents.

Regulatory and legislative intrusion may occur when an industry seeks to
standardize and improve operating standards among its members. The rationale for this change is the desire to reduce the bad-apple effect of the worst performers being used by activists to characterize the operations of an entire
industry. Although such efforts often have altruistic incentives, they also give
competitive advantage to the businesses within the industry that are most prepared to meet the standards that they seek to impose on their competitors.
Related to global human rights abuse, Misol (2006) argued that such "enforce-
able global standards are desirable, inevitable, and, contrary to received wisdom, good for business" (p. 1).

Associating issues management with public affairs, the Public Affairs
Council (1978) described it as "a program that a company uses to increase its
knowledge of the public policy process and enhance the sophistication and
effectiveness of its involvement in that process" (p. 1). The council endorsed
the now-standard issues management model that consists of (a) monitoring
the public policy arena to determine what trends will demand a reorientation
of corporate policy and communication process, (b) identifying those issues
of greatest potential importance to the organization, (c) evaluating their operational and financial impacts through issues analysis, (d) prioritizing and
establishing company policy positions by coordinating and assisting senior
management decision making, (e) creating the company response from among
a range of issue change strategy options, and (f) implementing the plans
through issue action programming.

More recently, the Public Affairs Council defined the discipline as the
process of prioritizing and proactively managing public policy issues, including reputation, than can affect any organization's success (Pinkham, 2003).

This definition is important because it suggests a breadth of response options and connects SIM with public policy and reputation, or what can be put under the umbrella of brand equity. The Public Affairs Council reasons that effective issues management can identify and work toward constructive response to opportunities as well as threats.

Speaking as chairperson of the Issue Management Association, W. Howard Chase (1982) offered a widely quoted definition:

> Issue management is the capacity to understand, mobilize, coordinate, and direct all strategic and policy planning functions, and all public affairs/public relations skills, toward achievement of one objective: meaningful participation in creation of public policy that affects personal and institutional destiny. (p. 1)

Chase (1982) stressed the proactive aspect of issues management that "rejects the hypothesis that any institution must be the pawn of the public policy determined solely by others" (p. 2). Maturing in his thinking, Chase (1984) later defined issues management as issue identification, analysis, change strategy options, action programming, and evaluation of results.

> An issue change strategy option is a choice among carefully selected methods and plans for achieving long-term corporate goals in the face of public policy issues, a choice based on the expected effect of each method of employment, cost, sales, and profits. (p. 56)

Ewing (1987) viewed SIM as a way to help fill the policy hole in the center of corporate management, "making it possible for the CEO and senior management to strategically manage their enterprise as a whole, as a complete entity capable of helping create the future and grow their company into it" (p. 18). Its greatest contribution is gained by early and proactive efforts "to intervene consciously and effectively and participate early in the process, instead of waiting passively until the organization finds itself a victim at the tail end of the process" (p. 19).

Issues management entails efforts to increase satisfaction between parties and foster mutual benefit. It fosters the interests of the stakeholders by helping an organization achieve its goals in a community of complementary and competing interests. For example, in corporate circles, the *double bottom line* is a relatively new phenomenon based on a private organization reaping profit and doing social good.

To achieve its potential, issues management must add value by allocating, defining, and distributing resources: human, financial, and material. It serves its sponsoring organization by engaging in a field in which each player seeks its own advantage. Although these competing and conflicting interests are such that all cannot be equally satisfied, issues management serves best when it assists in the planning, analysis, communication, and coalition-building efforts by which mutual interests are sought and appropriate resource allocation is achieved.

This section began by asking, what is issues management? The answer: It is the management of organizational and community resources to advance organizational and community interests and rights by striking a mutual balance with stakeholders and stakeseekers. SIM supports strategic business planning and savvy management by using issue monitoring to track and understand public policy trends, by meeting standards of corporate responsibility that are expected by key stakeholders, and by using communication to contest issues, foster understanding, and minimize or resolve conflict through collaborative decision making. It is not limited to media relations, customer relations, or government relations. It is expected to keep the organization ethically attuned to its community and positioned to exploit, mitigate, and foster public policy changes as they relate to its mission. It understands and engages in stake exchange with relevant stakeholders and stakeseekers.

SIM: Stakeholders/Stakeseekers

Since the 1970s, one of the central themes of SIM has been the role of stakeholders. The concern addressed in that seminal era featured the need to know how strong stakeholder relationships were, know where they were weak, and know how to correct or otherwise improve them. To that end, stakeholder and stakeseeker theory is essential to SIM. That theory can begin by noting that a public is some number of individuals, "who are linked by a common interest or problem" (Rawlins & Bowen, 2004, p. 718). One view of public opinion is that it is the collective thoughts, evaluations, beliefs, or opinions of many publics. These publics are defined by the kinds of relationships they have with various organizations, the opinions they share, and the power that they may hold.

Publics come in various kinds, shapes, and forms. They become serious players for those engaged in SIM when they become stakeholders and stakeseekers. Stakeholder and stakeseekers, as well as stakes, are the heart of the SIM process (Heath, 1994; Spicer, 2007). This proposition focuses on the fact that successful stake exchange is the most fundamental rationale for the success or failure of any organization, regardless of its type. Stakeholder theory is also vital to understand the *power resource* aspects of SIM as well as the *value compatibility/incompatibility* that focuses attention on standards and dynamics of corporate responsibility. Corporate responsibility standards arise through the expectations of various stakeholders and stakeseekers.

Any smart organization wants to know who its stakeholders and stakeseekers are (rarely in person, but certainly by category) and be able to understand whether the relationship with them is wholesome or dissatisfying

(Dunham, Freeman, & Liedtka, 2006). Issue managers need to realize, as well, that publics prefer to define and explain themselves and give the rationality, and even emotionality, of their concerns in their own words (Leitch & Neilson, 2001). Woe to the SIM team that willfully, openly, and indifferently makes public statements that interpret and frame key stakeholders in ways that are offensive to them.

Before going into the full logic of this opening position, we start with some definitions. Two factors are critical to the definition of stakeholders. One is that stakeholders are persons who have some interest in a matter, problem, issue, risk, or other concern. To this extent, they are cognitively involved to obtain, review, think about, and formulate attitudes and behavioral intentions about the matter. Second is that stakeholders hold stakes. In conflict theory, a stake is something of value. At the heart of resource dependency theory, the ability to hold or grant a stake is a key to the influence that a stakeholder can exert on some matter in which it has an interest (Ulmer, Seeger, & Sellnow, 2004).

Stakeholders are any persons or groups that hold something of value that can be used as rewards or constraints in exchange for goods, services, or organizational policies and operating standards. Stakeholders who have stakes that can directly influence the success of the organization are primary, whereas those whose stakes are less likely to be immediately brought to bear are secondary or indirect. *Stakeseekers* want something of value from stakeholders, the stakes held by those stakeholders. This logic applies to the marketplace as well as the public policy arena. Consumers can be stakeseekers and stakeholders; they want products and services of value. They hold resources, purchasing power that is sought by businesses. A mutually beneficial relationship operates if both sides are satisfied by the exchange. How these interests are balanced is the essence of stakeholder exchange and defines the extent to which the relationship is legitimate and mutually beneficial. Stakeholders and stakeseekers are "groups and individuals who can affect, or are affected by, the achievement of an organization's mission" (Freeman, 1984, p. 52).

Savvy managements want to know whether a legitimacy gap exists regarding each of its primary and secondary stakeholders/stakeseekers. A *primary stakeholder* has the potential of direct impact on the organization. A demographic category of customers can affect a business by deciding to pay for goods and services provided by the organization. Lawmakers are primary stakeholders for any government agency that needs revenue to operate. The people who would use the services of the organization are *secondary stakeholders*. Their influence over the agency is likely not to be exercised directly but indirectly by writing their congressperson or other such measures.

A *stake* is anything tangible or intangible, material or immaterial, that one person or group has that is of value to another person or group (Sellnow, Ulmer, & Seeger, 2004). It is something each party desires from a relationship.

Stakes can be transferable. They can be roughly divided into three types: instrumental, symbolic, and relational. A vote in Congress is instrumental; a behavior was enacted. Customer goodwill is symbolic; it is earned by the moral and ethical conduct of a business. The management of the arrangement of stakes is relational. The resources of a community and the degree of shared values and trust within it are relational, following Bourdieu's (1986) concepts of social capital. Relationships, as well as the power of those relationships, can be seen as one of several resources that actors use to pursue their interests and to position themselves. Ihlen (2005) suggested that Bourdieu's concept of social capital is a way to look at the power elements within a relationship between an organization and its stakeholders and stakeseekers on whom its success or failure depends. Whether instrumental, symbolic, or relational, stakes are important to the organization's brand equity. Willingness to give rather than withhold stakes suggests a positive relationship as defined by Sethi's (1977) concept of the legitimacy gap, which was discussed earlier in the chapter.

Keep in mind that in most cases, anyone engaged in SIM needs to be able to manage multiple stakeholder-stakeseeker relationships. Such is the case, for instance, even (or perhaps most especially) when stakeholders do not agree with one another. For example, a major petrochemical company is often confronted with stakeholders, especially activist groups that do not agree with one another. If the company creates a balance with one, it may have a more serious legitimacy gap with another. In fact, the two activist groups may suffer a legitimacy gap with each other.

Case in Point: Stakeholders and Stake Analysis for Salmon and Steelhead Fish

One of the major environmental efforts in recent years in the United States has been to protect salmon and steelhead fish populations (Fialka, 2006), which provides an opportunity to discuss planning and stake analysis. Through a mix of corporate responsibility, state and federal legislative action, and environmentalist pressure, the Bonneville Power Administration engaged in an experiment to provide access for upstream migration for these fish while continuing to use river water for hydrogeneration. The project cost: $8 billion. In any year, only 1% to 3.5% of the fish make the roundtrip from near Lewiston, Idaho, down through the Snake and Columbia Rivers and then return. Experts had hoped the efforts would at least double that rate, which is assumed to be necessary for the long-term viability of the species.

Natural predators, including large birds and seals, and Canadian fisherman account for some of the kill. Barges are used to transport the fish upstream around the murderous plant facilities, but that leaves the fish disoriented and subject to prey. Fisherman can obtain licenses to catch fish; policy allows for 50% of the

(Continued)

(Continued)

returning fish to be caught each year. Fish is served in restaurants; the tastiest of the salmon, Chook, sell for more than $20 per pound. Native Americans can fish for food as a cultural right. This doesn't even mention the commercial fishing industry that is represented by special interest groups, such as the Northwest Sportfishing Industry Association.

A direct stakeholder relationship is one in which stakeholders can exercise stakes directly on one another. An indirect relationship results when one or both stakeholders must rely on the other to represent the case for the distribution of stakes. In the case immediately above, the utility company and the governmental entitles have direct stakeholder relationships, whereas others, especially the wildlife, have an indirect relationship with the primary stakeholders.

Before continuing, consider and outline the stakeholder-stakeseeker relationships in the previous case example. We have these at least: federal government (agencies and legislators), state governments (agencies and legislators), Native Americans, fishermen (sport and commercial), environmentalists, electric rate payers (cost of the species protection project is passed on to the people who use and pay for electricity), and Canadians (fishermen and legislators/agency personnel). Of interest here, the salmon and steelhead are stakeholders (their flesh is a stake to be obtained) and stakeseekers (safe passage to spawning grounds). Seals, bears, and large birds are also stakeseekers and stakeholders. What is the mutually beneficial relationship between these stakeseekers and stakeholders? The complexity of this case demonstrates the need for stake analysis, as well as the rationale for the underpinnings of SIM: systems theory, rhetorical theory, and social exchange theory.

A symmetrical relationship exists between stakeseeker and stakeholder when stakes are perceived to be equal in worth and both parties are willing and able to exercise them. Thus, for instance, the ability to purchase gasoline at a pump and the ability to deliver it constitute an equal exchange between the driver and the gasoline station. An asymmetrical relationship exists when stakeholders hold stakes of different value or participants are unequally able or willing to grant stakes. Thus, a large retail discount company is asymmetrically able to pay a fine for not complying with a city ordinance prohibiting outside sales. In an effort to force merchants to make a city more attractive, city officials may pass an ordinance that would prevent retailers from storing sales goods and selling them in their parking lots. A multinational company can easily pay the $200-a-day fine rather than build a proper storage building. A small merchant could not afford that fine, and a city cannot tailor fines to the size of the company.

So we can have primary and secondary stakeholders/stakeseekers, who weigh into one another with instrumental and symbolic/moral stakes that can be used as power resources for sanctioning and rewarding legitimate or illegitimate exchanges. The power differential between various players can be small or great. Standards of corporate responsibility rest on knowing and being able to adjust to the power and moral and ethical obligations that exist within the mix of stakeholder/stakeseekers in any specific context.

One response to the mix of stakeholders/stakeseekers is to achieve harmony with them and reduce conflict. This is a cybernetic approach to SIM. A more constructive approach assumes that, through collaborative decision making, the parties can make society more fully functional, thereby maximizing the quality of decisions and advancing the quality of community. Either model assumes that SIM provides the means and ability to work together. The central challenge is to be willing and able to do so.

We can think of each organization, regardless of the kind and size, as negotiated enactments of stakeholder/stakeseeker interests (Heath, 1994, see Chapter 6). As much as these relationships may be defined by the discussion above, one additional point needs to be made. A stakeholder or stakeseeker may be the ideology (perhaps defined as a cultural archetype) that is central to some crisis, risk, or issue. For instance, in 2006, an *Escherichia coli* bacteria scare occurred, with many people across several states becoming ill (one died) from eating organic spinach. A central archetype in this case was the "good and healthy meal." Perhaps few archetypes of ideology are more central. Each society prizes healthy food. Mom's table set with good food is one of the most enduring archetypes. But that archetype can be put under pressure if tainted food is discovered in the marketplace. What can be done to ensure food safety? The archetype is strained if the cause of the contamination cannot be found, and therefore no lesson is learned from the crisis. As Mitroff (1983) argued, the quality of a relationship is often defined by an archetype, in this case, healthy and safe food. That standard seems beyond compromise. This archetype defines the relationships food companies have with customers, as well as those state and federal regulators (such as the Food and Drug Administration) have with citizens. The archetype either guides the relationship or must be changed. The healthy food archetype resists change for many obvious reasons. Thus, the pressure is greater than it otherwise might be for the industry and regulators to locate the cause and thereby demonstrate willingness and ability to deliver the stakes of food safety to the stakeseekers, persons who prepare meals. These customers hold the stakes of purchase dollars as well as pressures on regulators through legislators.

Let's flesh out the logic of stake analysis a bit more before we proceed. Issues managers are expected to identify key stakeholders, ascertain the quality of relationship between them and the organization, and determine what can be done to enhance that relationship based on stake exchanges. In this analysis, it is imperative that the persons doing issues analysis understand the position the various stakeholder publics hold on key issues. The quality of relationships predicts that stakes will be granted in support of the organization or used to punish it. The issue position reveals what changes need to be made, whether by one or more stakeholders and the organization conducting the analysis. Changes may occur in regard to issue position as well as actions, including the strategic business plan and the standards of corporate responsibility that are sensitive to various positions on the issues. This list, then, is illustrative of the generic types of stakeholders:

- Activist publics: collectivities that band together to increase stakeholder leverage
- Intraindustry players: other members of the industry
- Interindustry players: members of other industries
- Potential activist publics: persons, identifiable by demographics or opinions, who are likely to become activists if they recognize that their self-interests are harmed or helped by actions of an organization
- Customers: persons and entities that exchange stakes for goods and services
- Employees: persons who exchange time, knowledge, and skills for financial reward
- Legislators: persons who create a law or ordinance that prescribes which actions are rewardable or punishable
- Regulators: persons who implement law and ordinance by setting performance standards
- Judiciary: persons who interpret laws and ordinances
- Investors (and other financial supporters, such as philanthropic donors to non-profit operations): individuals and entities that offer financial support for enterprises
- Neighbors: individuals who live in proximity to organizations and whose interests may be positively or negatively affected by operations in the vicinity
- Media: reporters, editors, and news directors who are expected to understand, report, and comment on issues and events
- Social media: individuals, such as backpack journalists, who create and distribute information via new communication technologies without traditional gatekeepers to process the content or distribution

SIM: Bringing More Than Communication

One of the important realities is that interest in SIM is not limited to communicators but in fact arose in large part from strategic concerns by management experts. A quarter century ago, Buchholz (1982b) discovered that 91% of *Fortune* 500 companies had issues management programs. The vast majority of respondents indicated that such programs are extremely important (23.8%) or very important (50.0%). One indicator of executive support for the function was that the number of personnel assigned to it had increased by 47.1% during the 3 years prior to Buchholz's survey. Issues managers were responsible for identifying, tracking, analyzing, and prioritizing issues as well as formulating policy positions in response to them and implementing response strategies. A few respondents reported that issues management was vital to the long-range planning of their companies. Nearly 70% saw it as a function of growing importance. Approximately 40% believed that it would become part of corporate strategic planning. About 20% thought the future of issues management depended on whether the business-government climate continued to call for more regulation. Only 13% believed that issues management was a fad. Nowadays, issues management is commonly found throughout *Fortune* 500 companies as a strategic communication management function.

A survey of 1,001 large- and medium-sized firms by Post, Murray, Dickie, and Mahon (1983) revealed that the amount of influence public affairs exercised depended on four factors: (a) Advice is more influential when it focuses on the near term rather than long-term issues; (b) the influence is greater in companies that are highly regulated and worry about their operating environments; (c) in companies that genuinely use long-term planning, public affairs is more vital than in companies that plan only for the short term; and (d) large companies rely more on public affairs than do small ones. Among the many corporate communicators who complain that strategic planning often ignores public affairs is Bergner (1982), who blended the two functions, particularly for multinational businesses.

Rather than indicting the innovativeness of issues management, Post et al. (1983) condemned executive recalcitrance and the role or lack of one played by many public affairs and public relations practitioners in the issues management process. Once issues management is associated with organizational strategic business planning and efforts to enhance corporate responsibility, it may become distinguished from rather than integrated into routine public affairs or public relations activities limited to working with the media.

Public relations practitioners will play an active and valued role in executive management teams (J. E. Grunig & Grunig, 1989) in proportion to their ability to influence strategic business planning and management in ways that enhance the bottom line (Ewing, 1987; Wartick & Rude, 1986). The lack of consensus regarding the term *issues management* is captured in Miller's (1987) observation: "Issue management isn't quite public relations. Neither is it government relations, nor public affairs, nor lobbying, nor crisis management, nor futurism, nor strategic planning. It embraces all of these disciplines, and maybe a few more" (p. 125). Issues management entails key, integrated functions that each organization needs to perform to profit through mutually beneficial stakeholder relations (Chase, 1982). Communication experts move into executive discussions as they help improve their organizations' ability to avoid criticism of their policies and actions and to take advantage of opportunities presented by public policy trends.

As much as some might view an information-sharing or exchange approach to SIM, especially its communication function, others believe that approach is narrow and even naive. According to tradition, in 1977, Chase coined the term *issue management,* which he designated as the new science. He drew on his corporate experience and on the innovation of John E. O'Toole (1975a, 1975b), who is argued to have coined the term *advocacy advertising.* This loose partnership launched the efforts to create an embracing and responsible response to business critics. The innovation featured issue monitoring and advocacy but soon grew beyond those functions alone.

Addressing the need for a new communication philosophy, Bateman (1975) advised companies "to move from an information base to an advocacy position in their responses to their critics and to build relationships with key publics" (p. 5). This stance, he rationalized, was needed because "companies should not be the silent children of society" (p. 3). By 1976, terms such as *issue advertising* and *advocacy advertising* were being used in business publication discussions of the aggressive op-ed campaign made famous by Mobil Oil Corporation (Ross, 1976). At about this same time, the International Association of Advertising, in its global study of issues communication, urged adoption of the less contentious term *controversy advertising* (Barnet, 1975).

Dozens of articles published in the late 1970s and early 1980s discussed the new role of corporate communication and the strategic responses companies needed to take to counter their critics. In September 1978, Kalman B. Druck, chairman of Harshe-Rotman & Druck, Inc., told the Houston Chapter of the PRSA that "enormous opportunities await those who are willing to make the commitment, to apply professional management and public relations skills to the bitter confrontations industry is now facing" (p. 114).

Critics such as Sethi (1976a, 1976b, 1977) strenuously argued that merely explaining the corporate point of view could never be efficacious. Companies that shout loudest often may deserve regulation most. Discussion of what companies do in the face of changing social issues increased managers' sensitivity to changing expectations that members of the public had regarding responsible and reflective business practices (Heath, 1988).

A major proponent of business planning as the centerpiece of SIM was Archie R. Boe (1979), CEO of Allstate Insurance Companies (1972–1982) and later president of Sears (1982–1984). He created a Strategic Planning Committee in 1977 and an Issues Management Committee in 1978. The two groups had interlocking memberships. The Issues Management Committee was chaired by a vice president who also was a member of the Strategic Planning Committee.

As these examples demonstrate, issues management, in its struggle for prominence, has not relied exclusively on communication options; many leaders who helped form the discipline recognized the need to integrate planning, public policy analysis, and ethics along with various approaches to communication.

The Public Affairs Council (1978) was quick to see the limits of a narrow approach to the management of issues and offered sound counsel in a pamphlet titled *The Fundamentals of Issue Management*. According to the Council, "Issues management is a program which a company uses to increase its knowledge of the public policy process and enhance the sophistication and effectiveness of its involvement in that process" (p. 1). What were the functions required of issues management? The council listed these: "identifying issues and trends, evaluating their impact and setting priorities, establishing a company position, designing company action and response to help achieve the position (e.g., communication, lobbying, lawsuits, and advertising, etc.), and implementing the plans" (p. 2). Communication was the heart of issues management:

> Public affairs has increasingly come to mean not merely a response to change, but a positive role in the management of change itself in the shaping of public policies and programs, and in the development of corporate activities to implement change constructively. (p. 2)

Sponsored by the Conference Board's Public Affairs Research Council, Brown (1979) conducted a research project to determine how public affairs practitioners and corporate executives defined issues management. It featured strategic business planning as the centerpiece of effective issues management. The study argued that issues management must be integrated and focused on the central task of helping the company by improving the quality of its strategic management. What tasks could achieve this goal, according to Brown (1979)? The answer: planning, monitoring, analyzing, and communicating.

An early effort to identify the key functions of issues management reasoned that it involved three activities: "issue identification, corporate proaction, and the inclusion of public affairs issues in established decision-making processes and managerial functions" (Fleming, 1980, p. 35). Business professors, such as Fleming, led this innovation, and communication specialists and scholars joined later. Business faculty members, in particular Post (1978, 1979) and Buchholz (1982b, 1985), produced seminal studies to expose the need for companies and other organizations to recognize the important roles public policy and societal ethics play in their planning efforts and operations.

A milestone in this line of reasoning was *Issues Management in Strategic Planning* by Renfro (1993). A pioneer in the theory and practice of issues management, he worked to define the factors that predict how issues emerge and become worth considering. He stressed the need to identify and monitor issues as preliminary to strategic planning. "The field of issues management emerged as public relations or public affairs officers included more and more forecasting and futures research in their planning and analysis of policy" (p. 23). In this sense, "Issues management is an intelligence function that does not get involved in the 'operations side' unless specifically directed to do so" (p. 89). Despite its need to support business activities, this function "is not closely connected to immediate operations and the bottom line, and therefore, it is difficult to determine the effectiveness and value of an issues management capability" (p. 89).

As it has emerged, issues management has been a reaction to activism and the increasing intraindustry and interindustry pressure to define and implement higher standards of corporate responsibility as well as to debate in public what those standards should be. Similar struggles occur between nonprofits, especially those engaged in activist and government agencies at all levels. The strategic advantage of effective SIM is that it encompasses *all* efforts organizations must make to create mutually beneficial relationships with key players in the marketplace and public policy arena by sensing changing standards of the norms preferred by key publics, especially those that have become activists. Such efforts can be reactionary or proactive.

As this review demonstrates, issues management can be limited to a communication model or a commitment to high ethical standards, but leaders in the discipline have long recognized the need to integrate strategic planning, public policy analysis, and communication (Marx, 1986). Savvy companies have used issues management to determine which product lines are advisable in light of public policy trends (Fleming, 1980; Stroup, 1988). Seeing sound reason to connect issues monitoring and strategic planning, Stroup (1988) observed, "Early knowledge of these trends would give the company more time to change negative attitudes toward business or to adapt business practices proactively if attitudes and expectations could not be swayed from the identified path" (p. 89). Thinking of this kind, demonstrating how issues management matured from a publicity and press agentry activity to one involved in strategic business planning, is captured in Figure 1.2. It summarizes how over the years public relations and other related activities have combined with executive decision making to make the organization more effective in working with advocates of diverse opinions. The centerpiece in the process is savvy management and ethical decision making.

Proponents of issues management assert that it is vital to strategic management in four key ways: (a) Systematic issues identification, scanning, monitoring, and analysis allow firms to intersect the zones of meaning that form public opinion at formative and crucial stages. (b) Issues management helps organizations be proactive rather than reactive in their stances of corporate responsibility. (c) Issues management uses issues monitoring to supply executives with ample quantitative and qualitative analysis to solve strategic planning problems. (d) Two-way communication can reach constituencies in a way that is collaborative and long range rather than short term. It is not limited to periodic press releases, media relations, and publicity strategies but rather features the processes of dialogue. SIM assumes that organizations must achieve harmony by influencing

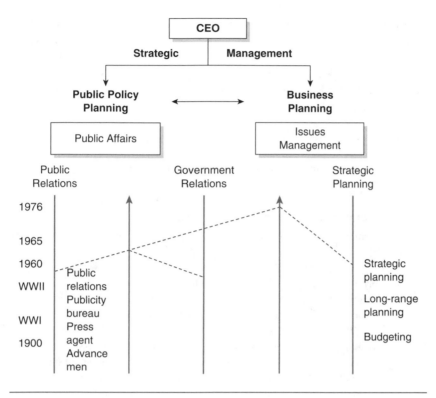

Figure 1.2   Evolution of Issues Management

as well as accommodating public policy stakeholders, although it never abandons the stewardship role organizations must play by asserting and defending their interests (Ackerman & Bauer, 1976; MacNaughton, 1976).

Extending this viewpoint, Arrington and Sawaya (1984) claimed that the heart of issues management "is reconciliation of conflicting internal interests on public policy issues of strategic importance in order to make a coherent external advocacy" (p. 150). This activity requires analysis and planning of public affairs options that should be viewed as analogous to corporate planning and research and development as a strategic process to help realize the basic objectives of a company. Wartick and Rude (1986) claimed that issues management loses its identity and credibility when it is not positioned to implement comprehensive programs. It is most useful when it interlocks with strategic information management because corporate culture fosters the acquisition and use of information in strategic planning (Ansoff, 1980;

Heath, 1991a, 1991b). A survey by Post, Murray, Dickie, and Mahon (1982) discovered that a critical phase in a company's (or any organization's) effort to adjust to its environment is the decision to integrate a public affairs perspective into corporate planning and management. A workshop held in 1993 concluded that a SIM program might not reach its potential, for six reasons (Tucker et al., 1993):

- Executives worry that the effects of issues management programs are too long term in a planning tradition in which management philosophy keeps executives focused on quarterly results and near-term solutions to long-term problems.
- Much needs to be accomplished to refine the ability to quantify the impact of issues management on corporate bottom lines.
- Communication is not the only function of issues management that often requires reactive and proactive corporate policy and practice changes to avoid collisions with public policy or to seize the opportunities it creates.
- The discipline is not owned by public relations practitioners and can be thought of too narrowly as a means for achieving publicity or working with the media rather than concentrating on issues of law, corporate policy, strategic business planning, and technical operations changes as well.
- It does not serve an organization adequately when it is not a corporate-level function that injects careful consideration of public policy planning options by seasoned senior corporate members involved in executive discussions.
- Traditional public relations training and experience often leave practitioners too narrow in their visions of what they can offer to a company to think beyond communication solutions to problems that cannot yield to information exchange and messages designed for external publics.

As Ewing (1987) concluded more than 20 years ago and still holds true today, "Issues management is about power" (p. 1). Organizations, as the collective expression of individual interests, engage in reward-loss (risk/benefit) analysis regarding the expediency of opposing or yielding to power pressures from stakeholders who can impose sanctions. The equation works like this: Assuming accuracy of understanding between the parties in contention with one another but suffering an unchangeable difference in evaluation, companies, regulators, or activist groups have the option of exerting influence or opposing the influence efforts of others. Issues management serves organizations when it assists executives to foster the bottom line by enhancing the quality of relationships with stakeholders in a power arena. To do so requires that organizations must not only engage in their own risk management but also must foster societal risk management.

To avoid collision that can become unproductive, SIM requires and fosters a variety of constructive adjustments, both reactive and proactive. Not only is issues management interested in the substance and impact of public policy, but it also can lead to the creation and implementation of policy internal to an organization. The resolution of the differences between organizational planning and management and external publics' expectations constitutes the dynamics of the legitimacy gap. Internal policy should meet or exceed key public expectations if the organization is going to avoid suffering the consequences of a legitimacy gap. Based on the discussion reviewed in this section, issues management consists of four core functions: engaging in smart business and public policy planning, playing tough defense and smart offense, getting the house in order, and scouting the terrain to gain early warning about troublesome issues (Heath & Cousino, 1990). To this end, SIM is a set of departmental activities, a culture of thinking smart to minimize conflict and maximize collaborations, and a philosophy of responsibility and reflectiveness that optimizes the quality of community interests.

SIM: Cornerstone of Strategic Business Planning

In short, what is happening around the organization can affect its ability to receive and use the resources it needs, in its resource dependency, to achieve its mission and vision. SIM weighs in when managers set out their mission, vision, and objectives. It is vital to how managers budget and supervise. It focuses attention on the balance and strains between the business arena, the generation of revenue, and the public policy arena, the formal and informal policies of society that define what is acceptable and unacceptable organization behavior and thereby help steer the organization through strategic business planning (Hillman, 2001; Schuler, 2001).

Strategic business planning (regardless of the type of organization) is always the starting point for SIM since the question is this: How can the business plan be achieved in light of marketplace and public policy positions? A quick glimpse can offer illustrations of the sorts of issues that affect the likelihood that a strategic business plan can be successfully implemented to obtain the needed resources:

- A country that might be engaged with another country in trade discussions that affect whether companies from either country can do business in and/or with companies in the other country
- Regulatory standards that may require that a company spend more as part of its strategic business plan to reduce toxic emissions or increase worker safety

- Health and safety standards that can require key businesses (and even other types of organizations) to spend more to comply with those standards as a requirement for operation
- Workplace issues that affect how organizations enact their business plans, such as age of workers, compensation (minimum wage), immigration status, and health and safety standards
- Governmental agency regulatory standards such as those implemented at the federal level by the Environmental Protection Agency and the Federal Drug Administration
- Raised vehicle mileage standards
- War on terrorism, which can create changes for security reasons
- Changes in finance policy, including borrowing and lending practices
- Changes in lifestyles, which might include environmentally responsible, sustainable, humane, and renewable practices as replacements for previous business plans
- Housing construction standards, as well as changes in drainage, traffic patterns, and even safety from wildfires, earthquakes, violent storms, floods, and mudslides
- Infrastructure improvements, repairs, maintenance, and construction, such as bridges and highways
- Outrage factors, such as unfair or unsafe labor practices, inhumane farming, and threats to public safety/health

Such a list often stresses the threats to organizational planning, but they also offer opportunities. For instance, as environmental regulation increases, it creates a market for equipment and services needed to meet higher standards.

In this way, SIM rests on the development and implementation of four kinds of activities. Each of these can be viewed as a requirement or pillar of a total issues management approach to organizational success:

1. *Strategic business planning:* Whether a business, a government agency, or nonprofit organization, issues management can help managers/planners to know the environment in which they operate, what strains and opportunities are at play, and how the organization can best be positioned to achieve its mission and vision.

2. *Strategic issue monitoring:* This plan is developed and executed to help management to know what issues exist, who supports and opposes them, what they mean for the future of the organization, how they are changing, and how deeply supported they are.

3. *Strategic corporate responsibility adjustment:* One of the axioms of issues management is that the strain of issues debate grows from differences over what makes an organization one of quality. What leads people to respect

or condemn and criticize each organization, individually and by type? If there is a legitimacy gap between what an organization does, how it does it, and what others believe it should do and how, then management must understand the challenge, know the criticism, and respond to it through planning, operations, or communication.

4. *Strategic communication planning and execution:* Debate, controversy, difference, and collaborative decision making are the lifeblood of issues management. If everyone agreed on every matter, issues management would not exist. It is the result of various kinds of disagreement that ultimately shape and reflect preferences of society. It rests on platforms of fact, value, and policy.

Preceding sections of this book have laid the rationale for making management and planning more savvy and reflective by increasing the organization's ability to listen to and regard the opinions of its stakeholders and stakeseekers. The objective of effective planning is to create as much harmony as possible while minimizing friction between the organization and those persons and groups whose favor the organization courts in the dynamics of power resource management. Unwise conflict can be costly. For this reason, SIM cannot have full impact if it is not part of strategic business planning—end of argument. This section explains the strategic planning process and demonstrates how issues management can enhance that process by tailoring it to the public policy arena as well as to the marketplace. In this section and throughout the book, strategic business planning is treated as a generic process by which revenue is generated and allocated to achieve the organization's mission. This process operates in every kind of organization, not just businesses. This section begins with a discussion of the rationale for including SIM in strategic business planning and then walks through the steps of this process.

The effect of the public policy arena, a vital theme in issues management, has changed over the years. Reflecting this trend, Brown (1979) observed that in the 1960s, according to a prominent consultant, 80% of planning was concerned with what management desired and 20% with how the world affected the company. "Now the figures are reversed or at least ought to be. Hyperbole perhaps: but the trend is unmistakable, and doubtless irreversible" (p. 3).

This observation is relevant today because regulation and legislation continue to affect private-sector activities. As well as creating constraints, public policy promotes business revenue and generates initiatives as well.

Strategic management entails an organization's ability (whether profit making or nonprofit) to generate the revenue it needs to survive and grow. Nonprofits and governmental agencies depend on revenue flow from stakeholders who want something in return. For that reason, management is optimal when it engages in the strategic acquisition and use of human and financial resources to create mutually beneficial relationships with stakeholders and stakeseekers. This planning process consists of delineating that complex series of independent and dependent variables that lead to the final planning objective of the organization, that dependent variable that is the product of all other variables, the acquisition and maintenance of resources. In many ways, the final dependent variable is support rather than opposition by its various publics. That planning model can guide strategic business planning and management regardless of whether the organization is profit making or not for profit. Each organization exists to the extent that it generates and wisely uses revenue.

As captured in Figure 1.3, strategic planning is the complex and creative process of goal setting and strategy selection whereby, for instance, a business seeks to optimize profits or any other type of organization seeks to maximize its resource acquisition and use. On one hand, then, we have revenue maximization. On the other, we have cost reduction, which can result from minimizing the interference of stakeholders in the strategic use of those resources.

Strategic planning is a systematic process that consists of (a) defining an organization's mission, (b) setting the objectives that must be accomplished to achieve the mission, (c) engaging in tactical programming and budgeting to accomplish the objective, (d) managing resources during the period required to achieve the objectives, and (e) monitoring progress and making adjustments during the implementation of the strategic plan as required by situational analysis of the circumstances that impinge on it. Plans require different time

Figure 1.3   Integrating Strategic Planning and Issues Management

frames, but they usually are "rolling." That means they are constantly refined but projected to guide management for 2 to 3 years and even as long as 10 to 15 years. All matters flow from the organization's mission and strategic business plan needed to accomplish that mission.

Strategic planning entails knowing short-term and predicting long-term trends and conditions. Such knowledge is achieved by conducting situational analysis, estimating strengths and weaknesses of the organization and the industry vis-à-vis marketplace and public policy forces, and engaging in creative decision making and resource allocation intended to accommodate or exploit the situation. All of this involves developing, repairing, and strengthening stakeholder relations.

What specific planning role does SIM play? Arrington and Sawaya (1984) concluded that it can enable an organization "to participate effectively in the shaping and resolution of public issues that can help or harm its operations" (p. 148). They see this function as a complement to public affairs that may otherwise be "confined to reactive, 'fire-fighting' conduct." Because it is inseparable from basic business concerns, SIM "is simply never unrelated to bottom-line consequences" (p. 148). Therefore, they proposed that issues management should perform "three concurrent activities: foresight, policy development, and advocacy." Foresight involves identification, monitoring, analyzing, and prioritizing issues. But it "is neither futurism nor forecasting; it is pragmatic, recurring judgment about external factors critical to company success" (p. 149).

Policy development, Arrington and Sawaya (1984) believed, is "the routine 'heart' of issues management." It requires reconciling "conflicting internal interests on public policy issues of strategic importance in order to make a coherent external advocacy" (p. 150). The final function, advocacy, includes communication efforts used to reach targeted audiences and achieve campaign goals. Such advocacy is best when it is designed to make society more fully functioning by fostering constructive dialogue rather than merely seeking to gain the advantage of one organization at some loss to its stakeholders or stake-seekers. In all of its facets, these authors reasoned, issues management supports strategic planning: "Strategic planning must ensure that various operating company plans are mutually consistent. Policy development in issues management must resolve differences among operating divisions on key public policy issues" (p. 153).

The planning process is invigorated by SIM functions: (a) anticipate, analyze, and prioritize issues; (b) help develop an organizational position on each vital issue; (c) identify key publics and influential persons whose support are vital to the public policy issue; and (d) identify desired behaviors of publics and influential persons. These functions support each organization's mission (Tucker & Trumpfheller, 1993). Broadly applied, these functions can empower communication specialists. Narrowed only to communication functions, it falls short of being a management activity vital to strategic planning and operations. Those who want to be issues managers need to engage in smart planning, scout the terrain, get the house in order, and enact tough defense and smart offense, the processes of collaborative decision making and responsible advocacy (Heath, 2007a).

Strategic business planning requires analysis and foresight of trends in the political economy that shape marketplace and public policy environments. The political economy expresses the value premises that comprise the ideology of each society. It reflects market trends and defines economic well-being of the members of society. It is an expression of policy guidelines regarding what organizational practices are acceptable and what are not. The political economy defines what players, whether in business trends or in policy formation, shape markets and public policy. The political economy defines the issues that confront each organization as a challenge or an opportunity.

Public policy and marketplace concerns tend to be based on one or more of the following issue motivators: security, equality, environmental quality, and fairness (Heath, 1988). *Security* is a measure of the extent that business operations, products, and services are believed to pose intolerable risks for those who come into contact with them. *Equality* is a judgment of the extent to which persons are treated the same, for instance, as defined in terms of civil rights. *Environmental quality* is a value judgment on preferences regarding standards typically associated with environmental regulation. *Fairness* is an estimate of the value received for what is given in exchange; for instance, a service (such as the cost of electricity) can be thought to be too expensive. All people, according to this set of motivators, could be treated unfairly by the pricing of products or services even though each customer would be treated equally. Reducing issues to their essence helps persons engaged in issues monitoring and analysis. Insights into these motivators sharpen strategic planning and shed light on how publics recognize and define problems.

Concerns connected to these motivators are the heart of the legitimacy gap, the extent to which key publics differ with executives regarding what constitutes sufficient security, equality, fairness, or environmental sensitivity. Trouble or opportunity can result when key publics believe that a problem arises from the difference between what exists and what is expected. This gap can demand a corrective communication campaign or changes in business operations, especially elevated standards of corporate responsibility, needed to mitigate or take advantage of the difference. These options are at the heart of the strategic business planning process that, if applied properly, obtains and uses information and judgment in ordinary and turbulent situations.

If planning is properly executed in normal times, it lays a foundation for unexpected events in turbulent times. Renfro (1993) summarized the prime tasks of strategic management as a means to understand the current and future operating environment, define organizational mission and goals, identify options, evaluate and implement strategies to achieve the mission and goals, and evaluate actual performance to lead the organization with a vision of the future.

MISSION AND VISION STATEMENTS

Mission and vision statements are stated in terms that position each organization in its operating environment: its marketplace where it competes for revenue, its organizational character and culture, its standards of corporate responsibility, and the dynamics of the public policy arena. Simply put: "The corporate mission is the purpose or reason for the corporation's existence" (Hunger & Wheelen, 1993, p. 14). The statement should differentiate each organization from all others. "A well-conceived mission statement defines the fundamental, unique purpose that sets a business apart from other firms of its type and identifies the scope of the business's operations in terms of products offered and markets served" (p. 15).

Mission statements translate into objectives toward which all management activity is directed and by which results of the organization's activities are assessed. The statement is most serviceable when it can be empirically measured to determine how well the mission and vision are being accomplished. In the judgment of Bowman (1990), mission statements should reflect the "claims of relevant stakeholders" (p. 6) and express key company and community attitudes, such as those regarding growth, innovation, and quality. Issues managers are challenged to bring to bear on these discussions the sociopolitical and public policy factors.

ENVIRONMENTAL-SITUATIONAL POSITION ASSESSMENT

Planning and management do not operate in a vacuum. Environmental scanning and situational analysis can locate and understand threats and opportunities created by public policy forces. Issues managers are expected to help assess the value assumptions and operant principles that shape stakeholder expectations. Such insights influence executives' sense of the preferred standards of corporate responsibility and accountability that differentiate rewardable from punishable actions and ones that build or harm relationships. "Situational analysis requires that top management attempt to find a strategic fit between external opportunities and internal strengths while working around external threats and internal weaknesses" (Hunger & Wheelen, 1993, p. 157).

Issues analysis must not only be sensitive to potential effects of public policy on the organization's policy and operations but also needs to look for market advantage. The most important counseling that can be done by issues managers is to offer advice on community opinion and public policy trends. Of interest are trends that are likely to (a) constrain current organizational policy and thereby increase operating costs; (b) pose strategic advantage for organizations that can seize the opportunity to change policies and operations, thereby offering new products or services, reducing costs, and making other strategic business alterations; (c) offer options for improving relationships with key stakeholders; and (d) provide new means for fostering community interests.

Situational analysis needs to determine which stakeholders think the operations and policies of the organization are legitimate. Central to situational assessment is the image or reputation of the organization. In this sense, image (and even brand equity) is a stakeholder's attitude toward an organization (its officials, personnel, policies, operations, products, and services). This attitude is a composite of the beliefs (subjective probabilities) that the organization is associated with certain attributes and the evaluative valence (positive or negative) of those attributes. Such evaluations are basic to predictions that stakeholders will act favorably toward or against the organization in exchange for what is thought to be actions that reward or harm the stakeholder (Ajzen & Fishbein, 1980; Fishbein & Ajzen, 1975). Part of image is an assessment of how well it meets stakeholders' expectations; another consideration is the extent that it favorably differentiates the organization from others, especially those in competition for the same resources (Bowman, 1990). As Renfro (1993) observed, "The issues management system provides a forum for input throughout the organization into the policy and strategy development process" (p. 95).

BUSINESS-ECONOMIC TRENDS AND FORCES

Although other members of the executive cadre are likely to have equal or greater expertise to monitor and analyze business and economic trends and forces, issues managers must understand those forces. They need to examine how shifts in policy can affect the acquisition and allotment of human and financial resources as well as shape markets and competitive advantage. They should help formulate policy changes to support the acquisition and use of financial and human resources.

PUBLIC POLICY TRENDS AND FORCES

In cooperation with executives, staff members, and operating personnel, issues managers monitor and analyze public policy trends to determine how shifts in norms, values, and legislative or regulatory codes offer market opportunities or threats. Focal points of this analysis are governmental bodies (legislative, regulatory, and judicial), industry policy bodies (typically trade associations), activist groups, academic and scholarly bodies and associations, and journalistic reporting and editorial agendas. As policy is refined by persons who are members of identifiable organizations, it goes through iterations that allow issues managers the opportunity to calculate the opportunities and constraints that it poses. The change in policy can be pressed by the organization as well as by other governmental, activist, or industry groups. Such options become addressed in the formation of the organization's public policy plan.

STRATEGY FORMULATION

The organization can enhance its economic gain and minimize its costs resulting from unproductive conflict and relationship damage by looking for advantage and points of leverage, either by continuing operations or altering them. Strategy formulation should be based on strategic positioning to achieve objectives derived from the mission statements and organizational self-assessment. Mission statements are implemented by the formulation of objectives, the creation of strategies, and the use of programs to achieve the strategies (Hunger & Wheelen, 1993). SIM applies the strategic planning process to comprehend and voice the standards of corporate responsibility that prevail in the community.

MARKET-DRIVEN DECISIONS IN STRATEGIC PLANNING

Some of each organization's planning is cast in response to market and other economic trends. (The following list is illustrative rather than complete.)

- Undertake, abandon, or modify a product or service.
- Target new markets for a product or service or abandon current ones.
- Increase or downscale quality of a product or service.
- Diversify or consolidate operations or holdings.
- Change methods of acquiring financing to enhance economic advantage.
- Change resource allocation or use.
- Adapt to changing tastes (attitudes that have market impact).
- Change vendors as a result of price or value.
- Change labor practices as a result of market forces and employment trends.
- Change operating procedures to become more profitable.

PUBLIC POLICY-DRIVEN DECISIONS IN STRATEGIC PLANNING

Strategic planning is improved by candid and honest consideration of strains and advantages created by the debates that are ongoing and thereby shape the public policy environment. Internal policy decisions may follow or work to lead opinion formation in public policy trends that increase the opportunity to satisfy stakeholder expectations. (The following list is illustrative, not complete.)

- Take a public communication stance on key policy issues.
- Engage in actions to create, change, or defeat legislation or regulation.
- Change operations and other market-driven decisions to adapt to public policy trends.
- Change mission to adapt to or take a leadership role in public policy issues.
- Change image to adapt to public policy trends.
- Change operating standards (corporate responsibility) to adapt to public policy issues.
- Alter employee performance criteria and procedures to adapt to public policy issues.
- Change product or service lines to adapt to public policy issues and standards of liability or public expectations.
- Change resource use in response to availability, cost, and prevailing attitudes of key publics or public policy.
- Reassess and alter planning assumptions to conform to changes in priorities and definitions of premises fundamental to the political economy.
- Change vendors as a result of public policy.
- Change methods of acquiring financing as a result of public policy.
- Change labor practices as a result of public policy trends.

STAKEHOLDER RELATIONSHIP DECISIONS IN STRATEGIC PLANNING

The desire and effort to build solid, long-term, and mutually beneficial relationships with stakeholders should drive the strategic planning process. This planning seeks to create, strengthen, repair, or build stakeholder relationships.

- Ascertain and work to achieve mutual interests with stakeholders/stakeseekers.
- Engage in communication campaigns to redefine or reassert company image to demonstrate conformance to stakeholder expectations.
- Foster constituent relationships with stakeholders based on mutual interests.

STRATEGY IMPLEMENTATION THROUGH TACTICAL PROGRAMMING AND BUDGETING

A strategic plan has little meaning and no chance of success until tactics have been selected and budgeted. The strategic business plan comes to life through the allocation of resources to generate and wisely use revenue to benefit the organization and its stakeholders. Business plans are sensitive to standards of operations that are shaped in the public policy arena. Examples of these standards include liability, financing options, service quality, personnel requirements, and import-export procedures. Public policy changes are created by dramatic fluctuations in the economy as well as by legislative initiatives of key groups. Policies may occur due to actions at the federal, state, county, and municipal levels. These changes pose threats to current and planned activities as well as open opportunities.

A counterpart to the strategic business plan, the strategic public policy plan, entails the allocation of resources to create, change, take advantage of, mitigate, or defeat public policies through legislation, regulation, or litigation. This plan is a tactical option to engage in governmental relations to help create a climate favorable to the organization's strategic business plan while seeking to advance the interests of the stakeseekers and stakeholders of the organization.

A third plan, the strategic communication plan, becomes meaningful when resources are allocated to reach key publics with properly designed messages to meet these publics' needs to understand and formulate appropriate opinions and behaviors in the mutual interests of all parties. This plan is a tactical option to foster agreement and understanding of the facts, values, and policies vital to the organization's strategic business plan. The objective is to communicate openly and honestly with the intent of building harmony with interested parties in ways that lead them to cognitively and materially support the organization's efforts to achieve its business plan.

If one of the major strains in its environment is the legitimacy gap with its stakeholders, each organization needs a strategic management of operations plan that calls for an allocation of resources to lessen that gap. This plan requires allocations to accomplish several refinements. One requirement is to constantly refine standards of corporate responsibility. Organizations should consider in their strategic management the advantage to be gained by creating and maintaining long-term, mutually beneficial relationships. They are wise to use training and development programs to help employees achieve standards of social responsibility. As standards are ascertained, they need to be communicated to employees and other key publics. Operating units need to engage in issues management. To do this, they need to establish and implement controls to prevent other functions, such as marketing and advertising, from creating stakeholder relationship problems, such as overpromising the attributes of products or services in ways that cannot be met, making untrue product or service claims, and adapting to market or policy forces in ways that offend the standards of corporate responsibility held by key publics.

Strains occur not only from what the entire organization does but also from actions by its operating units. For this reason, executives need strategic development of unit missions and strategic plans. What each unit does must support the corporate goals and mission (Hax & Majluf, 1991). To do this, each unit must create mission statements that specify the role it plays in the firm. Cognizant of the corporate strategic plan and in conjunction with strategic plans of other departments, staff and operating units need to develop their own strategic plans and determine how to achieve them through operations and policies. Based on how many resources each unit needs to support its strategic plan, budgets are developed and implemented. Without doubt, unit plans are enhanced by being integrated into the principles of the entire organization.

PERFORMING STRATEGIC ADJUSTMENT AND RELATIONSHIP DEVELOPMENT

The adjustments and tactical shifts used by an organization need to be constantly adjusted to meet the changing needs and desires of the stakeholders as well as changes in the organization's mission and vision. Strategic management ensures that operations and communication efforts are devoted to determining which stakeholder relationships are sound or need development, either by changed operations or enhanced communication. Stakeholder interests are likely to be at odds with one another, in varying degrees. One role of issues management is to open the organization to stakeholders so that their opinions can be ascertained and analyzed for implications regarding changes in operations, policies, or messages. Stakeholders are likely to have interests that are at odds with one another. For instance, investors like the organization to maximize its profits, an interest that may be at odds with environmental activists or consumer groups that oppose certain approaches to the generation of profit. Issues management is expected to reconcile these conflicts to the extent possible within current market and public policy forces.

EVALUATING THE EFFECTIVENESS OF THE STRATEGIC BUSINESS PLAN

Organizations set a vision and determine what objectives and tactics are needed to achieve that vision. Constant monitoring centered on key measures can determine whether tactics are achieving the plan. These measures need to address the success of the total plan and its successful implementation by levels and units: Applying a management-by-objectives model, tempered with a commitment to the fostering of mutual interest, assessment entails the generation of empirical data to determine whether resources expended in the implementation process were sufficient to achieve the goals and whether the goals were met. Analysis also needs to be qualitative. It must assess the quality of stakeholder relationships. Success is measured by the extent to which stakeholders reward the organization's policies by granting them support or oppose those policies and work to constrain or redirect the organization to alternative standards (see Table 1.1 for putting this all together).

SIM: Advocacy, Dialogue, and Collaborative Decision Making

Success does not occur in a vacuum. Perhaps the best way to describe the robustness of the debate over policy options is to think of it as a wrangle in the marketplace of ideas (Heath, 1992). The heritage of issues management has been a journey to understand how success depends on the ability to forge harmony between each organization and others. At times, the logic of SIM has featured communication options primarily and even exclusively. That view is narrow, even dysfunctional. It reflects the virtue of robust issue debate but ignores the possibility that if the organization cannot convince key stakeholders of the merit of its case, it will have to adapt to the preferred view of operations (Hill, 1963).

Out of this logic, such organizations can foster a strong and collaborative sense of community (Hallahan, 2004, Kruckeberg & Starck, 1988). Such adaptation is likely to require reflective management (Van Ruler & Vercic, 2005) and responsible advocacy (Heath, 2007a). Such reflectiveness and advocacy, internal and external, can enrich the dialogue, thereby leading to collective decision making necessary for a sound community. Stressing the connection between ethics, dialogue, and community, Leeper (2005) reasoned,

> The communitarian approach to ethics seems to be a virtue approach, which puts the emphasis on character development and on Aristotle's golden mean. The teaching of this approach would necessarily involve dialogue as to what it means to be virtuous. What it means to be ethical would not focus on rule following but on the situation and the interaction of the parties involved. (p. 170)

To that end, SIM can help organizations to make society more fully func tional (Heath, 2006b). Because it is a systematic management process as well as a culture or state of mind, SIM requires a complex of multidisciplinary functions. Savvy managements learn that these functions work best when they are brought into play as early as possible, while they can take advantage of or correct the organization's position in relationship to its stakeholders. In this effort, according to L. A. Grunig, J. E. Grunig, and Ehling (1992),

> Public relations is most likely to contribute to effectiveness when the senior public relations manager is a member of the dominant coalition where he or

Table 1.1   Integrating Stages of the Monitoring, Planning and
Communication Functions

Monitoring Options	Planning Options	Communication Options
1. Identifying stakeholders/ stakeseekers and stakes.	1. Develop corporate and unit missions and goals.	1. Establish communication goals and issue positions.
2. Identifying mutual interests, strains, conflict, disagreement, agreement, and cooperation.	2. Integrate SIM into business planning and management.	2. Select key audiences and engage in communication, including collaborative decision making.
3. Analyze issues and determine issue priorities.	3. Select and structure issues personnel matrix.	3. Select and refine message content and issue positions.
4. Identify facts, premises, and conclusions.	4. Budget for SIM.	4. Design messages.
5. Audit communication campaign.	5. Apply learning from monitoring to refine code of corporate responsibility.	5. Select channels and communication venues—mediated, group, interpersonal, collaborative.
	6. Incorporate public policy issues into corporate planning.	6. Implement campaign and continuously engage in collaborative decision making.
	7. Formulate public policy stances and implement public policy plan.	7. Reevaluate goals.
	8. Incorporate corporate responsibility principles into organizational and unit reviews.	8. Reassess strategic options.
	9. Reassess organizational stance on public policy and strategic issues and its fit with internal and external policy issue positions as well as stakeholder/ stakeseeker interests.	9. Reassess strategies.
		10. Redesign campaign.
		11. Continue campaigns with refinements.

she is able to shape the organization's goals and to help determine when external publics are most strategic. (p. 86)

Symmetry is an ideal. It can be seen in several ways. One is to assume that each side of a controversy yields some of its control over the debate to achieve something of the sort of power parity. This is often a nice ideal but difficult to achieve. Typically, during issue controversy, each side believes strongly (despite the fact that some sides are multinational corporations) that it lacks the power to fully assert its influence and voice its point of view. In fact, SIM operates out of a power resource management model, typically one that features efforts by the "power have not's" to gain and exert power against what they believe to be the "power have's."

Featuring symmetry only as a matter of power can overly assume the power that a large company has against a smaller, more rhetorically skilled adversary. Perhaps few greater examples of this have occurred in recent years than the changes in smoking policy created by antismoking advocates. They even exacted billions from the tobacco companies in the Master Settlement Agreement. Similarly, relatively small activist groups have changed environmental policy and other aspects of the public policy arena over the past 3 decades in the United States. So, instead of power as the only view of symmetry, we can feature the dynamics of the competing issue position, the wrangle of ideas. Each idea advances against a competing position. Especially given the dynamics of governmental hearings, lawsuits, and the Internet as a venue for conflicting ideas, each advocate sets for an idea, knowing that it will be met with a counterposition.

The centerpiece in the debate is the character of the organizations and individuals. SIM rests on the assumption lauded 2,000 years ago by the famous teacher of speech in Rome, Fabius Quintilian (1920–1922), that rhetoric requires people (or organizations in our era) to be good—of sound character— as the first step toward being an effective rhetor, a responsible advocate. As Burke (1973) said, democracy institutionalizes "the dialectic process, by setting up a political structure that gives full opportunity for the use of competition to a cooperative end" (p. 444). The dialogue consists of statement and counterstatement. In the best of worlds, it moves forward based on the refinement of fact, value, and policy. Advances also include the refinement of identifications and co-created narratives (Heath, 2006a). In essence, the goal of the many sides of some controversy centers on increasing or narrowing the legitimacy gap.

Since the era of Aristotle, rhetors have been challenged to aspire toward a display of character that creates credibility because the values they associate with their lives and arguments demonstrate sound character (Bostdorff, 1992). Such character brings admiration rather than condemnation. At the corporate level, it translates into high standards of corporate responsibility. At the rhetorical and power resource management level, it works for the infrastructures in which debate can transpire to the end that society is well served and community strengthened because of the quality of idea that emerges.

Conclusion

Operating in mutual interest with stakeholders and with a commitment to achieve social responsibility is vital to maintaining or restoring management's authority to guide its organization's destiny with minimum external constraint. Society consists of the assertion of interests. Interests have marketplace importance as well as roles in the public policy arena. Policies are means by which personal and corporate interests are achieved. The key, whether for individuals or organizations, is to achieve harmony between internal policies and standards expressed by external groups. This fit is fundamental to the rationale for issues management.

What future lies before issues management? Its prospect is bright, concluded Wartick and Rude (1986), if it can positively affect corporate performance by enhancing the firm's responsiveness to environmental change. Satisfactory outcomes require the careful linkage of issue priorities to corporate objectives and the development of action plans to make the firm more competitive (Littlejohn, 1986). Issues managers are challenged to capture the critical changes in the public policy environment and to integrate that information into the strategic business plan and management strategies. This information can offer business opportunities, justify the curtailment or change of business activities, and guide the standards by which the organization operates.

SIM Challenge: CSR and Long-Term Planning

In the past several years, business news has focused attention on the looming presence of China as a manufacturing and financial center for the 21st century. What often receives less attention is the sort of challenges it will face as the century continues. In fact, based on the experience in the United States, China will, at least for a while, sacrifice the health and well-being of its citizens (and indirectly the global population) for general prosperity and individual wealth. It is receiving internal and external calls for reform because of its business practices. Seeing parallels between the industrial growth in Great Britain and other countries in the late 19th and 20th centuries, Oster and Spencer (2006) pointed to the fundamental challenge as a SIM challenge:

> Now, China is confronting the same "trade-off between short-term profits by industry and the long-term profits by industry and the long-term burden of human and environmental costs," says Bruce Lamphear, a professor of environmental health at Cincinnati's Children's Hospital Medical Center. (p. A6)

Many of the industrial problems and issue challenges facing China were given top-of-the-hour attention during 2007. Some of that news started in 2006, after a boy died from swallowing a metal charm provided as a gift with Reebok sneakers. Reebok International Ltd. recalled 300,000 sneakers in the United States and a total of a half million in 25 other countries and committed to more carefully review products (U.S. Consumer Product Safety Commission, 2006). Chinese manufacturers use lead because it is abundant, adding it to products, including herbals, that are more valuable because they are sold by weight. The U.S. Consumer Product Safety Commission is one of many stakeholders pressuring change. So is the central Chinese government, after decades of ignoring this kind of problem. One is stricter monitoring of workplace standards. "Yet central authorities have found their efforts stymied by local officials whose promotions are based on growth in their local economies" (Oster & Spencer, 2006, p. A6). Lead has been a public health issue around the world for decades. Events such as the one above, however, have brought close scrutiny from government regulation. Typical of that SIM challenge is the headline of a recent story in *The Wall Street Journal:* "U.S. Moves to Tighten Rules on Lead in Children's Jewelry" (Munoz, 2006, p. D9). This crisis continued with the identification of lead and other toxins in toys, poorly manufactured tires, toothpaste containing toxic materials in large amounts, and deadly substances in pet food. False documentation and unwillingness to comply with industrial standards were the two primary motives, both linked with that nasty premise: Profit corrupts. As this issue neared crisis stage, China responded. The response was summarized in the opening line to a major news story in *The Wall Street Journal:*

> A death sentence meted out to the former head of China's food and drug watchdog, together with the announced formation of a national food-recall system, suggests Beijing intends to send a stern message amid a series of contaminations that has drawn international attention. (Zamiska, Leow, & Oster, 2007, p. A3)

Is China taking on new standards of CSR to support its robust strategic business plan? How will it work issues in a global market, especially one where parents are aggressive in the management of children's risks: safety as a motivator? Is it fair for advanced industrialized societies to push for stricter regulations on developing economies? What is SIM's role in the answer to these questions?

Summary Questions

1. What is the heritage that created and sustains the need for SIM?

2. How is SIM best defined?

3. What functions are needed for a fully developed SIM program? Why are these vital to the optimal outcome?

4. What are the logics of stakeholder/stakeseeker analysis? Why is it a cornerstone of successful SIM?

5. What are the stages of strategic business planning? Are these the same for non-profits and governmental agencies?

6. How can SIM add value to organizational planning and implementation, regardless of the type of organization? In this regard, does SIM "occur" even if it is not planned, systematic, and striving for the highest and best resolution of various legitimacy gaps?

7. How does this view of SIM combine planning, monitoring, refining corporate responsibility, and communication?

2

Historical Foundations

A Search for Order

Vignette:
Westinghouse Versus Edison

Imagine the last 2 decades of the 19th century, when electric lights were a new invention, even a novelty. Houses had no appliances. That array of inventions, which we take for granted today, was on the horizon. Electric motors were increasingly being put in use. Marketing of electricity was designed to sell "electrified" homes rather than those using natural gas for illumination. One marketing campaign implored people to notice how their "modern" neighbors' homes were safer, and illumination by electricity made for brighter rooms. As more people began to use electricity, cities became crisscrossed with a spider web of increasingly dense networks of copper wire carrying electricity from generators to customers. This then fledgling industry of electricity produced one of the most interesting issues management campaigns in U.S. history, one that pitted two industrial titans against each other: George Westinghouse and Thomas Edison.

Issues management is often seen as consisting of controversy between an organization, typically a business or industry, and one or more activist stakeholding publics. In Chapter 1, we indicate that issues can occur within industries, as well as between them. In this intraindustry battle, George Westinghouse and Thomas Edison each had a vested interest in establishing public policy regarding competing electrical generating and distribution systems. Westinghouse preferred alternating current (AC). Edison advocated the use of direct current (DC). The resulting "battle of currents" formed the policy that regulates the modern electricity industry. Although Edison is synonymous with the electrical generating and distribution industry, Westinghouse

(Continued)

(Continued)

won the battle. How he did that is illustrative of two relevant strategic issues management (SIM) themes. Have a superior business plan and be able to advance it with successful public policy and issue communication campaigns.

George Westinghouse and Thomas Edison debated the issue of whether AC or DC should be the accepted technology. Such public policy decision would give that technology a monopoly. During the debate, messages became curious, furious, and even bizarre. In this campaign, "events," a public relations staple, were used to demonstrate the power, and even horror, of AC. The essential concern featured in this campaign was security or safety. Knowing that the public would prefer the safer technology, Edison campaigned to demonstrate that AC was dangerous.

The barons of the industry knew that if one standard prevailed, and they owned that technology, they would rule the industry. Such a single standard would be worth a fortune. This battle began innocently. After he invented the incandescent light bulb in 1872, Edison's DC became the standard of the industry. It worked well for incandescent lights and electric motors. Once he had products that could be sold, Edison turned to the generating side of the industry. Soon, lines carrying direct current began to lace cities.

All was going Edison's way until Nikola Tesla, a young inventor who came to America to work with Edison, invented and championed a superior technology called AC. It was his dream as he arrived in New York City at age 28. He was nearly penniless but held a letter of recommendation from Edison. By then, electricity had been a growing part of modern life for 2 decades. As often occurs, invention is only 50% of the proposition of what makes an industry. The other part is marketing and, in this case, the ability to use public policy to define an industry. The battle of currents was nothing less than a war over standardization. Although the war took many routes, it culminated in the decision as to whether Edison or Westinghouse would illuminate and energize the Columbian Exposition, the Chicago World's Fair.

When he arrived in New York City, Tesla was shocked to see what he thought was a shabby electricity distribution system that was being installed and maintained to use Edison's direct current. He had theoretical insights into ways to create a superior form of electricity, AC. Tesla wanted to offer his inventiveness to Edison and thus sought employment with this luminary. Edison was satisfied with his DC but offered Tesla an opportunity to conduct research at Edison's labs and even offered an incentive of $50,000 should the technology prove successful, an outcome Edison found unlikely. When the technology proved to be successful and appeared to rival direct current, Edison reneged on the deal, saying he had made the offer as a jest.

As it helped to define the industry, the flaws of DC were becoming apparent. DC was quite difficult to transmit because copper wires often overheated and broke. The quality of the current fluctuated. Equipment did not operate properly. The greater the demand on any system, the more likely it was to fail. A different standard, an alternative technology, was needed. Tesla's ideas were coming of age and came to the attention of Westinghouse, who was an inventor but also a marketing genius. He struck a friendship with Tesla and bought the rights to Tesla's technology. This was a truly beneficial business partnership. As an aside, although Tesla revolutionized electric technology, with discoveries that are still fostering advances today, he died nearly penniless.

Edison quickly recognized this threat to his growing empire. His brand equity and fortune were on the line. He started the battle of currents using publications of various types to tout the virtues of direct current. Beyond that, he and his issue allies stressed the threat of AC, which they framed as a safety issue. In addition to publications, he managed a series of events. Many of these included the electrocution of stray animals, cats and dogs. Next in line of animals used to prove the terrible power of AC were some horses and, more famously, Topsy the elephant on January 4, 1903. Topsy, a domesticated elephant with the Forepaugh Circus at Coney Island's Luna Park, was considered a threat because she had killed several men in as many years. Edison captured the event on film and would release it later that year under the title *Electrocuting an Elephant.* Edison, through an agent, convinced the state of New York to use AC as a means for capital punishment. The first attempt was botched. After two tries, the victim was dead. One commentator said using an axe would have been less gruesome. Such "events," standard public relations efforts, were used in this public relations campaign to offer proof of the dominant issue theme of safety. In short, the campaign was designed to scare people from supporting AC adoption.

The battle led to the formation of another corporate public relations department, as was becoming the trend in this era. One was established in 1889 by Westinghouse. Using the sort of public relations specialist of the era, Edison had sponsored a book titled *A Warning* to scare the public into favoring DC. It argued that alternating current is too lethal. Its appendix listed persons who had been killed by electricity. In 1889, Westinghouse countered with *Safety of the Alternating System of Electrical Distribution,* which extolled the virtues of that technology (Cutlip, 1995). One of the interesting elements of this debate was that each of these industrial barons lent his name to the brand equity of the industry.

Despite fear tactics, AC was adopted and licensed for the Columbia Exposition. It was the superior technology. Its merits withstood the Edison assault. Eventually, Edison adopted AC because he could more easily admit that he had lost a battle than to stop his industrial war.

As well as leading a technology to be accepted, SIM also helped create a new product of the burgeoning mass production society, the regulated monopoly. This public policy advance allowed state or local government to grant a monopoly to a local utility company. Although this was a time of rampant competition, business leaders and government officials recognized that competition was counterproductive to such industries. Each city or rural area was better off with a single service provider that would be regulated by city, county, or state law rather than marketplace conditions. Otherwise, a city, for instance, might become a tangle of power lines or telephone lines, each set of which was provided by a competitor. In the case of telephone competition, a family might not be able to call a neighbor if they did not subscribe to the same telephone service. AT&T was a leader in advancing regulated consolidation of the telephone industry, for instance.

By helping form this business technique for the electricity industry, Edison's business secretary, Samuel Insull, was able to obtain a 50-year electrical utility agreement with the Chicago City Council to operate as a regulated franchise. Insull brought his conviction in the regulated utility monopoly to his term as president of the National Electric Light Association. Although regulation might hold rates down from an optimal level, Insull argued successfully that it kept competition from entering a community and threatened the stability of a company (Olasky, 1987).

In the study and practice of issues management, a few key themes seem central to the argumentative foundations of public policy, that matter of contest that defines issues. Issues seem to group around a few common themes. One of those is safety, or security. Given its potency, it is amazing that Westinghouse did not lose the battle to such a potent line of argument. Perhaps his team was able to defend itself on that issue, or perhaps Edison went too far along that line of reasoning. Also, we can imagine that a general population that was worried about safety lobbied policy makers who built their decision on different principles.

Chapter Goals

This chapter serves as a transition between Chapter 1, which featured the definition and management aspects of strategic issues management (SIM), and the rest of this book. It takes a historical trip through several of the key moments in modern issues management history. It features key challenges and themes that started during the Industrial Revolution, when America quickly became a leader as a mass production/mass consumption society, which led to the social awareness that forced organizations, especially businesses and governmental agencies, to acknowledge and work with activist publics as had not been the case before the 1970s. This discussion centers on issues management, which started as an effort used by large companies to search for order in business practices but then led to having most issues raised by socially aware activism in the 20th century. In this effort, government has been reactive more often than proactive, following an agenda set by companies or critics. By the end of this chapter, you should have an understanding for and appreciation of the dynamics of public policy debate that has pitted companies against companies, as well as activists against one another and against companies. In this entire contest, government is a meeting ground and a warrior. The chapter ends with a quick look at some of the daunting issues that are likely to persist for the future. Safety, fairness, environmental quality, and equality have been key values in this debate. However local or national they have been, they are quickly going global. We can be fascinated by colonialism as a key part of the 19th century, for instance, which has a lot to do with international public policy debates in the 21st century. What is over the horizon?

What motivated the discussion of issues in the last half of the 19th century was the growth of a mass production/mass consumption economy. But issues debate was not initiated then; it is as old as human society. When a prehistoric tribe debated which trail to take or when and where to camp, it engaged in issues management. When an agrarian society partitioned land, negotiated tasks, shared or kept the rewards, assisted each other in times of crisis, and paid money for civil protection, it engaged in issues management. Differences needed to be reconciled for the good of the group. That model defines SIM today. In fact, over the past few years, we have argued that risk management is the collective incentive of the advancement and even survival of society. This paradigm defines this chapter on the modern history of SIM, a search for order (Wiebe, 1967).

Throughout history, in numerous and eclectic ways and often by inventive means, human society has been deeply engaged in discussions to try to understand, interpret, mitigate, and manage risks, supporting Mary Douglas's (1992) notion that society is structured essentially for the cooperative management of risk. How well societies engage in issues management determines their ability to manage risks and survive at least and thrive at best. Alarm, anger, and outrage can result when people believe they are exposed to technologies that distress or harm, whether they live and labor near the risk or encounter it while using or consuming a product. A primary motivator of activism is people's desire to be safe and healthy coupled with their vigilance for problems of that sort that need remedying. They are sensitive to the fairness and equality of risk distribution. They don't like to bear risks that benefit others. When organizations are seen as abusing the privileges given to them by their constituencies and other publics who effect and are affected by them, individual and community responses and governmental controls and regulations can and should sanction the capacity of organizations to continue to operate. According to R. Jones (2002), "The emergence of the powerful consumer and the critical public is not coincidental but a symptom of the emergence of the risk society" (p. 49).

However connected issues management was to other dominant institutions presently or historically, such as government and religious organizations, it is currently connected at the hip with corporate activities and policies. Every time the corporate operating climate becomes turbulent, issues management's popularity soars. Business executives continue to learn by trial and error that they must shape as well as respond to political conditions (Buchholz, 1982a; Divelbiss & Cullen, 1981; Weinstein, 1979). Typical of that rough and tumble in the marketplace was Westinghouse and Thomas Edison's fight over the standard of electricity for domestic, urban use as described in the opening vignette.

Opinions Shape Operating Environments

Public opinion and public policy go hand in hand. Business and other organizations have recognized this link for centuries. Trends in public opinion, therefore, predict, follow, or lead efforts to create and change public policy. In a generic sense, the term *public opinion* is a concept broadly useful for issue monitoring and analysis, strategic business planning, issue communication, or ascertaining key publics' standards of corporate responsibility. Yet, in complex ways, decisions by corporate entities, courts, legislators, and regulators reflect a choice between opinions. As expressed in legislation, regulation, or legal interpretation, an opinion is the public's opinion; one view is better than others. The struggle between businesses, governmental agencies, and activists is a search for order, an effort to standardize public policy and related practices through informal agreement as well as legislative, regulatory, or judicial action (Wiebe, 1968). Summarizing this struggle for order at the turn of the 20th century, Galambos and Pratt (1988) concluded

> The rise of the large corporation in J. P. Morgan's era marked a decisive shift in the nation's business system. In manufacturing, transportation, communications, and distribution, giant corporate combines were organized to bring order to their industries' markets and to exploit major technological innovations. (p. 2)

Cutlip (1995) captured the spirit and content of this shift by focusing on "the melee of the opposing forces in this period of the nation's rapid growth" (p. 187). The focus of Cutlip's history of public relations shifts noticeably from an interest in puffery and ebullient publicity to a serious tone when he addressed the clash of the robber barons and key members of the populist and progressive media. Activism rose to battle monopolistic capitalism. Capitalist titans fought one another. Carving corporate capitalism out of a small business and agrarian society was neither easy nor pleasant. Stressing this point, Cutlip (1994) reasoned that "only through the expertise of public relations can causes, industries, individuals, and institutions make their voice heard in the public forum where thousands of shrill, competing voices daily re-create the Tower of Babel" (p. ix). The origin of issues management was and continues to be a weapon wielded in the battle for order.

The move toward order, industrialists realized, must be supported by governmental policy: "The government's role shifted decisively in three major areas in this century: single-industry regulation, cross-industry regulation that set rules under which all businesses operate, and government-directed activities that indirectly shaped the nation's business climate" (Galambos & Pratt, 1988, pp. 2–3). One residue of this effort, Tedlow (1979) observed, was that by the 1950s, public relations "had helped to alter permanently the public vocabulary of business" (p. 163).

Public policy advocates are faced with an array of options, including accepting policy changes wrought by others, mitigating the effects of those policies, analyzing the opportunities they offer, or creating policies favorable to their own interests. In such efforts, advocates seek wide acceptance of key premises that can influence how people think about the policies, products, and services of corporations and other large institutions. These premises provide the rationale for how companies plan and operate. Portending promise or peril for strategic resource management, those premises translate into strategic business plans (Sawaya & Arrington, 1988; Stroup, 1988). In this regard, SIM has responded to battles between competing voices, as activists have criticized industry, for instance. But issues management has and will continue to play an interindustry role.

Case in Point: Interindustry Search for Order and Sustainable Energy

Throughout the past 130 years, energy has increasingly come to play a dominant role in private-sector decision making, business planning, geopolitics, and environmental battles. One of the interesting aspects of this battle has been the engagement of the standard players in the integrated, multinational oil and gas industry and the integrated, multinational agricultural products companies. Today this battle has become defined as one over alternative fuels, global warming, and industrial standards. In such battles, a company's (an industry's) issue position and strategic planning can proactively foster advantages by adopting the proper image and adapting to key premises accepted by engaged publics, activists, nongovernmental organizations, and legislative and regulatory groups. The issue in this struggle has taken many twists and turns over the past 3 decades as companies, activists, and governmental officials work to balance the U.S. consumer's insatiable desire for petroleum and chemical products while protecting the environment. One

(Continued)

(Continued)

premise that is fundamental to public policy and many corporations' strategic planning is this: That product or process that pollutes least, all other factors being equal, is preferred to its alternatives.

This premise was the foundation of a strategic planning and governmental affairs effort by Archer-Daniels-Midland Company (ADM), which, in the early stages, dominated the federal policy debate over requirements that ethanol be included in all gasoline to reduce environmentally harmful automobile emissions. ADM is an agriculture giant that makes between 50% and 70% of the ethanol, a derivative of corn, which is manufactured in the United States. The 1990 Clean Air Act required service stations in the nation's nine environmentally dirtiest cities to reduce automobile pollutants by using either ethanol or methanol mixed with gasoline—or some other method. The science behind this public policy and marketplace battle focused on ways to increase the efficiency of gasoline combustion. One means was to use an additive that brought more oxygen into the combustion process.

This struggle over public policy resources was part of ADM's strategic plan to create a huge market for its products. ADM achieved a requirement that 30% of each gallon of gasoline must be ethanol, which is made from farm products such as corn. Reporting on ADM's campaign, Noah (1993) observed, "One reason ADM did no lobbying on this ethanol policy is that it didn't have to. Instead, its case was pressed by the Renewable Fuels Association, a trade group that lobbied the White House for months on the issue" (p. A10). This issue was one of President Clinton's campaign promises and is in the mutual interest of other producers of ethanol. The policy was advocated to reduce foreign oil imports and to please environmental groups. It is a case of public policy working for a company and an industry in the mutual interest of other vital segments of the nation, including farm belt interests (farmers, taxing authorities, farm equipment suppliers, financial institutions, etc.).

Reasoning from the premise on that which has less negative impact on the environment is preferred, ADM needed to ascertain whether ethanol would have a positive impact on the environment and economy, without undesirable side effects. If the facts were there, the conclusion was evident. ADM's expedient policy grew from this argumentative stance, which was challenged by advocates, especially in the oil and gas refinery industry, who argued that ethanol in hot climates and at summer temperatures actually creates more pollution. They also argued that harvesting corn requires the use of substantial amounts of hydrocarbon fuels.

Because of the market stakes involved in this controversy, the oil and gas industry used an issue advertising campaign to stress the superiority of reformulated gasoline (RFG). This additive was designed to have less environmental impact than would competing products, including ethanol. The oil and gas industry preferred to use a petroleum-based methanol derivative, MTBE. The industry also engaged in lobbying and filed a lawsuit over the requirement. In April 1995, a federal appeals court set aside the Environmental Protection Agency (EPA) rule that 30% of environmentally friendly gasoline would be ethanol. The decision was based on reasoning that although EPA can set performance guidelines, it cannot prescribe the recipe. In the summer of 1995, EPA vowed to appeal this decision because it believed that its original decision was legally sound and technically defensible—it was also an embarrassment for a regulatory body to lose its authority to be regulatory.

In the late 1990s and early 2000s, this public policy battle took an interesting turn when substantial amounts of MTBE began to show up in ground water around the country, most notably California. MTBE is not a known health hazard, but it makes water stink. Because water is a compound based on hydrogen and oxygen (H_2O), the MTBE bonded with water and did not release that bond easily. It was doing what it was designed to do, but with water rather than gasoline. Ethanol became a preferred additive and then a preferred energy source. Government subsidies poured into the industry, and ethanol plants popped up around the country. Detroit had made cars that would burn ethanol, but it was not widely advertised. So the market was in place, and now the supply was supported by the public policy arena. As a part of the mix of science, public policy, and business policy, the energy industry changed. SIM played a major role in that change in the interindustry battle. Activists played their role, but the real heavy lifting came from industry coffers. This case helps lay a foundation for the discussion that follows. It argues that over time, society changes and perhaps evolves by changing opinions, fostering and defeating key premises, and forming public policy that supports or constrains business planning and policy. This case emphasizes how businesses and entire industries turn to the public policy arena to shape the marketplace in which they produce and sell products. This clash results from two industries' search for order.

Much of the rest of this chapter examines the search for order. Before getting into additional details from the mix of business, activism, and government, it is wise to spend a bit of time examining how thoughts shared as zones of meaning throughout society support or oppose various business planning models.

Argument Structure in Public Policy Debate

What assumptions should guide our approach to the public policy debates in this country? The structure of public policy communication is dialogic in nature, a process of give and take—statement and counterstatement—between interested parties (Heath, 1993). The ethical dimensions of this dialogue are captured by Pearson (1989b):

> Dialogue is a precondition for any legitimate corporate conduct that affects a public of that organization. The prime concern of those departments is the constitution and maintenance of communication systems that link the corporate with its publics—those organizations and groups affected by corporate actions. The goal of public relations is to manage these communication systems such that they come as close as possible to the standards deduced from the idea of dialogue. This is the core ethical responsibility of public relations from which all other obligations follow. (p. 128)

Such dialogue examines and voices key premises. These premises become refined, abandoned, and created over time as conditions change. One of the realities of SIM is a constantly changing terrain of business activity.

Facts are an essential element of these dialogues. How they are generated and interpreted is never independent of basic premises that tend to feature themes of safety, equality, fairness, and environmental quality. Policy debates voice relevant facts, reason from them by applying evaluative premises, and draw conclusions based on those facts and premises (Toulmin, 1964). To endure by satisfying the needs of society, public policy positions require a foundation in verifiable fact and evaluative premises that allow satisfying conclusions to be drawn. So, sound science counts, but so does the cultural premises that forge and evaluate the role of science and the conclusions it draws.

This approach to the argumentative structure of policy analysis and debate is supported by the research and theory of Fishbein and Ajzen (1975; Ajzen & Fishbein, 1980). Their theories of information integration-expectancy-value and reasoned action argue that people hold attitudes of varying degrees of strength depending on how strongly they associate evaluative attributes with some object, situation, or action. The strength of these associations depends on the information (facts) the person holds and the evaluation (premise) associated with the premises. What premises people use and how they use them to make decisions depends on normative behaviors influenced by opinion leaders. For this reason, organizations seek to influence normative beliefs and the motivation key stakeholders have to comply with them.

Such analysis conforms with Burke's approach to rhetoric. Meaning created and expressed through discourse constitutes what Burke (1951, 1966) called *terministic screens,* which shape and limit people's interpretations of reality and prescribe what behaviors are normative. Terministic screens, especially those embedded in idioms, constitute zones of meaning once identifiable groups of people subscribe to them (Heath, 1991b, 1994). Viewed this way, all of the observations people make "are but implications of the particular terminology in terms of which the observations are made" (Burke, 1966, p. 46). On this point, Burke reasoned that "*each of us shares with all other members of our kind . . . the fatal fact that, however the situation came to be, all members of our species conceive of reality somewhat roundabout, through various media of symbolism*" (p. 52, emphasis added). Each idiom contains a unique view of economic, political, social, corporate, personal, and community interests. How each person identifies with the competing opinion leaders can influence the sorts of terministic screens adopted and how they are applied in the support or opposition of various business and public policy issues.

This conclusion is fundamental to Parenti's (1986) charge that business discourse invents the opinion that members of society often enact without much critical judgment of it. Taking a less ideological stance, Andrews (1983) pointed out that "a prime function of rhetoric is to interpret and make meaningful what is in the process of happening" (p. 9) in society. By the same token, multiple voices emerge in society, the essence of issues as being debatable and contestable. At the same time when robber barons were seeking to justify their business practices, including increasing business consolidation and the clout that followed, alternative perspectives were advocated. For instance, Griese (2001) noted in his examination of public relations giant Arthur W. Page, "In 1902, Progressive economist Henry C. Adams argued that publicity was the solution to the problem of trusts" (p. 24).

The importance of issues management is missed if we only think of an issue as being contestable. An issue is worthy of attention when it can have an impact on the organization (Dutton, 1993; Wartick & Mahon, 1994). The contest has implications for the distribution of resources as stakes that are held, sought, and granted or withheld. Herein lies the rationale for resource dependency theory, conflict management, and collaborative decision making.

Propositions of policy only come about after changes and analysis of platforms of fact and value. The logic, from the standpoint of an activist, is this: Companies are doing this (Y facts), which violates X values; therefore, they should be regulated in the following manner (Z policy). An effective issues analysis system focuses on where in this equation debate is at the moment and what strategic response allows for greatest leverage. To move toward agreement on policy, people need to share a set of facts that accurately define some relevant problem based on causal or correlation links between actions, attributes, objects, and situations. How the facts are interpreted and policies are formulated depends on values and premises that are current in the minds of the policy decision makers. Public policy needs to be founded on the best available facts if it is to serve the public interest.

In a similar effort, Exxon (now ExxonMobil) Corporation undertook a communication campaign to challenge the conclusion that long-term environmental damage had occurred in Prince William Sound. A key aspect of this campaign was to reinterpret the databases created by the government in its attempt to assess the damage done to the water, sediment, and marine life. Exxon wanted to be sure that the alleged facts were indeed accurate enough to be used for crucial interpretations and assessments of liability for damage. One point of contention by Exxon was that some of the alleged samples of pollutants were actually diesel fuel that was mistaken for Exxon crude. A key analytic methodology, called fingerprinting, was employed in the controversy between Exxon and government officials. This technique analyzed the levels of individual compounds in a substance. This methodology enabled researchers to identify which pollutants came from each source. Once the fingerprint of the crude oil carried in the Exxon *Valdez* was identified, it was compared with all other samples to determine which ones came from the spill (C. Solomon, 1993).

In this sense, argumentative structure of opinions, however broadly held and by which identifiable groups, consists of facts, values, or evaluative premises, which lead to conclusions, including which policies (whether pub-lic or private) are preferred—the best solution to any problem as defined. This decision process allows key publics to predict the liabilities and benefits of constraining or fostering admittedly complex corporate activities. It can be framed in terms of expedience, as interpreted by the political economy at a given time in history. This analysis explains why underregulation can result in socially irresponsible behavior on the part of individuals and organizations. Overregulation, on the other hand, can lead to a stifling operating environ-ment that works against needed increases in productivity and job creation.

In these dialogues, businesses and other organizations are rhetors that enact *personae* as well as affect meaning and identification (Cheney & Dionisopoulos, 1989). As well as being advocates, they are targets of external rhetoric between supporters and critics. Such analysis has been applied to the nuclear generating industry at Three Mile Island (Dionisopoulos & Crable, 1988), the Task Force on Food Assistance (Coombs, 1992), the key assumptions of industries vying for leadership in the information age (Gandy, 1992), and the rationale for conducting modern warfare (Hiebert, 1991). Olasky (1987) argued that industries define themselves and generate support for those definitions.

To understand the importance of the creation of such zones of meaning, one might turn to P. H. Weaver's (1988) analysis of the problems U.S. corporations are having in adapting to the international marketplace. Despite their claims to the contrary, U.S. businesses gained a lot of favorable regulation and legislation that defined and fostered their domestic operations. By gaining this kind of control, they created their operating environment and adapted it to them and them to it. Tariffs, subsidies, official monopolies, tax breaks, wage controls, defense spending, and government-sponsored research—such policy lulled executives into lethargy and weakened their ability to adapt to the robust international marketplace.

This review suggests the nature of public policy dialogue, the impact lan-guage has on judgment, and the structure of argument: facts, evaluative premises, and conclusions as competing and conflicting zones of meaning. With this set of ideas in mind, the remainder of this chapter reviews the history of key efforts by private-sector organizations, governmental agencies, activists, and professional associations. Each of these has worked to create and imple-ment, through informal and public policy, key definitions of what they think is most favorable to their interests.

Robber Barons and the Making of Mass Production Society

Near the end of the 19th century, regulation of business activities tended to be local. Fairly little national policy had been formed beyond tariffs and central banking. Federal powers were limited. Nevertheless, the country was developing a national mentality made possible by improvements in transportation (such as canal and rail systems) and communication infrastructures (typified by the telegraph). Far-sighted business leaders could see that postreconstruction industrialization would lead to lucrative mass markets and would require business operations that would support the systematic operation of large organizations and a less distanced government.

The Civil War in the United States had provided the incentive to mass produce. Nowhere was this more evident than the ability of manufacturing to create interchangeable parts of military firearms. No longer was an artisan needed to repair a rifle; it could be repaired by using a replacement part. In the artisan system, days were required to produce a rifle, but now rifles could be mass produced by the hundreds in the same amount of time (Morris, 2005). These advances allowed machines, rather than skilled workers, to create. Thus, production changed, and so did consumption. So did the concept and status of labor.

At the close of the Civil War, the nation was fertile land for growing corporations. The war had cost the nation dearly in money and labor force. Corporations had provided needed war matériel. After the war, they underwrote financial development for expanded industrial production. Kingpins who could generate money, sometimes by bold stock fraud schemes, were destined to shape the last 30 years of the 19th century and even the early years of the 20th century.

Corporations evolved through trial and error rather than by calculated design. As a first step toward business concentrations, several manufacturing plants, small railroad companies, or oil refineries were brought together under committees that managed them in a trust. This system increased their efficiency and decreased competition. Through absorption and amalgamation, for instance, 138 companies were combined into United States Steel (Kolko, 1967).

John D. Rockefeller, founder of Standard Oil, was a pioneer and master of the business practices and rationale needed to accomplish horizontal and vertical integration of business activities. Horizontal integration involved bringing several companies performing the same function, such as refining oil, into one corporate leadership. Vertical integration was accomplished by drawing to that structure a mix of functions that supported refining, such as crude oil production, transportation, wholesaling, and retailing (Galambos & Pratt, 1988; Morris, 2005). Even this master could not survive the scrutiny of ever more strident critics. In 1911, the Standard Oil Trust suffered the injunctive force of a federal judge and a federal antitrust lawsuit (Cutlip, 1995; Morris, 2005). Morris (2005) reasoned that Rockefeller was not as ruthless as muckrakers claimed, but he lacked the personnel and public opinion support to effectively mount a defense.

The nation's infrastructure began to burgeon as local markets were displaced with national ones. The slow metamorphosis from rural-agriculture to urban-industrial society demanded that farm produce reach the urban-industrial areas. This made farmers victims of railroad companies that often charged them more for local shipment than they charged large wheat-processing or meatpacking companies for long-distance freight.

Against roughshod industrialization arose the voices of farmer Populists in the later years of the 19th century and urban professional Progressives who, during the early years of the 20th century, effectively argued that corporations should be constrained by energetic governmental action. These two movements, made up of farmers, lawyers, small businessmen, ministers, and laborers, worked through legislative, judicial, and administrative channels to derail the robber barons that were creating an aristocracy of wealth. Populist stakeholders revised state constitutions as a means for controlling the economic giants that appeared bent to destroy their livelihoods. As reform interests gained strength in legislatures, they demanded that corporations act according to a higher standard of corporate responsibility by changing their operating procedures to satisfy their critics and by communicating more openly and honestly with their publics.

No ideological blueprint existed for the development of policies regarding corporate concentrations in manufacturing, railroads, and utilities. Standards had to be forged on the anvil of public debate, which increasingly gave voice to activist protest. How large should a corporation be? Should the government regulate industry, or was that task left solely to "rational" market forces? Could competition be maintained while small companies were being engulfed by larger ones or driven from the marketplace? To what extent should any corporation dominate a market by setting prices and establishing labor practices?

The dominant philosophy of the era, Social Darwinism, championed unbridled tooth-and-fang capitalism. Face-to-face relationships that had characterized commerce were being replaced by distant corporate managements who knew little and cared less about the men, women, and even children who worked for the company, lived in its vicinity, bought its goods, and used its services. One characteristic of corporate policy in these robust years was that the less "outsiders" knew about corporate behavior and policy, the easier it was for business leaders to arbitrarily make decisions. Armed state militia and Pinkerton agents (nowhere more dramatic than steel industry strike busting) were means by which corporations communicated their policies to labor. Business-to-consumer communication often consisted of product and service advertising fraught with factual inaccuracy and hyperbole.

This information and policy vacuum presaged the need for pioneering issue communicators who, during the 1880s, tended to call themselves publicists, and their skills were demonstrated in the ability to help forge new policies that limited the rampant price cutting by railroad lines that threatened the industry in the 1880s. Public relations–minded executives coupled with expert communicators forged an alliance between railroad industry leaders and politicians to bring order to the industry through the creation of the Interstate Commerce Commission in 1886 (Olasky, 1987).

Corporate spokespersons fought to maintain support for an ostensible laissez-faire attitude against challenges by increasingly sophisticated lobby efforts of labor leaders and middle-class Progressives. Federal and state government officials learned that powerful corporate leaders did not want unlimited free competition, as evidenced by a variety of fundamental changes in the way they conducted business. One monumental effort to systematize business practices resulted in the standard 4-foot, 8-inch railroad gauge, making possible an efficient national transportation network.

Debates over the implications of corporate size and power resulted in the Sherman Antitrust Act in 1890. Whereas Progressive forces were successful in invoking federal and state regulation through a series of other important bills passed between 1890 and 1914, the agencies generally proved more cooperative than combative toward business. This cooperation demonstrated the widespread endorsement of premises favorable to corporate preferences (Morris, 2005). Kolko (1967) contended that shrewd industry barons quickly recognized the virtue of business concentration and used government to protect industries; they realized the reformist zeal of Progressivism could assist in these efforts. Part of the reason for this acceptance stemmed from the efforts of business publicists.

Although not immune to criticism, corporations have become a permanent part of the social, political, and economic fabric of the country simply because their size and technological proficiency slowly forged a mass consumption society. More and more people could have more things because of mass production. For instance, before the mass production of soap occurred, women had to make soap if they could not afford the refined soaps made by artisans (Morris, 2005). Mass production society was a mixed blessing. To examine the tension between public sentiment and corporate behavior, Galambos (1975) investigated the opinions several key occupational groups held toward corporate growth. He discovered that few individuals held rigid views. Members of these groups were not always at war with corporations; indeed, often corporations were viewed as vital to prosperity. For instance, from 1879 to 1892, engineers saw their economic interest inseparable from the growth of corporations. One gripe by engineers, especially against railroads, was their miserable safety record. They argued that standards should be imposed to make rail travel and transportation safer for workers and passengers.

During this period, Protestant ministers applauded corporate growth as evidence of the realization of a divine mission. They broke out of their conservatism periodically to suggest a few social welfare programs. Southern farmers felt a sense of economic disparity created by corporate growth, but they appreciated the access to markets provided by large rail transportation networks.

Midwestern farmers, too, appreciated this access but worried that railroads used government to shore up the industry. For this reason, farmers supported the Interstate Commerce Act. Of these groups, laborers were the most concerned by growing business concentrations.

Passage of the Interstate Commerce Act of 1887, Sherman Antitrust Act of 1890, and Safety Appliance Acts of 1893 was a landmark in consumer regulation. The Interstate Commerce Commission was first and was created to lessen the likelihood that railroad rates would be established by distant railroad czars. Wiebe (1967) observed that a few railroad "executives actually welcomed it as a protective cover" (p. 53). At the turn of the century, Progressive small businessmen and professionals lobbied for revisions in the Interstate Commerce Act that would take even more power from the railroads—by then, deeply in debt. Railroads tended to raise rates to offset these debts, a practice resisted by middle-class Progressives who did not want to shoulder new costs at the expense of their own businesses. The Interstate Commerce Act was important to railroad executives who were fighting deteriorating finances. This legislation allowed railroad executives to set rates, control competition, and revamp freight classifications in ways similar to what could be accomplished by the organizational tactic of pooling (Olasky, 1987).

Despite these trends, Galambos (1975) concluded that in 1892, "few signs indicated that the concentration movement would produce a major crisis in America's middle cultures" (p. 78). The depression of 1893 caused many to reconsider the liabilities associated with the unbridled pursuit of wealth by industrial combines. Farmers, especially, championed financial reform. In addition to their growing anger at the economic clout of bankers and other plutocrats, farmers had mixed feelings about the urban growth corporations were causing. Young people were being lured to the big cities far from their rural origins. "While the farmer was thus capable of conjuring up some highly abstract enemies, he lavished most of his animosity on those industries and firms with which he had direct economic relationships" (p. 96). Farm groups saw their influence erode. Their role as a counterbalance to corporations was being taken over by labor organizations.

By 1901, farmers had become less angry toward trusts than other occupation groups, particularly engineers and laborers. Unskilled labor realized the battle lines had been drawn, particularly after the bloody rioting and harsh use of Pinkerton strikebreakers at Andrew Carnegie's Homestead steel mills near Pittsburgh in 1892. Homestead proved to labor that corporate giants, such as Carnegie, were determined to destroy labor unions and would kill to accomplish that end (Morris, 2005). Ensuing strikes were often violent. In contrast to the lower paid workers, skilled laborers looked on corporations positively because they offered promise of economic well-being, but they recognized corporations' power was not to be taken lightly. By the turn of the 19th century,

Galambos (1975) argued, the nation had begun to establish a coherent set of beliefs and attitudes toward the regulation of corporations. These opinions caused the regulatory measures of the later Progressive era to be more legally exact (Morris, 2005).

During the first decade of the 20th century, corporate America lost one of its strongest supporters—the clergy. Doubts were raised whether corporations returned to the people as much as they took. Bremner (1956) observed that in contrast to other countries, ours has never accepted the assumption that some people must be in poverty. A dramatic change of opinion around the turn of the 20th century was the discovery of poverty. The Social Darwinism of the previous century argued that poverty persisted only among the lazy and spend-thrift. This was no longer accepted as fact, particularly by religious reformers who observed that low wages caused laborers to suffer despite their energy and frugality. Many social evils were laid at the doorsteps of business, as ministers became incensed at the poor health and living conditions typical in corporate towns. Clergymen believed that where morality and corporate growth had been positively related before, they were now at odds (Galambos, 1975).

Names such as J. P. Morgan and John D. Rockefeller Sr. raised the ire of citizens who believed that the foundations of the society were being eroded because so few had so much power and wealth. The number of regulatory measures passed in the opening decades of the 20th century indicated that the Progressive search for order was becoming more robust. Presidents of the United States joined the advocates for corporate reform, sometimes out of fear of losing a valuable portion of the electorate. As he did with other groups, Theodore Roosevelt encouraged farmers and other supporters of trust busting to renew their attacks on businesses. Passage of the Bureau of Corporations Bill in 1903 established the Department of Commerce and Labor; this marked for many Progressives the beginning of an important era of regulation. However, Kolko (1967) concluded that the measure was enacted with strong conservative support by industrialists who saw it as a way to lessen competition. Many battles were fought over wages and working conditions, at first and, later, over the quality of goods and services. Even though the debate was in its infancy, the public along with business was confronted with the need to formulate standards of responsible corporate behavior.

Companies did little to create a safe and comfortable working environment. With rare exception, wages were at a subsistence level that was achieved only by working long hours. Typically, entire families, including children as young as 6 or 7 years old, had to work to survive. Some employers favored the labor of children who could work in small and cramped quarters, particularly important to save unnecessary excavations in coal mines. Railroad companies typically subjected employees to extremely dangerous working conditions. To oppose such conditions, workers could strike. Bosses worked to prevent this collective action. For instance, coal was often stockpiled by coal companies to prevent the possibility that a strike could be effective.

Abuse always sparks opposition. Muckraking journalists led by David Graham Phillips, Lincoln Steffens, and Ida Tarbell exposed the irresponsibility rampant in industry, particularly during the first 2 decades of the 20th century. Books such as Frank Norris's (1903) *The Pit* and Upton Sinclair's (1906) *The Jungle* fostered discussion that helped lead to the Pure Food and Drug Act of 1906 and the Federal Meat Inspection Act of 1906. This latter act was the culmination of an effort to reform the meat industry, which began as early as 1865 when Congress banned importation of diseased cattle and pigs. Meat reform was supported by some of the largest packers who, unlike their cut-rate competition, maintained sanitary plants and routinely inspected their product. The bigger firms wanted to extend government inspection to all packers to establish equity of quality—and expense. Similarly, the Pure Food and Drug Act was endorsed by the National Pure Food and Drug Congress, which included trade groups and industry representatives such as the Creamery Butter Makers' Association, Brewers Association, Confectioners' Association, Wholesale Grocers' Association, and the Retail Grocers' Association (Kolko, 1967).

Magazines were the major mass medium by which muckrakers reached their audience, the U.S. middle class, which was increasing in size and political importance. Steffens and Tarbell, in conjunction with Ray Stannard Baker, made *McClure's Magazine* the leading outlet for reformist material. Other key journals included *Everybody's Magazine, Collier's, Arena, Success Magazine,* and *Cosmopolitan.* All joined the reform battle out of conviction and the desire to increase circulation. Influential muckrakers found much to criticize about corporate behavior. Tarbell's (1904) *History of the Standard Oil Company,* first published in *McClure's,* was one of the first statements on corporate responsibility to find its way into middle-class living rooms. Steffens's (1904) *The Shame of the Cities* (also released that same year) provided another landmark exposé. In the face of the challenges by muckraking journalists, Cutlip and Center (1982) observed, "The corporations, the good ones along with the ruthless ones, had lost contact with their publics. For a while, they sat helplessly by, inarticulate and frustrated, waiting apprehensively for the next issue of McClure's magazine" (p. 76).

No public opinion change was necessary to condemn the consumption of tainted meat. When reformers alerted the public to unsanitary meatpacking conditions, it was ready to demand reform. An informed populace had well-established premises by which to evaluate such information and draw conclusions. Such dramatic changes in stakeholder opinions underscore the reality that issues management can never ignore what others believe and prefer. The opinion battleground is the struggle between corporations that attempt to do business, for the most part, in ways that coincide with accepted standards of behavior and the public interest. If business loses public support, it is doomed to fail or change dramatically. According to Galambos and Pratt (1988),

> The political economy of the United States was beginning to change in the Progressive Era in ways that gave business leaders pause, if not reason to fear for their future. As single-industry regulation became more prevalent, as cross-industry policies were implemented, as government-directed activities increased, executives sensed that they were losing contact with and control over their political and social environments. (p. 92)

Stridsberg (1977) approached the connections between corporate responsibility and brand equity as he analyzed an advertisement titled "The Penalty of Leadership," used by Cadillac Motor Car Company in 1915. It advocated the need to maintain high standards of manufacturing quality. The ad masked the fact that the original 51 Cadillac model was not very reliable. In this advertisement, the company proclaimed its commitment to quality by asserting, "In every field of human endeavor, he that is first must perpetually live in the white light of publicity" (p. 41). It continued:

> When a man's work becomes a standard for the whole world, it also becomes a target for the shafts of the envious few. If his work be merely mediocre, he will be left severely alone—if he achieves a masterpiece, it will set a million tongues a-wagging. (p. 41)

The theme, apparently, was that if people are critically discussing the quality of the Cadillac, their talk is motivated by envy, not justified criticism of inadequate engineering and manufacturing. Such cases can yield to fact.

By World War I, increasing numbers of corporations employed wordsmiths to explain to key publics the importance of business in underwriting modern abundance. Walter Lippmann (1918/1961) noted in *Drift and Mastery* that effective execution of a series of such opinion campaigns by skilled public relations practitioners Ivy Lee, Edward Bernays, and others led to growing recognition for the field and dramatically changed people's attitudes.

Because magazines and books were the primary media used by those seeking corporate reform, they were used by public relations practitioners. Public relations specialists wrote articles extolling the virtues of a company or an industry while railing against pending regulation. Each case was presented as though it resulted from objective journalistic research. For instance, George Gunton was a popular economist who championed the free enterprise system in his capacity as editor of *Gunton's Magazine*. While in that position, he received a $15,000 annual retainer from Standard Oil (Kolko, 1967). As early as 1880, the railroad industry was being encouraged to recognize the value of public relations (Raucher, 1968), which was having a difficult time understanding and developing issue communication strategies that would conform to excellence in issues management.

Industry barons sometimes entered the fray as J. Ogden Armour did. He used *The Saturday Evening Post* (Armour, 1906) to defend some of the practices of the meat industry under attack, to invite public visits of his facilities, to describe sanitation efforts his company was taking to ensure high quality, and to support passage of inspection legislation. Several large packing concerns, including Swift & Company, published a series of advertisements to present a favorable image of them and proclaim their commitment to healthful meat-processing conditions.

Another utility giant increased control over its industry in the last decade of the 19th century. Frederick P. Fish, who became president of the Bell Telephone System in 1900, recognized the need for his growing company to take its case to the public. The apprehension was that if the public did not understand the advantage of a monopoly (albeit a regulated monopoly), it would seek regulation or oppose monopolization. Either stance was contrary to the growth goals of the company. Raucher (1968) concluded "that by 1906 the American Telephone and Telegraph Company had a general policy designed to placate public hostility and had methods for broadcasting the news about that policy" (p. 49). That policy was aggressively continued by Theodore Newton Vail when he became AT&T president in May 1907. He sought to insulate the communication utility from public control by convincing Americans the phone company was operating in their interest. One of the first issue advertisements, put out by AT&T in 1908, emphasized the bond between the company and its customers:

> The Bell System's ideal is the same as that of the public it serves—the most telephone service and the best, at the least cost to the user. It accepts its responsibility for a nationwide telephone service as a public trust. (Garbett, 1981, p. 40)

By 1910, Vail had converted these ideas into a consistent long-term campaign stressing the advantages of a privately run, publicly minded system (Schultze, 1981). The rationale featured several key premises, one of which was that an integrated, regulated monopoly allowed people in different parts of town and in different cities to talk to one another (Olasky, 1987). To accomplish this end required public goodwill (Cutlip, 1995) because the standards of corporate responsibility achieved by each company met or exceeded the expectations of its key stakeholders.

One of the first major tests of this opinion formation strategy came in 1913, when the Justice Department initiated an antitrust suit charging that AT&T had created an impermissible monopoly through its control of Western Union. AT&T defended itself with a newspaper series that was started under the name of Vail beginning in *The New York Times* on September 4, 1913. The case collapsed. Part of AT&T's campaign was to avert governmental regulation, but another threat involved direct government ownership of utilities. By May 1928, AT&T Publicity Director Arthur W. Page could announce that their educational efforts had successfully convinced the public that the phone industry was best handled as a regulated monopoly. But he also prudently cautioned company executives over still-lingering concerns (Raucher, 1968; see also Griese, 2001). Thus, even though a victor in many battles over the years, AT&T never completely won the war for public confidence. This conclusion is best justified by the eventual breakup in the 1980s. One irony in this long history is the reemergence of a combined telephone company under the name of Bell in the mid-2000s. The name and concept of the company have enormous brand equity, an issue position that sustains itself through performance effectively communicated.

In the early years of the 20th century, public relations practices by utilities and railroads gained popularity with manufacturing companies that feared antitrust legislation. To protect International Harvester Company, George Perkins, at the direction of Cyrus H. McCormick, fought governmental action by the Bureau of Corporations in 1906. The publicity firm of Parker and Lee also joined the fray. The argument against antitrust legislation was couched in what had become the standard premise of "the benefits of largeness," an attempt to publicize the economics of mass production. The argument continued that corporations pay better wages than do smaller businesses. The campaign had some success because the Roosevelt administration dropped the case in 1908 (Raucher, 1968).

The Rockefellers drew heavily on public relations to protect Standard Oil against Ida Tarbell's claims that John D. Sr.'s philanthropy was "tainted money" and charges of violent strikebreaking in labor relations at their Colorado Fuel and Iron Company. Despite his efforts on behalf of the Rockefellers, Ivy Lee was soundly criticized for presenting one-sided, factually inaccurate material in his bulletin titled "Facts in Colorado's Struggle for Industrial Freedom" (Raucher, 1968, p. 27). Lee was of service to key industrial groups that sought to improve their image and challenge efforts to regulate them. He defended the Anthracite Coal Operators by reasoning that competitors should be excluded to ensure the production of high-quality coal (Olasky, 1987). He assisted the Cotton Yarn Association, which argued that constraints of trade prevented cotton producers from putting out low-quality products, regardless of price (Olasky, 1987).

Advertising agencies, shortly after the turn of the 20th century, offered their services to the beleaguered corporations. Following New York State's Armstrong Committee exposé of insurance industry corruption, the New York Mutual Life Insurance Company hired N. W. Ayer to conduct an advocacy campaign to restore confidence in the industry. Communication efforts were never separate from attempts by the Theodore Roosevelt, William Howard Taft, and Woodrow Wilson administrations to regulate industry. Public relations practitioners were brought into the fray to correct false information, champion traditional values, and argue that regulation was detrimental. During the first decades of the 20th century, Raucher (1968) observed, increased corporate responsibility and ethical behavior became commonplace public relations themes.

Like many other aspects of the reform period, considerable discussion revolved around definitions of "good" and "bad" business concentrations, including the ways organizations advertised products and services. Discussion of the need for the Federal Trade Commission (FTC) began to surface in 1911. The National Civic Federation discovered that the idea was broadly favored in an opinion poll conducted in 1911. The Progressive and Republican Parties endorsed it in 1912, and by 1914, the FTC was created to replace the Bureau of Corporations. As is true today, one of the hardest parts of achieving responsible corporate performance involves deciding what it is. The task is often assigned to the membership of regulatory bodies that often have representatives of the industries to be regulated serving on them.

Industries rightly have the information needed to assist the creation of such definitions. Soon after the creation of the Interstate Commerce Commission, the members realized that the data needed to ascertain the fairness of rates would have to be obtained from industry (Galambos & Pratt, 1988). In a similar fashion, the FTC was headed by the avowedly pro-business Edward N. Hurley. It was supported by and greatly influenced by the National Association of Manufacturers (Kolko, 1967). This association has engaged in extensive public relations battles that Cutlip (1995) believed have often failed and have not been cost-effective.

The period from 1901 to 1939 was one of flux, as a corporate commonwealth was forged to replace the era of single corporate leaders, such as J. P. Morgan or John D. Rockefeller. The goals for national public policy were often blurred, and input came from an ever more diverse array of players. At issue was the laissez-faire approach, which "rested on the traditional American faith in the marketplace as an effective regulator" (Galambos & Pratt, 1988, p. 45).

World War I did not bring an end to reform and concern over corporate America. "The clergyman, the engineer, the farmer, the laborer—all found cause for distress in the immediate aftermath of the First World War" (Galambos, 1975, p. 193). Labor's attitudes remained negative. With technological change making jobs obsolete, the greatest challenge facing the laborer was to protect his or her craft. A new twist in corporate issues management was the presence of Bolshevism; now, corporate representatives claimed that criticism of corporate America was unpatriotic and communistic. Businessmen recognized that the flow of immigrants was bringing many people to this country who neither understood nor appreciated the economics of free enterprise. Business had no intention of letting competing economic systems gain a foothold.

This section has featured corporations as struggling and often battling to respond to pressures between themselves as well as those applied by activist groups. Despite the widely accepted view that large corporations dominated society at the turn of the century, activist groups played a major role in the first quarter of the 20th century in the United States.

The Great Depression and the Redemption of Capitalism

The era of the Great Depression demonstrated how improper business policies lead to such damaging consequences that communication strategies are unable to rectify them. Only by making massive changes in the way business was done could society rebalance public and private interests. As a result of this loss in faith, new argumentative principles arose that have guided business practices and allowed for expanded governmental oversight and often intrusion into those activities. In the post-Enron and WorldCom scandals (1990s) and investment and mortgage scandals (2000s), additional standards have been added to ensure accuracy and openness in financial communication. That issue continues rather than being settled in the years after the Depression.

The financial collapse of the country during the Depression strained the relationship between the public and corporations and seriously damaged the public's support for business principles. It raised anew questions as to whether large companies could and would serve the public interest. Because of the need to rebuild financial and industrial institutions, the public championed increased federal powers. Many in the clergy argued that one of the solutions to the Depression was to break up the corporations that had become too powerful. Rather than being totally at odds, government and business worked with surprising cooperation to return the nation to prosperity. Despite the impact on farm prices, the farmer emerged from the 1930s supporting large corporations that could buy produce and inexpensively sell equipment needed for future plantings and harvests (Galambos, 1975).

One telling result of this period was a loss of autonomy on the part of business executives. New legislation expanded into boardroom executive decisions. During the period, price stabilization was more important than fostering competition. One goal was to restore the ability of companies to meet payrolls and avoid massive layoffs. Legislators were less interested in consistency of policy than in its effects; piecemeal regulation resulted. The incentive was not to stop industrial policy that generated profits but to ensure their wise use in the public interest. According to Galambos and Pratt (1988),

> Although management of individual firms initially decried many of these changes in the economic functions of government, most would gradually adapt to them and discover that there were in fact many advantages to a corporate commonwealth that was more stable economically. (p. 126)

The 1930s and 1940s witnessed a series of issue ads stressing the virtues of capitalism to counteract prevailing doubt about whether business could provide general prosperity. Business leaders feared the public no longer believed in the free enterprise system that had left them without work and dashed their hopes of prosperity, even survival. Galambos (1975) concluded,

> The values and attitudes of the new culture clearly emerged intact from the 1930s. By that time most Americans saw antitrust as a dead or dying issue. They were coming to accept—in varying degrees—a different outlook embodying modern, organizational norms and a new image of the large corporation. Gone was the deep hostility of the 1890s, the progressive era, and postwar crisis. By 1940 the corporate culture had largely supplanted the individualistic-egalitarian outlook of the nineteenth-century. The era of the organization man had begun. (p. 249)

To justify corporate influence in policy matters, some companies engaged in issue advertising. In 1941, one campaign for Warner & Swasey compared the French worker's life with his U.S. counterpart. "Wonder What a Frenchman Thinks About" exemplified how the company used the threat of Nazism to rekindle patriotic commitment to U.S. capitalism. It argued that the French laborer's greed led to the plight of working "53 hours a week for 30 hours' pay." Warner & Swasey voiced the regret of the typical French worker in these words (Stridsberg, 1977):

> I wish I had been less greedy for myself and more anxious for my country; I wish I had realized you can't beat a determined invader by a quarreling, disunited people at home; I wish I had been willing to give in on some of my rights to other Frenchmen instead of giving up all of them to a foreigner; I wish I had realized other Frenchmen had rights, too; I wish I had known that patriotism is work, not talk, giving not getting. (p. 103)

This sad plight could be interpreted as directing the U.S. worker to support the interests of a united corporate America faced with an emerging fascist danger in the midst of the Depression.

Marshaled in the face of heated debate regarding the ability of U.S. capitalism to provide jobs and ensure the public economy, the theme of the importance of free enterprise has remained remarkably consistent over a nearly 50-year period (Garbett, 1981). Developed were Warner & Swasey ad themes, such as "Where do your wages come from?" (1944), "To cure a headache, you don't cut off your head" (1947), "If you own a hammer, you are a capitalist" (1948), and "They don't keep feeding you cheese after the trap is sprung" (1950). These ads discussed the problems of the welfare state and the virtues of U.S. free market enterprise. This theme was exemplified in the 1970 advertisement, "What's right with America?" In one 1971 ad titled "Business men are like the bashful boy who sent his girl a valentine but didn't sign it," Warner & Swasey justified the use of issue advertising. Pointed out were facts on how business "taxes support America's schools 1½ days every week." Business contributes to charities and provides community support. Through its research, the nation is made better. Business is cleaning up the slums, training the unemployed and unemployable (Garbett, 1981). Ironically, 35 years later, many of these problems persist. Some advocates still believe that the private sector will solve these problems, or they must be blamed on the lack of the character of people who suffer poverty.

The end of the Depression and new prosperity in the aftermath of World War II diverted attention from the problems of corporations. In place of problems, Moore (1982) concluded that business during the 1950s enjoyed a honeymoon. People were thankful to have work. The private sector again offered financial security for the average citizen. Beneficial changes in working conditions and an apparent new level of corporate ethics seemed to indicate that businesses had learned to be good community citizens. These changes, combined with upbeat popular culture publicity surrounding wartime efforts (for instance, the "Riveter Annie" mystique), helped free corporations from the degree of regulatory scrutiny typical of previous decades.

In the Eisenhower years, little regulatory legislation was passed. The predictable economic recessions came and went without residual hostility or massive public interest activism. In general, this was a period of good feeling between the public and corporations that provided jobs and supplied goods and services to a people desiring to forget the difficulties of the 1930s and 1940s. Massive research and development efforts fostered by the war effort, and often funded by public taxes, led to the availability of new products that reshaped middle-class lifestyles. New synthetic products, such as nylon and rayon, replaced silk as fabrics for clothing and components of other products. The era of chemical manufacturing was gaining ascendancy. The general public experienced positive change from this mass production.

The cold war with the Soviet Union helped blunt corporate criticism and led to prosperity in defense industries that were funded by public taxes. One harbinger of future nuclear regulation was the Atomic Energy Act of 1954. People's awareness of the danger of nuclear energy was born when they learned that devastating atomic weaponry had been used against Japan. Nuclear power as well as new industries, such as the space industry, grew out of the international struggles of this era, all of which led to new regulatory issues.

Old issues continued in perplexing ways. Corporations still directed issue communication against labor. For instance, Ohio Consolidated Telephone used an ad titled "The Case of the Amputated Telephone" in its efforts to discredit striking telephone workers by blaming them for damaging telephone lines: "Since July 15, [1956] when the strike against Ohio Consolidated began, more than 50 cables have been cut, slashed, burned, hacked in half—interfering with the phone service of more than SIX THOUSAND homes and businesses!" This ad could alienate the public against the strikers, who were compared with dedicated employees: "Supervisors manning local and long distance telephone boards—trying desperately to keep the lines open to you—have been harassed, threatened, intimidated, even shot at!" The ruthlessness of the vandalistic strikers was portrayed even more dramatically: "More than ten offices have had to be closed down for short or long periods—due to vandalism or because police protection was not adequate to handle the danger to operators and equipment!" (Stridsberg, 1977, pp. 106–107). Such issue advertising—a blatant labor-management power play—used scapegoating and blatant fear appeals.

Less combative, General Electric innovated in the 1950s and early 1960s by recognizing the value of keeping employees and other constituencies informed regarding corporate plans, management efforts to be responsible, and pending issues that could affect profits and employee interests. Timken Roller Bearing Company and Caterpillar Tractor demonstrated their citizenship by participating in issue discussion. For example, Caterpillar asked employees and surrounding communities to understand the need to "Hold the Line on Wages" to remain competitive—especially in foreign countries and against foreign competitors. By anticipating union attacks on the company's contentions, Caterpillar muted labor's negative influence (Bateman, 1975).

During the early 1950s, the tobacco public health issue started to gain steam with the release of critical reports by medical experts and epidemiologists. This issue continues to today and has taken many interesting twists. By 2006, what was essentially a public health information campaign by researchers took another twist where cities, counties, and states had banned public smoking. Substantial increases in taxes raised the cost of a pack of cigarettes to a level intended to discourage smokers from continuing and nonsmokers from starting. The principal founder of Hill & Knowlton Public Relations, John Hill, became associated with this controversy when he took the industry as a client in 1953 and helped create the Tobacco Industry Research Council. This entity had two primary missions: to fund research to better understand the connection between tobacco consumption and health and to engage in communication activities designed to ensure that science favoring the industry's side of the issue got its place in media discussions.

This campaign became part of the litigation battle over the 1980s to 1990s. The allegation was that the information supplied by Hill & Knowlton misled the public, even confused them, so they ignored or did not believe the health statements by the critic experts. The truth is that the issue was contestable until at least the 1964 Surgeon General's report. Second, the evidence is clear that despite the huge clout of advertising dollars on media, negative attention of the

industry outweighed positive comments. Press releases and other public relations messages carried statements by prominent public health experts who
refuted the claims of the tobacco critics. Third, large numbers of the public in
1954 reported having heard the criticism of the product and believed that it
posed a health risk.

Issue ads often addressed the self-interest of the company more than that
of key publics. Private-sector management did not understand how little the
public knew about operations and the requirements of finance, product development, liability, and pollution control. Feeling little pressure from the public,
business leaders built new relationships with government. They believed government could be a source of revenue for products and services as well as
research and development. Companies, such as those in the steel industry, used
the war years to expand and modernize because they had a ready market for
their products. They fought efforts to nationalize the industry during times of
war and price controversy. Government contracts steadily became more and
more important to many industries.

The questioning of private-sector behavior, prompted in the post–World
War II period primarily by the civil rights movement, blossomed during the
1960s. The history of issues management parallels the tumultuous growth of
corporations, marked by an ongoing public policy contest between business critics and supporters. Supporters stressed the ability of corporations to create jobs
and provide products and services. They opposed regulation, unless it stabilized
the marketplace and boosted profits. Executives believed that if key publics
understood the plight of business, they would not champion restrictions.

Critics argued that companies must comply with ever-changing public
expectations of responsible behavior. Under pressure, corporations began to
reexamine themselves, but the road was not an easy one. Public policy revolu-
tions always occur when massive reevaluation focuses on an era's underpinning premises. The euphoria of the late 1940s and 1950s misled corporations.
Most were unprepared for the hostile outbursts of social reexamination that
occurred during the 1960s and 1970s. Business leaders had failed to keep in
tune with public expectations. Companies had not fostered a platform of fact
or affirmed key value premises. New premises arose with startling speed to
reinterpret existing information about environmental quality, fairness of business practices, product and operating safety, and equity in hiring and promotion. Rather than seeing the merits of involving critics' concerns in corporate
planning, firms tried to keep them outside plant and company boundaries and
marginalize their voices.

In the face of these challenges, some companies assumed the trouble would
go away once the outrage burned itself out. They hoped the difficulties could be
communicated out of existence. Many business leaders repeated stock claims
about the damage of regulation and the destruction of the free enterprise

system. They thought these statements might convince bleeding-heart agitators, and if not, they would be marginalized. Few if any industries realized that a new search for order was in the making.

Dissent Flowers in the 1960s

During the Depression of the 1930s, the power of business was substantially blunted by a larger government that many citizens believed was preferable to irresponsible capitalism. Even so, people wanted to trust the inherent good of business ethics. By the 1960s, this value premise had changed; beneath the good feeling was a deep layer of skepticism about corporate performance. During the postwar era of "good times," growing dissent in the African American community and changing values publicized by the beat (as in beatnik) generation were signaling the most massive challenge to standard business practices witnessed in this country. Many institutions—government, business, family life, organized religion, and education—were carefully scrutinized. The rift between critics and companies obtained full articulation when civil rights and antiwar protests became front-page news. The war in Vietnam became a forum for reexamining corporate behavior.

The era of change began when new facts were laid before the U.S. public regarding the harm business was doing to the physical and human environment. Product safety and employment practices were two of the many corporate policies that changed as a consequence of new premises. A new definition of corporate responsibility altered business planning and management. New definitions of risk and safety focused on operations of nuclear generation and use of pesticides, as well as new environmental ethics for harvesting timber and producing oil and chemicals. Critics examined financial institutions, automobile safety, and air transportation. In these turbulent times, "government was more likely to be a partner or helpmate than an opponent of the modern corporation" (Galambos & Pratt, 1988, p. 154).

Coupled with the search for values that continued after the antiwar years, reform interests pushed for a broad reorientation in business ethics. *Corporate citizenship* became the major public affairs theme during these decades. Quality of life and businesses' contribution to it took on new meaning, once people who had not been politically and socially aware before the 1960s came to believe that they could no longer take business policies for granted. Labor unions demanded higher wages and benefits. Accelerating the breakdown of this social contract were record unemployment and bankruptcies, the uncertain government response to foreign sales in the country, deepening trade deficits, and a declining manufacturing base as the United States moved haltingly toward a postindustrial economy. Invention of the personal computer, effective software, the

Internet, and all the advances in communication and information technology and desire for ever cheaper goods led to a new economy.

Professional communication had to reach an ever higher standard and impress these new challenges on a basically recalcitrant cadre of senior management. Businesses' images and sales slid when company spokespersons tried to cover up embarrassing facts. Attempting to restore credibility, a number of CEOs stepped forward to personally represent their companies and be visible on matters of public interest, even though image masters sought to (re)present companies as image rather than substance (Cheney, 1992). The private sector became interested in applying sophisticated social science techniques not only for product sales but to market ideas. Companies undertook campaigns to politically educate and foster participation by employees, shareholders, customers, and other allies. They became involved in grassroots programs and sought to build constituencies to marshal support for issues relevant to the needs of their firms. Trade associations and political action committees (PACs) became valuable means for expressing the corporate position without individual businesses having to be visible.

Until 1971, corporations were expressly forbidden from contributing to federal candidates and their party organizations. The Federal Election Campaign Act of 1971 and its amendments in 1974 and 1976 allowed corporations, unions, and industry special interest groups to form PACs and use them to funnel dollars into political campaigns. The Bipartisan Campaign Reform Act of 2002, also known as the McCain-Feingold Act and an amendment to the original Federal Election Campaign Act of 1971, was an attempt to monitor and control fundraising and the use of campaign contributions in relationship to the elimination of soft money. Soft money is contributions to political parties and political action committees that enable large donors to circumvent federal limits on direct contributions to candidates. New modes of injecting money into campaigns, by companies and individuals, became notorious in the 2004 presidential election. Now election spending has reached the multi-billion-dollar level. Public interest groups, such as Common Cause and Move On.Com, were troubled by corporate and special interest PAC contributions to political campaigns. Campaign chests overflowed, and voters became weary of negative campaigning.

During prior wars, businesses that supplied matériel and armaments had been seen as making a heroic contribution to the country's security. Activists against the Vietnam War reversed that equation. Dow Chemical, for instance, was singled out for attack because it produced napalm. Napalm is a gasoline-based military weapon that incinerates what it touches—including innocent men, women, and children. Before Vietnam, Dow had been viewed as a good company for which to work. College graduates had lined up for job interviews, but antiwar sentiment changed this. By the 1970s, Dow's favorable image was replaced by that of a warmonger, indiscriminately destroying nonmilitary targets. Students scorned job interviewers and made the purchase of Saran Wrap synonymous with incinerating innocent men, women, and children.

Environmental quality became one of the major public expectations, now made more salient by concerns over global warming. Such concerns began to get voice in 1962, when Rachel Carson stunned the nation with a series of articles in the *New Yorker* titled "Silent Spring," later published in book form. She alleged that insecticides and herbicides have serious side effects as silent killers. For the first time, the public learned how heavy metals, such as mercury and lead, seep into the water systems, where they are picked up by the simplest forms of life. As each higher level of life eats each lower one, the poisonous metals are stored in fat tissues; these poisons are ingested in ever more concentrated amounts when little fish, which eat plankton, are devoured by larger fish. Eventually, the poison concentrates in humans who eat the larger fish. DDT became associated with declines in bird populations. This chemical continues to receive scrutiny today; some scientists and economists believe it is quite beneficial, especially in combating malaria, and is not as harmful as once claimed. Science, in these ways, has become increasingly politicized as we continue to understand risk management and communication.

Ecologists argued for a "spaceship Earth" concept in caring for our planet. Pollution was characterized as a form of global suicide. Biologists and allied groups pronounced rivers and lakes dead and held national rallies to protest the destruction of the environment that the agitators argued was a common legacy. Popular musicians and singers participated in this effort, lending visibility to the problem and building a popular culture that rejected corporations. Positive contributions made by chemistry can be obscured by the discovery of the impact of toxic waste and related issues. Events such as the Cuyahoga River catching fire in Cleveland dramatized the seriousness of chemical pollution. Ecologists mobilized to conduct memorial services dedicated to the past beauty of the countryside.

The terms *biodegradable, returnable,* and *recyclable* became hallmarks of responsible "green" product marketing. Today these terms have been replaced by *sustainable, renewable, eco-friendly, natural,* and *organic.* People learned that plastic containers, which seemed so convenient, would last in landfills long after they themselves had died. Nuclear generation and nuclear waste disposal became issues made more salient by the Three Mile Island nuclear generating facility incident. Chernobyl, a nuclear generating facility in the former Union of Soviet Socialist Republics (USSR), went critical and discharged tons of radioactive materials around the globe. Children in Europe have been closely watched to see if their exposure has led to increased health problems. Legislative acts made executives personally liable for ensuring that their companies complied with standards relating to toxicity and clean air and water.

Acts went so far as to state that executives did not have to have direct information regarding noncompliance; they would be liable for creating an organizational culture that allowed noncompliance by subordinates.

How the private sector responded to these new facts, premises, and policy conclusions determined whether it could avoid more stringent regulation and win back public trust. When even soft drink containers became a political issue, the question shifted back to corporations. One of the most famous Advertising Council public service campaigns was the "people start pollution, people can stop it" effort financed by Keep America Beautiful, Inc. It featured a Native American shedding a tear for the fouled landscape. By drawing attention to the need for individual (as compared with collective) responsibility in combating litter, the series adroitly sought to reposition the pollution issue by downplaying its industrial origins and deflecting efforts to punish business. This theme is not surprising, because the volunteer coordinator of the Ad Council campaign was W. Howard Chase, then with American Can Company. Board members of Keep America Beautiful also included representatives of soft drink companies, brewers, glass bottlers, and aluminum can manufacturers (Barnouw, 1978).

Ralph Nader helped spawn this consumer concern in 1965 when he proclaimed that General Motors's Corvair compact was "unsafe at any speed." New standards of automobile safety were imposed on the car industry, in part by consumer interest groups but even more resoundingly by the massive automobile insurance industry. This group wanted car manufacturers to implement automobile designs that would lessen the costs of injury, death, reconstructive surgery, and rehabilitation.

Angry consumers, educated by advertising to desire high-quality products at low prices, gave birth to consumer interest groups. Critics demanded that corporations deliver all that they promised in their product and service advertisements (Richards, 1990). Large consumer coalitions, such as the Consumer Federation of America, drew their financial support and membership from across the nation. Opposing sophisticated corporate lobbying efforts, consumers borrowed strategies refined by other activists who had learned to use government to reshape corporate performance. Tactics have included media blitzes, class action suits, boycotts, defiant rallies, injunctions, and grassroots lobbying of government agencies. Since the 1960s, the consumer movement has turned its attention to virtually every aspect of human life touched by business. Massive class action lawsuits have become a standard part of issues management. One of the largest was the Master Tobacco Settlement that accounted for about $280 billion to be contributed to participating states. The purpose of getting the funding was not only punitive but also intended to be spent on educating young people to prevent them from initiating smoking. Many of these dollars, however, were spent by greedy state legislators on completely unrelated projects.

Of the 35 major health, safety, and environmental laws that had been passed by 1982, starting with the Dangerous Cargo Act in 1877, 26 came into being in the 1960s and 1970s (Renfro, 1982). These cover tobacco and alcohol abuse, flammable fabrics, poison prevention packaging, mine and railroad protection, water pollution control, clean air, noise control, lead-based paint restrictions, food quality control, and myriad other issues that introduced a new vocabulary and an accompanying set of values. The National Environmental Policy Act of 1969 required environmental impact statements. In slightly more than a decade, environmental acts were passed regarding endangered species (1973), safe drinking water (1974), transportation of hazardous materials (1975), toxic substances (1976), solid waste disposal and resource conservation (1976), surface mining (1977), hazardous liquid pipeline safety (1979), and environmental compensation and liability (1980). Recent additions to this list include the Hazardous and Solid Waste Amendments (1984), Superfund Reauthorization Act and Emergency Planning and Community Right-to-Know Act (EPCRA, 1986), Water Quality Act (1987), Lead Contamination Control Act (1988), Ocean Dumping Ban Act (1988), offshore production and transportation legislation of 1990, and the Clean Air Act (1990). Many aspects of corporations' and citizens' lives are affected by a deluge of legislative acts: Highway Safety Amendments (1984), Age Discrimination in Employment Act Amendments (1986), Americans With Disabilities Act (1990), Asbestos Hazard Emergency Response Act (1986), Civil Rights Restoration Act (1987), Commercial Motor Vehicle Safety Act (1986), Comprehensive Smokeless Tobacco Health Education Act (1986), Drug-Free Workplace Act (1988), Education of the Handicapped Act Amendments (1986, 1990), Fair Housing Act Amendments (1988), Cash Management Improvement Act (1990), Older Workers Benefit Protection Act (1990), and Social Security Amendments (1983, 1991). This list continues to grow.

Revolutionary changes in employment, hiring, salary, and promotion practices dramatically redefined the standards of corporate responsibility. Resulting from efforts by the civil rights and women's movements, firms were required by federal law to become "equal opportunity employers." Employees' rights to speak out publicly on controversial issues were protected, as was the right to disclose illegal actions by their employers.

The relationship between employer and employee became more regulated. The Occupational Safety and Health Act established an administrative agency charged with ensuring that workers not be subjected to unsafe or unhealthy working conditions. Asbestos became a major corporate political issue, particularly when it was learned that companies involved in mining and processing asbestos had covered up evidence linking it with cancer.

Privacy emerged as a major employee and consumer policy issue. Frustration with massive and impersonal databases, computerized mailing lists, electronic banking, and computerized telemarketing and children's access to adult material have played a part in the consumer push for government oversight of information industry practices. A landmark piece of legislation pertaining to potential government abuse was the Freedom of Information Act of 1966, amended in 1974, which gives the public access to many federal records. This act also made public certain information that corporations have on individuals. The Privacy Act of 1974 balanced this by specifying that documents regarding employee performance must be guarded from scrutiny by unauthorized individuals. Later, the Foreign Corrupt Practices Act (1977) reflected congressional concern that information and guidelines were needed for corporate behavior overseas. The act specifies that companies operating abroad must implement adequate internal measures to prevent illegal payments to obtain business.

Many governmental agencies have the power to demand information from corporations and make it public. These agencies include the Securities and Exchange Commission, Federal Trade Commission, Federal Communications Commission, U.S. Postal Service, Occupational Safety and Health Administration, Office of Economic Opportunity, Nuclear Regulatory Commission, Consumer Products Safety Commission, Organisation for Economic Co-operation and Development, and EPA. The terrorist attack on the World Trade Center towers, the airlines, and the Pentagon led to a new era and the formation of the Homeland Security Agency. Hurricane Katrina, the most devastating storm in modern U.S. history, demonstrated how even with newly created agencies such as Homeland Security, which subsumed the Federal Emergency Management Agency, could fail to serve the citizenry.

Of special interest for SIM is the U.S. Uniting and Strengthening America by Providing Appropriate Tools Required to Intercept and Obstruct Terrorism (USA PATRIOT Act) Act of 2001. The terrorist attacks of September 11, 2001, led to heavy reassessments on whether information about potential targets for terrorists should be disclosed in any way. According to Jacobson (2003),

> The issue has generated fierce debate between environmental activists and industry representatives. The focus of the debate has been on the conflict between dissemination of information to the public and attempting to keep potentially harmful data out of the hands of terrorists. (p. 329)

Babcock (2007) suggested that the events of 9/11 brought into sharp focus the clash between safety and other values such as the right to a healthy environment. According to Jacobson (2003), soon after the attacks, many governmental agencies began to pull sensitive information from their Web sites and other sources. The U.S. Geological Survey, for example, recalled a CD-ROM containing information on bodies of water and asked all recipients to return it (Associated Press, 2002). With the introduction of the USA PATRIOT Act in

October 2001 and the Critical Infrastructure Information Act of 2002, many corporations used the excuse of protecting sensitive targets from terrorist attacks to stop providing information about hazardous materials to communities under the EPCRA (Chekouras, 2007). Babcock (2007) described how the USA PATRIOT Act undermined many provisions of the Freedom of Information Act and EPCRA, among many other environmental laws about right to know and access to information. And the battle continues.

Acquisition of information is only part of the policy effort. In regulatory efforts, debate always centers on which criteria should be used in determining what constitutes responsible business behavior. Corporations have much of the technical expertise and information necessary to discover the best methods for solving problems, but until pressured, they are often reluctant to use this knowledge.

Political pressures, however, are brought to bear by activists who have become institutionalized in the past 40 years. Today, they have substantial lobbying presence in Washington, the various U.S. states, and around the globe. For instance, in some countries, Greenpeace is the 800-pound public policy gorilla. Activist groups spawn activist groups. They select outrage issues, supply information to define problems, help establish the agenda for debate, preempt "moral" arguments by convincingly couching their case in public interest rather than self-serving commercial terms, and engage in relentlessly well-organized and tactically intelligent campaigns attractive to media reporters. They are quite capable of engaging in the "sound bite" war of public policy debate. Environmental groups, for instance, matured from ragtag operations to boast memberships in the millions and reach around the globe. They acquired money to engage in research, establish wildlife preserves, and create partnerships to protect the environment.

One of the major corporate responses has been the science- and policy-based trade association. Because of uncertainties surrounding nature and toxicology, the American Industrial Health Council was formed in 1977. Approximately 200 companies and trade associations provided support for the shared interest in monitoring toxic waste and materials issues. The council represented an array of industrial concerns, including pharmaceutical and petrochemical companies. The council drew together those interested in metals, textiles, and other consumer goods that could be toxic or that produce toxic wastes. The members shared the commitment to better understand the nature and control of toxic materials. In recent years, the Chemical Manufacturers Association became the American Chemistry Council. The U.S. Council on Energy Awareness (USCEA), started in the 1980s, followed on the heels of the "Atoms for Peace" initiative during the Eisenhower years.

For example, to counterbalance the drive for regulation of disposable aluminum cans, industry companies and municipalities have sponsored recycling programs. Not only did this campaign help abate the move to outlaw throwaway containers and impose returnables in their place, it also supplied aluminum companies with a cheaper resource that requires less electricity to process than does the refining of raw materials. Poll data suggest that the general public favors recycling and hopes that their friends and neighbors actively support the movement. Thus, values become separated from behavior.

The Alaskan pipeline and controversies over offshore drilling and access to the Alaskan National Wildlife Animal Refuge denied energy industry board-rooms the freedom to disregard the environment. A visit to oilfields in this country allows anyone to witness environmental devastation that is more than 70 years old. A similar visit to contemporary oil drilling and production sites offers tangible evidence of the marked improvement in corporate responsibil-ity, albeit forced by regulation. Industry spokespersons have not been reluctant to point to these accomplishments in an attempt to refurbish their tattered cor-porate images. There is little doubt that the oil and gas industry has the tech-nology to shock the skeptical public with its ability to produce oil without pollution. That fact is even admitted by Greenpeace, which nevertheless believes that industrial performance can only provide part of the solution. People must change their personal lifestyles. Today's counterpart to these types of controversy that has global impact is global climate change.

Three decades of energetic criticism and robust development in issue communication, plus the prospect for future challenges, provide the context for the study and practice of issues management. Those who manage, design, or critique issue campaigns have learned that they cannot assume that these tactics will establish mutual interests with all stakeholders. They have come to see the virtue in negotiation and collaborative decision making. They have learned the lesson that issue communication cannot solve problems and abate criticisms that require improved business operations. "Government officials who had tolerated business's foot-dragging for several decades responded to mounting public pressures by demanding immediate solutions to a series of difficult problems" (Galambos & Pratt, 1988, p. 213).

One victim of the turbulent past 3 decades is the assumption, promoted by public relations pioneer Edward Bernays (1955), that consent can be engi-neered. Business historians Galambos and Pratt (1988) reflected on the dislo-cating transition for business in the 1970s: "Just as the Vietnam War forced the nation to reassess its military and political power in international affairs, how-ever, so the energy and environmental crises forced difficult reassessments in the nation's business system" (p. 2). Regardless of the interest of any person or organization in this drama, the long-term goal of society and the organizations that conduct or regulate business is to achieve sufficient order so they can strategically plan and systematically achieve those plans. If companies cannot always manage issues, they can implement effective strategic business plans, engage in useful communication, and manage their public policy plans.

The Present and the Future

This section offers a brief summary of themes discussed earlier and looks briefly at current issues that are likely to continue with variation into the future. These we list briefly, but we also suggest themes that become increasingly complex because they often result in a collision between science, operating policy, and societal values. As will be seen in the chapters on crisis and risk, issues interconnect with the other two (see Figure 2.1). Any issue may result from a crisis, which is a risk manifested. A risk may create an issue, especially once it has become a crisis. Issues become contested interpretations of risks and crises. A crisis may become an issue.

One of the basic themes of this chapter is the recurrence, persistence, and redefinition of premises on which issues turn. Central to each issue is one or more molar values that is vital to how people interpret risks and crises. Four molar values seem central to all issues, although any issue may involve one or more of them: environmental quality, safety, fairness, and equality.

Biotechnology. Advances in food supply, quality, production, and medical breakthroughs can result from the scientific advances housed under biotechnology. For instance, new medicines and therapies can be created by genetic modification. Food production can be advanced by genetic modification.

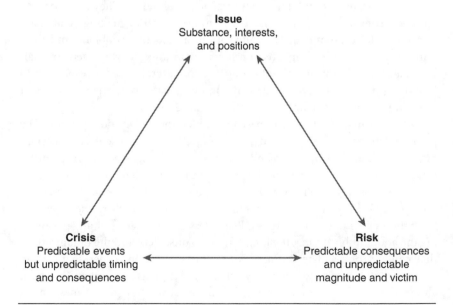

Figure 2.1   Interaction Between Crisis, Risk, and Issue

Knowing this, people become concerned about the safety of such technologies, if not environmental quality, fairness, and equality.

Public Health. How healthy can a society be? What can be done to make people healthier? Does business practice add to and work against health improvement? What should the role of government be? How do high-profile products, such as alcohol and tobacco, as well as pharmaceuticals and medical practices help or harm the steady advance toward increased quality of health, in the United States and around the world? Is the automobile and traffic safety a greater threat to countries such as the United States than international terrorism? Does the marketing of food in countries such as the United States lead to a healthier society or merely sustained or greater profit?

Energy. Do we have enough hydrocarbon fuel to go around, or is the sole resource of a few countries often extracted through geopolitics from other countries? Can we have "affordable" energy and a safe environment as well? Can we create renewable and sustainable resources? Can we develop a national and international energy policy? Is every major military and political battle of the foreseeable future tied to energy? Is nuclear again on the table as a viable alternative? Is all of that debate muted by the prospect of global warming?

Environmental Quality. What is environmental quality? How safe are people from toxics such as EPA-listed chemicals and heavy metals such as lead? Can we protect species and wildlife, or are population explosion and resource exploration on a collision course with Mother Nature?

Postcolonial Civil Society. Can people live together in peace and harmony? Can we learn to use civil society to solve problems, or must we continue to arm, maim, and kill in the name of peace? Popular culture continues to raise issues such as the causes and perils of global warming, arms dealing (*Lord of War* observes that the nations of the UN Security Council are the world's leading arms dealers), and the use of impoverished people of the world as medical guinea pigs (*The Constant Gardener*). Can the wealthy nations maintain themselves without colonizing the rest of the world?

Work, Working Conditions, and Immigration. Boundaries seem to be vulnerable to easy passage. Jobs are being created in many countries that deny that work to U.S. residents. Some of those moving about have terrorist intents. Most are looking for work and a better life. Labor has become global, but worker safety may be the victim of xenophobia and profit. How can fully employed people in rich nations be held to poverty existence? Has the world solved the workplace problems tainted by race, gender, and age? How much unemployment and underemployment occurs in some nations because of labor costs in others?

This brief summary undoubtedly slights many issues, but it suggests that issues management has a solid future as interests are pitted against one another and contestable issues are bountiful because of available fact, value, and policy position choices.

Conclusion

This chapter described how key publics' and organizations' contest for order is an ongoing, robust debate. Interested participants seek to provide facts, shape premises used to judge those facts, and draw conclusions from that combination. Individual statements blend into collective opinions. If chaos reigned, companies and other key segments of society could not conduct their activities. For this reason, a primary rationale for issues management, the dialogue in society, is a search for order. Such order occurs because people share zones of meaning whereby key premises connect to facilitate agreement and concurrence.

SIM Challenge: Science or Sham?

The SIM challenge at the end of Chapter 1 looked to the current and future business practices relevant to China, which may dominate much of the world's business activity in this century. Instead of the future, this chapter, dedicated primarily to historical review, looks back to 1953, when the tobacco/public health issue gained traction as it had not before.

Public health and tobacco was a longstanding issue by the time Christmas plans were well under way in 1953. But that year was a crucial one for the tobacco industry, as well as the professional practice and reputation of John W. Hill, the principal head of Hill & Knowlton, which by that time was the largest public relations agency in the world. John Hill was well associated with the challenges of representing industry and industries. He helped create and hone the use of trade associations. He was an unabashed believer in the private sector, but so were other giants in the public relations profession (Cutlip, 1994). Two major private agencies already had a tobacco company as a client, especially Tommy Ross of Lee and Ross and Ben Sonnenberg. Hill & Knowlton joined the team in 1953, and within just a few days, Hill and his key people had interviewed leading executives, public relations professionals, and scientists for the tobacco industry. The question: Could the industry be properly represented by an agency on matters of scientific claims that smoking posed serious health consequences?

Before getting more details on the issue and the challenge, let's explore the public relations philosophy of John Hill. His campaign and others he worked on came well before the 1970s with the emergence of the new concept of issues management and the coinage of that term. He retired in the late 1960s, but he influenced a generation of practitioners on the management, ethics, and social responsibility of issues campaigns. Hill wrote two books, *Corporate Public Relations: Arm of Modern Management* (1958) and *The Making of a Public Relations Man* (1963). In those books, he expressed his professional philosophy, which guided his practice for the tobacco industry, which in part included the development of a trade association. What did Hill think about what constitutes the public interest?

> It is not the work of public relations—let it always be emphasized—to outsmart the American public in helping management build profits. It is the job of public relations to help management find ways of identifying its own interests with the public interest—ways so clear that the profit earned by the company may be viewed as contributing to the progress of everybody in the American economy. (Hill, 1958, p. 21)

> In attempting to guide its enterprise in keeping with the public interest, corporate management is confronted with the problem of determining just what is meant by 'public interest.' It certainly does not mean catering to every passing popular whim, nor does it carry the implication that management should toss aside all its deeply held precepts and principles. At the same time, management cannot assume that it is always right and that serving the public interest means convincing other people to go along with its views. (Hill, 1958, p. 166)

> Where hostility in public opinion exists, its roots should be uncovered and steps taken to correct it. If policies are unsound or out of step with the identifiable public interest, they should be studied and, if possible, corrected. Quite often the remedy called for is more information to the public together with forthright explanation and interpretation. (Hill, 1963, p. 230)

Hill believed that companies and governments, no matter how powerful, could not dictate what people should believe, value, or support. Support, rather than opposition, had to be earned by sound policy and effective communication. Failing either or both, the organization had to adjust itself to the public expectations, exactly the point made in the discussion of the legitimacy gap in Chapter 1. Thus, Hill (1958) concluded the following: "Public relations is an outgrowth of our free society, in which the ideal of an enlightened and rational public opinion is brought ever closer as understanding increases between groups and individuals" (p. ix).

One of the milestone years in the tobacco/public health case was 1953. In December 1953, research-based articles and speeches aroused grave concern among the leaders of the industry. The December 1953 issue of *Cancer Research* carried an article by Ernst Wynder, Evarts Graham, and Adele Croninger at

Sloan Kettering Institute in New York that reported the results obtained from painting tobacco tars—smoke residue—on the skin of mice. This publication was not the first of its kind. The widely read *Reader's Digest* had done so for years, and it would continue to publish articles pointing to this public health problem. On December 8, 1953, Alton Ochsner spoke about his research findings in New York City. Ochsner was a major medical researcher whose fame and notoriety rose as the issue gained traction. These presentations and articles, as well as the likelihood of more, motivated industry leaders to hire a public relations agency that was prepared and able to perform what were essentially SIM tasks. One was to conduct a national communication campaign, starting with a major ad that ran around the nation on January 4, 1954.

What happened in the last 2 weeks of December help us focus on the role and challenges of issues management: strategic business planning, issue monitoring, issue communication, and corporate responsibility.

• Despite fear that they would be charged with violating antitrust sanctions that had been placed on them, on December 10 and 11, 1953, presidents of all but one of the major tobacco companies met at the Plaza Hotel, at the invitation of Paul Hahn, president of the American Tobacco Company.

• Shortly thereafter, these executives invited John Hill to consider being public relations counsel for the industry. The goal was to combat the public health charges, which were hurting sales. These executives acknowledged that the smoking critics were professionals of unquestionable integrity and motive who were sincere in their belief on the issue (Kluger, 1996).

• On December 15, 1953, John Hill, Bert Goss (Hill's chief associate), and other senior members of the firm met with tobacco industry representatives. They would meet again on December 29 to finalize the ad and campaign launch. In the days just prior to this meeting, senior Hill & Knowlton executives were forging ideas, but more important, they were working to know the tobacco industry representatives, company, and scientific validity of the claims. Recall that Hill & Knowlton had no tobacco client, so this was a quick but deep learning curve. One key theme in the planning documents was a commitment to be sure that the public received true and useful information on the potential health hazard. Hill & Knowlton's planning documents noted that no trade association was in place to represent the industry as a whole.

• During meetings with the industry, Hill insisted that the name of the industry (tobacco) or product (cigarettes) had to be in the title of the organization. His ethics led him to be sure that people knew the communicator because the character of the communicator (motive, for instance) was crucial to the quality and impact of the message. The identity could not be hidden. This could not be a front. Moreover, the industry had to have and share with

Hill & Knowlton a true, unbiased, and defensible knowledge and interpretation of the facts on the health issue. Facts are facts. Finally, in the planning, Hill and his key personnel told the industry that people were fully and honestly entitled to their public health concerns; they could not be dismissed or downplayed. They had to be addressed in fact by people of high character since allegations were being made by medical scientists of high character who put in front of the public facts as they were known.

- Out of this planning arose the Tobacco Industry Research Committee. It would consist of scientists broadly interested in the topic and with solid credentials. Funding initiatives would be invited to explore in detail not only the claims being made by the critics but other alternative interpretations of the causes of lung cancer and heart disease. Findings would be published for all to see. Surveys and epidemiological studies were to be considered but had to be treated as presenting correlations, not causes. The committee wanted to fund research that could empirically decide the issue.

- With these agreements and assurances, the issue campaign began. It was sustained through various permutations for decades. During that time, press releases were issued by Hill & Knowlton and other agencies that challenged scientific findings. One of the goals of the industry was to be sure that if critics made a claim, an opposing position had to be published if it existed. Whether honestly or cynically, this was to be a sound science campaign. Whether that was true is up to others to consider, as they have.

Here our point is not to debate the merits of the campaign. Was it ethical? Did it confuse people? Did it unfairly stall sanctions against the industry? Such questions are addressed by many others. Here we want to use this case to point out the workings of SIM. We have a risk-based issue, public health, that over time became a crisis for the industry. However much any critic might focus on the campaign, the reality is that steadily, public policy sanctions have been brought against the industry and are likely to continue. Substantial numbers of people in 1954 knew of the research alleging a connection between health and tobacco use. A sizable part of the population smoked, and smoking was a rich part of the popular culture of society. It was considered by many to be sophisticated.

No matter how long this public policy battle has gone on, it indicates that even a rich and powerful industry cannot dominate an issue. However, it also proves that the quirks of human nature are at play. For instance, did putting a health warning on packages make the product more attractive to risk-taking teens who are prone to engage in taboo behaviors? Do generations of young people suggest that they like to do what they are told not to do? If fact is the only basis of public policy, why does it tend to fail, but having said that, can public policy survive without fact? Thus, we have the eternal battle between scientific interpretation of risk and the cultural interpretation.

Summary Questions

1. Name at least one product or service whose history is defined by a public policy battle. Explain the battle, the themes, players, and outcome. Account for why the battle culminated as it did.

2. How are facts, evaluations, and policy positions connected? How do marketing and public policy battles often rest on terministic screens and shared or competing zones of meaning? How do beliefs and attitudes, influenced at least in part by significant others, lead to behavior or behavioral intentions?

3. Why did the robber barons need new public policy to foster their innovations of mass production that eventually led to a mass consumption economy? How did critics battle against these industries by shaping alternative premises on which to evaluate the legitimacy of their policies and activities?

4. Explain why the Great Depression led to public support of heavy-handed measures against industry. Explain how these feelings of goodwill led industry to be so unprepared for the criticism launched against them starting in the 1950s and gaining impetus in the 1960s.

5. Why was so much public policy created to restrain industry after the early 1960s and throughout the end of the century?

6. What three broad issues seem more likely to make work for issues managers in the 21st century?

7. Was John Hill standing on solid principles when he took the tobacco industry as a client in 1953? Which of those principles would best inform your practice today and why?

3

Scouting the Terrain

Scanning, Identifying, Monitoring, Analyzing, and Priority Setting

---

Vignette:
The Greening of Nuclear Power

In the 1970s, a substantial number of nuclear-powered electric generating stations were built in the United States and elsewhere. They rode two conflicting currents. One was the popular culture myth that it was the energy source of the future. Such power was at the heart of U.S. and Japanese experience at the end of World War II. It produced most of the heat behind the debate of the cold war. Many countries built nuclear facilities with increased safety measures, but costs increased after Three Mile Island and Chernobyl events created a crisis of opinion and safety. Risk manifested itself over other factors driving public policy. The industry in many countries went on as always, but in the United States and some other countries, the prospects for nuclear generation slowed. Its death was announced by critics with great applause.

In the early 2000s, President Bush began to advocate this power source following the logics used by advocacy groups such as the U.S. Council for Energy Awareness: Safety; environmental impact reduction, especially in contrast to coal; and reduced dependence on foreign oil at a time when it became more closely associated with nationalism on the part of oil-producing countries and international terrorism. This has been an interesting trend. The popularity of the fuel as an energy source has fluctuated. By 2007, the U.S. government was even proposing $8 billion in subsidies to restart the engineering and construction of such facilities. Applications for licenses came forward by the dozens.

(Continued)

(Continued)

This industry is totally dependent on public policy because it is licensed by the federal government. U.S. public opinion was essentially split but more favorable than unfavorable on this energy source in 2005, according to Gallup Poll data (strongly favor, 17%; somewhat favor, 37%; somewhat oppose, 22%, and strongly oppose, 22%). As is typical of risks, however, the NIMBY (not in my backyard) syndrome was evident when these same people were asked if they would support or oppose a facility in "their area" (strongly favor, 11%; somewhat favor, 24%; somewhat oppose, 19%; and strongly oppose, 43%). In the early 1990s, three fourths of Americans thought the energy source was important for the future. Looking back to 1979, the nation was split on whether it would support or oppose nuclear as a way of dealing with the coal and oil supply. On this issue, a contestable matter of value and policy, the trend seems to reflect willingness to keep this energy option alive but is best used "in someone else's backyard."

This is a quick overview of how the nation is thinking about nuclear power, a very complex issue. But in terms of strategic issues management (SIM), we are wise to look beyond and beneath the broad generalizations of public opinion polling to address other questions:

- Who believes what, and how much influence do these people (including the organizations they influence) have on each relevant issue?

- How powerful are the advocates for and against some issue? What gives them their power that allows them to play the stakes they hold?

- Is support for the issue position increasing or decreasing, as well as how many and who are attending to the issue and believing one side or another?

- What do the influencers and advocates believe? What facts do they assert, values they prefer, and policies they advocate? Who listens to and believes them? Who are their followers and supporters? What advocates are generating information, evaluations, and policy positions on the various sides of different issues and on specific issues?

- Has the dialogue reached a point at which certain issue positions have become ossified, or is there still chance for change for or against some specific issue position? Can the change be created by adopting new organizational policies and/or by responsible advocacy and collaborative decision making?

In all of these matters, as we stress throughout the book, the issue is not what all people believe but what some believe—and believe strongly—to exert effort and pressure to bring their positions into public policy arenas and marketplaces. In politics, for instance, a majority opinion accounts for the outcome of elections. Such majority opinions may be a complex of minority opinions. And whereas public polls tell us what many people think, public policy battles often turn on what a few energetic, articulate, and dedicated advocates believe and desire. That theme should be quite evident from the discussion in Chapter 2 and will become clearer as we discuss activism and social movement dynamics later in the book.

Chapter Goals

After reading and understanding this chapter, you should be able to explain the conditions of public opinion, the stages of issue monitoring, and the ways in which teams are assembled to bring depth and breadth to issue monitoring. This chapter establishes a rationale and tactics for issue scanning, identification, monitoring, analysis, and priority setting. It sheds light on how issue analysis should look for conflict and mutual interests between a firm and its stakeholders and stakeseekers. The key is to ascertain as early as possible what issues need attention and determine how they can be used in a company's strategic guidance system. One concern is estimating which issues may yield to communication and which ones require new procedure or policy to repair, maintain, or strengthen relationships with stakeholders. The goal is to identify and understand incompatibilities between cultures—zones of meaning—to seek ethical and harmonious resolution of frictions that arise from opinion differences.

Public opinion can be conceptualized as shared perspectives on key matters, including the public interest. John Hill (1958), the principal founder of one of the largest international public relations agencies (Hill & Knowlton), noted the following (introduced in Chapter 2):

> It is not the work of public relations—let it always be emphasized—to outsmart the American public in helping management build profits. It is the job of public relations to help management find ways of identifying its own interests with the public interest—ways so clear that the profit earned by the company may be viewed as contributing to the progress of everybody in the American economy. (p. 21)

Hill (1963) succinctly stated, "No one person, and no one group, is entitled to determine arbitrarily what is in the public interest" (p. 253). Public opinion and the definition of public interest arise through dialogue—no different than other issues exemplified in this book. SIM is wise, therefore, to listen to and understand the dialogue. It is privileged, even obligated, to communicate its agreement and disagreement. Any business, or other organization, is one voice among many.

In addition to its other business responsibilities, organizations are expected to help create through dialogue, not monologue, the public opinion that would govern its actions and define the relationships with its markets and publics. Failing that balance, a company would stand accused before the court of public opinion. As Hill (1958) wrote, "In a nation such as the United States, where public opinion is both judge and jury, any segment of the public is free to question management's wisdom, integrity, and good human intent in handling responsibilities that amount to a public trust" (p. 25).

Opinion landscapes shape market forces and affect operating costs. Change happens; a competitor presses for new product or manufacturing process safety guidelines or product quality standards. A market changes dramatically because key opinions favor or disfavor it. A regulator alters ground rules, which can add to the cost of doing business or change what motivates people to contribute to a charity or vote for or against a candidate. An activist group challenges established premises by offering new and startling facts or reasoning from different premises than a business or governmental agency does. Some nut tampers with a product, causing a crisis. Workers, such as coal miners, are hurt or killed when safety standards are inadequate or improperly implemented. A reporter writes an accurate (or even inaccurate) and embarrassing feature story.

The person who wants to be a vital part of any executive team needs to understand his or her organization and the context, such as market or public policy arena, well enough to know what changes can add costs to how business is done or where business advantages can be obtained (Reeves, 1993). Viewed this way, "An issue becomes strategic when top management believes that it has relevance for organizational performance" (Dutton & Ashford, 1993, p. 397). Often, one or more members of the organization recognize the nature and seriousness of an issue and sell their analysis and conclusions to management. As management comes to share the sense of opportunity or harm drawn from this analysis, it moves to name the issue, collect information about it, discuss it, and assign key individuals to monitor it. Managements are more likely to find subordinates willing to watch for an issue and bring it to executives' attention when the management cadre is open to and rewards such initiatives (Dutton & Ashford, 1993). In this way, issue monitoring works best when it is part of each organization's culture.

Things Go Bump in the Dark

Effective issues managers engage in environmental-situational position assessment. Simply stated, they want to know what is going on; they want to know trends, facts, and opinions that have consequences. One of the differences between effective proactive issues management and crisis management is not waiting for "things to go bump in the dark." Savvy issues management and proactive risk and crisis managers work to be knowledgeable early in any learning curve.

Communication practitioners and scholars (as well as persons from related disciplines) for decades have advocated the use of social scientific systems to observe and monitor issues at stages when firms still have adaptation options. A quarter century ago, Renfro (1982) reported that at least 200 *Fortune* 500 corporations had established management-level groups to monitor and formulate corporate responses to public policy issues. More recent studies suggest that most major corporations use some type of situation analysis to monitor issues and their corporate responses.

The initial view of modern issues management advocated that organizations were wise to look for and take actions on *emerging issues.* Such advice is sound, but it also led to at least two realizations. One, a plethora of issues emerges that fail to draw significant attention or do not amount to much. Two, many important issues just don't fade away. To develop and execute their plans, executives must be committed to situational analysis that can help them avoid the unexpected and respond quickly when it happens. To define that process, this section lays out a rationale and structure for integrating strategic business planning and issues monitoring.

Issues monitoring and analysis shed light on which beliefs and attitudes are held by each stakeholder, which can affect the future of an organization in a positive or negative manner by the way stakes are granted or withheld. Issues monitoring and analysis seek to know what facts, premises, and values key publics use and what conclusions they draw from them. Much of the general public knows or cares little about most issues that can affect the prospects of an organization; nevertheless, the opinions of key publics are crucial to an organization's success. Opinions may be unfounded, incoherent, ill-defined, unproven, and inconsistent or perfectly on track; nevertheless, stakeholders' opinions are vital to the success of the organization.

Opinions of key publics can affect corporate decisions related to marketing, product development, operating standards, options for financing business activities, consumer protection, transportation and manufacturing safety standards, and environmental protection. If planners and strategists make incorrect assumptions about this landscape, they are likely to steer their companies on a collision course with the expectations and preferences of key publics.

Issues monitoring and analysis need to be strategic. Jaques (2000) suggested that no organization can identify, track, and respond to every issue. It cannot afford to bog down in issues identification, scanning, monitoring, and analysis so that it defaults in the public policy process because it tries to do too much with every issue and accomplishes too little with the ones that truly make a difference to the success of the organization. Some issues are easy to track. Once they enter legislative, regulatory, or litigation processes, they can be tracked through formal channels.

Some issues focus only or primarily on values, but others center on scientific processes and technical facts that leave the realm of public discussion to be debated or negotiated in legislative, regulatory, or judicial chambers by experts for companies, governmental agencies, and activist groups. Stem cell research is a recent good example. Most people, whether for or against based on values or morals, have little knowledge of the science of stem cells. Those who support it may do so on the principle that scientific research offers hope, even though they may not or cannot understand the technical aspects of the research.

Whatever the nature of an issue and related threats and opportunities, the real importance is the potential or real impact on strategic business planning and future operations. As we have stressed throughout this book, issues management entails the skilled balance of four functions: (a) strategic business planning with a vigilant eye to public policy trends; (b) scanning, monitoring, and analyzing issues to understand the terrain; (c) communicating in ways that create a good offense and tough defense; and (d) being sensitive to changing standards of corporate responsibility and adapting to those standards. Fundamental to all elements of the process, strategic planning must consider internal and external circumstances that will affect how and whether the business plan can best be accomplished, if at all.

To assist strategic planning, issues managers, in coordination with key persons throughout an organization, must (a) scan the environment to ascertain what public policy issues are arising and progressing; (b) identify them and know their substance, as well as understand why they are staying alive and what players are sustaining them; (c) keep watch on them (monitor their trends); and (d) learn from the analysis what course of action is best. These steps, explained in the next section, lead to priority setting. Surveillance may give organizations time to change business policies, undertake a communication program, negotiate differences, collaboratively make decisions, create a platform of fact, propose the best values by which to judge the issue, or counter unwise policies. Scanning and monitoring can give technical experts and managers time to develop a stance to take advantage or lessen the impact of emerging or changing issues (Krippendorff & Eleey, 1986). As we try to understand where we are in the dark, so too do savvy organizations try to know what goes bump in the dark, trying not to hit their head or be caught off guard.

Logics of Issues Monitoring

Building on the logic of the chapter to this point that monitoring is strategically sound, this section suggests the rationale for key steps that are integrated into a model for monitoring issues. The logic begins by recalling Chase (1984), who reasoned that "an issue is an unsettled matter which is ready for decision. Trends, on the other hand, are detectable changes which precede issues" (p. 38). In similar fashion, R. H. Moore (1979) defined an emerging issue "as a trend or condition, internal or external, that, if continued, would have a significant effect on how a company is operated over the period of its business plan" (p. 43). Reflecting on such definitions, Crable and Vibbert (1985) stressed the importance of treating trends, issues, and policies as quite discrete concepts. So, SIM requires systems that can knowingly and strategically scan, identify, and monitor trends and analyze in ways that foster priority setting. According to Palese and Crane (2002), "It is about having the capacity to act quickly in order to seize opportunity or to avert risk before impact of implications become relevant to your business's operations and/or reputation" (p. 284).

For what should we scan? What is the evidence or data that would prompt an issue monitor to say, aha, I think I am on to something important? As noted in the first two chapters, an issue is a contestable point, a difference of opinion regarding fact, value, or policy, the resolution of which has consequences for the organization's strategic plan and future success or failure. It is a matter of concern that results from what is thought to be true (factual), of value, or wise policy. A trend is the trajectory an issue takes because of the discussion it receives and the sociopolitical forces that impinge on it. A policy results when an issue is resolved through governmental action or voluntary actions by a company or industry, a negotiated agreement among opposing sides, or social convention.

Trends result from relatively small to significantly large shifts in known facts, beliefs, and attitudes that can redefine corporate performance standards or result from the awareness that such standards are being violated. Trends probably do not yield to corporate communication and may not involve specific issues that a company needs to consider in its business, public policy, or communication plans. Changes can also occur in the sorts of terminologies and identifications individuals and organizations use to define their political economies.

An issue is more focused. It has the potential, once key groups begin to promote it, to require resolution—the expression of one set of standards in contrast to others or one solution in competition with others. An issue is defined by those public advocates who have an interest in it. If the issue is large and complex, as in the case of global warming or global human rights, discussants of much kind, interest, and quality will engage in the dialogue.

Issues exist in a hierarchy of abstraction. For instance, the issue of environmental quality embraces thousands of narrow issues of fact, value, and policy. Each large issue is divided by categories; for instance, the environmental issue is divided by chemicals, plants, animals, and agricultural practices. In recent years, a new dimension of this trend discussion has been added: biotechnology. Chemicals can be divided into categories, such as toxic and carcinogenic. Plants can cover an array from giant redwoods and firs to swamp and marshland growth. Animals are divided by types—for instance, water turtles and wolves. Even in that regard, the issues related to them are different. Turtles, for instance, are an issue when their ability to survive as a species is threatened by shrimp-harvesting measures. In contrast, wolves are not threatened by otherwise routine agricultural events but by farmers and ranchers taking overt actions to kill them, ostensibly to protect livestock. Viewed in this complex hierarchy of generality and interest, the status of each issue is derived by its place in each key public's issue agenda and something we might image as society's issue agenda. Even in that regard, we confront related issues, such as the need for wood for houses and paper or the use of endangered plants for needed medicines. International trade can complicate such discussions. Nations, such as China, which are currently in a dramatic industrial growth, are, at least for a while, willing to sacrifice environmental quality for low production costs for goods. Recall the attention we focused on the lead issue and China in Chapter 1.

Issues may be universal, affecting much of society and requiring the intervention of government or massive changes in industrial policies or procedures. Issues may be narrow in the interest placed on them and their impact on society. Most environmental issues tend to be universal, for instance, but often have very localized impact. For instance, nuclear waste management is a universal issue but has tended for years to be much more relevant in the United States to proponents and opponents of locating a storage site in Yucca Flats, Nevada.

Some are advocacy issues, those identified by and promoted by activists or some other special interest voice. These may entail shifts in values or the adoption of new perspectives favored by the advocacy group. If such issues are quite narrow or local, they are selective. They can grow or fade, depending on their seriousness and the rhetorical competence of the group. They fade, are dealt with by the stakeseeking group, or grow into advocacy issues. Technical issues are those that often are identified, analyzed, and solved by specialists with special training or expertise. Depending on its nature, an issue may change types (Reeves, 1993).

Issues are not just trends or unsettled matters but contestable points that concern the self-interests (even altruism) of key stakeholders that lead them to support or oppose corporate actions and public policies (Heath & Douglas, 1990, 1991). For this reason, issues monitors should define key publics, not based on demographics but on opinion positions people hold, their issue involvement, and their communication patterns (Berkowitz & Turnmire, 1994). As several scholars have argued (J. E. Grunig, 1989, 1992; J. E. Grunig & Hunt, 1984; Leitch & Neilson, 2001), issues managers should be interested in what key publics recognize to be a problem, believe to affect their self-interests, and feel constrained to take actions. Of central importance is the fact that persons work hard to obtain information, talk about it, and form opinions on issues related to their self-interests (Petty & Cacioppo, 1986).

As well as understanding factors crucial to situational analysis, issues managers need to know the components of such analysis. In this regard, Renfro (1993) highlighted four intelligence activities: "(1) scanning for emerging issues, (2) researching, analyzing, and forecasting the issues, (3) prioritizing the many issues identified by the scanning and research stages, and (4) developing strategic and issue operation (or action) plans" (p. 64).

A widely adopted model, presented by Chase (1984), features issue identification, analysis, change options, and action program. Acknowledging the influence of Chase, J. Johnson (1983) offered a model that Hainsworth and Meng (1988) used to feature scanning-monitoring, identification-prioritization, analysis, (strategy) decision, implementation, and evaluation. Johnson said that strategy-decision is "the pivotal stage." What are the options? Management "might decide to 'hold the fort' and take no action, or it might decide to implement a full-blown action plan in an attempt to 'kill' or mute an issue before it 'takes off'" (p. 26). Taking this stance, Johnson's model is communication oriented, featuring messages as the answer to public policy problems. This model depends on early intervention using communication to blunt issues before they do harm. It begs the following question, however: What if analysis determines that a new or established product is associated with a provable health risk or that it has serious side effects?

The Public Affairs Council offered a version of issues management functions that consists of five building blocks: (a) identification, (b) evaluation, (c) priority setting, (d) corporate response, and (e) implementation. This model does not integrate these issue activities into strategic business planning and management or create standards of corporate responsibility (Armstrong, 1981).

One contingency model, provided by Wartick and Rude (1986), features identification, evaluation, and response development. Even though this model is broad and assumes that these functions are continual, not linear, it does not capture the breadth of functions needed for issues management. It omits the key function of creating and implementing standards of corporate responsibility. A contingency model encourages issues managers to not think defensively about how to protect the company from public policy changes but to look for opportunities and to use public policy to create them.

Supporting this view, Arrington and Sawaya (1984) claimed that the heart of issues management "is reconciliation of conflicting internal interests on public policy issues of strategic importance in order to make a coherent external advocacy" (p. 150). This activity is proactive if public affairs is "viewed as analogous to corporate planning and research and development—as a strategic process to help realize the basic objectives of a company" (p. 158).

Emphasizing the contingency approach, Stroup (1988) observed, "Early knowledge of these trends would give the company more time to change negative attitudes toward business or to adapt business practices proactively if attitudes and expectations could not be swayed from the identified path" (p. 89).

This view makes issues management vital to corporate planning and management. Ewing (1987) reasoned that strategic information management should be part of the systemic processes and culture needed to acquire and use information in planning. Various scholars agree (Ansoff, 1980; Dutton & Duncan, 1987; Dutton & Ottensmeyer, 1987; Lauzen, 1994, 1995). However, this process is best conceptualized as four interlocked functions that operate simultaneously and contingently: (a) strategic planning and management; (b) development and implementation of standards of corporate responsibility; (c) issue identification, scanning, monitoring, and analysis; and (d) issue communication. Without all four functions, issues management is unlikely to achieve its potential to empower personnel to exert influence on behalf of their organizations.

Underpinning assumptions needed to guide issues identification, monitoring, and analysis are provided by co-orientation. One co-orientation model features three dimensions of a relationship: understanding or agreement, congruence, and accuracy (McLeod & Chaffee, 1973). Broom (1977) proposed that the image or issue position preferred by a corporation be compared with that held by key publics. He suggested that

> a public relations problem exists if there is a discrepancy between the corporate definition of an issue and the views held by members of an important public. Reducing or eliminating this discrepancy then becomes the motivation for the informational and persuasive messages directed to the public. (p. 111; see also the legitimacy gap, Sethi, 1977)

Co-orientation assumes that no absolute standard for issue truth, corporate image, or ethical behavior exists because such standards are formed by the dialogue between an organization and each of its stakeholder groups. The extent to which these opinions diverge can result in magnitudes of dissatisfaction on the part of the corporation and its publics. If their positions converge, both parties should be satisfied. By applying this analysis, issues managers can estimate degrees of satisfaction and accuracy as the basis for calculating whether harmony or friction exists and for formulating options to increase harmony and reduce friction.

Accuracy is an expression of the extent to which the leaders of an organization and members of stakeholder groups hold the same opinions on key points and know what each other believes. For instance, if both sides wrote down what they thought the other side believed on key issues, what was written would be the same if they understood one another. Satisfaction is a measure of the degree to which both sides evaluate (positively or negatively) what they know in the same way. For instance, a timber company and an environmental group might agree (know accurately) that the company engages in clear cutting, a means for harvesting timber. The two parties might not be equally satisfied that the practice is environmentally sound (Heath, 1990).

This section demonstrates how many versions, often overlapping and complementary, exist to explain the importance of issue monitoring and set forth the key steps in the process. It answers the question "Why monitor?" by indicating how managerial or communicative actions can do more to address issues in their early stages than if they are already mature.

With this logic in mind, the next section addresses the key steps needed for issue monitoring: issues scanning, identification, trend monitoring, analysis, and priority setting. These functions assist responsible managers in spotting issues and determining appropriate responses to reduce friction between their organization and their stakeholders.

The Systematic Stages of Issues Monitoring

To refine strategic management information systems (Ansoff, 1980; Dutton & Duncan, 1987; Dutton & Ottensmeyer, 1987), organizational structures and functions must be designed and empowered to deal with the ambiguity of information that produces uncertainty (Huber & Daft, 1987). Palese and Crane (2002) described issues management as a team sport that requires effective communication, coordination, and collaboration. Uncertainty predicts information seeking because uncertainty is uncomfortable. Key elements of uncertainty are doubts and predictions about what will happen, what the effect will be, and what response will occur, either on the part of the key public or the organization (Gerloff, Muir, & Bodensteiner, 1991). As well as looking outside of the organization, issue managers must look inward to understand its culture, organizational and political structures, and strategies of public policy issue analysis. Thousands of issues emerge but do not mature into concerns that require much, if any, response by the company. Even without comprehensive issue identification and response techniques (see Figure 3.1), an organization tracks changes in key issues and attempts to ascertain how their resolution can affect its business, public policy, or communication plan.

The ostensible value of scanning, identifying, and acting quickly on emerging issues assumes that such issues mature from a felt concern on the part of many people. One difficulty regarding emerging issues is deciphering which ones will become the mission of key and powerful groups or media, including social and nontraditional, and achieve sufficient vitality to deserve an organization's serious attention. Many issues die a natural death and never amount to anything. Few issues mature. Telling the difference is vital because no organization has the resources to scan, monitor, and respond to all issues. As Renfro (1993) observed,

> Most issues become credibly foreseeable only when they have become so stable as to be impervious to outside forces, including those generated by a

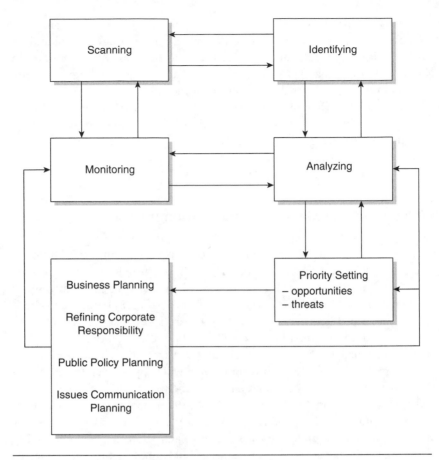

Figure 3.1   Issue Alert and Response Process

corporation's issue action program. In other words, by the time an executive has enough confidence in a forecast to justify expending his or her limited resources, it is often too late to have any real impact. (p. 12)

Although issue scanning, identifying, trend monitoring, and analysis should be continuous, they need to be phased into the normal planning patterns of the organization if they are going to have their maximum effects. Drawing on years of work with sophisticated issues management systems and senior executive discussions, Renfro (1993) observed, "Usually, successful issues management systems are built to run on the strategic management cycle, often an annual process" (p. 103).

Thus, Renfro (1993) reasoned, for issues management to be a vital part of strategic planning and management, it must begin with a "recognition of the need for faster, clearer, earlier intelligence on emerging issues," no matter how "minimal, unarticulated, disjointed, confused, and tardy it may be for getting information about the changing environment into the organization" (pp. 104–105). The ability to scout the terrain means getting the best available information as quickly as possible and making the most of it to understand the opportunities and threats the public policy environment poses for corporate plans, policies, and operations.

ISSUES SCANNING

Issues scanning can be compared with the radar monitoring of storm trends that gives us weather predictions based on the physical and meteorological trends. Scanning entails constantly watching for issues to emerge and become salient. Scanning involves looking for reports of facts, scientific conclusions, credible discussions, scientific discoveries, or concerns that could be important to the organization's planning and operations. At this stage, the issues manager is more interested in spotting figures when they appear on the horizon than in determining whether they are friends or foes and deciding whether they will last only a moment or stay for a while. Issues identification, tracking, and analysis call for sustained efforts to use benchmark data as starting points to extrapolate formation and change of opinions by key publics. Indicators of issue shifts can include the number of people who are aware of an issue, whether it is serious enough to warrant corrective action, and the strength and variety of opinions that agree or disagree with issue positions of the company.

Where do we look for issues? They might emerge in obscure publications and outlets. Nowadays they often emerge on the Web via social networks or other new information and communication technology developments, as well as through videos produced by backpack journalists posted on such sites. One safe generalization is that by the time an issue has reached the point of being discussed in mainstream daily newspapers or national news magazines or appears on local or national news, it has emerged through various nonmainstream media and other venues such as forums. Issues can first appear in reports of scholarly research: masters' theses, dissertations, convention papers, scholarly journals, quasi-scholarly publications, opinion publications, underground press, underground Internet discussions and chat rooms, specialized narrow-viewpoint journals and papers, cause journals, special interest newsletters and other publications, conferences, voiced concerns of nonmainstream political candidates, and ungeneralized comments in a community. The next layer of publication outlets includes books, industry journals, trade publications, larger circulation scientific or social scientific journals, call-in talk shows, letters to the editors, and bellwether newspapers or other mainstream media outlets. Issues often emerge in publications that are read by members of the company other than issues managers, such as lawyers, human resource personnel, or chemical plant technicians.

Issues arise from diverse sources: special interest advocates, media commentators, governmental agencies, industry leaders or bad apple companies, bloggers, backpack journalists, technical experts, community leaders, and other industries. Companies that have a lot of contact with customers, such as utilities or retail outlets, may find it useful to arm telephone service representatives or salespersons with guidelines that allow them to record and report customer concerns and complaints. Ultimately, organizations need to develop ways or let systems grow organically where members of a community can voice their concerns into an early warning system. With Web technologies readily and widely available, organizations can solicit comments and reports. Organizations can actively, transparently, and responsibly work to understand social media norms by scanning issues on the Web. Today, experts have information technology software and applications that are and will be ever more increasingly vital to issues scanning efforts.

An issue should be placed into the company issues monitoring system only after it meets three criteria: (a) It is listed in standard indexes, suggesting that journalists have come to believe that it is legitimate and worth general public discussion; (b) a case can be made that the issue will threaten company operations or offer opportunity for market advantage; and (c) the issue is associated with at least one identifiable group (whether business, government, activist, or media) that has the track record, or the potential, of bringing it to the legislative agenda.

Shifts in values, expressed concern, research findings, calls for solutions to problems, some of which people did not think of as problems before: These discussions may very well begin on the fringe of thought in a society. To visualize this process, think of the opinion of the public on any issue as constituting a bell curve of opinion both in terms of extremes of issue positions and degrees of awareness of each issue. The ends of this curve constitute cognitively involved proponents and scoffers regarding an issue (J. E. Grunig, 1989; Heath & Douglas, 1990, 1991). The middle population knows less about the issue, has fewer thoughts and opinions about it, and takes it less seriously. The mainstream may shift to where the fringe once was. However, the middle is rarely likely to have sufficient concern to voice opinions and create an issue that comes to have public visibility. For that reason, issues scanning requires looking at the edges of opinion rather than at mainstream thinking. The latter is more important for the processes of trend monitoring.

ISSUES IDENTIFICATION

Issues identification involves determining whether a problem or concern (a contestable point, difference of opinion, legitimacy gap) exists that could affect (positively or negatively) an organization's ability to achieve its strategic business plan. An issue may result from changes in evaluative criteria such as a new sense of corporate responsibility. Another source of an issue is the discovery that a company or industry is doing something offensive, in violation of current expectations by key publics. An issue may result from a trend, such as a general move to make publicly traded companies provide more and better information relevant to their stock performance.

Issues at some point in their life cycle acquire a name. The identification step typically entails giving a name to an issue or learning all of the names that its various discussants give to it. Each name is likely to suggest how the issue is being framed by various interests. Those typically are part of a larger concept. So, the issue of a species, such as the polar bear whose fortune has been indicated to be bleak because of global warming, gets identity by definition and association. Political discussions of the past decade have given names to issues such as "death taxes" for estate taxes and "family values" to oppose issues such as equal rights for gay and lesbian citizens. Framing is a key part of identifying issues. We often see data, but the data take on life and character once they are named, categorized, and assigned a positive or negative valence.

Identifying issues is difficult because of complexity—the number of variables that affect the emergence and growth of an issue. Turbulence increases as the issue environment becomes more unstable, less predictable, and more uncertain. Issues are more difficult to identify when the information load increases, requiring that more data must be obtained and analyzed than an organization may have resources to accomplish. Analysis is more demanding when issue positions are ambiguous and complex, when the number of participants and issue positions are high, and when participants have many opinion options because the issue has not become well defined. Interdependence can be a stabilizing or destabilizing factor in issues identification. The destabilizing aspect of interdependence results when individual players or issue positions do not respond in thematic or predictable ways, thereby making issue extrapolation difficult or impossible (Huber & Daft, 1987). One activist tactic is to be unpredictable and constantly changing, to keep the company guessing. Critics often make incremental changes that slowly erode the acceptance that once existed regarding a company's or industry's operations, policies, products, or services, a rhetorical strategy that has been called incremental erosion (Condit & Condit, 1992).

During issues identification, Renfro (1993) advised the use of issue briefs that (a) define and explain the issue; (b) explore its various positions, sides, and options as well as the parties that have an interest in it; (c) determine the nature, timing, and mechanisms of the potential impact of the issue; and (d) guide attention to additional sources of analysis regarding the issue. These briefs are thinking documents that precede the formulation of issue position papers, which, based on the data captured by the briefs, assert the position and tactics executives are going to take and use on the issue.

Identification may result in the awareness that a new issue is emerging, a concern exists that may mature into an issue for several reasons, or an issue has existed for some time but has avoided detection or taken a new turn. The issue may find the organization rather than it finding the issue. For that reason, savvy organizations constantly monitor issue trends.

TREND MONITORING

Issues monitoring assumes that some issues pose threats or opportunities and therefore should be watched to see how they develop, which advocate takes a particular position, and the extent to which the issue achieves public and opinion leader visibility and credibility. Issues are tracked to ascertain whether and when they become associated with established and powerful advocates who have the potential to sustain the discussion and press an issue to its logical outcome, such as change in regulation or legislation. Issues do not sustain themselves. Part of strategic monitoring is knowing the factors that sustain each issue and observing whether they are working for its development or demise.

Issues monitoring includes issues forecasting. One problematic aspect of issues monitoring and analysis is foretelling the future of an issue—whether it will increase or decrease in salience, whether advocates will increase or suffer a decrease in their influence, and whether its consequences for the organization are likely to be more or less serious. Forecasting entails making extrapolations as to whether (a) the trend will continue, stabilize, increase, or decrease in momentum; (b) change will occur in the breadth and depth of coverage and discussion by the media, governmental agencies, activists, and others in business (intraindustry and interindustry); (c) a rise or decline will take place in terms of the number of people (segmented into key publics) who favor or disfavor a particular issue position, who adhere to key premises and values, and who know and believe crucial facts; (d) change will be seen in the number, degree of conviction, composition, and role played by opinion leaders; and (e) trends of these kinds will lead to or away from legislative action.

Issues may be watched at two levels of abstraction. One level is the shift in basic principles or premises that results from extensive discussion, typically requiring much or all of a decade or more to reshape taken-for-granted assumptions about the "way things are." Two powerful examples quickly come to mind. One is the shift that has occurred whereby individuals feel less responsibility for their own actions and blame negative consequences on someone else; for instance, 4 decades ago, if a person were hurt using a power tool, he or she would feel foolish for not being careful or well prepared to use it. Now, the lawsuit begins before the blood is stanched because the fault is assumed or alleged not to lie with the user—who may have been careless or drunk—but with the manufacturer, who should have designed the tool so that even a drunk, incompetent fool could not be hurt using it. The second powerful shift in basic premises is the result of environmentalists arguing that progress does not give governments, individuals, or companies license to take actions harmful to the environment.

This last point underscores the second level of analysis on which a trend monitor should focus. As large principles or assumptions change, new frames of mind become important for the particular application of those general principles to individual cases and decisions. For instance, changes in environmentalism may have quite different implications for the food industry, bringing implications for packaging or agricultural methods to the forefront of debate. In contrast, actions of the chemical industry, although scrutinized by environmental principles, may be affected in quite different ways, and therefore it needs to monitor issues differently.

Values translate into the premises by which people draw conclusions based on the data with which they are familiar. For instance, previous to the 1960s and 1970s, consumers were usually considered to be "unsafe" or "foolish" if they were harmed while using a product. Now the tables have turned, and public value systems hold corporations responsible. When values change, the probability of regulation increases. Class action suits occur frequently. The consumer movement has created a trend where caveat emptor is dead; fair warning is often not enough to protect an organization against liability. Even within the limits of statistical probability for product safety, few are willing to be the statistical victims. Such trends have daunting importance for standards of corporate responsibility.

Monitoring issues is easier if the players stay on the same trajectory. They often don't. Monitoring can be divided into distinct but interrelated phases. The first assesses the situational environment of the organization, the second monitors issue trends, and the third determines whether the organization's efforts (strategic business planning, communication, or public policy positioning) make a difference in the direction and outcome of the issue. Many organizations fail to conduct pretest or benchmarking and posttest analysis to determine the success of their communication or other adjustive efforts. Determining the company's or industry's image or polling for public sentiment on certain issues may not enable an issues management team to determine what a campaign contributed. Campaigns by various players target a variety of audiences, but in truth, most assume they are most effective when they influence opinion leaders.

Of substantial value to any issues monitoring team is Renfro's (1993) contention that issues progress through six stages: (a) birth (the result of key changes), (b) definition (some persons or groups characterize the issue), (c) name (attach it to a few terms that give it identity), (d) champion (key players become identified with and advocate the issue), (e) group (interested parties become definable as a demographic or interest group), and (f) media recognition (editors, reporters, and news or program directors believe the issue is worth reporting because it has or deserves status of news). A crucial stage is naming: "Those who define the issue win the debate," which can lead to the complementary advice: "Redefine the issue to win a new debate" (p. 40). This truism is one longstanding reason for analyzing and publicly discussing an issue early, in a proactive manner, rather than allowing reactive strategies to limit a group's response options.

Discussing the focal points in the monitoring process, Ewing (1980) advised issues managers to conduct private discussions with leaders who are sensitive to public opinion trends, particularly those below the surface of mass media visibility. In addition, the issues manager should monitor newsletters, books, and reports of special interest groups, foundations, and governmental agencies. Monitoring should include analysis of popular entertainment sources, such as plays, movies, novels, and television programs. Themes expressed through entertainment, especially television programming, follow the formation of opinion and constitute a period where it seems to be becoming firmly established in popular culture. For instance, in 1994, the mother in the cartoon strip "Sally Forth" spent a week of anguish over whether her daughter would become a smoker as the result of selecting the controversial marketing icon Joe Camel as the subject of her art project. By 2007, there was no evidence that she had taken a puff of tobacco smoke, but she had flirted with a punk look because of a peer. Another comic strip that has contained antismoking comments is "Doonesbury," which periodically has featured Mr. Butts as a pro-smoking advocate, lobbyist, and beleaguered smoker who suffers because of corporate or governmental policies regarding smoking.

Needed information can be extracted from existing research studies, syndicated studies, industry sources, and customer studies. Research methods include watching for information and opinion, printed or broadcast in traditional or nontraditional media or social media, that relate to the company or industry. Methods can range from discussions with experts and opinion leaders to the use of focus groups and content analysis as well as opinion surveys. Merely obtaining and subscribing to activist publications or corporate publications, reading blogs and Web sites, and tracking new stories in the general and opinion media count. Over the past 10 years, opinion media, especially talk and opinion radio programs, have played a key role in helping trend monitors to track trends.

One feature of the Internet is the availability of electronic databases that can be used to scan, monitor, and track issues. Electronic databases can be used internally so that key issues personnel can communicate with one another through alerts to indicate changes in issues and in the company's response to them. These internal databases can be used by members of the issues monitoring and analysis team to keep up to date with the status of each issue. Forms such as that shown in Table 3.1 can be entered into company databases and shared among individuals, who update the information in the form on a routine basis. This form is designed to capture all aspects of an issue. It assumes that issues are promoted by key stakeholding publics and can take a trajectory that leads to new laws and regulations. The form can indicate who has been assigned responsibility for each issue. It focuses on mistakes the company or other organization has made that may have caused the emergence of the issue. It addresses response options and focuses on the cost impact of the issue.

Few changes in trend monitoring have changed more since the mid-1990s than has occurred in online research. The Internet has made databases and reports instantly searchable and retrievable. Important information can also be instantly analyzed, searched, and retrieved from Web sites, blogs, and other social media sources. Proprietary research sites abound, as do membership sites that provide information to members. Rather than each member tracking trends, now it is easy for subscribers to hire others to do that, at least in part. Master search engines such as Google and Yahoo provide access to an immense body of literature. Tracking can occur through special interest Web sites that are constantly changing. Such information helps issue process stewards (Palese & Crane, 2002) to bring detailed and useful information to the attention of others. Together, they are more able to use the details to foster and refine strategic planning efforts of their organizations.

Online discussion has rich implications. The Web offers the power of dialogue, the equivalent of a town meeting where issues advocates can meet. In this arena, corporate money (deep-pockets spending) becomes less important to getting out messages than does the simple act of framing a cogent message and getting it set for search engines to find. Getting data quickly and easily meets only part of the challenge of trend monitoring. The other part is being able to perform trend analysis, which is making sense of the data to have a sense of where the trend is and where it is going. Part of just evaluation is solid social science. Mix in intuition, a bit of crystal ball gazing, and hard work: Now you have the ingredients for making trend analysis, which often entails making projections leading to actionable intelligence (Palese & Crane, 2002).

Skills of futurists came to play a role in SIM in the 1970s. To improve trend projections, futurists continue to refine monitoring and forecasting strategies. Nearly 2 decades ago, Ewing (1979) discovered 150 forecasting techniques, although only a few were widely used then or are employed today. Coates et al. (1986)

Table 3.1   Issues Monitoring and Analysis Form

1. Name of issue
2. Issue steward who is primarily responsible for monitoring and analyzing the issue
3. Internal liaisons (personnel who support the effort of the issue steward)
4. External liaisons (external individuals and groups who support the effort of the issue steward)
5. Relationship between this issue and other issues
6. Influential persons, opinion leaders, and special interests who are taking a stand on the issue, as well as the stand each is taking, the support for the stance, and its rationale
7. Stage of issue development
    a. Priority 1: Legal-administrative litigation
    b. Priority 2: Legislative watch
    c. Priority 3: Prelegislative
    d. Priority 4: Potential legislative
    e. Priority 5: Emerging issue
8. Implications of this issue for the organization's mission (with cost impact or profit generation estimate) SWOT (strengths/weaknesses as well as opportunities/ threats) analysis
9. Implications of this issue for organizational standards and ability to comply with standards of corporate responsibility (with cost estimate and possible revenue advantages)
10. Alternative operating procedures (with cost estimate and possible revenue advantages)
11. Overall SWOT analysis
12. Public policy plan
13. Issue communication plan
14. Changes in corporate responsibility
15. Measurable outcomes for managing this issue
16. References and supporting documents

shortened the list to 25 means for getting and making sense of data: networking, precursor (bellwether) analysis, media analysis, polls and surveys, juries of executive opinion, expert panels, scanning and monitoring, content analysis, legislative tracking, Delphi, conversational Delphi, Consensor, cross-impact analysis, decision support systems, computer-assisted techniques, small-group process, scenario building, trend extrapolation, technological forecasting, decision analysis, factor analysis, sensitivity analysis, trigger event identification, key-player analysis, and correlation-regression. Some of these are methods for obtaining information; others feature statistical analysis. All can be expensive; some are very expensive. All have their problems, limitations, and strengths. Some overlap and complement one another, but the following ones deserve special consideration.

News hole analysis employs content analysis of newspapers, magazines, and electronic media and works on the principle that the dominant public opinion issues and topics are those that command proportionately larger amounts of space or time. Naisbitt (1982) made a splash in *Megatrends,* where he projected public opinion changes occurring in the 1980s that would dominate attention for the foreseeable future, based on the proportion of news coverage devoted to each issue. This analysis assumed that what is discussed predicts what key publics will be thinking. It reasons that coverage in news outlets leads in the formation of issues awareness and position formation. Naisbitt and other consultant/researchers have generated business by selling their trend-monitoring skills.

Doing analysis by actually reading a sample of newspapers and news magazines is quite time-consuming. One variation on this content analysis is to use one of the newspaper and news magazine electronic databases. Using a search engine as well as searching within specific online versions of publications, a trend monitor can find news stories that contain the keyword. Once this list of references has been acquired, the issues monitor can analyze content of the stories and determine whether the interest in the issue is local, regional, or national. By tallying and monitoring the trends—more or fewer stories—over a period of time, a trend monitor can estimate whether interest in the story is growing, remaining stable, or declining. Such analysis can also track the content of the discussion. What facts, values, and policy positions are being discussed?

Trend extrapolation assumes that media agendas change slowly, as do issue trends. Current issues can be projected a few years into the future with a reasonable degree of reliability. Such projections are often adequate because most issues never reach the point of being formed into legislation. Those that do are subjected to long and tedious discussion that becomes more narrow and focused as the issue enters the legislative arena. In contrast to this slow, orderly development, some major events, especially disasters, can have a dramatic effect on public policy formation. Predicting disasters is difficult.

Trend impact analysis takes advantage of the ability of computers to store and analyze vast amounts of data that are used to project the short-term future. Monitoring consists of collecting brief summaries of issues created by specialists who read specialized and general publications to sense trends and estimate the intensity of issue discussion.

The *Delphi technique* draws on experts' opinions to sense important developing issues. Once this information is gathered, it is submitted to the people who were surveyed to determine whether they agree with individual estimates of issue trends. Related to the Delphi method is the snowball interviewing technique, whereby people are asked to name influential people on an issue. Those people are contacted and asked the same question. Through repeated inquiry, the network of key players becomes evident. That group is used to generate data.

Forced rankings are used to allow the members of the survey to place the issues into priority, based on their learned judgment of their importance. Cross-impact analysis assumes that a trend will come true. The purpose of this technique is to estimate the ripple effect that would result if it did.

Computer simulations have been used to combine data gathering and trend projection. With increasing sophistication, computers can help answer "what-if" kinds of questions based on extrapolations of historical information that is placed into a matrix of weighted variables. For instance, a computer projection can compare technological development, trends in public sentiment, economic-condition projections, and issue extrapolations. "What-if" questions can be answered by examining the impact on the other variables that would result if one issue changed.

Focus groups consist of specially or randomly selected groups of demographically important citizens or issue specialists who engage in topical discussions led by facilitators. One advantage of focus groups is that the conversation of one or more members can spark thoughts and comments in other members. Unlike surveys, which reveal only opinions they are designed to disclose, focus groups can elicit candid and unpredictable responses. They can estimate the outrage factor in issues, as the American Bankers Association used them to discover the anger persons felt toward the 10% withholding-tax provision proposed by the Reagan administration (Elmendorf, 1988). Focus groups can obtain opinions from key stakeholders regarding what they find acceptable or offensive regarding corporate policy (Heath, 1987–1988).

Standard survey techniques are useful. Trend monitors need to specify what the study is supposed to discover, what populations are to be included, and how to develop and execute the instrument and report data. In addition to identifying where issues are arising, monitoring may discover whether key segments of the public believe an issue constitutes a problem. The issues manager needs to know whether stakeholders hold inaccurate beliefs.

Archival research is increasingly useful, whether manual but especially through electronic databases. It can be conducted to determine whether articles discussing an issue are based on information that can be refuted or is accurate and whether the basis for arguments is legitimate. The issues team should compare the facts as it understands them with those believed by key publics and asserted by critics. Such research may include candid diagnostic studies of the organization's strengths and weaknesses.

At a given time, hundreds of pieces of federal, state, and local legislation—to say nothing of regulations by agencies—are in the hopper to be discussed.

Any or all will (or at least could) affect various organizations' operations or missions. Because of online access, many of these pieces of regulation and legislation are available by the click of a mouse. The key is to find and track them; looking for the following two dimensions is vital: likelihood (probability that an issue can grow to affect the organization) and its impact on the organization (see Figure 3.2). For each issue, the issue steward and the issue management team need to develop means for creating likelihood and impact estimates. What is the likelihood that an issue will mature into legislation or regulation with wording that offers opportunity or poses threats? The impact statement addresses the effect an issue could have if it is brought into legislation or regulation. Out of both kinds of monitoring, a firm can develop its strategic response when, based on likelihood and impact estimates, cost-effectiveness statements are prepared.

Issue trends on the Internet may be difficult to monitor, but they can take dramatic turns. Coombs (2002) called this issue contagion. Issue discussions disseminate quickly because of the multiplier factor, which results when one person comments to others who comment to others who comment to others. Data and commentary can go around the world at Internet speed. Anyone can inject comments and pictures into the dialogue. Blogs have become a new factor in the contagion, both as a focal point where people offer fact and opinion as well as where they obtain facts and opinions. Through this variety of contagion, like that of a viral illness, damage can spread quickly.

As may have been apparent in the discussion provided in this last section, issue trend monitoring and analysis necessarily blend. Nevertheless, specific

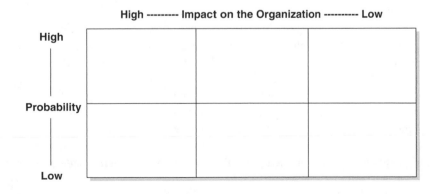

Figure 3.2   Impact and Probability of Occurrence Matrix

effort needs to be allotted to analyzing issues to understand the motives of advocates, the merits of the arguments, and the implications for threats and opportunities. Analysis should also lead to what seems to be the best strategic options. This last step is crucial if analysis is to be effective.

ISSUES ANALYSIS

Scanning helps discover issues, which then are identified. Trend monitoring and analysis estimate their intensity and intellectual or sociopolitical viability. Issues analysis examines facts, premises, conclusions, and policy recommendations that are employed by discussants of the topic. What facts are central to the discussion? Are they accurate? Are the premises that are being used to interpret the information widely held, newly forming, or under attack? Which values are basic to the issue discussions, as determined by whom? Are these values the appropriate ones to draw correct conclusions and then create the best policy changes?

Of importance to the analysis of issues is an understanding of the argumentative content of the macro-issues, the changing premises and principles of society. Macrosocial shifts in principles such as environmentalism may have dramatically different implications for different industries and various nonprofit and government agencies.

Issue analysis requires an understanding of (a) the public policy process; (b) anticipated social, economic, technological, and political changes; and (c) each issue advocate's objectives as well as the quality of the argument being made. Such analysis must understand and appreciate the rhetorical substance and strategies of the various advocates and the quality of the exchange, statement, and counterstatement (Heath, 2001). Important analytical focal points are the trajectory and salience (immediacy and prominence) of each issue (Chase, 1984; B. L. Jones & Chase, 1979). Renfro (1993) featured several dimensions of issues: objective-subjective, external-internal, and location of the interest (national-regional-local). Whether an issue is external or internal is a matter of how the information comes to issue trend monitors, whether by internal persons or external sources such as scanning/tracking services. John W. Hill (1958) focused his public relations counseling on many principles that connected acceptance (legitimacy) with meeting others' expectations. For instance, he wrote, "In creating and enhancing economic values, today's management may never forget that these exist solely by public assent and consent. All values measurable in dollars rest ultimately on nothing more than value judgments inherent in public opinion" (p. 15). This statement, made 50 years ago, is as true today as then.

Rather than treating opinion as mere response items on a survey, one preferred approach is to understand how response items cluster into arguments.

Researchers may create survey response items so that they dissect the content of arguments that constitute public opinion. To understand opinion, issues managers should comprehend the depth and breadth of the opinion positions as sustainable arguments (Davison, 1972; Dillman & Christenson, 1974).

Issues analysis entails careful consideration of whether the facts underpinning an issue are accurate, given the best available analysis. Analysis may weigh the appropriate methodology to use in making the judgment. It evaluates the premises central to the positions taken on the issue, the facts on which it is based, the kinds and quality of reasoning, and the conclusions that are being drawn based on existing or advocated principles and premises. Premises may be well established (taken for granted), in the process of being formed, or under pressure to change, or they may be held narrowly by serious issues advocates or fringe groups lacking and unlikely to attract a following.

Issues analysis is often difficult because the data needed to understand the issue may be incomplete or conflicting and the evaluative premises may be contestable. The history of many products and industries lends support to that conclusion. For example, a 50+–year battle continues over the link between health and tobacco. Periodic attention focuses on the public health implications of food and alcohol. Such discussions are often or at various times problematic to draw hard conclusions because of inconclusive and even conflicting studies. The climate change battle is at least a decade old. Even today, religion and science collide. Some advocates who rely heavily on religious interpretations believe that humans were given responsibilities as they were given dominion. Others believe that humans have no role in such matters because all is in the hands of God.

Not only should analysis examine the arguments in the issue debate, but it should also investigate the character of the players engaged in the dialogue. Issues managers should consider experts' and key publics' experience with the issue. Because they play instrumental roles in how issues form and how information about them is disseminated, opinion leaders and media gatekeepers should be located in the process so they can concentrate on elected and appointed government officials. The major concern is to locate people who are friendly and unfriendly to the issue position. Companies often lack credibility in defense of themselves because people assume they take a stance to defend products even at the risk of harming public health. As will be discussed in Chapter 5, corporate responsibility is a struggle for legitimacy, including the credibility of positions taken. Self-interest and profit are alleged to corrupt the character of corporate advocates.

Along with concern over who is saying what about which issues, issues analysts should consider the pathways of influence. Which spokespersons have access to media reporters and editorialists? Which players are likely to or actually have influence over legislators or regulators? Which members of the dialogue are mute or lack a voice because others are ignoring their statements or drowning them out? Which players are credible? Who considers them to be credible or doubts their credibility? What voices can be trusted? This analysis acknowledges that information and influence diffuse throughout a community through a communication infrastructure.

Renfro (1993) saw issues analysis as playing a major role at the corporate level, where senior management uses it for proprietary strategic management. At lower corporate levels, issue discussion keeps other executives involved in the input, processing, and output of issue positions and strategic planning options. Analysis involves dialogue with customers, clients, and other key stakeholders.

> A corporation does not stand alone but in an environment composed of its customers, clients, and suppliers. Where emerging issues are forcing change in the immediate environment, it is essential that the corporation include input from its customers, clients, and suppliers in both its scanning and its issue detection system, as well as communicate its issue concerns and research to them. (p. 95)

This communication often occurs through issue newsletters, issue-relevant activism, and trade associations.

Analysis needs to examine trends. Ewing (1980) explained the five-step issue trend analysis system adopted by Allstate Insurance, which is still used today by many organizations:

- The first stage is problem recognition, the belief that some problem exists—a gap between what is found or thought to be the case and what is expected.

- The second stage occurs when dissatisfaction gets a name and becomes topical.

- During the third stage, media pick up the issue. Often, the second and third stages are inseparable. Critics give the issue a name, form it into a slogan, and make it visible, especially by gaining attention of the media. The outrage factor can be estimated by noting the number of articles on a topic and the kinds of publications in which they are printed.

- The fourth stage Ewing identified occurs when pressure groups take note of the topic and add it to their list of grievances. In some instances, pressure groups raise issues and give them visibility; in other instances, these topics become developed by one or more persons and may be adopted by larger or allied pressure groups.

- Issues have matured to the fifth stage when legislators or regulators discuss them and formulate policies about them.

Although this model focuses on activists, they are not alone in moving issues through their evolutionary trends. Many other organizations, including other companies within an industry or other industries, create the impetus for issues sustaining themselves to the point of public policy changes.

As individuals work to bring their analyses of issues to the attention of executives, they are likely to meet greater success when they can demonstrate the payoff or harm that can result from skillful or inattentive responses. Of related interest is the recommendation for actions in regard to the issue that can be taken, proactively or reactively (Dutton & Ashford, 1993). Managements that are capable of high levels of information use are more likely to strategically achieve positive outcomes and control the organization's reaction to the issue (J. B. Thomas, Clark, & Giola, 1993).

Analysis is meaningless if it does not translate into action. It helps to inform organizational management of the threats and opportunities and suggest when action is needed, as well as the nature of that action. Not all issues need action at the same time. Priorities need to be set. Such priorities grow from the analysis.

ISSUES PRIORITY SETTING

Issues priority setting entails taking the intelligence achieved through monitoring and analyzing it to determine what issues constitute opportunities or threats to the sustained implementation of the strategic business plan. Based on this priority, additional resources may be allotted to create and enact an issue response program that features the threats or opportunities involved in the issue. As that decision is made, the response is affected by changes in the strategic business plan, the standards and implementation of corporate responsibility, the public policy plan, and the communication plan. After all of the data gathering and analysis, priority setting focuses on the best response at this time in the life of each issue.

An issues response action program involves elements of strategic business planning, communication initiatives, public policy planning, and refinements of corporate responsibility designed to correct the situation. It begins with setting or refining goals and discussing what strategies can effect the desired change. That matrix comes into full effect because a variety of disciplines is needed to determine the best issue response (Buchholz, 1982a). Response analysis may determine the targeted audiences, message design, and channels needed to reach the audience. A strategic response may include negotiation and collaborative decision making—or even issue advocacy. It may require a change in the business plan, if it is determined that how the organization operates is the source of offense: Thus, a change in corporate responsibility may be in order. For instance, if the conflict results due to a business policy, that policy can be changed voluntarily rather than waiting for change to be imposed.

Note that the strategies of priority setting depend on the status of the issue. For instance, once an issue has made its way into the legislative process (legislative watch), strategic action will center on knowing the preferences and influence of key legislators, key lobbyists, administrative executives, and the major influence brokers. Under those circumstances, the priority action might entail little more than maintaining contact with legislators, legislative aides, conference committee members, and key watchers of the political process, such as legislative-beat reporters. It could call for proposals to be included or omitted from legislation or regulation.

In setting priorities, analysis needs to focus on legal trends. No better example exists than that which occurred during the 1970s. During that time, responsibility for product liability became more focused on what companies must do to fairly and clearly inform persons who buy and use products on how to use them safely. This right to know extended to workers, such as those exposed to asbestos or chemicals. Such warnings extended to residents who lived and worked near such products and processes. From a time when executives had no obligation to inform and warn, a trend occurred in the United States whereby full responsibility came to rest on the shoulders of companies. At first, they set priorities to resist such responsibility, but the public opinion trend was such that they were wise to adapt rather than to avoid responsibility. During the 1960s, debates had centered on warnings, especially on tobacco products and alcoholic beverages. Such warnings have become dire over the years, especially on tobacco products. Some countries allow warning of death. Others allow for pictures of damaged lungs and livers.

Creating an Issues Monitoring and Analysis Team

Issues are too complex and difficult to spot and monitor for any individual or group to perform this task properly. A serious problem facing persons engaged in issues management for a company, trade association, activist organization, government agency, university, or nonprofit group is the limitation of time, knowledge, and analytic insights. Issues management requires that issues be observed as soon as possible so they can be monitored to ascertain whether they offer threats or opportunities for the organization. For an organization, this task is daunting. The issues manager needs to know how to create a monitoring and analysis team, the topic of this section. Each issue needs a steward to be primarily responsible for keeping an eye on the issue, as demonstrated earlier in Table 3.1.

One grave mistake issues managers make is to assume that they, individually or in conjunction with key staff members and executives, can identify and analyze public policy issues early enough to take appropriate proaction to exploit opportunities and avoid collisions with criticism and unfavorable policy. Issues monitoring and analysis ought to be systematically diffused throughout an organization rather than be the responsibility of a single concentrated group. Organizations characterized by participative management cultures prefer to use issue teams, persons drawn from various parts of the organization. The team may exist informally and be quite fluid (Lauzen, 1995).

An organization has many people in positions where they can watch for issues, monitor their growth, and analyze potential impacts on the unit or the entire organization. A systems approach to this task assumes the presence of input (what goes into a system), processing (how the input is handled), and output (the result of processing). For instance, organizations take in issue-relevant information.

Planning and issues analysis does less good when it remains local to the unit engaged in them. Issues managers often serve as the links between persons who discover and interpret issues and the executives who engage in issues response (McElreath, 1980). However, it does not take long for many issues to rise and move horizontally as units share their issues monitoring, analysis, and planning efforts with other staff or operating units as well as executive management. Figure 3.3 indicates the vertical levels needed to create an integrated issue monitoring/analysis team. It requires input from those responsible for strategic business planning and needs to draw on experts from each of the organization's key operating units. The input from that team needs to be integrated into and coordinated with the public policy team and issues communication team efforts.

To do the best job it can for the organization it serves, issues management needs to be a staff function with carefully selected and designed matrix interfaces between units and programs. As Renfro (1993) advised, "The executives who participate in the issues management process need to reflect the range of interests of the corporation" (p. 122). He continued,

> For this reason, members of the issues management group are often drawn from across the organization in all major dimensions—organizationally, geographically, divisionally—in the style of the matrix management concept. This assures the richest flow of emerging issues information. (p. 123)

Issues management can reside in one department or be diffused throughout an organization and embedded into its planning, operating, and communication decisions. If a company has a highly pyramidal structure, the primary responsibility for issues management is likely to be assigned to one major officer who works with a matrix of experts to monitor the trends in public policy, advise the corporate planning process, and communicate with constituencies. If the company has a diffused managerial system, many people may be simultaneously responsible for aspects of issues monitoring. In both situations, a matrix management system seems to be typical, whether the activity is concentrated or dispersed.

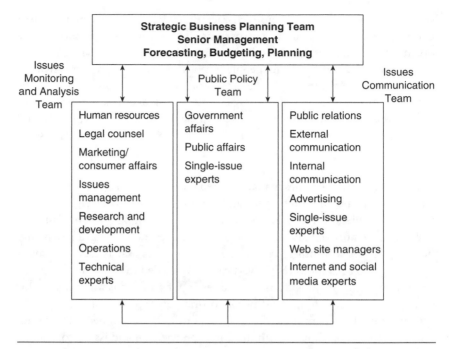

Figure 3.3   Issues Monitoring, Analysis, and Priority Planning Matrix

This process confronts management, issues specialists, and unit members with key challenges. Successful implementation requires training and coordination as well as a participative culture that fosters discussion of issues rather than stifles such concern. This process offsets a common complaint about the training and performance of persons in organizations—that they understand and concentrate only on the operations or market side of matters. Issues management requires that internal partnerships be created so that many eyes and minds are engaged in the process. Such efforts demonstrate two valuable points to members of organizations. One, issues management is everyone's responsibility. Two, solutions to potential public policy issues reside in how the organization meets or corrects stakeholder expectations and works in conjunction with the disciplines vital to its operations.

As issues move through the planning process, they become visible to individuals who would otherwise be less likely to observe them as quickly, if at all. Persons at the operating unit level are probably better prepared to identify and analyze any relevant issue, interpret its implications for stakeholder relations, and engage in the kind of analysis needed to estimate the potential of the issue for or against the organization. The ability of people at the unit level to make their issues visible depends on their training—their understanding of issues, their analysis of the impact they could have on the organization, and their recommendations for correcting or exploiting the issue. This is a rhetorical process, whereby personnel need to present their issue analysis in ways that call attention to it.

One step is to imagine how operating units in the company or other type of organization should be informed of the process as well as trained and empowered to participate in it. Training begins with helping key members of these units, perhaps through their strategic planning efforts, to understand the importance of this issues management task and to understand how they can contribute to it. They often need the basics of scanning for and identifying issues. They need a means by which they get that information into the SIM monitoring system. Such systems may not need to be terribly complex, just functional. One issues manager for a utility company held brown-bag sessions once a month; during these sessions, she explained the process and collected names of persons who volunteered to support the project. Admission to a session required that people indicate an awareness of an issue that might offer threat or opportunity. In a sense, it became a contest to see who could spot various issues.

How people are trained to be part of this process and how their information is used determine the impact that issues management can have on the organization. J. E. Grunig (1978) discovered that people who have constant contact with members of a public may develop a distorted view of the public's attitudes toward the organization and key issues. Unless extraordinary effort is exerted, little accurate information flows from management to and from interested parties under these conditions. Issue positions can be trivialized and dismissed. What is worse, biases can contaminate what is sought, what is received, how it is interpreted, and how it is responded to. The individuals with the most accurate information about the public's attitudes toward the company are those who are minimally involved with the public and who have to exert extra effort to find such information. These individuals are ones least likely to serve as liaisons with the public.

This section has provided research and guidance to help make the monitoring process more effective by creating a team composed of the appropriate people. This group needs issues expertise and the support from management.

Issue Content: Basis for Issues Analysis

Issues take on content as a result of the opinions, facts, evaluations, and conclusions advocated by the parties engaged in dialogue. This section examines the content of issues and sheds insight into how they can be interpreted and framed. SIM teams are interested in not only facts but how they are framed and how responses can be framed in response. Hallahan (1999) reported seven models of framing: situations, attributes, choices, actions, issues, responsibility, and news. The nature and argumentative implications of these frames will be discussed in Chapter 6.

Underpinning issues analysis are at least five constructs: the need persons have to reduce uncertainty (obtain and understand information) about factors that affect them, evaluation (judgment) of those factors, power influence, cognitive involvement (attentiveness to issues related to self-interest), and balance between rewards or benefits and costs. At heart, this social exchange model assumes that key publics weigh the benefits they receive from their interaction with an organization against the costs of that relationship (Heath, 1990; Prior-Miller, 1989). This logic is the essence of the stakeholder/stakeseeker approach to issues management and power resource management.

Issues can be analyzed rhetorically by featuring their argumentative content and structure. Rhetorical analysis features propositions of fact, value, and policy. Facts are verifiable and objective; value judgments center on subjective assessment of what is right and wrong. Propositions of policy result as persons and groups interpret issues and ponder ways of solving problems. Each proposition is instrumental in building understanding and satisfaction, the basis of relationships between publics and organizations.

People filter, distort, and ignore information that does not confirm their attitudes, including those toward businesses, a premise of social judgment theory (Sherif, Sherif, & Nebergall, 1965). People who champion corporations will likely excuse most instances of corporate misbehavior because "you can't make an omelet without breaking an egg," or they will ignore the information as tales told by a biased media. At the extreme, this kind of logic can lead to dysfunctional analysis that reasons business interests are more important than public interests. The extension of this logic is to oppose all policies affecting business because "it will lead to a loss of jobs."

Attribution theory and cognitive involvement theory reason that people who question the performance of private-sector organizations willingly accept facts that confirm their predispositions. Those who have negative attitudes toward businesses are ripe for information on issues that can lead to regulatory constraints. Those who support, almost without question, the private-sector interests as being paramount often work out of the opposite logics. Both sides of this paradox need to realize that values, as well as the premises that express them, change over time, bringing about new standards of what publics will accept or reject. Although persons may reject information they do not find agreeable to their opinions, that does not mean that they are unwilling to know that information or to be aware of related opinions and arguments (Petty & Cacioppo, 1986).

Fishbein and Ajzen (1975; Ajzen & Fishbein, 1980) demonstrated that individuals process information into attitudes that consist of weighted and interconnected evaluations and beliefs. Each proposition is a belief measured by the extent to which it is thought to be true. To each belief is attached an evaluation. This approach to cognition assumes that individuals (or groups targeted by issue campaigns) may believe many propositions about companies, activist groups, products, services, industries, or issues. They will have many accompanying attitudes. This approach helps issues managers decompose complex issues or images (Denbow & Culbertson, 1985).

We can explore this line of reasoning by imagining a company about which one or more key publics hold four beliefs: It sells a safe product, exploits its laborers, damages the environment, and supports public school events through its community relations. The first question we would ask is how firmly any individual (collectively analyzed as members of various stakeholding publics) believes each of those attributes to be associated with the company (0%–100%). The extremes of this scale indicate that the individual does not believe the attribute is associated with the company or that the attribute might be absolutely associated with the company (100%). The next question is whether a positive (+), neutral (o), or negative (–) valence is associated with the attribute. We might assume that safe product and support for athletics are associated with positives, whereas exploitation of labor and damaged environment are likely to have negative valences. On one hand, the stakeholder may support this company in the marketplace by purchasing the product or may oppose the company and buy from its competitors. The person in question might want the company to be prevented by public policy from polluting or exploiting labor. The person might not feel these attributes are a problem needing correction and want to see solutions negotiated or collaboratively decided.

Issues analysis can focus both on the perception of the organization and others like it—an industry, for instance, or a set of governmental agencies. Such judgment affects the perceived credibility of the organization to address issues, a component of its reputation. On the opposite side of the coin, the perceived credibility affects stakeholder/stakeseeker perceptions of the quality of issue stance taken by the organization. An organization needs to be good (demonstrate high standards of corporate responsibility) to be an effective communicator on the issues. This is a two-way sword: Issue position affects perception of organization and vice versa.

Issues analysis can determine whether all publics operate from the same platform of fact and whether it is accurate. A review suggests the diversity of issues of fact that provide insight into beliefs about a firm's operations and business plan requirements:

Cost of production, including research and development

Harmful or beneficial effect of products

Impact of regulation on costs of products or services

Impact of the industry on environment (physical, social, and economic)

Quality of employee workplace

Place in global economy

In addition to facts, analysts must address values, the premises publics use to interpret how people evaluate facts:

Virtues of regulation or deregulation

Willingness of the organization to work with others to solve problems

Demonstrated standards of corporate responsibility

Willingness to achieve mutually beneficial outcomes

Ability to understand and respond to others' values and interests

Analysis reveals what strategic management principles each organization stresses as being essential to their productivity, profitability, and progress. It identifies points of departure and agreement between companies, for instance, and their critics.

On the basis of the interaction of fact and value, advocates argue for or against policies. The logic is this: If certain facts are true and if specific values prevail as key premises, a policy is thought to be reasonable or unreasonable. Such policy positions are subject to debate by opponents and supply discussants and collaborative decision makers with information about the advantages and disadvantages of various issues perspectives.

As well as addressing the various kinds of issues and their status in the dialogue, issues managers need to be attentive to the kinds of voices operating. We should not think, for instance, that the dynamics are just company versus activist. In fact, some of the greatest battles occur within an industry or between activist groups and even between governmental agencies. We have, then, intraindustry, interindustry, activists and other nonprofits, and government agencies as players. In that array of players, issues managers are wise to be concerned about understanding the dynamics of the various publics and the dynamics that motivate them. Hallahan (2001) reasoned that there are four kinds of public, each of which responds to different categories of motives and acts in unique ways in response to two primary motivators (knowledge and cognitive involvement): active (high knowledge and high involvement), aroused (high involvement and low knowledge), aware (high knowledge and low involvement), and inactive (low knowledge and low involvement).

Various players can be plotted on a matrix that locates them on the two dimensions of knowledge and cognitive involvement. By a similar but additional logic, the playing field can be plotted using the logic of field dynamics. Springston and Keyton (2001) reasoned and offered empirical data to demonstrate how players in a controversy can be plotted on additional dimensions, such as friendly-unfriendly, to a proposal and whether they are community or self-oriented. Such analysis demonstrates that issues analysis needs to understand the substance of issues, the knowledge and involvement that exist on the part of various players, and how they array for or against one another in the playing field of each issue, as well as all complexes of issues. At the focal point of such issues also arises the matter of whether each organization is seen as being favorable or unfavorable to the issue and its resolution.

Each public's desire for legislation or regulation can be understood by realizing that people seek to maximize their gains or minimize their losses. For these reasons, segments of the public may favor or oppose governmental intervention and constraint. The most powerful incentive for regulation occurs when individuals attempt to minimize their losses. Such incentives have come in the form of protection against asbestos, acid rain, visual or air pollution, noise, dangerous toys, flammable garments, or cars that are unsafe. Looking at an entire community, one is likely to find a curvilinear relationship between cognitively involved supporters and cognitively involved opponents. In a case concerning a controversial plastics plant in Texas, 67% of the community voiced support of the plant because of its financial benefits, whereas 17% opposed it on economic or environmental grounds (Heath, Liao, & Douglas, 1995).

Issues content is the meaning each issue takes on as it is discussed in the public forum, as well as the perceived character of the various players (Bostdorff, 1992). The views of people grow from the self-interest and altruistic interests they feel about the issue. The savvy issues manager listens to the issues positions espoused and looks to see how his or her organization needs to adapt to the issue, collaboratively resolve conflict, or take advantage of the issue's trends and implications. Analyzing an issue is the prelude to forming a response to it. Such analysis is basic to the rhetorical heritage that has defined the issues playing field for centuries (Heath, 2001).

Conclusion

Issues management functions must be performed strategically to achieve corporate public policy and strategic business planning goals. They require surveillance to observe issues that have potential impact on the business plan—as threats and opportunities. To do the best planning, issues managers must obtain data about trends and analyze issues to determine their potential impact on the business plan, public policy plan, and communication plan. They also need to understand the issue positions, rationale for those positions, and substance of the issues of the various players. Analysis needs to understand the knowledge and environment as well as rational orientation of each player. A variety of response options are available to issues managers. The best feature positive options needed to resolve conflict in the mutual interest of all relevant parties. Finding and achieving that balance is never easy and perhaps impossible, but it is a worthy goal.

SIM Challenge: NAACP and Issues Monitoring

The 20th century heard many voices that addressed the roles and conditions of African Americans in American society. The National Association for the Advancement of Colored People (NAACP) was and remains one of many strong voices engaged in the dialogue on race. In the formation and change of public opinion, no organization dominates. Many compete with one another to shape opinions. The NAACP offers an interesting case study of an organization that monitors issues but also works to affect the trend of those issues.

The NAACP was formed in 1909 through the efforts of many leaders. Among them was W. E. B. DuBois, a writer and educator who aspired to create a leadership organization that brought out the talents and fostered the ideas of the black middle and upper classes. The development of leadership continues to be vital as the organization nears its 100th birthday.

The NAACP has assaulted legal constraints against the interests of African Americans. Litigation was a primary tool in this battle, coupled with its ability to debate key issues. The leadership of the NAACP realized that laws must be challenged and changed to break the old public opinion of White domination and bring about an era of racial equality and harmony. It fought to end segregation and discrimination in housing, employment, public transportation, public accommodation at hotels and motels, voting rights, and education.

Slowly, the federal courts began to embrace the principles argued by the NAACP attorneys, suggesting a shift in public opinion among leaders in the public policy arena. One of the iconic cases that helped to co-create public policy was *Brown v. Board of Education of Topeka* (1954). This Supreme Court decision reversed the public opinion expressed in *Plessy v. Ferguson* (1896) of "separate but equal." In the *Brown* case, the Court held that public school segregation was unconstitutional because segregation is predicated on the assumption that separation is inherently unequal. Argued by attorneys such as Thurgood Marshall, who later became the first African American Associate Justice of the Supreme Court, the case was made that segregation laws violated the equal protection guaranteed in the 14th Amendment.

The NAACP celebrated such cases and worked to attract publicity for the ruling and the implications for public policy. One of the major public relations tools used by the NAACP was its publication, *The Crisis,* founded in 1910. One of the first contributions of this public relations tool was to report in detail the number and horrors of lynching that occurred at various locations in the United States. *The Crisis,* including its online version, continues today to serve many publicity purposes to draw attention to problems, events, and successes.

The Crisis provides a record of important happenings and events. It offers opinion and editorial commentary on the problem of interracial tensions. Those activities are part of its business plan. The NAACP Web site serves as an issue communication vehicle for disseminating and cataloging press releases by year and topic.

The public relations efforts of the NAACP help support this mission, which continues to be the protection and enhancement of the civil rights of African Americans and other minorities. To advance these ends, the NAACP has a youth leadership development program, a Washington office that engages in governmental relations, and a legal branch that uses litigation, especially through class actions, to fight barriers to the social and economic advance of minorities. One of its major programs is voter empowerment, which believes a people without the vote are a people without hope.

The Web site features this sense of the public opinion success and challenges that face the NAACP in its efforts to accomplish its mission.

> The history of the NAACP is one of blood sweat and tears. From bold investigations of mob brutality, protests of mass murders, segregation and discrimination, to testimony before congressional committees on the vicious tactics used to bar African Americans from the ballot box, it was the talent and tenacity of NAACP members that saved lives and changed many negative aspects of American society. While much of its history is chronicled in books, articles, pamphlets and magazines, the true movement lies in the faces— black, white, yellow, red, and brown—united to awaken the conscientiousness of a people, and a nation. This is the legacy of the NAACP! (http://www.naacp.org/home/index.htm, accessed August 14, 2007)

This legacy was a vital voice in achieving changes during the 20th century and continues in the 21st century. These challenges and evolving public opinion will require continuing issue management efforts by the NAACP.

Summary Questions

1. For what reasons should issues managers monitor issues?

2. What are the stages of the monitoring process?

3. Why is monitoring best when it results from matrix analysis?

4. How does the Internet foster issue contagion?

5. What molar concepts constitute the life blood of issues?

6. What are the dynamics of activists and the competition with other players in the public policy arena?

4

Corporate Social Responsibility (CSR)

Getting the House in Order

Vignette:
Wal-Mart's Makeover?

Wal-Mart is the largest private-sector employer in the United States and one of the largest around the world. It advertises its mission to sell products at lower prices. It is the largest trading partner with many product companies, as many as 60,000 worldwide, and even a larger trading partner with China than many individual countries. Its logo and corporate culture presence are felt negatively and positively in small towns and large cities around the country. What is its standard of corporate social responsibility (CSR), as defined by its sense of its role in many communities and making society more fully functioning?

It is protested and prevented from entry into communities because many believe Wal-Mart damages or destroys the local small business community that cannot compete. If Wal-Mart tires of a location, it abandons the building after its cost has been amortized. Such abandoned buildings are so large they are often hard to lease for other purposes. It often flaunts local community planning and zoning ordinances against outside sales (gardening products) and outside storage. Wal-Mart stores are often so unwelcome that the arrival of a planning team to set a site for another store is often met with varying degrees of local, regional, and national activist protest.

Such reputation results from how well or badly Wal-Mart meets key publics' standards of corporate responsibility. It demonstrates how legitimacy is a key factor in CSR and its ability to create mutually beneficial

(Continued)

(Continued)

relationships with key stakeholders. Metzler (2001) concluded that "establishing and maintaining organizational legitimacy is at the core of most, if not all, public relations activities" (p. 321). This case vignette also demonstrates the separation between strategic philanthropy and corporate social responsibility. Wal-Mart engages in charity, such as giving to educational institutions. It provides school supplies and funds college and university programs. But is that enough to allay the anger of its critics?

Probably or obviously not. So, Wal-Mart started a new CSR program in which it is seeking to be a more "green" company and also encouraging its supplier/vendors to be more "green" as well. This CSR effort encourages suppliers to eliminate nonrenewable energy from products and manufacturing processes. Wal-Mart couples that request with a promise to eventually power its operations with wind and solar power, which is part of the company's "Sustainability 360" initiative, which responds to claims that the world is suffering from a warming trend due to accumulative amounts of carbon and CO_2 in the atmosphere. Wal-Mart is cooperating with companies such as General Electric and Siemens in energy efficiency initiatives, such as the Personal Sustainability Projects. This initiative includes encouraging employees to live as sustainably as possible and improve their personal health with weight loss and smoking cessation programs. Whether this initiative improves employee relations is one question, but it is likely to meet with environmental groups' approvals (Hudson, 2007).

What's the value of these programs on the company's reputation/brand equity, legitimacy, and bottom line? Do these CSR measures mute critics, increase sales, and make Wal-Mart a more attractive business and employer in town after town around the world? Do they create mutually beneficial relationships and meet its critics' CSR expectations (Epstein, 1987)? Do they foster sales and profits? Do they motivate stakeholders to give stakes, rather than withhold them? Do these measures satisfy key stakeseekers' interests? Is the change substance or image? Is it genuine, an expression of character? Is it developing and implementing CSR standards that respond to outside-in logics of being willing and able to be a good community neighbor, one that community members welcome for what it adds rather than protest for what it detracts? Do these CSR efforts increase the likelihood that Wal-Mart is a good organization that thereby can communicate effectively? The answers to these questions in principle constitute the substance of this chapter.

Chapter Goals

After reading and understanding this chapter, you should be able to understand and appreciate how important mutual interests are to standards of corporate responsibility and how such standards are the fodder of dialogue and the rhetorical interaction of statement and counterstatement. Such standards become the foundation for helping management of all types of organizations to be more reflective about the role and impact of their organization in the communities where it operates as well as their global responsibilities. Once the standards are known and used reflectively, the organization is prepared to be a good organization that can communicate more effectively.

The problem: As much as has been written and said about organizational responsibility, especially CSR, anyone who engages the challenge realizes two salient points. One, no universal standards of CSR can be applied to the satisfaction of all stakeholders and stakeseekers, for whom CSR is "in the eyes of the beholder." Second, standards are central to the perceived legitimacy of the organization, and those standards are routinely contested by the "beholders." So, proceeding with efforts to achieve and enact CSR is always like walking on sand, but is it "quicksand"?

If a pet food company gives money to pet rescue and promotes adoption (and uses those facts in product advertisement), it is meeting its CSR? If a nonprofit group is not as responsive as critics think, did it fail to demonstrate its organizational social responsibility? If a major company funds arts, does that demonstrate its CSR? If a government agency spends tax dollars on a project that a church or health group is morally against, has it met its social responsibility expected by that organization or has it failed miserably? If a company or industry engages in the teetering balance between profits, managing payroll, cost of products, and environmental responsibility, at what point does it fail to exhibit sufficient CSR on any or all counts?

Questions of these sorts pop up in leadership discussions of corporate, nonprofit, nongovernmental, and governmental organizations each day. Public relations and issues managers are sometimes, and perhaps often, asked to assist organizations in knowing what standards should be, helping to understand how the organization meets those obligations, communicating those standards, and using those principles and values as character foundation for issue debates.

The character of the organization, its perceived legitimacy, affects issues trends and the credibility it has during issue debates and efforts to make decisions collaboratively. Conventional wisdom reasons that CSR can help defend an organization during crisis or be its downfall. It requires normative behavior, in the sense of social exchange theory. As an organization meets or exceeds the normative expectations others hold of it, it enjoys a high reputation and likely benefits in numerous ways. For instance, the logic of strategic issues management (SIM) is that stakeholders give rather than withhold stakes based on the degree to which the organization meets or exceeds its CSR standards.

To frame the discussion in this chapter, we should consider some premises at the outset to serve as thinking points for this complex topic. CSR is often either taken for granted or assumed to be easy; neither stance is wise:

- Successful issues management programs avoid a defensive stance in regard to changing expectations of stakeholders and prefer to look proactively for competitive, bottom-line advantage by meeting or exceeding stakeholder expectations. This approach to corporate responsibility takes us beyond typical feel-good community relations programs. Innovative issues managers seek advantages by establishing harmony with stakeholders in ways that lessen unwanted intrusion into strategic business planning and management of the organization while fostering mutual interests.

- Authors, primarily conservative economists, have argued that CSR is unethical if it harms profits, let alone does not foster them. Such arguments assume that stockholders are the only stakeholders whose interests are worthy of consideration in these matters. The arguments may also confuse strategic philanthropy and CSR. Research suggests that CSR can sell products (Gildea, 1994–1995) but has the potential of being biased if sales drive CSR instead of savvy CSR strategic planning leading to increased sales and reputation management. Carroll (1991) argued that CSR pays for itself. Other assumptions relevant to the bottom line include (a) reducing the propensity and rationale for overlegislation/overregulation, (b) temporarily protecting reputation during a crisis and reducing various costs such as litigation, and (c) increasing the likelihood that nonprofits and governmental agencies get funding because they are accomplishing a mission that stakeholders support. Using social identity theory, Cornwell and Coote (2005) found that if supporters of a nonprofit organization know of a mutually beneficial relationship between it and a company, that knowledge and the identification with the nonprofit will predict consumer purchase intentions. Barone, Miyazaki, and Taylor (2000) found a positive connection between cause-oriented marketing and consumer relations.

- An outside-in approach requires sensitive and reflective understanding of community standards. Such standards must be responded to by an ethical position that is greater than the mere majority or prevailing opinion. For instance, what does a company do if it operates a manufacturing facility in another country that is in desperate economic conditions, in which the culture suggests that child labor is perfectly acceptable or that women can and should be paid much less than their male counterparts? CSR requires a multiple stakeholder approach but assumes that ethical standards must be discovered to achieve mutually beneficial benefits, even in a hostile opinion climate. As Brummett (1995) warned, the opinions held in a community may actually stifle better thought rather than liberate it. People may resist change by arguing that some position, advocated perhaps by an interest group, is contrary to conventional wisdom of the community and therefore wrong. Because there are no absolute standards of CSR, organizations need to be sensitive to community standards and public expectations, but those expectations can be in conflict with one another (Ackerman & Bauer, 1976). Savvy CSR sees the high ground in such conflict.

- CSR poses many paradoxes, and one of these is that ethics is traditionally thought to be a higher standard than legal requirements (Bowen & Heath, 2005). Legal requirements often can be the lowest acceptable political decision. Again, savvy CSR sees the high ground in such conflict.

- Strategic philanthropy can be a vital part of CSR but is not its essence or limit. Philanthropy needs to be more than cosmetic, driven only to promote image and sell products. It must express the essence of the organization. For instance, Enron used strategic philanthropy to create a favorable image to increase its ability to hire and retain employees and to gain favorable business relations. But those eventually were discovered not to be mutually beneficial. In fact, its history of giving nearly destroyed several charities that had come to depend on its largesse. In contrast, Avon products are associated with advocacy for women's health issues. Strategic philanthropy can have an economic advantage but achieves the highest standards of CSR only when it serves multiple beneficial interests.

- Responsible and viable CSR includes understanding community standards and can be ascertained through research techniques, including focus groups (Heath, 1987–1988), ethnography (Palenchar, 2008), and other methodologies, but must reflect ethical principles that are more than situational.

- Effective CSR standards result from monitoring internal and external opinions through the open flow of information advocated by systems theory. However, values do not define themselves. Settling on the best value perspectives and implementing them responsibly is a process central to the rhetorical heritage (Heath, 2001). Such dialogue must balance utilitarian and deontological ethics and achieve perspectives that meet or exceed the highest values (but not all values) in the community of opinion in which the organization operates.

- There is good reason to connect SIM, risk management, and crisis management when discussing CSR. One of the key frames for CSR discussion is to view organizations as serving to add value to the collective management of risk (certainly rather than creating risks, which is likely to foster crisis and issue debate). For that reason, public relations can serve to help organizations work for a more fully functioning society (Heath, 2006b).

Any organization that operates in a manner that is indifferent to or flaunts the CSR performance expectations held by key publics can suffer substantial legislative or regulatory penalty—pressures to reestablish legitimacy by lowering the gap between what is not and what is preferred. No business or other stake-dependent organization can operate—create and implement a successful business plan—if it loses complete control to one or more external constituents. Chapter 3 emphasized the importance of issues monitoring to learn what concerns and opportunities could affect strategic planning and management. This chapter demonstrates how the information acquired from surveillance can be put to wise use. The objective of issues management is not merely to prepare for guests when they are arriving but also to act in ways that would lead unexpected guests to be pleased by what they find.

The quandary of CSR is, whose standards? To whom should the organization be responsive and responsible? Different stakeholders/stakeseekers hold different issues to be important and have different positions on those issues. Consensus does not prevail or easily emerge from the analysis, yet the organization is expected to find and enact that center as its brand equity and the essence of its CSR.

CSR is not a feel-good topic limited to philanthropy; it is a power resource challenge (Pfeffer, 1981, 1992; see also B. K. Berger & Reber, 2006; Carroll, 1999). Stakeholders prefer giving their stakes to stakeseekers who do the most to achieve a balance of mutual interests. That vital principle reminds us that SIM requires power resource management, not merely external opinion change. To manage issues, an organization needs to reduce the difference between what it does and what its stakeholders expect it to do. When organizations' operations offend key publics' expectations, legitimacy gaps foster the desire to correct those operations (Frederick & Weber, 1990; Sethi, 1977).

CSR can be achieved through carefully formulated, reflective management policies and operating procedures that are refined and maintained by constantly reviewing plans, operations, and personnel who are trained to ensure that they help achieve corporate responsibility (Van Ruler & Vercic, 2005). Central to this discussion is an analysis of the rhetorical rationale for corporate responsibility, the means by which an organization senses shifting standards, which it uses to refine its culture and management philosophy and which it communicates to attract stakes. This analysis starts by examining how the effort to achieve mutually satisfying interests with stakeholders begins with a search to know the appropriate standards of corporate responsibility. Such analysis grows out of the challenge of aligning firm-stakeholder interests (Heugens & van Oosterhout, 2002).

As noted previously, the conservative economics approach to CSR sees it limited to generating profits. As Paluszek (1995) championed,

> Business is increasingly in society not only in its traditional role of improving the standard of living—by generating jobs, offering products and services and paying taxes—but also via an overlay of sensitivity that supports employees,

empowers customers and investors, and relates to the needs of local, national and international communities. (p. 49)

Although this observation may overstate the achievement of new corporate personae, it captures the trajectory of change that has occurred in the past 4 decades (Carroll, 1999). The bottom line: Regardless of the type of organization, its CSR standards are only as good as management's ability to implement them with its strategic business plan. Thus, for instance, if the plan is to raise some operating standard, how will it be budgeted, implemented, monitored, and measured? That's why SIM must be comprehensive, a reflective approach to management that at some point requires putting "the money where the mouth is."

Mutual Interests: The Basis of Corporate Responsibility

Organizations have traditionally claimed to operate in the public interest. Whether business, nonprofit, or governmental, organizations' missions/visions focus on serving some socially valued purpose. That is the foundation for incorporation. It is the essence of any government's purpose to service the general welfare. Nonprofits receive their right to operate by petitioning to serve the public interest. Glacial shifts in the ideology of society reshape the standards by which companies and other types of organization must eventually learn to operate (McGuire, 1990).

Enhanced standards of CSR strengthen the design and implementation of the strategic business plan. If preferred standards of CSR exist but are not widely accepted or implemented under the guidance of the organization's mission, a public policy plan can seek to have them translated into legislation or regulation. That plan may be invoked by the organization or its critics. One way to respond positively to stakeholder expectations is to stop doing that which is offensive. As simple as that sounds, it is not easy. The National Rifle Association is the champion of some interests and a much-hated organization by others. The same is true of the American Civil Liberties Union. In a very real sense, the business plan is the means by which an organization implements its license to operate.

Polishing the ethical performance of an organization or industry requires many interrelated activities: monitoring key publics' opinions to assess changing standards, integrating issues management into corporate strategic planning, updating codes of conduct, and informing key stakeholders regarding the standards the organization has achieved. Savvy management prefers to draw favorable rather than unfavorable attention. For this reason, organizations' efforts to establish and implement CSR should not be static.

Case in Point: Think Before You Pass Regulations

Substantial attention has recently focused on illegal immigrants—more often than not narrowly limited to Spanish-speaking persons who came across the U.S.-Mexico border. As a slap at illegal immigrants, outraged citizens prompted city ordinances in several communities around the United States that prohibited the use of any language but English for matters of public business and activity. Whether viewed as the correct course of action or as fundamentally unjust, these new city ordinances passed by elected officials or through direct voting measures were a new standard of organizational responsibility for local governments. However, for example, police could not use interpreters since the victim, witness, or suspect could only speak or write in English. Foreign businesspersons could legally conduct public business only in English. Would language programs at the local public schools and public colleges be banned? City- or county-employed doctors could not question non-English-speaking patients. Ooops! Recall the Latin terms on U.S. currency. Would official currency be banned in those cities? Having high standards of organizational social responsibility is a political, legal, social, and ethical challenge.

Four points demonstrate the difficulty of defining and implementing proper standards of CSR. First, a multiple-stakeholder approach to issues management recognizes that each stakeholder may have different expectations of how the organization should operate (see Figure 4.1). For instance, individuals who invest in a company (investment dollars as stakes) may have less concern than activists (regulatory stakes) for its ability or willingness to meet high standards of air or water quality. In the timber/wildlife/stream pollution controversy of the Pacific Northwest, complex and interconnected interests exhibit varying degrees of compatibility and conflict: timber companies, loggers, communities dependent on wages and revenue produced by the industry, conservationists, animals, and persons desiring to purchase lumber or housing at the lowest cost. As runoff became more of an issue caused by logging, water pollution harmed municipal water quality downstream from logging activities.

Second, no absolute standards of corporate responsibility exist; they are defined by each generation and may differ for each stakeholder. For instance, standards of product safety have become more demanding during this century. Some seemingly obvious standards—such as the principle that companies are best when they provide information openly and candidly—may not be universally appropriate. For example, companies are allowed to protect proprietary processes and are required by law to protect the privacy of employee records (Simms, 1994). Insurance companies, medical facilities, and other types of organizations are prohibited from making key types of information known.

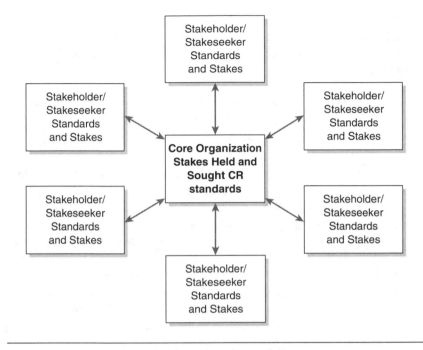

Figure 4.1   Multiple Stateholder/Stakeseeker Analysis

Third, executives are outraged by accusations that they prefer unethical business practices. Whether insensitive or truly noble, they are not easily persuaded that their business judgment is legitimately subject to what they may see as carping comments by persons who have no knowledge of business processes. Executives are more likely to see the wisdom of achieving a higher level of ethical performance when they realize that their operations could be more successful by doing so; they rely on utilitarian ethical standards when making their business decisions (Premeaux & Mondy, 1993).

Fourth, public policy standards are contestable. Contests focus on questions such as, "Does a problem exist?" "How serious is it?" and "What needs to be done to solve it?" Priorities of operating standards require the definition and ranking of standards of performance (Black & Hartel, 2004). A "public interest first" strategy is complicated when executives are reluctant to respond proactively to external, nonmarket forces. Many operations personnel fear that issues managers will interfere with the orderly performance of their jobs. Because of these internal political problems, issues management programs need the commitment and participation of executives.

To define and implement standards of CSR, issues managers can follow several steps. Improved standards of corporate responsibility can be used to increase harmony with stakeholders and increase the organization's strategic business advantage.

- Ascertain the standards of corporate responsibility held by key stakeholders.
- Compare those standards with those preferred and used by the organization.
- Determine whether differences exist and, if so, whether they strain the relationship.
- Ascertain whether differences in facts account for the disparity in expectations.
- Decide whether value differences constitute the disparity between the organization and its key stakeholders.
- Budget for change options, whether communication strategies, public policy efforts, or redefined strategic business strategies, to respond to stakeholder expectations.
- Alter performance or operating standards to lessen the legitimacy gap.
- Take a communication or public policy stance based on correct facts or preferred values when the community interest would be better served.
- Eliminate misunderstanding and disagreement by supplying facts or redefining standards vital to the community interest.
- Incorporate preferred standards of corporate responsibility in strategic business planning, and communicate with key external stakeholders.
- Integrate standards into individual, unit, and corporate performance review, including efforts to achieve total quality management.
- Use improved standards of corporate responsibility to achieve competitive advantage.
- Integrate these standards into product, service, and organizational reputation messages.
- Achieving mutually beneficial interests is not easy in a multiple-stakeholder environment.

Not all stakeholders see the world in the same way. Interests often conflict. Priorities differ. By achieving high standards of corporate responsibility through fostered mutual relationships, issues managers can attract stakes and avoid costly conflict. Good performance is a bottom-line issue.

Standards of Corporate Responsibility: A Rhetorical Rationale

CSR standards are the product of advocacy, a debate that addresses the standards by which key organizations are judged (Heath, 2001). To appreciate this struggle, this section delves into the rhetorical structures that form the content and appeals for new and improved standards of CSR. As opinions are formed by and yield to rhetorical challenges, society forges new performance standards. One of the perplexing challenges for issue managers is not only to understand CSR in their own culture but to do so in a global marketplace. Not all languages easily translate the concept, certainly not with 100% accuracy, or the standards by which an organization is evaluated. Even broad concepts such as human rights and fraud differ across various parts of the world.

Each organization's CSR standards are affected by macrosocial principles as well as by premises key stakeholders hold. The same can be said for the actions of governmental agencies, activist groups, and nongovernmental and nonprofit organizations. Each set of premises is subject to rhetorical contest. Key premises are used to evaluate the practices of public-sector and private-sector organizations. These premises are used to interpret information from competing perspectives (Heath, 1992). They drive the assumptions used to create public policy (R. Pearson, 1990). They underpin efforts to negotiate differences and collaboratively solve mutually interesting problems.

Broad principles of organizational performance change slowly. Once they become widely accepted, they provide the framework that all mutually interested parties use to judge corporate responsibility. For instance, during the past 3 decades, the locus of responsibility for safely operating power equipment or electrical appliances has shifted from the person using them to the companies that design, manufacture, and market them. Even toys have become a focal point for refined CSR standards. Those who design and manufacture toy guns are wise to make them distinguishable as toys rather than real weapons to prevent unfortunate confrontations between children and police. One last illustration focuses on the premise of freedom to use products that are not illegal; the tobacco industry challenges legislative control of its product, such as prohibiting smoking in company or public buildings.

SIM and CSR are a way for people and organizations to be involved in the marketplace of ideas, the free exchange of ideas. Part of the free exchange of ideas includes knowledge of source, funding, and intent of discourse within the marketplace of ideas. A foundational component for this discourse through advocacy is Burke's (1969a) iconic wrangle in the marketplace or the human barnyard. For rhetoric, advocacy is a fundamental concept within humanity, and that wrangle is the point, counterpoint of advocacy, negotiation, discourse, conversation, or, more broadly, communication.

As a part of CSR, corporations have the right to advocate their interest from the perspective of a good organization communicating well, which we have talked about before. Advocacy from this perspective is an ethical, strategic management and communication approach to addressing public relations problems. According to Heath (2007a), advocacy is based on engaged dialogue where participants discover and learn the merits of others' positions and how the interplay and refinement of these ideas transpire in public communication. "This paradigm assumes that ideas grow in quality through dialogue as a win-win outcome" (p. 43). According to Heath (2007a) and Fitzpatrick (2006), the challenge for public relations practitioners is the utilization of advocacy and related skills so that it serves society as opposed to only narrow interests that look to position their perspective central and superior to others for their own advantage.

Rhetoric is a process for the free exchange of ideas and one of the fundamental communication theoretical orientations that guides public relations research and practice. Rhetoric is fundamentally about persuasive speech, a product of intensive systematic reflection (study of what works and why) for identifying best arguments for (and against) one's position. According to Burke (1966), rhetoric is the use of language as a symbolic means of creating cooperation in beings that by nature respond to symbols. When we seek agreement, there is a bilateral emphasis on open communication. There are a great many rhetorical situations in which communicators are likely to conceal some aspects of their views while emphasizing others (advocacy). Cultural norms regulate what are permissible omissions. But fundamental to advocacy is that we do not expect them (in this instance, the sponsoring organization of a front group) to deliberately misrepresent the fact that they are partisan advocates. The speaker (sponsor of the front group) within discourse and drama should be known to the audience.

Rhetoric is instrumental in that one person engages another in an exchange of symbols to accomplish some goal. It is an attempt to coordinate social action but not manipulate social action (Hauser, 1986). Ethics plays a fundamental component within rhetoric, though not as an attached element or theory but as an inseparable, intertwined construction. Philosophers and scholars have defined ethics as the study of what is right or wrong, fair or unfair, just or unjust. Others have argued that ethics is in essence morality. While a thorough review of ethical orientations is not the scope of this chapter, such models are based on historical philosophical perspectives such as Aristotle's golden mean.

Aristotle's golden mean advocates that a person of moral maturity would naturally seek the action that would further moral character. Moral maturity is defined as one who is of good character, which comes about by developing the habits of good character, thus gaining sound moral reasoning. This moral mean lies somewhere between excess and deficiency, but it does not advocate starting with extremes and identifying the mean—this would lead to mediocrity rather than excellence. The moral mean is different for each person and is acquired through good character, moral maturity, and the ability to perceive a situation accurately as it pertains to the individual (Apostle, 1984). Within public relations, this approach can be taken to form the basis of a good organization communicating well based on the developing habits of good character and behavior (Palenchar & Heath, 2006). This rhetorical heritage of Western civilization offers a rationale for the ethical practice of public relations:

It explains how public relations participates in the creation and implementation of value perspectives that shape society. It supports the practice of public relations in the marketplace and public policy arena, where values are brought to bear on economic and sociopolitical matters. The rhetorical heritage of public relations features the role of public discourse through which ideas are contested, issues are examined, and decisions are made collaboratively. In this way, concurrence is achieved to guide personal and societal decisions. (Heath, 2000, p. 69)

Within the field of public relations, scholars and practitioners advocate various perspectives on incorporating ethics into the study, pedagogy, and practice of public relations. For example, Fitzpatrick and Gauthier (2001) modeled their own professional responsibility theory of public relations ethics that is based on practitioners' dual obligations to serve client organizations and the public interest. Bivins (1980, 1992) and R. Pearson (1989a) advocated for an ethical paradigm for public relations based on moral philosophy.

Palenchar and Heath (2006) suggested that at the core of public relations, rhetoric, and ethics is the individual and community right to know, to involve stakeholders in risk assessment and decision-making processing. They identified public partnership, shared control, uncertainty environment, community decision making, trust and collaboration, individual values, community relativism, and community narratives as at the heart of ethical and responsible public relations. Responsible advocacy occurs when public relations practitioners make a case that reflects the arguments and claims of concerned citizens and employees. This is an internal voice for external interests. This management positioning of public relations does not demand that it is contentious toward management preferences but gives fair and honest vetting to concerns voiced by employees, customers, and neighbors.

Organizational standards should be based on genuine attitudes and actions of the organization, as well as resulting behaviors that are perceived and recognized by stakeholders and the market as credible, ethical, and beneficial, rather than an image that is inconsistent with organizational operations (Palenchar & Heath, 2006). "The character of this market recognition is therefore largely one of social agreement, i.e., one constructed by shared communication" (Spickett-Jones, Kitchen, & Reast, 2003, p. 69). This perspective is consistent with R. Pearson's (1989b) contribution to public relations ethics that maintaining a communication relationship with the public is essential and that the quality of those relationships is improved through dialogue.

The Arthur W. Page Society's 2007 report, titled *The Authentic Enterprise*, based on a survey of chief executive officers (CEOs), examined the rapidly changing context for global businesses and society. The CEOs surveyed for this report "underscored these converging forces—technology, global integration, multiplying stakeholders and the resulting need for transparency—as the most important communications challenges facing their companies" (p. 14). The report's acknowledgment for *authentic* business practices underscores a fundamental element of rhetoric.

A powerful rhetorical force behind the development and implementation of CSR standards is the expression of self-control. Although ostensibly self-imposed, control is prompted by forces outside. Many people—for example, those confronted with risks associated with chemical companies—do not believe that such businesses would voluntarily implement standards of self-control that would meet community expectations (Nathan, Heath, & Douglas, 1992). Technical experts who work in the industry believe chemical companies voluntarily exert high standards of control over hazardous processes, whereas technical experts who do not work for the chemical industry have less faith in its sense of corporate responsibility (Gay & Heath, 1995).

Authenticity is not so common anymore, at least from the perspective of the general public; the public's confidence in corporate managements' honesty and ethics has tumbled. Four decades ago, in 1966, 55% of the public had "a great deal of confidence" in the capability and moral qualities of corporate leaders. By 1976, the confidence level had fallen to 16% (Kelly, 1982). Today the numbers are even worse. The public cannot decide whether it distrusts government, the media, or big business more. Gallup Poll data reveal low regard for many of the key professions in society, including government officials and professional communicators, including reporters. A majority of the polled public believed nurses (84%) exhibited very high or high standards of honesty and ethics. Below that pinnacle were druggists/pharmacists, veterinarians, medical doctors, dentists, engineers, clergy, college teachers, and police officers. Bankers, journalists, and state governors rated between 22% and 37%. The following scored in the teens: business executives (virtually unchanged for decades), lawyers, stockbrokers, senators, congressional representatives, insurance salespeople, HMO managers, and advertising practitioners.

One likely explanation for the loss in confidence of corporate performance is the fact that expectations forged through public debate are higher today than they were 4 decades ago. Part of that change, at least in terms of environmental impact, has resulted from more sophisticated measures of pollutants and some more refining data about health links and exposure to chemicals and other environmental toxics. If we assume that the key concepts of CSR remain roughly the same—variations of key terms such as *fairness, equality, safety,* and *environmental quality* (the latter even more broadly defined as quality of lifestyle)—we see the trends defined in Chapter 3 as relevant to the development of refined CSR standards. These standards yield to reasoning presented rhetorically by statement and counterstatement, the dialogue of interested parties. Through investigative reports, violations of public confidence become widely known. Firms participate as citizens in a changing political environment. Championing this spirit, Chase (1982) wrote,

> The noblest aspect of freedom is that human beings and their institutions have the right to help determine their own destinies. Issue management is the systems process that maximizes self-expression and action programming for most effective participation in public policy formation. (p. 2)

Companies and other organizations address the standards of corporate performance, working to change those that are unwise and adopting those that foster the community interest.

Three decades ago, Sethi (1977) believed many corporations fell short of prevailing standards of corporate responsibility. He worried that the media would be unable to manage the space and time available so the public would have adequate access to all viewpoints. He wondered whether people would have the time and patience to wade through the flood of information to become well informed. In retrospect, even the more demanding critic of corporate behavior is likely to acknowledge that a higher standard prevails today than Sethi imagined would occur.

One reason for such change is the ability of activist publics to create their own media or turn to special publications and Web material created by like-minded groups. Anyone becomes a reporter and sharer of information, offering additional voices that never had access to other publics and the opportunity to voice contrasting perspectives. For instance, environmentalists prefer to get detailed information on those issues from environmental sources, including Web sites and magazines. Persons who are concerned about the economic benefits and harms that result from the operations of a chemical plant in a small community tend to monitor the local media for information on that issue. But they also demonstrate a strong interest in obtaining information from interpersonal contact, government publications, the company executives (Heath, Liao, & Douglas, 1995, see also J. E. Grunig, 1980), and others who share their thoughts on their daily blogs. In this way, highly involved publics exert special effort to obtain the quality information they need to form opinions that satisfy and protect their interests.

The public cannot count on reporters, editorialists, and news directors to be critical of private-sector marketing and advertising practices. The ability of marketers and advertisers to wield the club of advertising dollars has muted some critics, so discovered the Center for the Study of Commercialism (Zachary, 1992). Despite reporters' and editors' claims to the contrary, Zachary concluded, "In interviews, both happy advertisers and concerned journalists say several converging forces have meant softer coverage of advertisers" (p. A1).

Words alone will not convince the public of the CSR standards that strengthen the community. Seeing the mutuality of need is to recognize and act on the mutuality of interests. Boe (1972) credited these ideas to General Robert E. Wood, former president of Sears who spearheaded the Sears program to open retail stores outside of urban centers:

> Had a sign over the front door and it's still there. It says, 'Business must account for its stewardship, not only on the balance sheet, but also in matters of social responsibility.' We have incorporated this philosophy in our advertising efforts. (p. 3)

As do companies, nonprofit organizations take stands on issues in the regulatory marketplace. They may advocate issue positions that challenge companies, governmental agencies, and even one another's policies and practices. The National Rifle Association (NRA) champions ownership and legal possession of guns, pistols, and rifles. Antigun/firearm activists oppose measures long on the support agenda of the NRA. The debate continues.

One principle that has become increasingly central to business planning in the past 3 decades is that if companies want to minimize externally imposed standards, they must self-regulate by ascertaining and implementing appropriate standards of ethics. Market forces alone do not shape the fate of corporations; public policy change plays its role. For this reason, corporate planning should couple with the formulation of business ethics (Buchholz, 1982b, 1985; Post, 1979).

One way to study standards of corporate responsibility is to view them as themes that run throughout a story, a narrative. In this sense, life—personal and organizational—is envisioned as exhibiting narrative form and content. The assumption: All of what people and organizations do must fit into a narrative, where characters enact themes that motivate their actions and serve as the rationale for what they do. In this sense, discourse is inherently narrative, exhibiting two traits: narrative fidelity (a story should conform to known or assumed facts) and probability (a story should be internally consistent and coherent) (Fisher, 1985a, 1987).

Sharing narratives, cultures, dominant themes and principles, and concerns/solutions leads to identification. Part of the rhetoric of SIM entails the creation of identification as shared views on corporate responsibility (Heath, 2006a), including strategic philanthropy (Cornwell & Coote, 2005). As Burke (1973) said, democracy institutionalizes "the dialectic process, by setting up a political structure that gives full opportunity for the use of competition to a cooperative end" (p. 444). Rhetoric deals with "the ways in which the symbols of appeal are stolen back and forth by rival camps" (Burke, 1937, p. 365).

This view of the standards of corporate responsibility assumes that all of what an organization does or is perceived to do communicates to audiences' powerful statements about the organization's CSR standards. Actions speak as loudly as words (or more so). Enactment is the performance of narrative form and content, a means by which a company, for instance, becomes to its key publics as an actor presents its persona to an audience. Such performance becomes the experiential data audiences use to determine whether the organization exhibits values that the stakeholders favor or reject (Heath, 1988, 1994). Through public dialogue, CSR standards are asserted, contested, and forged. Standards change. So must organizations' strategic management principles.

Changing Organizational Policies: Getting the House in Order

Issues management begins by getting its house in order, a point driven home vigorously during the 1960s and 1970s. The first step toward being an effective communicator is to be good, exhibiting the character that supports and augments the positions advocated in public discourse. Expectations of how organizations should perform change over time. They are unlikely to be universal and timeless. "Reshaping the corporate citizenship debate poses challenges to both the advocates and critics of corporate social responsibility. But it is where the debate should occur" (Heineman, 2005, p. B2). Advocacy over standards is likely to occur within as well as outside of each organization (B. K. Berger & Reber, 2006; Heath, 2007a). The simplest standard of corporate responsibility is captured in that timeless bit of advice: "Don't do anything that you do not want reported on the front page of the newspaper or the top-of-the-hour news report." Be known for doing good by being good. This section addresses that challenge, looking to the strategies that organizations can use to put their house in order—to meet or exceed stakeholder expectations.

For many years, as Chapter 2 demonstrated, large companies dominated this debate and created a definitional hegemony that biased decisions in their favor. The past 100 years have demonstrated that standards of corporate responsibility are not absolute; they change as the product of complex rhetorical enterprises engaging scholars, activists, corporate executives, reporters, and government officials. The product forged from this discourse operates at a macrosocietal level (broadly generalized abstract ideals that are used in specific cases) and microsocietal level that is unique to each company, industry, nonprofit entity, or government agency.

In response to the turmoil surrounding corporate ethics in the 1970s, the Business Roundtable commissioned a study of corporate ethics that culminated in *Corporate Performance: The Key to Public Trust* (Steckmest, 1982). This book was developed "to provide a forum for the examination of economic issues facing the nation, to develop reasoned positions on those issues, and thereby to contribute to the formation of public policy" (p. ix). The project evidenced a willingness by corporate leaders to debate such issues as corporate performance and governance, consumer and employee rights, and the difference between legal and ethical requirements.

Through hard experience, firms discovered the subtle but profound distinction between legal and ethical behavior (Bowen & Heath, 2005). For too long, corporations attempted to hide behind the veil of legality without realizing that the public makes a real distinction between the two. Insensitive managements could claim an action, procedure, or policy was legal, even though it markedly violated public expectations of trust and morality. Issues managers learned the harsh reality that key publics are the final judges of corporate behavior.

Violation of publicly held standards can only lead to public condemnation and public policy constraints if such results are discovered by nonindustry researchers. Scandals associated with such research result because instead of obtaining and using information to guide ethical business policy, some companies deny the findings, destroy them, or suppress them as well as fire the researchers. Some executives are frustrated by the prospect that others can "dictate" how they will operate their companies. Unwillingness to acknowledge the presence of critics ignores the reality that some of them have legitimate beefs that can be persuasively disseminated to publics as the first step toward increased legislation or regulation.

Where do savvy issues managers focus their attention in their effort to identify, monitor, and define ethical concerns? Four categories of concerns stand out: political economy, management concerns, stakeholder motivators, and issues of corporate responsibility (see Table 4.1).

The broadest set of ethical concerns arises from the organization's economic, social, and political interests (Wartick & Cochran, 1985). Each political economy defines these interests. In this regard, dramatic shifts occur in a society. As N. C. Smith (1995) observed, "Marketing strategies are increasingly subject to public scrutiny and are being held to higher standards. Caveat emptor is not longer acceptable as a basis for justifying marketing practices" (p. 85).

On the basis of their definitions of these concerns, managers are responsible for implementing several considerations: ethical, conceptual, technical, functional, and operational. Operational management refers to the means to satisfy customers or other stakeseekers (such as nonprofit supporters and persons who expect governmental agencies to serve their interests), improve products or services, and husband assets wisely. Functional management involves maximizing revenue, minimizing costs, and optimizing returns; parallel analysis relates to the wise stewardship of public funds or nonprofit revenue. Technical management requires the involvement of all relevant people in decisions, the wise use of information, and the application of technology. Conceptual management is accomplished by setting objectives, gaining advantages, and building competencies.

Table 4.1   Focal Points for Ascertaining Stakeholders' Expectations of Ethical
               Performance

Political Economy Concerns	Management Concerns	Stakeholders' Motivations	Corporate Responsibility
Economic	Ethical	Security	Economic
Social	Technical	Fairness	Legal
Political	Functional	Equality	Ethical
	Conceptual	Environmental	Philanthropic
	Operational		

Ethical management assumes the ability to gain commitment, expand cooperation, and create community. Done singly, any of these management challenges would fall short. Combined, they provide a substantial statement about corporate responsibility (Hosmer, 1991).

Definitions and implementation of CSR standards must embrace the spectrum of issues: economic, legal, ethical, and philanthropic (Carroll, 1991). Legal concerns become the foundation for legal argument and judicial decisions. Economic issues are inseparable from considerations of corporate responsibility, whether carefully scrutinized or not; companies do not operate in an economic market without making decisions on how to balance profits and the interests of the marketplace. Philanthropy can become a show for image's sake rather than an honest expression of the organization's commitment to community interests; philanthropy is more profound when it mutually benefits the community and the sponsor. Independent of situation assessment are dominant themes of moral consideration. Taken together, these factors translate into axioms that Carroll (1991) argued serve the good of the company and community: Do good for the community, be ethical, obey the law in spirit as well as principle, and make a profit (or generate revenue regardless of the type of organization) that is put to proper purpose. These bits of sage advice need to be considered in combination with stakeholder/stakeseeker interests.

Policy analysis and ethical considerations need to be based on key motivators that seem to be universal to stakeholder concerns and public outbursts on matters of corporate responsibility: security, equality, environmental concern (quality-of-life issues), and fairness (Heath, 1988). People want to be secure from risks—at least those they believe to be intolerable. No longer will key segments of society tolerate unequal treatment, although achieving full equality is an endless battle. Groups such as environmentalists demand that companies have a positive rather than negative effect on the environment. People want to be treated fairly, however contentious the definition. Standards such as these are pivotal points when looking for issues that will prompt activism and governmental intervention.

The focal points featured in Table 4.1 need to be central to planning and operations while making every effort to meet bottom-line requirements through strategic planning decisions. The desire is to seek to add value to each organization's operations by fostering mutual interests with key stakeholders. For instance, one cost benefit for seeking higher ethical standards is to avoid the expense of dealing with regulatory agencies. Although reactionary mitigation can be used to demonstrate savings, making a cost-effect case for proactivity may be more difficult. Despite the belief by Weissman (1984) and Chrisman and Carroll (1984) that corporate responsibility pays for itself, Cochran and Wood (1984) found a low correlation between corporate responsibility and financial performance. The degree of corporate responsibility exhibited by companies corresponds to the age of their manufacturing facilities. For instance, factories built before 1960 are more likely to pollute and cost more to bring within federal and state standards.

Research findings are worth the attention of executives engaged in strategic business planning. CSR can affect people's willingness to engage in business transactions and stakeholder loyalty (Owen & Scherer, 1993). Makeover (1994) claimed that corporate responsibility is good for business. Herremans, Akathaporn, and McInnes (1993) found that business reputations correlate positively with financial performance. Examining the trend toward sustainable resources, Elkington (1994) concluded that companies are integrating environmental values and competitive strategizing. Another reason for increased sophistication in monitoring public standards is the growing number of court awards against companies. The financial magnitude of such cases is substantial and often leads to frustrations.

Advocating making planning skills systematic, McGinnis (1984) observed, "Intelligence is the firm's ability to simultaneously scan and interpret its external environments, monitor itself, and communicate effectively with itself" (p. 46). To achieve balance, a company should "be centralized and decentralized simultaneously" (p. 46). Issues management can help departments concentrate on the internal and external policy implications of their activities. A common set of operating standards and an awareness of public policy implications offer managers in diverse parts of a company a collective sense of their operating environment constraints.

Corporate planning requires that each major department develop an issues analysis and response plan. This effort begins by reviewing highlights of the previous year and identifying the key challenges the company expects to face in the coming months and years—based on trend analysis. The next step is to specify how these challenges will be met in conjunction with all other departments. Putting this plan together requires internal discussion and coordination. At the end of the effort, a master plan summarizes how each department will perform and how it can count on specific actions from other departments.

By sharing information in this manner, issues managers can have proactive input into operating activities early enough to matter—a matrix management approach that brings the best and brightest into play. Communication support can be realistically budgeted, and operations and financial managers have a ground floor opportunity to consider and authorize the funding of the issues communication. One of several benefits that arise from this planning process is the increased awareness of external scrutiny of their efforts—a means for making them conscious of operating expectations that others have of them. Operating units become more sensitive and willing to self-impose publicly acceptable standards of ethical behavior once they are forced to consider such eventuality in the planning process.

As the Post et al. (1983) survey revealed, public affairs thinking can have its greatest influence on short-term problems faced by corporations rather than long-range planning. In fact, "The influence wanes unless great care is taken to interpret the long term to line managers so that it has immediate relevance" (p. 147). This limitation seems predictable, given companies' quarterly planning mentality. The survey also disclosed that public affairs is more likely to be influential on corporate strategic planning in highly centralized companies. The authors concluded, "Companies using long-range, strategic planning of a qualitative nature are far more likely to have influential public affairs offices." This seems "intuitively logical because strategic planning tends to examine the environment more broadly and systematically than do operationally focused and/or less formal planning systems" (p. 147).

Such planning makes operations people aware of the public policy consequences of their business decisions and alerts communication experts to possible dangers of business policies and procedures. In this way, issues management is infused into corporate planning and evaluation. By continuing careful coordination, line and staff executives have the opportunity to make adjustments during the year by monitoring how well the plan is working and whether it continues to coincide with management thought, business opportunities, and public expectations. Issues management fits comfortably with management by objectives.

Planning can include estimates of the kinds of groups that will make a positive or negative reaction to company and industry policies and actions. Such estimates can be made issue by issue and group by group. Each group can be placed on a pro-con continuum. Some groups are valuable because they are willing to buy products or services. Other groups are important because they are willing to take sides on public policy debates. Sometimes, sizable groups of individuals fall into both categories. After identifying each issue by group, the company can determine what information each has and the attitudinal impact of the information. The logic expressed here connects in thoughtful and reflective ways the tools of issues monitoring and reflective management (Van Ruler & Vercic, 2005).

Corporate decision making, Schwenk (1984) argued, follows three stages: goal formulation/problem identification, strategic alternatives generation, and evaluation and selection. That logic underpinned the discussion of strategic business planning in Chapter 1. Issues management has its strategic corporate planning role at each of these three stages. In the first stage, issues managers can help corporate planners determine the public policy implications related to corporate goals by isolating and weighting input-output variables that impinge on operations. In the second stage, issues management seeks to clarify the effect of key publics' expectations on specific corporate practices. The third stage requires that the cost-benefit analysis of the first and second stages be resolved so that strategies can be selected to foster corporate profit and image goals. Planners estimate the complex of variables that includes marketplace competition, production costs and schedules, transportation, acquisition of materials, capital improvement, labor conditions, and financing costs. The standard worst-case scenario equation goes like this: What reaction will occur if chemical plant operators allow periodic discharges of toxic or noxious fumes? Is such an industry as responsible for abating obnoxious odors as it is for toxic releases?

Issues managers must recognize that the more their recommendations are complex and risky, the less likely they are to be successfully implemented (Fidler & Johnson, 1984). As Brodwin and Bourgeois (1984) demonstrated, few executives get beyond their short-range problems to articulate long-term projections. Compromise is essential to success, even if it means abandoning optimal plans. Corporate culture contains value judgments, such as ethics in marketing, product design, employee relations, quality of work, and competition; they are vital to matters regarding how each company treats its customers, neighbors, and employees (Drake & Drake, 1988). Unwilling "cooperation" by managers coerced into supporting projects they do not really believe in generally leads to failure, even when the proposal has merit.

Diagnostic studies determine the opinion environment and how to use it to reconsider the corporation's performance strengths and weaknesses. Unless CSR is integrated into organizational structure, its issues campaigns will flounder once investigative reporters or shrewd activists discover that message claims are narrowly self-interested or mask unethical corporate performance. To avoid such gaps, one should use social audit to look for legitimacy gaps, the differences between expectation and action. If a performance gap is discovered, the audit can determine what action is needed and how messages can help or hinder such action. To prevent being unduly myopic, issue monitoring, Brown (1979) concluded, "must include external validation" (p. 34).

Getting the house in order requires that sensitive and reflective individuals be challenged to ascertain those changing expectations that are likely to be imposed on an organization or industry if they are not self-imposed. Sometimes companies and other organizations employ ethicists. Perhaps no industry uses wise counsel more successfully than does the field of medicine. Because of the complexity of modern organizations, a matrix-planning arrangement is needed. Codes of performance need to be created and implemented in ways that attach them to the performance review of personnel, operating units, and the entire organization. Despite their ostensibly heightened awareness of what such codes should contain, public relations practitioners seem to be less involved in the development and implementation of CSR than they should be (Heath & Ryan, 1989). This is the case even though public relations practitioners have good standards of business ethics that can support this effort (Ryan, 1986; Ryan & Martinson, 1983, 1984, 1985; see also B. K. Berger & Reber, 2006).

The degree to which a company's values disagree with those of its stakeholders is likely to reflect the profitability of the firm (profitable firms are more ethical than those that are desperate to survive), its size (larger firms may differ more from stakeholder expectations), the amount of product diversification (the more products supplied by the company, the greater its chances for differing with key publics), and the speed of growth (a slower growing company may exhibit fewer differences) (Cochran & Nigh, 1990). The profitability of the pharmaceutical industry and the enormous profits reported by the oil and gas industry become lightning rods destined to attract criticism. This is especially the case when stakeseekers believe that the high cost to them is the basis of the profitability.

Self-regulation begins with an honest, objective, and candid assessment of the behavior of the industry as a whole and of its component companies. Industries establish groups to monitor issues and attempt to regulate behavior industry-wide. Founded in 1974 by 11 major chemical companies, the Chemical Industry Institute of Toxicology (CIIT) receives contributions from its constituent companies and other sources to study and commission studies regarding toxicity. It features itself as conducting nonprofit research on the potential adverse effects of chemicals, pharmaceuticals, and consumer products on human health. To demonstrate its CSR, this organization has to be independent and committed to managing risk experience by customers, not just the litigation potential of its sponsors. CSR arises from mutually beneficial interests. Organizations such as the Energy Production Research Institute are designed to help sponsoring companies increase their performance, including the ability to understand and respond intelligently to technical, social, political, and economic issues.

In another example, publics' concern has put pressure on the alcohol industry to create and implement higher standards of ethical performance. Central to this controversy is the Washington-based Center for Science in the Public Interest, which includes the 5.5-million-member National Parent-Teacher Association, the United Methodist Church, and the National Council on Alcoholism. These groups are protesting televised advertisements of alcoholic beverages that play up themes of fun and irresponsibility. Under pressure, the three major networks have tightened their standards on advertisement copy. Critics of alcohol advertising have attempted to place the same product stigma on alcohol that was placed on cigarettes.

Systemic changes are often needed in companies, nonprofits, and governmental agencies seeking higher CSR standards. One mark of maturing professions and industries is the formulation of codes of ethics and efforts to be more proactive in solving problems and reducing risks. Many industries have learned the market and image advantages of establishing codes that guide and regulate business activities. They understand the advantages for seeking mutuality in collaborative problem recognition and solution. Another mark of ethical maturity is the realization that an organization is not a moral agency and that personal ethical responsibility cannot be ignored by anyone who becomes part of an organization. Ethical responsibility is the burden of individuals, no matter how many are joined into a single enterprise, a point that society has demonstrated by requiring criminal penalties for managers who willfully violate statutes (Dunn, 1991).

Platitudes are likely to foster as well as frustrate efforts by organizations to discover that CSR standards truly make a difference in and often define their relationships with key stakeholders. One goal is to achieve the common good (Mahon & McGowan, 1991), to achieve community (Heerema & Giannini, 1991) and mutual benefit. The challenge is to know how the interests of the organization merge with those of its stakeholders. Achieving corporate responsibility requires a constant search for ways to maximize mutual interests, the ability "to act with rectitude, to refer their policies and plans to a culture of ethics that embraces the most fundamental moral principles of humankind" (Frederick, 1986, p. 136).

Think positive and be proactive. Those guidelines are more than platitudes. They suggest, according to cognitive categorization theory, that if managers think negatively about an issue, that perspective will persist, perhaps leading to a downward spiral of ever more dire predictions and hostile, reactive responses to the proponents of the issue or the cause of the threat. In contrast, a positive, opportunity-seeking stance fosters individuals' efforts to be proactive, looking for and consequently finding positive responses (Dutton & Jackson, 1987). When issues managers adopt a positive view of the concerns that arise in their environment, they are more likely to adopt ethical, community-oriented responses than is predicted if they see only threat, which motivates defensive responses.

Where should some of the focal points issues managers and corporate responsibility monitors look for potential strains on the legitimacy between their organization and key publics?

- Quality of products and customer service (including hidden or known risks)
- Fair pricing policies and practices
- Ethical and responsible advertising and promotion
- Timely and proper equipment and facility maintenance and repair
- Timely and appropriate resolution of customer complaints
- Responsiveness to the community in which the organization does business
- Demonstrable commitment to society
- Increased access to society and its benefits, especially through schools and community services
- Provision of jobs and economic advantages in excess of harms to the community
- Enhancement of the environment through reduction of energy consumption, proper disposal of wastes, recycling, the use of recycled goods and materials, and contracting with environmentally conscious suppliers
- Demonstration of concern by performing periodic social audits

Does doing good enhance marketing? Gildea (1994–1995) reported a national survey conducted in 1994 regarding how a business's social performance affects decisions by customers, employees, and investors. Based on ranking data, the following list was compiled, ranging from most important to least important factors in making decisions relevant to a specific company: business practices, community support, employee treatment, quality, environment, service, price, convenience, and stability. Purchasing behavior includes, but is not limited to, considerations of behavioral intention. Analysis revealed that 34% of the respondents would avoid buying a product or service from a company they perceived as unethical. Sixteen percent seek information to consider a company's business practices and ethics as part of their decision making. Of substantial importance, 50% intended not to purchase a product or service from a company they considered not to be socially responsible. Put those data before management, and see whether issues management can help businesses with strategic planning and bottom-line performance.

What, then, should companies do? Gildea (1994–1995) drew four suggestions from the report, all of which have profound issues management implications.

1. Study the scope of your corporate responsibility.
2. Closely analyze your reputation and those of your competitors.
3. Measure and manage what "drives" the perceptions of those reputations.
4. Put the findings to work for you in the marketplace. (p. 21)

Findings and logics of this sort lead to a rationale for coupling SIM and reputation management and the fostering and protection of brand equity (see Chapter 10).

Ascertaining changing standards of corporate responsibility is daunting. Efforts to change can have positive outcomes for the organizations that do the most to meet key stakeholder expectations. Conflict, the cost of friction and dissent, is the cost of not learning to change. The advantage is an increase of legitimacy, as well as a decrease of its gap between key publics' expectations and the reality of the organization's ethical judgment.

Corporate Responsibility Partnerships: Communicating Ethical Performance

An organization needs to make its CSR improvements known as they happen. This section addresses the communication of ethical performance, recognizing that such announcements are often distrusted or mistrusted. For instance, as Nike sought to resolve the confrontation and controversy over work policies characterized as sweat shop conditions, it encountered another. That led to a California Supreme Court case, *Kasky v. Nike* (Cal. 2002), which even limited Nike's ability to debate standards, enforce compliance, and announce its changes (see Collins, Zoch, & McDonald, 2004). At this nexus occurs public relations' major contribution, defined as

> the management process whose goal is to attain and maintain accord and positive behaviors among social groupings on which an organization depends in order to achieve its mission. Its fundamental responsibility is to build and maintain a hospitable environment for an organization. (Broom, Lauzen, & Tucker, 1991, p. 223)

The goal is to do this not with the public but with many publics, each of which may have slightly or profoundly divergent expectations of what the organization should be doing and how.

Rather than fear the comments of critics, working with critics gives them less incentive to go to the press when they experience concern or outrage regarding some aspect of an organization's activities. Critics' greatest power comes through inflamed statements carried by media. Organizations such as Greenpeace look for moments when they can hold a press conference that is designed to embarrass one of its targets. Such statements demonstrate that something is so wrong with a company that it deserves criticism and is guilty of malfeasance. Such attacks are one of the reasons for effective crisis planning and response. Effective media relations can use reporters as issues watchers— issues monitoring. When someone in the media calls, his or her questions signal the presence of an opinion or concern that could grow in consequence.

Companies can weaken their ability to present themselves as honest and ethical either by dismissing their critics' concerns or by making inadequate although ostensibly positive responses. Framing strategies for communicating about corporate responsibility, Sims (1992) offered the following sage bits of advice: (a) Be realistic and do not promise what the organization or industry cannot delivery, (b) encourage organization or industry-wide input into the standards and the best means for accomplishing them (as well as the stumbling blocks), (c) allow diversity, (d) allow whistle-blowing, (e) provide ethics training, (f) recognize the ambiguity that is inherent in ethical standards and their implementation, and (g) integrate ethical decision making into employee and operating unit appraisal. This advice supports the rationale that CSR is dialogic and collaborative.

Issues communication is best when it fosters mutual understanding that can foster trust and trust that can foster mutual understanding. This communication must be two-way and collaborative. Companies need to address issues of concern felt by key publics and report accurate information about their operating problems and conditions. The more those organizations meet key publics' need for information, the more likely they are to be praised rather than criticized. Taking a position such as this challenges corporations to open the "windows of vulnerability," whereby they can increase public understanding instead of blind compliance.

Communication alone cannot solve problems where corporate behavior differs significantly from key publics' standards. One mistake companies have made is to develop codes of responsible behavior and tout them to key stakeholders before they were fully incorporated into operations. Failure to achieve and maintain the standards so publicized can embarrass the company when someone—a vigilant activist, a reporter, a disgruntled employee, anyone—reports that the code was never translated into action and employees knew they could not be penalized or might even be rewarded for failing to comply with the code.

One response to unfavorable or inaccurate reporting begins with good media relationships. If media relations personnel foster good relationships with reporters, they can call on that rapport for a payback. The reward of doing business properly and being candid and responsive with reporters is the legitimate expectation that a favorable story will be written to feature some significant change in how the firm operates in an attempt to set or meet appropriate standards of responsibility. This response strategy is more than just doing community relations, although that can count for something and always demonstrates the news value of human interests. It results from changes in the way business is conducted in the name of meeting higher levels of ethics to meet or exceed community stakeholder expectations.

A second means for getting the point across is to use paid image advertising in ways that address issues of common interest between the organization and its stakeholder/stakeseekers. During the 1980s, Chevron Oil Company's "People Do" campaign won the favor of environmentalists (Winters, 1988). The campaign reported how industry activities fostered rather than harmed the environment. Several ads focused on how drilling and seismic activities were conducted at a time when they did not disturb wildlife. Another focused on how a plot of ground on a refinery had been planted with buckwheat for a species of butterfly. It, along with other oil companies' advertising, has demonstrated the measures firms will take and are taking to be more responsive to public expectations beyond merely turning a profit and paying taxes and wages.

A third opportunity for communicating new standards of corporate responsibility is through financial documents, such as the annual report and CSR annual reports. Financial stakeholders appreciate companies' ability to generate profits in ways that demonstrate preferred standards of responsibility. Such claims are strengthened when they demonstrate how improved ethical standards increase profits, especially by avoiding increased amounts of regulatory constraint, limiting legal liability, increasing market share, or operating efficiently. Sometimes, companies realize that by improving their engineering standards, for instance, they can use more of the feedstock materials they purchase while reducing environmentally damaging wastes and emissions, thereby avoiding unnecessary regulatory constraints. Companies can tout the reduction in raw materials used, the improvement of processes to lessen environmental impact, lowered accident rates, and other practices that mark financial and ethical improvements. In publications and at their home pages on the Internet, companies and other organizations routinely tout their standards of corporate responsibility and how they meet those standards. Perhaps no communication vehicle is more important than the Web for such statements, which are available 24/7 for the inquiring individuals. It is wise as well to continually report on progress and be willing to combat against unsupported or biased claims to the opposite.

Another means for communicating increased standards of corporate responsibility lies in the array of vehicles used to reach employees. Organizational culture is vital to the way employees conduct themselves and perform their work. If standards are being implemented that meet or exceed key public expectations, such information is useful for employees who use it to achieve a sense of empowerment and organizational identification that results from thinking about how well they are doing their jobs and achieving organizational success. In this sense, employee empowerment is a post hoc kind of analysis, whereby they look back on their efforts with a sense of achievement (Albrecht, 1988). This achievement is fostered and reinforced when the organization demonstrates that employees' efforts achieve new performance standards. For instance, one chemical plant in the Texas Gulf Coast region has undertaken an aggressive employee empowerment effort to stress to its personnel, as well as report to the public, how well empowered engineering and operating personnel do in abating environmental discharges. Personnel benefit from improving the performance of their plant. When engineering techniques are proven and patented, the relevant personnel receive monetary reward when proprietary processes are used by other plants. The result: Although this is the largest plant in the region, its environmental emission levels are among the lowest. This favorable outcome results from a culture that empowers employees to improve plant operations. Employees are one of the best means for communicating CSR, as is the case for nonprofit supporters and government agency employees.

Despite the obvious advantages to be gained by building employees into the advocacy team, many companies take the stance that employees must be mute regarding corporate mistakes. Otten (1984) concluded, "Slowly but steadily, states are beginning to protect employees who blow the whistle on dangerous or improper business behavior" (p. 11). During crises, as well as other times, the voices of stakeholders must be public rather than muted in what the organization sees as its interest (Waymer & Heath, 2007).

Another means for communicating CSR is to integrate such claims into product and service advertising, as well as arguments by government agencies for funding and by nonprofits for fund-raising. Such claims demonstrate how the actions by the organization truly benefit its stakeholder/stakeseekers. As Post et al. (1983) pointed out, the central thrust of public affairs offices is "to narrow the gap between corporate practice and public expectations" by functioning "as a 'window out' through which management can comprehend the social and political environment and a 'window in' through which relevant external constituencies can understand the organization" (p. 139). Organizations face the difficult task of providing information about their activities and their executives so that key publics and audiences are fully and accurately informed. The standards of corporate responsibility that activists hold are inseparable from their willingness to champion, allow, or discourage legislation and regulation. Activism suggests that external force must be brought into the power dynamics to force responsible behavior on individuals who otherwise would not act in the public interest.

A final means for communicating CSR is to integrate such claims into the latest information technologies and social networks that are being used by stakeholders. While technology changes so rapidly, the basic intent of sharing good CSR actions, which are backed by legitimate behavior by corporations, is instrumental in getting the message across.

Ultimately, if executives are going to establish and implement meaningful standards, they must create a climate and culture that supports that goal. This logic agrees with a principle often repeated in this book: An organization must first work to be good to communicate well. That does not mean that effective communication is not needed during the time the organization works to improve itself. In fact, it only can improve itself through the effective ability to listen, understand, and appreciate when others think and say (Heath & Coombs, 2006).

Issues communicators engage in dialogue and collaborative decision making to ascertain what standards lead to best organizational practices, those that create mutually beneficial relationships. Standards of corporate responsibility are of vital interest to society. Thus, rhetorical challenges and definitions are aimed toward creating and refining them. Once they are in place, that fact is worth communicating to key external and internal audiences.

Conclusion

Issues management entails executive commitment to ascertain and comply with appropriate CSR expectations. Confronted with these conditions, issues managers can lessen the legitimacy gap by changing the organization's behavior rather than altering public expectations. Proactive change takes its value referent from "the body of sometimes dimly or poorly expressed but deeply held moral convictions that comprise the culture of ethics" (Frederick, 1986, p. 135). Organizational leaders incorporate issues monitoring into the organization's structure, scan issues development and public interest group activity, and work to achieve communication goals that blend corporate goals and the concerns of various audiences and key publics. All of this is easier said than done.

Over the years, the role of corporate responsibility has become better understood and more comfortably associated with revenue generation and cost reduction. Standards of rectitude move an organization favorably into a positive relationship with stakeholders/stakeseekers through achieving mutual interest and engaging in social investment. That thought can very much have a Pollyanna quality to it. But, pressed in the right way, it is a key factor in reducing the legitimacy gap and in fact increasing the legitimacy of the role and impact of the organization in its relevant communities.

SIM Challenge: Global Warming

On matters of CSR, the devil is often in the detail. Addressing the challenges to large multinational companies, Ben W. Heineman Jr. (2005) wrote on the topic as Senior Vice President for Law and Public Affairs at General Electric: "Corporate citizenship has three, interrelated dimensions: strong, sustained economic performance; rigorous compliance with fundamental accounting and legal requirements; and ethical actions beyond what the law requires, which advance the reputation and long-term health of the enterprise" (p. B2). Profit, legal requirement, and ethical standards: seems clear-cut.

For several years, scientists and others debated the extremely complex issue of global warming. The oil and gas industry was one of the key players, along with all other industries that use hydrocarbon-based energy. Since that is a foundation of economy, it necessarily was a topic of great interest to businesses of all kinds (including those that could create alternative energy sources); nonprofits, especially those concerned about the environment (including universities); and government agencies.

The SIM Challenge for this chapter focuses on this theme and the role played by ExxonMobil, the world's largest oil and gas company. Over the course of the CSR debate on global warming, various oil and gas companies either engaged in the dialogue or looked to the bellwethers. Certainly, ExxonMobil is a bellwether. Its management leadership was willing to spend money and reputation on determining the scientific basis for the claim that hydrocarbons were a contributing factor for global warming. ExxonMobil knew that its environmental reputation was on the line, as well as its leadership in the industry, which has reported staggering profits over the past several years as gasoline prices have soared. Its environmental reputation continues to be defined in popular culture by the crude oil spilled on March 24, 1989, from the Exxon *Valdez* in Prince William Sound, Alaska. During the global warming debate, a persistent rumor alleged that ExxonMobil was paying ostensibly independent researchers to discredit the global warming thesis.

One of Paul Krugman's (2006) syndicated editorials was titled "He Made ExxonMobil an Enemy of the Planet" (p. B9). The editorial focused on the recalcitrance of Lee Raymond, then former CEO, who had been paid $686 million for 13 years' service in that role. "Exxon, headed by Raymond, chose a different course of action: It decided to fight the science" (p. B9). Krugman charged Raymond's company with supporting false and misleading research. Did ExxonMobil play a decisive role in what Krugman believed was a public policy position so clear that it needed decisive action rather than recalcitrant opposition? Did that action make the environmental situation worse? No, said Krugman, "But the fact is that whatever small chance there was of action to limit global warming became even smaller because ExxonMobil chose to protects its profits by trashing good science" (p. B9). The role of the company balances General Electric's guidelines of profit, legality, and ethics in ways that at least worried and frustrated Krugman and others.

By 2007, ExxonMobil had shifted its position, perhaps because it realized it could not stem the tide or determined that the science was more sound than it had determined earlier in the dialogue. Instead of focusing on the factuality of the case (knowing it had to accept the evaluation of environmental quality), it decided to focus on policy: regulation (Ball, 2007). In early 2007, ExxonMobil announced a partnership with Stanford University to find cutting-edge technologies to balance the need for meeting energy demands while dramatically lowering greenhouse gas emissions.

A company of that size, operating globally, treads on many toes and is the hero of others. It even publicly addressed the "oil curse" in 2006. Many countries where oil exploration has produced huge reserves—and their profits—are in dire need for what humanitarian nonprofits believe to be higher standards of CSR. Although not singular, Norway is a model for how a nation blessed with huge oil income can create a trust and use the money for the quality of life of all its citizens. In African countries (and elsewhere), the model of oil and gas operation has long seen some prospering in princely ways, while others are at the margin of subsistence. Locals know they cannot petition their government for money, for schools and medical care, for instance. They turn to the multinational oil companies. Here we have the paradox and peril of strategic philanthropy as part of CSR. As Ball (2006) noted, local leaders petition companies such as ExxonMobil for social services. One peril is that such contributions lead to more requests. Once the flow begins, when can it stop? Thus, we see that one company's, even one industry's, CSR strategic philanthropy can create dysfunction or exacerbate it. They could do more, but they also could do less. What is the right action for them to take?

Summary Questions

1. What is CSR? What is its relationship to strategic philanthropic? Why is it best to consider it as more than philanthropy?

2. What key premises underpin the SIM approach to CSR?

3. Explain why a mutual interests approach to CSR is a good starting point toward understanding the concept and how it can be achieved.

4. Why is reflective management necessary for making the organization good?

5. Why is it important to take a multiple stakeholder/stakeseeker approach to identifying the stakes and standards of corporate responsibility?

6. What steps can be followed to identify standards and reconcile them with preferences and actions by the organization?

7. Why do we believe that a rhetorical approach occurs in matters of corporate responsibility? How are they debated, by whom, and to what end? Why is risk and crisis management central to this debate?

8. Why does CSR reduce the legitimacy gap when organizations work effectively "to get their houses in order"? What are the focal points? See Table 4.1.

9. How is profitability (increased or decreased revenue) related to CSR? Why is this as true for nonprofits and governmental agencies as for businesses?

10. What strategies and communication principles can be applied when communicating an organization's CSR standards?

5

Special Interest Activists as Foes or Allies

Vignette:
Fast Food—A Lightning Rod for Big Food Protest

Decades of television advertising joined low-cost food with the concept of attractive and healthy meals. A family can eat cheap if not healthy food that is industrially prepared, branded, and purveyed in establishments that also spend money to create a thematic brand equity. Packaging has been one battleground, and another source is cheaper beef from abroad. Is the growing girth of nations such as the United States the result of a lifestyle that includes fast food that can purvey fat and sugar, as well as preservatives, with industrial efficiency? Activists constantly challenge the industry to higher standards, some of which are no more clever than to prove that the advertising is not deceptive.

One of the pitfalls of being a brand leader is the fact that honor paints a target on your organization. Competitors use you as a target for their business planning and management execution. Activists single you out on the assumption that the bigger the target, the harder it falls, so if you can bring down the big player, then the smaller ones fall like dominos.

McDonald's became one of the fast-food (and big) food icons, and it was destined to be targeted for criticism. One of the ironies of McDonald's is that it not only spawned copy-cat fast-food companies but franchise buildings that are "signage" dotting our landscapes with expensive brand equity. So well established is the fast food industry that Americans can have their fast food when they travel abroad—it is our identity to travelers who come to this country. At the same time it has given this imprint to the world, it in fact has spawned alternative versions of staples such as hamburgers.

(Continued)

(Continued)

Thousands are sold each day in establishments that enjoy the branding of the hamburger but counter the fast-food giants with taste and nutrition.

Activist criticism has focused on McDonald's packaging; use of slaughtered animals (unhappy meals), fat (trans fat and saturated fat), and sugar; community beautification stakeholders who oppose theme-driven businesses whose buildings and signage stand out (intrude into) rather than blend into the quality of life in the community; and colonialism (global impact of huge multinationals), which includes buying abroad for beef and other products in ways that are indifferent to local interests and markets. Activist criticism points to the perils of brand equity and the issues management aspect of brand equity: To wit, if a company bases its brand equity on cost/value (amount of food for cost), taste, fun (happy meal), and nutrition (at least by implication through advertising), it becomes liable for attack. Such attack may focus on an industry leader, which becomes the lightning rod.

In the 1980s, packaging concerns were voiced in McDonald's business plan. Today, environmental activists point to the tons of paper and plastic that are used in packaging the products each day, especially polystyrene packages. McDonald's has worked with the Environmental Defense Fund to increase its environmental responsibility. As McDonald's forged alliances with activist groups such as the Green Business Network, other activists protested that connection as a "green" wash of McDonald's reputation at the expense of the credibility of the environmental movement. In 2000, McDonald's proudly announced that the Environmental Protection Agency (itself long a target of environmental activists) had granted it a coveted WasteWise Award.

Use of slaughtered animals is opposed with special vigor by People for the Ethical Treatment of Animals (PETA). It also protests the factory farming techniques that produce eggs. In its protest against the use of beef (as opposed to a vegetarian menu), PETA adopted a well-established brand component of McDonald's Happy Meal, which was renamed an "Unhappy Meal." PETA has distributed thousands of these protest boxes to protest the horrifying treatment of animals by what it calls "McCruelty." These protest boxes feature Ronald McDonald carrying a bloody ax and a cow breaking out of the box as though fleeing the slaughterhouse and a stuffed Ronald that is covered in blood and holding a bloody knife. The package offers antimeat stickers showing animals with their "throats slashed." Eventually, PETA's criticism of McDonald's lessened, and PETA now claims to work with it behind the scenes to reduce the most egregious suffering.

Public health had been an issues management theme for more than a century when critics achieved passage of the Pure Food and Drug Act. One problem: Definitions of what is healthy change over time and are even affected by evolving and changing lifestyles. The focus of criticism is fat and sugar, which are alleged to add to public health challenges. A movie was created based on the best seller, *Fast Food Nation*. In 2006, Eric Schlosser wrote *Chew on This* to appeal to 11- to 15-year-olds in an attempt to encourage them to eat a more healthy diet, which meant less fast food. This documentary called attention to what some scientists believe to be an unhealthy diet as well as an end to more small-scale farming.

McDonald's has used its Ronald McDonald character to invoke customers to live a more active, healthy lifestyle full of exercise. One of the most criticized villains in this era of health safety and fast food is the trans fat content of foods that are frequently used by the fast- and big-food industries. Cardiologists and other researchers reason that moving from trans fats is a productive way to reduce health risk. Getting a tasty and healthy substitute has meant that McDonald's lags many in the industry in this transition, leaving it open to the criticism that profit is more important than public health. The Food and Drug Administration has weighed in by requiring consumer notification of the fat and trans fat content of food. Is the change slow and responsive or something that motivates critics? In 2006, *The Wall Street Journal* carried a story titled "Trans-Fat Content in Fast Foods Varies Widely by Country, City." Findings reported in the *New England Journal of Medicine* formed the basis for the story, which observed, "Order french fries or hot wings at a McDonald's or a KFC in the U.S. and you're more likely to get a super-sized helping of artery-clogging trans fats than you would be at those restaurants in some other countries, the study found" (p. D3). What drives McDonald's and KFC's menu policy? "Local taste preferences" or activist pressures.

Buildings and signage have long been a challenge for the fast-food box industry. Community beautification activists and planning and zoning committees (often through architectural control) have attempted to regulate companies such as McDonald's. One of the great moments in the history of the company was when it agreed to locate in London, without its massive "golden arch," which was its marketing icon for decades. Today, casual observation indicates more willingness for McDonald's to conform to architectural standards as the price of entry into a market.

Colonialism and globalism have in the past several years become themes attached in several ways to companies such as McDonald's. First, they are willing to conform to local and national laws to gain entry into a market. Local businesses and those associated with any specific country realize that these behemoths will take a market share, and perhaps a huge one. One of the sticking points between McDonald's and the countries where it operates is the source of its products—so to maintain quality and to keep costs low, the company may shun the local agricultural products in preference for imports. The concept of franchise, which McDonald's perfected if not invented, leads to as much product uniformity as possible. As much as the company seems to conform to local conditions, it nevertheless has a colonial approach of

(Continued)

(Continued)

imposing itself into a market. Protest takes many forms, one of which in New Zealand several years ago was to paint defacing swastikas on McDonald's golden arches logos, which the company had plastered on trash cans as a marketing communication strategy for accomplishing name recognition.

One of the interesting paradoxes of big companies that are attacked by critics is the likelihood that their communication efforts with the activists are likely to become part of the rationale for protest and criticism. For instance, if McDonald's sues any activist for defamation, that legal tactic invariably is blasted as Goliath trying to squash David. Efforts to collaborate and cooperate can be framed as attempts to co-opt and stifle. Media outlets such as Fox News may seek to defend McDonald's as it did when it chided McDonald's for caving into the Keep Antibiotics Working Campaign, which criticized McDonald's and others for using chickens that had been fed fluoroquinolones, a class of antibiotics that supplements growth. The activists charged that the antibiotics in the meat work in such a way that children eventually cannot be effectively treated for disease with prescribed antibiotics. Fox News certainly wins little if any applause for McDonald's because it is associated with a conservative interpretation of science and business policy at a time when both are under attack. So, the debates, and there are many of them, continue.

Chapter Goals

This chapter gives special attention to the nature of activism and its role in creating social movements that lead to regulation and legislation. The modern era of issues management arose to address activist pressures that caught corporate America off guard. Discussion in this chapter will explain how activism focuses on power resource management through moral outrage. As such, activists seek to elevate the values that define corporate responsibility. This criticism focuses on strategic business planning and management, governmental agency policies, and other nonprofits, including other activist groups. The chapter explains how activism is strategic. Even riots are strategic and tactical. Long gone is the notion that activism is irrational outbursts of rage without mission and purpose. Five stages are suggested to explain the progression of activism and issue development. After that discussion, the chapter focuses on specific activist strategies, such as incremental erosion and identification. Activism uses a courtship rhetorical style to ask potential followers to join in the crusade. Companies and other organizations have an array of response options, including collaborative decision making. A central theme, however, is that activism is not inherently correct, nor is business, for instance, inherently wrong.

Against this background, the purposes of this chapter are fourfold: (a) to justify the contention that activism entails public policy resource management, (b) to describe the life cycles of activism, (c) to explain the rhetorical processes of activism, and (d) to suggest strategies that issues managers can employ to work constructively with interest groups. This discussion demonstrates that activists voice issues and empower individuals who otherwise would not likely be able to change key aspects of society. Therein lies the virtue of a rhetorical approach to strategic issues management (SIM), based on systems theory and social exchange theory.

Activism, the grassroots engagement in issues discussion and public policy formation, is a global tradition. Two hundred years after the Declaration of Independence, the United States still reveres a form of government that fashions policy through debate and activist politics. However, even in this reverence, one of the rhetorical tactics of what has been called the Establishment has been to simply point out that a critic is an activist as though that immediately discredits the cause and affirms the stance of the Establishment.

Because of the nobility of social activism, we often think of those few heroines or heroes who lent their name, thoughts, and sometimes even lives to a cause. A modification of this view occurs in the introduction to *Activists Speak Out,* where Marie Cieri (2000) observed that activists or at least engaged individuals

> are scattered throughout this country, coming from different backgrounds, walks of life, and points of view. They are known within their own communities and activist networks, but most are not famous and do not aspire to be. But they are heroes nonetheless. They are part of a little-recognized subculture, operating on the belief that dramatic, progressive change is needed in our society and willing to pay the often formidable price of being activist in America. (pp. 1–2)

The interviews reported in her book added depth to what other scholars of activism and power resource management had discovered. Activism is about the strategic use of the tools of change: "person-to-person organizing, employment of mass media, economic pressuring, public actions, skillful oratory, legal weaponry, quiet persuasion, education, steady vigilance, and even prayer" (p. 10).

A form of government based on debate, dialogue, and power resource management is not without problems. While helping frame the U.S. Constitution and the U.S. Bill of Rights, James Madison worried that factions would destroy the new republic. Nevertheless, he and other historical, political leaders established the First Amendment to foster expressions of controversial views as well as citizens' right to obtain information and opinion as precursors to changing their circumstances. Agitation, even revolution, is part of the American culture; that was a rallying cry of the antiestablishment movements of the 1960s. The ability of a society to collectively think and respond to prob-lems is the mark of civil society.

At times discordant, public policy contests between key groups are funda-mental to our sociopolitical power system; interest groups speak to reveal pro-blems and inject values into dialogues by which issues are judged and solutions are weighed. Activist groups arise, mature, and fade. They help people exert power collectively that they lack individually. Through refined insights, pooled information, shared values, and common goals, cooperative actions can bene-fit all parties. Strategic issues managers realize that this contest is for power resources.

Chapter 2 described how social movements have occurred and how activists have joined together to restrain the prerogatives and actions of organi-zations led by aloof, insensitive, and unreflective executives. The 20th century in most countries around the world saw the rise of activism that both rode and contributed to social movement change. This century has started with a burst of terrorism, which is not a stranger. We have had assassinations of major figures and genocide. Definitions play a substantial role in such matters. If a powerful nation bombs a city, that can be attributed to an act of liberty. If a local faction bombs a police station, that is defined as terrorism. In all cases, however, one theme runs throughout these matters. An activist group, by any label, seeks to leverage change, through argument, organization, and even violence.

At the core of this chapter is Coombs and Holladay's (2007) contention that "activism can be seen 'as' modern public relations" (p. 52), using an eclec-tic range of public relations strategies and tactics. They continued,

> It is not until the mid-1990s that public relations researchers considered activists to be practicing public relations rather than simply posing an obsta-cle. This realization was hailed as an epiphany in the field. Strangely, the evi-dence had been there for nearly a hundred years! (p. 52)

They also suggested that there are unseen contributions by activists to the field of public relations and, we would add to that, to the field of SIM. While many view SIM and public relations as inherently focused on corporate agen-das, an incredible amount of knowledge and insight can be gained from study-ing activists and their role in dialogue, decision making, and effecting change. "In reality, social activists were practicing public relations before large corpo-rations existed" (Coombs & Holladay, 2007, p. 75).

As L. A. Grunig (1992) observed, "The activist group's intent is to improve the functioning of the organization from outside" (p. 504). She noted that the groups intend "to influence and change a condition through means that range from education to violence" (p. 504). Each group works to make itself useful to its followers. It positions itself as speaking in the public interest. Either through issues communication or collaborative decision making, issues managers can prove to key publics that they do not need to rely on activist demands to achieve improved performance by the firm, governmental organization, or other activist targets.

What is an activist, activist group, and activism? M. E. Smith and Ferguson (2001) synthesized several definitions of *activist* to emphasize these attributes: organized around a common shared goal, issue oriented (sometimes called single issue or interest), and exerting pressure on entities that use communication strategically to achieve specific outcomes and to alter perspectives that dominate society. According to M. F. Smith (2005), "Activism is the process by which groups of people exert pressure on organizations or other institutions to change policies, practices, or conditions that the activists find problematic" (p. 5).

In the discussion of activists, one line of analysis refers to them as active publics. Such discussion must acknowledge that they are autonomous of their target in opinion and cannot singularly be defined by that target (Leitch & Neilson, 2001). They express their opinion, which the target may try to reinterpret and even denigrate. It is not for the target to decide the nature of the relationship or voice of the public but the privilege of the activist to define, express, and exert. Also, no sense of public can be appreciated as activist if the force of its stakes and ability to play them is not considered. In this way, the matter of stakes is paramount. The test is the ability to achieve influence, not merely to voice concerns, through processes of power resource management (Heath, 2007b).

As activists and others engage in a dialogue and power struggle, they collectively create a social movement. The sum of the organizations involved in a particular movement comprises a social movement (M. F. Smith, 2005). A key element of the shared substance, conjoined and divergent zones of meaning, results in ideology, perspective, and identity/identification. "A social movement becomes a social actor at the point where such an organization takes form" (Leitch & Neilson, 2001, p. 131).

Activists are typically nonprofit or nongovernmental organizations, but companies and government agencies can serve the activism/agitation role. Reporters, editors, bloggers, and commentators qualify as activists when they explicitly (and even implicitly) champion a point of view on some issue. An establishment in their own right, foundations and angry shareholders can seek to exert influence through proxies and various other battles, including lawsuits ("Foundations Test Proxy Power," 2007). As discussed in Chapter 2, for instance, the muckraking reporters and authors raised issues that alerted key publics to problems, suggested higher standards of corporate responsibility, and supported explicit policy positions.

Activists need legitimacy—the good organization communicates well. They, like any other organization, employ various communication strategies and tactics, as well as place facts, values, and policy positions into their own and the larger dialogue. An activist group is a rhetorical system, a part of larger rhetorical systems that grind issues into various policy applications (Heath, 2001, 2006a). They create legitimacy by creating positions that connect with other zones of meaning. They add to and alter such zones. They solve problems, gather resources, and sustain themselves as is the want of all other kinds of organizations. Theirs is a rhetoric of courtship (Burke, 1969b), inviting others to join and identify with their cause, their view of the world, and their solution to shared problems. In this dialogue, they strive to solve problems in competition or collaboration with not only their targets but also other organizations, often and especially other activist groups.

Influence exerted in the public policy arena results from the power that resources activists acquire and use efficiently (Blalock, 1989). Activist groups work to acquire and use stakes as a means for encouraging or forcing change. One of the stakes held by their targets is the ability and willingness to change. For instance, a stake might be a more environmentally responsible automobile. Standards can be set by government regulation, and competitors can design and manufacture more environmentally responsible automobiles. Viewed this way, issues management often entails balancing relationships with multiple stakeholders and stakeseekers, each of which has unique opinions and interests.

Dealing with several activist groups and other stakeholders can be difficult. For instance, in 1995, Shell created an advisory panel consisting of industry specialists, governmental officials, and prominent environmental scientists to determine the fate of a massive oil production tank, the Brent Spar, that needed to be retired from service. After substantial deliberation, this panel decided that the platform should be taken into deep Atlantic Ocean waters and sunk. Greenpeace protested, and the decision and decision process came apart. An alternative solution was created. The battle played out in various media, but on the Internet, the exchange between Shell and Greenpeace leveled the playing field. It could even be characterized as a "town meeting" (Heath, 1998; see also Coombs, 1998; Reber & Kim, 2006). This case reminds issues managers that "activist groups vary in size, range of issue involvement, tactics, and effectiveness—but all (especially the smallest, most active ones) are potentially damaging to the target organization" (L. A. Grunig, 1992, p. 513).

Although this chapter focuses on the nature and role of activists in the public policy arena and the SIM process, it does not ignore the fact that a substantial amount of legislative and regulative changes occur for reasons that may have little to do directly with activism. Public policy change also results from pressures between companies within an industry and between companies in different industries. However much pressure Ralph Nader exerted on the automobile industry, for instance, to make a safer automobile, the real pressure came from the automobile insurance industry. It wanted Detroit to make a safer automobile, thereby reducing the costs of medical expenses of accident victims and making automobiles more predictable as a sound business practice. Policy changes result from politicians' agendas and judicial decisions. Without ignoring these forces, this chapter focuses on activism, citizens banding to express their interests. The wise issues manager realizes that in a multiple-stakeholder environment, the concerns that must be addressed are not likely to be narrowed to the relationship between one company and one group of activists. Bridging differences and achieving mutual interests can be challenging, requiring the marshaling of a variety of resources through a business plan, a public policy plan, and a communication plan.

Moral Outrage

One of the traditional roles of activism has been to call for some higher standard, some higher value, to guide organizational decision making and behaviors. Such appeals can be seen as an annoying but positive advance to society. However, early interpretations of activism often believed these expressions of moral outrage were impertinent, even treasonable. Moral outrage can be looked at as placing blame for an inequality, and this blame is placed on either or both the structure/system and or multiple third parties. Fine, Weiss, Pruitt, and Burn's (2004) discussion of moral outrage and review of relevant literature suggested that there is no self-blame involved with moral outrage, which pushes for external efforts to effect change. Moral outrage thus should be a powerful motivator for efforts related to justice and equality. Their book noted that there has been very little research conducted on moral outrage as a relative advantage, noting a couple of German studies that determined there was a positive relationship between moral outrage and efforts at social change.

How we view special interest advocacy and agitation depends on who we believe activists are and how we define their sociopolitical role. Two early writers, Gabriele Tarde (1922) in *L'Opinion et la Foule* and LeBon (1925) in *The Crowd: A Study of the Popular Mind*, viewed activists as unworthy types who disrupt an orderly and well-managed society. This elitist notion arose from the belief that the best class deserved to rule without challenge, especially not by their social and moral inferiors. Activists were called rabble-rousers. That view was challenged by Saul Alinsky (1971), who wrote *Rules for Radicals* to empower the poor, disadvantaged, and concerned by giving them practical strategies by which to advance their cause. Some of these strategies were devilishly fun and difficult to defend against.

The pejorative word *rabble* may not accurately describe activists on environmental issues or religious champions of decency on television—certainly not pension managers or foundation heads leveraging their proxies. One doubts that the Religious Right, which has been such a recent political and social force in the United States, would think of themselves as rabble. Activist groups, especially in recent years, routinely draw members from every economic and educational strata of society. Membership can be fashionable (in fact, celebrities who associate with activist causes become a target). Members, as well as leaders, represent professions. Housewives protesting unsanitary food-processing conditions can hardly be characterized as rabble.

Small-business persons and neighbors who do not want their small communities to be damaged by large outsider corporations have resisted efforts to open Wal-Mart stores in an ever growing number of small communities and in established neighborhoods of cities. Local residents, some of whom had moved to the country to avoid crowds, resisted Walt Disney's efforts to locate a theme park near the hallowed Civil War battlefield in Manassas, Virginia, in 1994. The American Association of Retired Persons was founded in 1958 to advocate social service support for the elderly. Because of its efforts, it has raised the ire of conservative congresspersons who resented the lobbying efforts of this group on behalf of Medicare, Medicaid, and Social Security. This group's membership draws from the powerful voting-age population 50 years and older, which has not only increased in size and wealth but also developed sophistication in its dealings with Congress. Major environmental groups, such as the Nature Conservancy, raise money, buy land, receive land in trust, commission research, and have extensive grassroots lobbying efforts. Some pretty pricey pieces of Washington, D.C., property are owned by activists, who each day lobby federal legislators and regulators. Activism has become institutionalized; activists cannot accurately be described as rabble.

Activist groups are often portrayed as liberals who oppose practices of key businesses, among others. Activists may oppose one another: Common Cause versus Fair Government Foundation, Children's Defense Fund versus Center for Effective Compassion, Sierra Club versus Frontiers of Freedom, National Organization of Women versus Independent Women's Forum, and Public Citizen versus Project Relief. Other mainstream activist groups include Consumer Federation of America and Consumer Union. Pro-life advocates battle pro-choice advocates.

Any issues manager who thinks of the opposition as rabble is likely to be at a competitive disadvantage. Such stereotypical responses may swing the power balance to members of an interest group who understand how to use traditional or social media or position themselves as a voting bloc to pressure regulative or legislative bodies to act in what activists define as the public interest (Murphy, 1992). They may stall the granting or implementing of permits that a plant needs to operate; such measures were used by a handful of community activists near Galveston, Texas, in opposition to strategic planning efforts of Mitsubishi Corporation, one of the largest companies in the world.

Residents and fishermen (recreational and professional) feared the proposed copper plant would be a health hazard, due to emissions of lead, and a threat to property values (Heath, 1995).

When people become dissatisfied with their conditions, they join together to change them and thereby become an activist group. Successful groups are skilled at framing their cause in moral terms needed to obtain and wield economic, political, or social resources (Blalock, 1989; Gamson, 1968, 1975; Oberschall, 1973, 1978; Simons, 1970, 1972, 1976). Social conflict entails "the intentional mutual exchange of negative sanctions, or punitive behaviors, by two or more parties" (Blalock, 1989, p. 7). Activists and their targets have a mutual stakeholding and stakeseeking relationship that can be confrontational or collaborative. Activists not only work to create and use stakes against the organization but also seek stakes it holds.

A view of issues management that ignores the public policy power and rhetorical influence of activists is naive. And we must avoid limiting issues management to the negotiation of contested positions between one organization (a company or industry, for instance) and one activist group. Many issues management problems arise because multiple stakeholders and stakeseekers press an organization for specific concessions. Also, an issue can arise rhetorically, such as a concern over safety in living near a chemical plant, even when no group exists for the organization to negotiate with as a single representative of a community of concern.

This communication process can be one-way but is presumed to be better as dialogue—two-way interaction: statement and counterstatement. Issues communication, including issue advertising, is used not only by private-sector organizations but also by activists. Special interests rhetorically press government to intervene on issues that they help publicize in the media. In this way, activists have the power of exposé, the strategy of calling negative attention to some aspect of their target, which is designed to elicit moral outrage against it. Activists introduce issues into political campaigns. They use the moral outrage they can generate to solicit political contributions, motivate voting blocs, and gain or grant endorsements to encourage or coerce candidates to take stands on key issues. They use moral outrage to supply volunteers to assist in political campaigns. They make issues visible, sometimes by dramatic protest or by pressing them through referenda, by reasoning that change is justified by the outrage. In this regard, the rhetorical use of atrocity, a key part of the 1960s' civil rights movement, is used to demonstrate the need for action against the target.

Accustomed to doing business in relative tranquility prior to the robust growth of activism in the 1960s, corporate and governmental leaders tended to view such groups as threatening because of their expressions of outrage. Too often, a negative, reactive attitude toward such groups led businesspeople to the knee-jerk desire to defeat, even destroy, the "enemy." Shants (1978) described the combative attitude of members of the nuclear generating industry who wanted to fight antinuclear "activists not with facts but with closed factory gates, empty schools, cold and dark homes and sad children" (p. 10). This rhetorical stance implies the company is correct, protesters are wrong, and, through punishment, the public can be bludgeoned to understand and accept the difference.

A combative stance is ironic because many activists can use it as motivation and like nothing more than to punish private-sector and governmental organizations for causing the outrage. This adversarial, or win-loss, posture occurs when the sides presume to have an exclusive grasp of the truth and want to silence their opponents or bait them into making statements that key segments of the public will find offensive. Combativeness increases the likelihood of hostile polarization over value positions that can mature into confrontation. Visible issue combat can do little to improve some stakeholders' attitudes toward companies. When a company battles a group that seems to be acting in the interest of the "people," they appear to flaunt their contempt for the public interest. For this reason, some firms, such as large food companies, have wisely used activists to help establish the criteria of responsible performance, such as standards of wholesome food.

As Wallack, Dorfman, Jernigan, and Themba (1993) pointed out, activists use media advocacy. They combine "community advocacy approaches with the strategic and innovative use of media to better pressure decision makers to change policy" (p. xi). The media continue to look for community interest stories. Outraged charges and demonstrations of problems by activist groups have media appeal and cost activists nothing in terms of publicity for their ideas. Various kinds of problems become a foundation for media attention. They are of interest because they have a moral advocacy sense to them. "Advocacy is a catch-all word for the set of skills used to create a shift in public opinion and mobilize the necessary resources and forces to support an issue, policy, or constituency" (p. 27; see also Heath, 2007a, on advocacy).

Each activist group develops its unique view of what ought to be; these expectations can have implications for how private-sector organizations operate. Such groups form a culture that views the world and evaluates business activities in terms that may be at odds with preferences of company executives. This struggle can take at least two directions. One focuses on constraints that groups can impose on companies to limit what they can do and how they can do it. The second struggle is to alter the culture of society in ways that lead to some corporate actions being prohibited that once were allowed. Managed poorly, cultures of the enterprise and the group collide. Managed effectively, these cultures can lead to positive outcomes for both groups. Central to these strains are competing narratives of what is, what should be, what can be, and who supports or opposes these visions. Such is the essence of activist rhetoric that expresses expectations of how targets should think and act (Heath, 1994).

Through such give-and-take, culture changes. Such changes form the trends mentioned in issues monitoring and trend analysis in Chapter 3. The concept of culture can be used as a focal point for comparing the decision-making processes and expectations of companies and activists. If a culture is a way of thinking, persons who share that culture constitute a zone of meaning—a shared sense of reality. This analysis becomes clearer if we define culture as a way of thinking about ourselves, our identity and our actions, and the world around us. G. Morgan (1986) defined culture as "a process of reality construction that allows people to see and understand particular events, actions, objects, utterances, or situations in distinctive ways" (p. 128). This line of analysis reasons that culture is a defining variable that accounts for why different groups think of and perceive the world in unique ways, in ways that can be at odds with one another.

If zones differ sufficiently, conflict and negotiated settlements may be required (Heath, 1994). Central to activist efforts is the presentation of key premises that, if adopted in public policy decision making and dialogue, lead to conclusions different than before. Antismoking activists assert the premise that cigarette smoking is harmful to health, to challenge tobacco companies' contrary view. Environmentalists assert the premise that industrial processes that degrade air or water quality should be curtailed. If that premise becomes accepted by key publics, companies or other types of targeted organizations are expected or mandated to implement new operating standards—meet new evaluative frames. Thus, activism arises from moral outrage and leads to attempts to create and exploit power resources to change the offending practices and policies so that they meet or exceed the moral expectations from that outrage.

Outrage alone is unlikely to cause change. It needs to be coupled with and empowered by power resource management.

Power Resource Management

Conflict management builds on the rationale that power is brought to bear insofar as one player in a conflict can influence another through the granting or withholding of stakes. Activists use legislation, regulation, and litigation to limit business options. Early-warning, issue-scanning systems can alert organizations to emerging issues and identify highly motivated individuals who are attempting to focus attention on them. Many issues arise as the product of the effort of a few individuals who are troubled by some aspect of society or corporate behavior. By articulating the issue and demonstrating the extent to which it affects the interests of others, activists attract followers, make the issue visible, assert their own premises that they believe should guide public policy discussions and decision making, and employ power resources.

What resources are employed in this effort? Resources are stakes—something of value that a group has that is sought by other groups, whether corporate, governmental, or activist. Stakes can include the purchase of goods and services, the ability to engage in litigation, the casting of votes, and lobbying the legislative and regulatory process. Other stakes are community support or opposition for permits a company needs to expand or to continue operations. Favorable comments to reporters are stakes, as are complaints.

Issues managers should understand the cultures that surround their firms so they can determine how each one can affect executives' efforts to create and implement their strategic business plans. Each culture consists of premises that support or oppose the planning rationale behind a strategic business plan. A constructive solution to this problem is to plan for outcomes and reflectively employ management options that are compatible with the cultures and thereby satisfy mutual interests (Van Ruler & Vercic, 2005).

Aligned interests through compatible cultures are a reasonable outcome of dialogue, perhaps the rationale for and product of collaborative decision making. Issues managers may help change their firm's culture (its standards of corporate responsibility) so that it is more compatible with stakeholder expectations. Issues communicators may undertake campaigns to change external cultures to increase harmony. Thus, the essence of ethical and strategic SIM requires successful management of this friction to keep differences from manifesting themselves in public policy changes that lead to destructive solutions to problems.

This outcome requires that issues managers monitor for differences and mount appropriate planning, communication, or operational change offenses or defenses to seek mutually satisfying outcomes with key groups. Settlement of differences can prevent a concern from becoming an issue so compelling that the company is forced to accede to changes that are not constructive to the mutual interests of relevant parties. Accommodation may be required, but so might aggressive advocacy (Heath, 2007a).

Strategic business planning considers constraints and opportunities facing the organization. Two aspects are crucial: the revenue source by which the organization acquires the resources it needs to survive and grow and the public policy environment in which constraints are imposed or opportunities are created by legislative, regulatory, or judicial bodies. Activist groups can affect any of these. Hunger and Wheelen (1993) differentiated types of environments. The external environment consists of conditions that could affect a firm's ability to achieve its desired outcomes, as expressed in its mission, given the compatibility or conflict between its interests and those of persons outside of it. This environment, in turn, can be divided into two parts. The task environment "includes those elements or groups that directly affect and are affected by an organization's major operations. Some of these are stockholders, governments. suppliers, local communities, competitors, customers, creditors, labor unions, special interest groups, and trade associations" (p. 12). The societal environment "includes more general forces—ones that do not directly touch the short-run activities of the organization but that can, and often do, influence its long-run decisions," for instance, "economic, sociocultural, technological, and political-legal forces" (p. 12).

Issues arise from the societal environment (cultural, economic, political, and technological) and from the marketplace environment. This realization led Hunger and Wheelen (1993) to propose a planning acronym—SWOT: external environment (O = opportunities, T = threats) and internal environment (S = strengths, W = weaknesses). Planning assumes the ability to exert control over resources needed to achieve desirable outcomes. Activism rests on the ability to constrain the target's ability to have this control.

Power resource management entails the ability to employ economic, political, and social sanctions and rewards through means such as boycotts, strikes, embargoes, layoffs, lockouts, legislation, regulation, executive orders, police action, and judicial review. Power resource management assumes the ability of a nonprofit group, a company, or a governmental agency to give or withhold reward—stakes the target of this pressure is seeking. A boycott, for instance, can work if consumers who hold purchasing stakes (purchasing choices) withhold them from the business that seeks them. Part of this power resource management is public attention, which, according to Hoffman and Ocasio (2001), is a scarce resource that structurally awards corporations over power. However, it does not exclude activists from public attention, and as this book has argued throughout, especially historically, activists have done a remarkable job of getting public attention for their messages over the years to effect public policy and business change.

At one extreme, coercion entails granting or withholding punishment or rewards. Coercive persuasion draws its potency from the fear on the part of a group, company, or agency that punishment will be given or rewards withheld. At the other end of the continuum is accommodation, giving in to "be nice" and thereby get the stakes that would otherwise be held. Responsible advocacy and collaborative decision making are more toward the middle, the moderate approach, of this argumentative and power resource management model.

During early stages of activism, agents of change must acquire power. This point will be explained and expanded in the five-stage model that follows in this chapter. Mere outbursts or moral outrage are unlikely to foster issue development beyond the point of outrage. Activist power consists of the number of people who support the movement, alliances and other third-party assistance, media attention, and favorable responses by key people in power institutions, such as the judiciary, members of Congress, administrative officers, leading educators, or religious leaders. Persuasion is necessary to help obtain, maintain, and marshal power resources and to develop allies and opinion favorable to goals and strategies of the activists.

A dominant theory of power is that it consists of the ability X has to affect how Y achieves its goals. Barnes (1988) argued that this definition does not actually define power but merely indicates when it is present. The telling point is captured in the following question: What characteristics of X or the nature of the situation give X the ability to affect Y? The answer to that question addresses what power is in each circumstance. As a starting point, Barnes directed our attention to the focal point:

> Whether we talk of rights and obligations, or of roles and institutions, or of patterned social relationships, the import is much the same: we are talking of a presumed structure and orderliness in social activity, and a need to understand the nature and the basis of such structure and orderliness is implied. (p. 20)

Power results from value premises and social norms—expected and accepted patterns of thinking and acting: "The normative order must reflect not internal pressures within the psyche but the pressures people exert upon each other" (p. 42).

Meaning, which is a shared sense of social reality, is the basis of society and social order. One important reason for building SIM on the rhetorical tradition is to help explain how meaning is created and changed, as well as being brought to bear on issues and outcomes. Stressing this point, Barnes (1988) concluded, "Every society possesses a shared body of technical, manipulation-related knowledge, knowledge of nature, and a shared body of social knowledge, knowledge of a normative order" (p. 55). Power, therefore, results from shared knowledge— the norms and expectations that are captured in this collective view of selves, social relationships, privileges, and obligations. As interest groups and private-sector organizations contest assumptions and norms, they define and redefine power, "the structure of discretion" (p. 62). Power, in this sense, is the "capacity for action and the possession of power [is] the possession of discretion in the use of capacity for action" (p. 67). Issues managers need to sense the ebb and flow of social meaning (and its sense of preferred expectations) and the application of that meaning as means for obtaining and distributing stakes, the management of power resources.

Each power player seeks to privilege itself with the ability to address issues in ways that are self-interested or altruistic. Message strategies concentrate on types of evidence and propositions of fact, value, and policy. Despite their ostensible objectivity, media are prime players in these controversies. They may be little more than channels through which combatants communicate. At other times, they help wage the controversy. An underlying realization is that issues conflict is not only a matter of disagreement; it entails power resource management. Activist rhetoric entails efforts to obtain and marshal power resources that can be used to correct problems and make dramatic improvements by forcing change in the way a company or governmental agency does business.

One of the key arenas of the public policy marketplace is the political or referendum campaign. Power resources are votes and what moves them for or against a candidate and cause. In this arena, one important, although widely criticized, power resource is the political action committee (PAC). PACs got a boost in 1974 when the Federal Election Campaign Act outlawed large individual or corporate donors from giving money to candidates' campaigns. For this reason, corporations, unions, trade associations, and interest groups started PACs to channel money to candidates as a means for participating in the power game of established politics. These may be liberal, moderate, or conservative, for and against various issues and the candidates who champion or oppose them. This in turn created political pressures leading to passage of the Bipartisan Campaign Reform Act (BCRA), banning soft money expenditure by parties. Some of the legal limits on giving of "hard money" were also changed by BCRA.

Corporate PACs can keep employees and other constituents politically educated and give them opportunities to contact legislators. Corporate PACs can develop and circulate issues materials. Under other political funding devices, special interests can pay for advertising on issues or for or against candidates. On one side of an issue might be Move On.Com, a liberal organization that features its grassroots character as a family of organizations that brings real Americans back into the political process. On the opposite side of the fence might be Citizens United, which is closely associated in interest with its large industry contributors. Citizens United is positioned as a conservative research group that works to return government to citizens' control. The power resource challenge is not only to have a position that can be articulated but also to create or build a constituency or find one in place. One of the new communication tools in the arsenal of such organizations is the Internet and the blog.

This section has stressed the notion that as issues become more focused and people see reason to agree with some and oppose others, they are likely to be strategic stakeholders—issue constituents who withhold stakes as a means for gaining individual and collective advantage. Once this occurs, it has become a reality that issues managers need to use in their recommendations for strategic business planning.

Strain: Nexus of Issues, Risk, and Crisis

An essential theme in this book is the interconnectedness of issues, risk, and crisis (also discussed in Chapters 8 and 9). One of the primary motivators for moral outrage and strain results from a sense that a group (or some aspect of the environment, for instance) is being put at risk by the actions of an entity that becomes the target of activism. Key concerns focus on the presence of risk, the degree of the risk, the magnitude of suffering the risk, and the legitimacy that the persons or entities that are suffering the risk deserve to bear that burden (see Tansey & Rayner, 2009). The perception of risk is certain to lead to issue discussion and even to crisis. A crisis can in fact bring up the evidence of the risk. This theme will be advanced in Chapters 8 and 9.

The logic of activism grows from the nexus of issues, risk, and crisis. Activists focus attention on the risks created by or mismanaged by targeted organizations. Presentations of details about the risk call attention to the organization's crisis or create a crisis for an organization. Out of the challenge to do a better job of risk management, a clash is likely to occur over the nature of an issue and its management. The battle between activists and target organizations focuses on who has the best definition of a problem and recommendation for its solution.

A quick summary of recent events suggests the relevance of this approach to activism, as many cases in point:

1. The Katrina disaster demonstrated that the Army Corps of Engineers suffered a crisis for not building the levees in New Orleans properly, maintaining them adequately, and restoring them in a timely fashion.

2. Various government agencies leading up to the White House were found wanting in 2007 for inadequate service to current and past veterans.

3. Antismoking advocates continued to focus on measures to lessen the health effects of smoking. Similar efforts addressed the role and responsible use of alcoholic beverages in society.

4. Various pharmaceutical companies and the Federal Drug Administration came under attack for review and marketing of medications. Vioxx was especially problematic.

On a given day, hundreds of people feel discomfort about various aspects of their lives. To the extent they share this discomfort, they constitute a potential public. People may recognize problems as isolated instances such as when families suffer the tragedy of children losing their lives or being seriously harmed, perhaps due to improperly constructed toys, drunk drivers, or child predators. People may have difficulties concerning automobile warranties or failure of insurance companies to pay on policies in ways that seem predictable by the companies' product/service advertising. Children may develop cancer in patterns that seem to correlate that ailment with exposure to electromagnetic fields. Hydrocarbon emissions damage the atmosphere. Marketing philosophies create a consumer economy of immediate gratification and debt and not one based on saving. Jobs continue to be exported to other nations or wages are depressed (especially in contrast to executive compensation) so that the gap between the rich and poor increases and the middle class shrinks.

In their rhetorical positioning, activists express concerns about problems they find and solutions they prefer. Activists believe that as others learn the facts, values, and policy preferences, they will adopt a new set of expectations and demand improved corporate and government policy. Beyond knowing facts, they interpret those facts. Explaining the need for interpretation, Campbell (1996) compared the efforts of scientists for whom "the most important concern is the discovery and testing of certain kinds of truths," whereas "rhetoricians (who study rhetoric and take a rhetorical perspective) would say, 'Truths cannot walk on their own legs. They must be carried by people to other people. They must be explained, defended, and spread through language, argument, and appeal'" (p. 3). Activists may generate fact, but even more important, they put them into play and apply specific issue interpretation.

A timeless assumption of public policy battles supposes that once problems are recognized, the status quo is pressured to change. This sense of strain results from a comparison of what is versus what should be, a perceived impairment (Smelser, 1963). The rhetorical tradition has for centuries realized that problem recognition is a foundational assumption for indicting the status quo. This logic has more recently been applied to public relations theory (J. E. Grunig, 1989; J. E. Grunig & Hunt, 1984). Activists work to persuade others that their self-interest is being damaged, that norms have been violated, or that new values need to be applied to evaluate corporate behavior. In this way, they insert facts, values, and public policy solutions into the public dialogue.

Activists desire to change conditions that cause discomfort or prevent people from advantages they believe they deserve. "A social movement represents an effort by a large number of people to solve collectively a problem that they feel they have in common" (Toch, 1965, p. 205). The feeding ground of activism is "the ranks of persons who have encountered problems" (p. 9). Activists seek to convince potential supporters that strain is serious enough to warrant collective action to change it and thereby move toward equilibrium or comfort. One example of such rhetorical stance is the statement by the Humane Farming Association, which challenges what it believes to be inhumane farming techniques. Using a picture of a pig confined in a iron cage, the association points to the horrors of pig husbandry as well as alleges that the industry puts consumers' health at risk because of its "routine use of sulfamethazine, antibiotics, and other drugs that can be passed on to consumers." How is the typical pig treated? "Day after day, she rubs her nose across the front of her crate. In sheer desperation, she bites the metal bars."

Smelser (1963) viewed social change as the result of concerns that range from a relatively undefined interest, such as fads, to norm-oriented or value-oriented issues. Fads (crazes or panics) have little permanent impact on the social, political, or economic character of a society. In contrast, major movements result in dramatic change. For instance, the civil rights movement has struggled to implement the norms based on freedom, equality, and pursuit of happiness. The environmental movement has revolutionized lifestyles and notions of safety. Environmentalism changed values as a precursor to altering personal and corporate behavior and policy. For example, outbursts during the mid-1960s followed 2 decades of strong corporate growth and prosperity (Brown, 1979). Strain is most persuasive when established social, economic, or political norms are violated and expectations go unmet.

The extensiveness of support is another measure of the intensity of an issue. Strain can be measured by the number and kind of people who belong to a group or support the issues it promotes. Because activist leaders need large numbers of supporters as a power base, extensive and enduring support is crucial. Coincidental to this measure of effectiveness is the ability of the group to attract third-party support and form coalitions with other activist groups and legitimate members of a power bloc—a governor, mayor, president, religious leader, or celebrity.

Beyond ideas, activism may test the willingness of combatants to risk their lives, property, position, or economic stability. Corporations have an advantage in communities where people are unwilling to risk losing income. But if the risk of loss, such as the danger of radiation or toxic waste, begins to outweigh the economic loss, agitators may confront the company with a new set of dynamics. In these ways, persons calculate the constraints against their activism.

Strain is strongest when it expresses the self-interest of members, actual and potential, or their altruistic interest in the well-being of others or something as general as the environment. Groups create a sense of strain by showing how business actions violate the self-interest of segments of the population. Sometimes the problem is readily perceived, such as when companies improperly dispose of toxic waste. Activists "often are characterized by their motivation, fervor, and enthusiasm; they will persevere until they achieve their goal" (L. A. Grunig, 1992, p. 504).

Strain is expressed in rhetorical statements that blend emotional terms, the marshaling of evidence, and careful reasoning. Emotion gains attention; evidence and reasoning give an issue permanence. Out of conditions of strain, the group builds "a fire under its members by stressing the intolerability of their fate. . . . The result is to reinforce the member's conviction that he must take action" (Toch, 1965, p. 83). A "sufficient condition for the outbreak of collective behavior is communication" when united with "a shared culture and a common orientation among the discontented group." Activism focuses "attention on the same incidents and the shared culture ensures that a similar interpretation of those events will be made" (Oberschall, 1973, pp. 310–311).

A challenge facing corporate communicators and activists is to reach key publics with simplified versions of often complicated issues. During pollution battles, even the regulators and scientists may not understand and agree on the components of pollution, a safe level of chemicals emitted into the air, or the best technology to stop the emissions. Because issues may be complex, activists attempt to simplify and freeze attention on a few defensible statements, perhaps key examples, which followers believe to be true and can easily remember. An atrocity is vivid and easy to understand, it can be difficult to explain away, and the burden of proof has shifted to the corporations or to governmental agencies. Activist rhetoric is often most effective when it is expressed in hyperbole.

Companies, industries, and governmental bodies can redirect or refute claims that strain exists by managing certain issues, symbols, and rewards. Edelman (1964) suggested that "restiveness occurs when the state is not symbolically aligned with those who feel threatened" (p. 167). This requires that government either take the side of business or those who seek change. Activists often perceive the state to be an enemy to change. Throughout such battles, government must maintain the symbolic value of its presence. Individuals cherish "the images of society, of right and wrong, justice and injustice, success, and other moral components of their view of the world and where they themselves are situated in it" (Oberschall, 1973, pp. 83–84).

Activists—environmental groups, for instance—use prosocial rhetorical strategies to get audiences to comply with recommended actions. Such groups claim that rewards will be achieved if followers hold environmentally responsible opinions and take individual and collective actions recommended by environmentalists. In addition to positive appeals, environmental groups forecast negative outcomes that will result from irresponsible environmental behavior (Baglan, Lalumia, & Bayless, 1986). This tactic is intended to persuade followers and other targeted audiences to trust the advice and comply with the environmentalists who seek positive answers to questions and concerns in the public interest.

Activists work to foster useful relationships with "people of like mind, building alliances between organizations with similar goals" (Reber & Kim, 2006, p. 313) and creating goal compatibility (Werder, 2006). The Internet is a key tool in this regard, but the essence of the relationship is the building of shared control, trust, and dialogue, which Web sites seem to do better with followers than the media. Nevertheless, the media use activists as valued sources of information and evaluation on key issues (Reber & Berger, 2005).

Strain occurs not only when individuals and groups discover facts but also as they interpret those facts using current frames (such as concern for lead in paint on children's toys) and also work to create new frames or reshape current ones. In doing so, strain offers new premises by which facts are interpreted and used to draw conclusions. As such, frames "serve as bridges between elite discourse about a problem or issue and popular comprehension of that issue" (T. E. Nelson, Oxley, & Clawson, 1997, p. 224). As Entman (1993) defined the term, "To frame is to select some aspects of a perceived reality and make them more salient in a communicating text, in such a way as to promote a particular problem definition, causal interpretation/analysis, moral evaluation, and/or treatment recommendation for the item described" (p. 52).

In this definition, Entman (2007) featured four kinds of frames that are vital to SIM because they offer excellent insight into the kinds of arguments made by activists and other issue positions advocated: problem definition, causal interpretation, moral evaluation/judgment, and treatment recommendation/remedy promotion. These frames offer productive insights into the sort of discourse that transpires and to which activists and other nonprofit voices add. How issues are framed is an essential aspect of the SIM activities of businesses, nonprofits, and politics. The debate is about not only issues but also the ways in which they are framed. That is a vital aspect of the activist effort to voice the strain they see and use to motivate followers and to set the conditions for confrontation. With this analysis, we gain insights into the attitude formation aspects of framing (Nelson et al., 1997) as well as belief formation and salience (T. E. Nelson & Oxley, 1999). The entities that frame news and issues achieve and exert power because the way issues are framed predicts how they will be debated (Entman, 2007).

Framing is not something that only results from efforts by politicians or media reporters/editors. It also results from issue positions taken by companies, industries, and activists. As such, the frame advocated serves as a response to a rhetorical problem, and it likely creates a rhetorical problem for other voices. Even the frame is contestable; for instance, George W. Bush defined global warming and corporate response as something that hurt the economy and could/would only be addressed after emerging nations had also addressed the topic. The counterframe is that companies and governments have no choice and major countries need to lead, rather than follow. Herein lies the frames as contested shared social reality.

Stages of Activism

Writers have proposed various models to depict activist movement life cycles. For instance, L. M. Griffin (1952) identified three stages (inception, rhetorical crisis, and consummation), whereas Oberschall (1973) argued that movements progress from commitment formation, through mobilization, to confrontation. Stewart, Smith, and Denton (1984) proposed a five-stage model: genesis, social unrest, enthusiastic mobilization, maintenance, and termination. Some models tend to focus only on the activist group and do not ground their logic in the interaction of conflict. It takes two or more parties to have a conflict. After confrontation, what can happen then? Any list may be misleading because movements vary; without some sense of how activism develops, issue monitoring and responses to activists are likely to be unfocused.

Such analysis can become the basis for designing a monitoring and strategic issue response plan. For instance, the model used by a major southwestern utility company is based on the belief that issues develop through five stages:

- Vague discontent: A few members of the public and a few experts-agitators begin to discuss some topic that eventually receives media attention.
- Politicization: Groups begin to form and agitate collectively to increase the visibility of an issue, to propagate discussion and concern, and to attract followers and money.
- Legislative awareness: Legislators promote topics and generate bills.
- Regulatory guidelines: The campaign to control a company or industry reaches a crucial stage when an existing or newly created agency is assigned the responsibility for executing regulatory guidelines.
- Judicial debate: Corporations seek a court ruling against the regulation or law.

To keep on top of developments in each stage, the company (a) monitors issues, (b) discovers allies, (c) communicates with constituencies to lay a foundation of key public and employee opinion, (d) establishes coalitions with other groups, and (e) implements a lobbying campaign.

The value of any model is its ability to provide insight into how and where organizations can constructively intervene to reduce the strain that motivates activism. Regulation and legislation are created and imposed during confrontation, negotiation, and resolution. If an activist group never progresses that far as a group or on a particular issue, any monitoring system may be credited with doing its job so that strategic planning and perhaps changed standards of corporate responsibility or improved communication could adapt to and mitigate emerging issues.

This section features five stages that embrace the expected and sustained effort of activism based on the logics of social conflict theory: strain (problem recognition), mobilization, confrontation, negotiation, and resolution. Some groups mistakenly try to get to one of the later stages before the requisite foundation has been established; later stages may collapse because they lack the necessary support. Likewise, activists can fail if they are unable to progress beyond the first stages. Because of favorable circumstances, some activists succeed without going through all stages. Issues monitoring can use the stages of activism development as well as the trajectory of issues to track how individuals and unorganized publics become organized activist groups or become associated with organized activist publics.

STRAIN AND MOBILIZATION

Strain, which is a product of problem recognition, moral outrage, and cognitive involvement (Petty & Cacioppo, 1986), is activists' energy source and leveraging point. If it is sufficiently strong, people will join a group or at least support it with their approval and even with membership dues. However, activist groups do not exist long on fire and brimstone alone. If they are to be potent forces of change, they must achieve structure, conduct routine tasks, and maintain or increase membership. Activist groups require a division of labor, motivated supporters, and monetary resources—the resources of mobilization.

Mobilization occurs when activists begin to gather and marshal their power resources. Activists seek followers who sacrifice time, money, reputation, and, in extreme instances, personal security—even their lives. N. Fraser (2003) asked, "Why do so many movements couch their claims in the idiom of recognition?" Because this is required to marshal power resources discussed in the previous section. Part of these power resources is recognition and identity, the relevant aspects of identification, which consume the politics of legitimacy for activists. In essence, social movements argue for a position on various issues, and they ask potential followers and supporters, "Who are you and what do you stand for?" (Stryker, Owens, & White, 2000). Persuasion supplies ideals, emphasizes self-interest, and fosters identification sufficient to sustain the activist group. In this battle of wills, corporations and governmental agencies often have the advantage of being able to outlast the activists. Companies and agencies can simply ignore activists on the assumption that they will run out of the fuels of ideology and outrage. Defined in terms of the acquisition and use of power resources, power is the product of three variables: resources, the degree to which they are mobilized, and the efficiency of that mobilization (Blalock, 1989). The incentive for creating and employing power resources entails the desire for subjective expected utilities—gains through collective efforts. In such efforts, strategic issues managers realize that although the entity they represent may have some goals that differ from those of activists, the likelihood is great that both entities share goals that can be the basis for reconciling differences (Blalock, 1989) and fostering mutually beneficial relationships.

To build commitment, activists must win victories that evidence their ability to solve their followers' problems. Sage activist leaders may pick easy battles they know they can win, to symbolize power. They call on followers to participate in ways that do not go outside their experience or willingness to act. They minimize the perceived level of risk to be encountered by supporters and convince them that the rewards of participation are justified by the outcomes achieved (Alinsky, 1971). Over the years, according to Oberschall (1973), activist leaders have realized that "to be effective, they must show evidence of widespread support—hence, they frequently resort to mass rallies, demonstrations, petitions, and other forms of visible aggregation of the discontented groups and their sympathizers" (p. 308). Idle threats are the death knell of activist groups. Corporations and governmental agencies are barraged with so many complaints and appeals to change that they are willing to resist or ignore all but those that seem capable of ending business as usual.

During mobilization, activists seek media attention. Achieving favorable attention is sometimes difficult because activist voices often compete with one another for reporters' attention. Typical reportage consists of a quotation from an activist, a corporate spokesperson, and a governmental agency representative. The goal is to be prominently and favorably featured on front pages, editorial sections, and top-of-the-hour news reports. As well as using their own media to disseminate messages, activists work to appear favorably in the standard media and to at least seem to have broad and enthusiastic support.

Without doubt, the Internet and Web capabilities have been a boon to activists. They can engage in low-cost mass communication, both through e-mail and well-designed Web sites and blogs. The Web reduces the advantages that can come to well-funded companies and governmental agencies, which can have a professional staff and excellent media relations capabilities. Activist groups can become a spokes entity on an issue by creating a Web site that pops up high in the cue of a topic search. Their Web sites are available 24/7. Press releases can be posted; discussion sections can be created. Events can be announced. Atrocities can be featured using text, graphics, still pictures, and even video. Events or atrocities can be reported in real time. Anyone with digital communication abilities, such as the upload ability from a digital camera, can be a reporter for such sites.

Not only can activists develop Web sites that give them voice, but they can also connect with and tailor other sites to their cause. Delaney (2007) described, for instance, how environmental activists use Google Earth to monitor and communicate about environmental problems. They can use links to show the ways in which strip mining in West Virginia obliterates hills and creates runoff for valleys and streams. By using such tools, activists can monitor the sort of environmental damage they use to provide facts and define the strain created by offensive business and governmental activities. They can use images to mobilize followers and inform legislators as a means for creating confrontation. Such sites can appeal to those concerned about species such as chimpanzees whose habitat is being destroyed or about global warming. The latter debate centers on the changing shape of lakes, rivers, coastlines, snow caps, and glaciers.

Activist groups develop their own communication systems, which can include specialized software to use images generated at other Web sites. More traditional uses typically include a variety of newsletters, magazines, newspapers, videos, speakers bureaus, and the Internet. Typical of the sophisticated, slick magazines activists develop are *Audubon* and *National Wildlife*. Both are products of wildlife groups that engage in environmental lobbying. Such publications provide a wealth of information and pictures that appeal to readers, create identification, and feature either the beauty of nature or its ruination.

Each issue of *Audubon* is likely to monitor several issues, such as telling readers in a Q&A format whether they should be worried about eating swordfish, moving to biofuels, and the biodegradability of various plastics. It might dramatize battles between efforts to reestablish a dwindling or endangered species and its predators or factors that degrade its environment. An issue might champion the use of mulch. As an example of an atrocity, it would offer aerial photos of the devastation of hill-top coal strip mining in the Appalachian Mountains. In that story, it could indicate the mandated reclamation efforts as part of demonstrating the visual damage as well as the impact of soil erosion and runoff.

An issue of *National Wildlife* might include a monitoring story on the restoration of wolves in the West and the character of those animals that may be distorted due to misinformation and myth. It is likely to report on some global topic such as emission of CO_2 by country, making the point that the United States emits more global warming gasses than any other country in the world.

Reports of these kinds keep the positive-negative format of informative (fact-based) persuasion that can help mobilize followers. The organizations' followers are encouraged to continue their memberships, get active in terms of writing congresspersons, and contribute for special issues efforts, often including specific lobbying efforts on key issues and pending legislation/regulation.

During mobilization, activists must resist the dangerous tendency to factionalize, to fragment as leaders vie for followings. They challenge one another's resolve, boldness, and issue positions. They destroy one another in what they think to be the best interest of the total social movement. A test of power is the debate over slogans and symbols that foster identification and simplify the movement ideology. "To be a part of an organization viewed as potent is evidently to derive some feelings of effectiveness" (Edelman, 1964, p. 109).

During mobilization, an activist group is strengthened by its ability to achieve coalitions that add to its legitimacy. If judges, legislators, government executives, and regulators are unwilling to support the group's position, it is unlikely to mobilize appreciable power resources. For this reason, a power strategy is to threaten legitimate leaders of society with the prospect that they must support the movement or lose their own authority and position. Activists seek celebrities who identify with their cause and lend their names to make it visible and legitimate. Petition drives give an activist group a sense of legitimacy; they suggest that its cause has popular support. Activists seek alliances with other groups that have similar interests (goal compatibility) and take compatible stands on the relevant issues.

Corporations have used many tactics to resist special interest mobilization. They have worked to disrupt the sources of funds for a group. They might fund a competing group. For instance, as some Christian conservative leaders openly embraced the concept of the need for intervention to slow global warming as a theme inspired by the Book of Genesis, other conservatives opposed them. Some conservatives were actually hired as spokespersons by companies opposing global warming to argue that global warming is God's will and part of intelligent design and "evolution." Legitimate figures in society can be discouraged from endorsing the group. Corporations may increase laypeople's risk of supporting the group by threatening layoffs or shortages or by showing the costs that will result if the group's efforts are successful. Businesses or governmental agencies may argue that support of the group is not needed because it cannot solve the problems and activists' efforts are likely to be unproductive. Such tactics can lead to additional outrage and increased opposition.

The best long-term solution to difficulties with activists is to employ strategies that allow for both sides to win. That may entail even supporting activist efforts that align with the organization's interests. For instance, chemical manufacturing companies have sponsored wetland restoration and petrochemical companies have supported groups that plant trees as a measure of beautifying the environment and combating CO_2. So, organizations and activists can move to the level of confrontation or try to avoid that step by proactive and even collaborative engagement.

CONFRONTATION

Activists are ready to confront their enemy once they can marshal the requisite power resources. Confrontation occurs when a group attempts to force a corporation or governmental agency to recognize its legitimacy and acknowledge its demands. They use confrontation to polarize society to choose between their position and that of their corporate or governmental adversaries. "Radical confrontation reflects a dramatic sense of division" (Scott & Smith, 1969, p. 2). Confrontation tests whether the group can be ignored. By the time confrontation occurs, the situation may have gone so far that the company or agency must work hard to mend fences and build bridges. We need look no further in this age than to terrorism, which has become a salient theme that is employed in dramatic instances of heartfelt issue positions where the participants are dramatically different in power resources.

Jackson (1982) wisely observed, "Issues can't be 'managed'; confrontation can" (p. 212). Companies should avoid confrontation because conflict can legitimize activists and help them obtain or maintain momentum and enhance their fund-raising and membership drives. Issues managers should recognize when its opposition is strong because its point of view is legitimate, but they should not fear conflict when facts and solutions deserve analysis. Indeed, periods of conflict can be used to get the corporation's message across to key publics and put issues into the public policy agenda. Conflict can prove that activists are ill-informed or are employing shallow reasoning.

Rather than unwisely allowing an issue to mature to confrontation, Jackson (1982) advised corporations to identify and minimize their vulnerabilities. Once conflict begins, he observed, companies have several options: (a) "Stick to the issue at hand." (b) "Be able to admit you're wrong, or could be." (c) "Don't be afraid to alter your position." (d) "Find good things to say about others and their viewpoints." (e) "Present your views forthrightly and do not apologize for your self-interest." Flagrant use of legal authority or money can be counterproductive. Veterans of activist battles from whom Jackson drew advice cautioned companies to avoid counterattacking the credibility or personality of the activists; rather, they should focus on providing valuable information to help interested parties understand the corporate side of the issues. Companies may be hurt more than helped if they escalate controversy. Throughout Jackson's advice ran this theme: Maintain a win-win attitude (pp. 216–220).

During confrontation, each side fights for legitimacy and to be recognized as the preferred spokesperson on the issue. Activists struggle to be recognized as the bargaining agents for change by associating their power and issue position with the public interest and commonly held principles. Companies attempt to keep key publics' opinions on their side; they try to portray confrontation as likely to result in negative consequences. In contrast, activists work to keep their followers committed to the cause and attempt to maintain support by characterizing corporations in negative terms. They show their followers the virtues and necessity of confrontation. Activists argue that change can come only through their efforts.

Funding is a vital part of mobilization. Big bucks flow into various activist organizations, both through individual donors as well as the basic membership. Estate planning is now a vital part of activist mobilization. Hundreds of public interest groups operate in the federal government because of the tenacity of their leaders and their ability to get the money to sustain their causes.

Activists may use referenda and initiatives to require legislators to deal with issues they might otherwise avoid. Battles over propositions give them free and favorable press, but such contests can place them at a disadvantage. Once an issue is placed on a ballot, companies use advertorial advertising in all media. Activists gain power if they wage a successful proposition battle, but corporations often prove formidable.

In the 1980s, activists became more aggressive in the use of shareholder meetings as forums to criticize actions of targeted companies (Ingersoll, 1985). With sufficient numbers of shares of stock, they can gain the floor to address issues regarding corporate policy. Shareholder protest can attract media attention; reporters look for drama. Religious groups or state or city pension funds, which hold sizable amounts of stock and can acquire proxies, use this strategy to bring attention to their issues. One of the strongest groups, the Interfaith Center on Corporate Responsibility, represents Protestant, Catholic, and Jewish religious orders. This organization is primarily interested in social issues, such as public health and safety. In the 1980s, it was pleased to tout the total value of the proxies it held at $10 billion. By 2007, that figure had reached

$110 billion. Its membership included 275 faith-based institutional investors. This organization uses its proxy clout to sponsor as many as 200 shareholder resolutions in stockholder meetings of major companies each year.

In the aftermath of the Exxon *Valdez* oil spill, environmental activists used the Exxon shares owned by the New York City Employees Retirement System to introduce into a shareholder meeting what came to be called the Valdez Principles. Developed by the Coalition for Environmentally Responsible Economies, the list called for protection of the biosphere, sustainable use of natural resources, reduction and safe treatment of waste, wise use of energy, risk reduction, marketing of safe products and services, redress for environmental and personal damage, commitment to inform employees and the public, appointment of environmentalists to serve at the board and executive levels, and annual reporting and independent auditing of environmental performance. These principles became a standard list introduced at other companies' shareholder meetings and proposed during negotiations with petrochemical companies. The principles increased pressure for more environmental responsibility even if they were defeated by shareholder votes.

Davis and Thompson (1994) advised corporate managements to take a social movement, as well as an efficient market, approach to their dealings with shareholders. Increasingly, for instance, large pension funds and certain fund managers use corporate responsibility standards to assess whether to maintain a business's management team and whether to include the organization's stock shares in its portfolio.

One strategic advantage activists have is time, which to companies is money. For this reason, court and public hearings allow them a power resource. Injunctive intervention can be a powerful confrontational strategy. Activists can sue to have legal review of the wisdom of allowing companies to act as they prefer. For instance, activists prevented construction of a copper plant in Texas City, Texas, because they forced legal review of the operating permits the plant was required to obtain from either the state of Texas or the federal government. Eventually, the proponents of the plant abandoned their efforts to bring it into being (Heath, 1995).

During confrontation, power resources of the combatants are tested by the ability to exert pressure. Persuasion supports the resources needed to achieve confrontation by maintaining and marshaling resources, by intensifying commitment, and by drawing and contesting issues.

NEGOTIATION AND COLLABORATIVE DECISION MAKING

According to classic conflict management theory, conflict results from a clash over valued and scarce resources or positions as well as the opinions related to the value and distribution of those resources. It is heightened in proportion to the importance each combatant places on the outcome, the winning of the resources or positions. During confrontation, the relevant organizations can stay opposed to one another, one can accommodate the other, or they can work to solve the problem collaboratively. One side can even attempt to "destroy" the other actually or symbolically.

Conflict resolution can entail distributive strategies or integrative strategies. Distributive strategies promote individual over mutual outcomes. Integrative strategies do the opposite, leading to shared problem recognition and commitment to mutually beneficial outcomes. Such observation should not suggest that the environment of activism is inherently committed to mutually beneficial outcomes. Activists are willing to engage in win-loss outcomes if they are met with resistance. Sometimes, the issue position they take may indeed be unwise or offensive to a larger and more sound set of facts, values, or policy options. Making such choices becomes important to the spirit and strategy selection of conflict resolution.

If strain is the foundation of activism, then change is aimed at achieving harmony. Targeted organizations may be smart to accede to the demands of activists without waging open battle. Outcomes can be dire if organizations fight to defend unpopular policies and premises or adhere to operating procedures that contradict widely expected standards. If organizations refuse or are exceedingly slow to change or even engage in collaboration, they can be made to look like the villain in a political melodrama. The crowd is sure to hiss and boo.

One dramatic change in the role of activism in our society has been the increased use of negotiation and collaborative decision making. It centers on what interpretation of a problem or what solution is preferred. To answer those questions entails the uses of facts, values, and preferred policy positions that have been contested at previous stages in the activism process. Issues, such as those involving smoking or environmentalism, have become narrowed to the point that much of the dialogue transpires in courts and regulatory hearings rather than in the open press. Issues relating to dose response or parts per million (or billion or trillion)—concepts vital to discussing technical risks— are often not easily understood by lay publics and lack the kind of glamour that attracts journalists. For this reason, issue participants often express opinions and negotiate solutions out of the light of public attention, not because of a desire for secrecy but due to the failure of most reporters to be interested in arcane discussions. Much negotiation is unspectacular. It takes place in the halls of legislation and offices of administrators and regulators. Some negotiation transpires in courts and judges' chambers.

During negotiation, each side seeks to gain as many advantages or minimize as many losses as its power and argumentative ability allow. One of the frustrations at this stage is the unwillingness of either side to agree to specific points on which to stand firm. Companies complain that activists often are unwilling to settle on a specific solution or standard for drawing conclusions.

Activists may lose advantage once they have struck an agreement. One of their tactics is to constantly battle for increased standards. To settle on a standard would end their appeals for increasingly higher standards. Such tactics frustrate the negotiation process. They can mask a win-lose attitude. Key publics' opinions and their ability to grant stakes continue to be important during negotiation. The advantage each side in the controversy is capable of exacting depends, at least to an extent, on what key publics come to believe is fair.

Research by Murphy and Dee (1996) underscored the reality that negotiation and compromise are not easily achieved. Examining the relationship between companies and extremely polarized activist groups, they discovered that each of these groups espouses an ideological position that actually differs from their behavior. For instance, one side might espouse a particular environmental position but act in ways that do not correspond to that ideology. Of even more importance is the finding that the ideological positions espoused by the companies and the activists are very similar. Nevertheless, neither group wants to accept that similarity and use it as the basis for negotiating solutions. The differences between activist groups and the targets of that activism often seem to reach a point where the issues are personalized and compromise is a matter of losing face, not a pretty prospect for resolving public policy differences.

Public relations practitioners can play a useful role in the public debate of issues during negotiation. They can work to keep the media and other constituents apprised of the issue and the working of meetings. That is a standard public relations role. Recently, however, public relations practitioners are learning how to engage in collaboration. If they are limited in their view of public relations to media relations, they can miss a golden opportunity to take a leadership role. Heath and Coombs (2006, see p. 409, for instance) offer conceptual and theoretical, as well as practical, advice for collaboration. The central theme is to look for concurrence and mutuality of control as well as the distribution of resources in a win-win style.

Even in the announcement of the outcome of the negotiation, corporations or interest groups can characterize the situation to their advantage (or disadvantage if they intend to continue the fight). They may describe the constructive role they played in the development of effective legislation. Announcements of change, made in the public interest, can go a long way toward building a positive, supportive environment for future operations. At the end of negotiation, advocates need to persuade interested publics that solutions achieved will eliminate the problems that fueled the controversy.

RESOLUTION

If skillfully managed, issues communication by all parties can help resolve controversy and create or reestablish harmony. Such positioning necessarily assumes that neither side is likely initially to be correct and the other to be incorrect. So, resolution is a meeting point through collaboration. Once that meeting point has been achieved, either side is wise to communicate what has been accomplished and perhaps how that occurred. Resolution is not a time to personalize the outcome and claim victory. That stance is too integrative in approach to build and advance the rapport that is best under these controversies.

This phase in a controversy is vital, especially in a multiple-public, multiple-stakeholder model where competing interests must be satisfied and reconciled. The major requirement of this stage is to determine how society and the interests of key players can be adjusted to accommodate the results of the settlement. If trade-outs and decisions favor business most, activists have a hard time agreeing to them. The opposite is also true. If the negotiation is fair and open, conflict can end or be reduced, and the parties can gain support for the agreement.

Followers and others interested in the outcome of the controversy need to be convinced that an adequate settlement or collaboration has been achieved. They need to realize the way this settlement reduces the strains that led to the motivation for the controversy.

One problem in the resolution of conflict is the selection of the people who will administer regulatory programs. Isaac and Isaac (1984) found that as activists become a part of established governmental systems, they often take their political agenda with them and attempt to implement it. That kind of approach to conflict can tend to personalize the battles and champion distributive rather than integrative approaches.

Resolution may be difficult to explain because controversy can be complex. Many issue battles consist of a dialogue between technical specialists, particularly natural or behavioral scientists or engineers. Some researchers are unwilling to take stands on issues, whereas others join their sciences to issue politics. Interest groups have their own scientists, as do the companies. The government will have its cadre of specialists who give opinions. Science is often not definitive; new research findings may lead key players to reopen controversies once thought to be settled. For these reasons, trust and compatible goals are necessarily a key part of the communication process.

Even when prevailing opinion is for or against some issue position, the weight of scientific evidence and efforts of politicians will be key factors in how the regulatory battle will be played out. Politicians, whether representing a specific constituency on an issue or not, have their own agendas. Some will favor the interest group side of the issue on a technical question, and other politicians will take the corporate side. As in poker, how the regulatory or corporate responsibility battle plays out depends on the relative power and resource distribution skill of the players. It may be settled or redirected by election outcomes. One dramatic instance of that occurred in 1994 following the landslide that gave Republicans control of both houses of Congress. During much of 1994, Representative Waxman (D–CA) used his chair on a major subcommittee to grill tobacco executives about the health effects of tobacco on smokers and the manufacturing procedures that may include increasing the addictive components of cigarettes. Following the 1994 legislative election, the new chair of that committee, a Republican from Virginia, claimed that the tobacco industry had satisfactorily answered all questions and deserved no more restrictions over its operations. In 2006, the power shifted again in the House of Representatives to the Democrats, who again assumed chair positions of key committees. So the ebb and flow of hearings/investigation, legislation, and regulation goes.

This ebb and flow also demonstrates the vitality of adopting and understanding a power resource management approach to issues management. The battleground is one of legitimacy, not only of position but also of players. Who speaks for the best risk management policies of society?

From this review of activist theory, four conclusions are justified: (a) Without effective issue communication, power resources cannot be obtained or maintained; (b) tactics of inducement and constraint lose their effectiveness when they are not sanctioned by public opinion; (c) political pressure is likely to result once activists gain enough power; and (d) negotiation, collaborative decision making, and other forms of issue communication are needed along with new and improved policies to restore or achieve harmony among the interested parties.

Incremental Erosion

Throughout this discussion of activism—especially the previous section that outlined its stages—two themes are central: Groups work to obtain and use public policy power resources, and they rhetorically challenge their opponents' positions and justify their own. Organizations that lack power must draw on, or change, the assumptions and principles of society to empower themselves; those that have power must work to maintain it, in part by justifying the rationale for their power. "Established groups," Gamson (1975) observed, "must maintain the loyalty and commitment of those from whom they draw their resources; challenging groups must create this loyalty" (p. 140).

Whereas the previous section of this chapter stressed the efforts activists employ to obtain and marshal power resources, this section features a rhetorical component of that process. Of special interest is the rhetorical effort to privilege the policies and actions of some groups while undercutting the rationale for other groups' policies and actions. The best approach to issues management is to seek maximum harmony and agreement among the participants. Managing responses to and generating policies from a multiple-stakeholder environment is daunting. Through what they say and do, private-sector companies, government organizations, and activist groups work to justify themselves by adopting or creating assumptions that serve to rationalize their discretion. It can be defined as a battle over expectations and the extent to which each party meets or violates others' expectations (Heath, 1994).

Activists may chip away at the foundations of their enemies, one premise at a time. These assumptions may become generally accepted—part of the macrosocial opinions—or they may be narrower, localized to a specific interest. Persuasion is vital to social movements; it "is not so much an alternative to the power of constraints and inducements as it is an instrument of that power, an accompaniment to that power, or a consequence of that power" (Simons, 1974, p. 177). Power and persuasion support one another. Persuasion keeps people committed to the belief that groups that have power deserve to keep it and, therefore, their policies and actions are correct.

Successful critics make small demands and introduce a bit of information into the public commentary at a time. Using incremental erosion, activists chip away at their adversaries. Incremental erosion, as defined by Condit and Condit (1992), is the use of rhetoric by activists to slowly and steadily challenge and deny the assumptions on which their opponents build their case, justify their actions, and generate support. Activists create points of view to which targeted companies must continually respond; issues are incrementally redefined to the advantage of the attacker. Condit and Condit concluded,

> Working on different target audiences at different times, the activist group attempts to chip away at the various supports underlying its opponent's position. It makes a series of gradual and small moves designed to maneuver opponents into a position where they have no more rhetorical options. This is done by establishing rhetorical exigencies—needs, conditions, or demands to which the opposition must respond—while simultaneously establishing rhetorical constraints that limit the strategies available for response. (p. 242)

Each activist statement can attack specific principles that provide rationales for company policies and procedures.

One target of incremental erosion is the tobacco industry. For years, its advertising claimed that smoking made people attractive. Various companies even acknowledged the health theme and advertised that their product was less likely to produce a "smoker's cough." Critics featured the health and cosmetic hazards of smoking. The industry used ads to tell youths that smoking was adult behavior that they should not engage in until they were old enough. Critics claimed that instead of being expressions of corporate responsibility, such ads gave young people incentives to smoke as a means for demonstrating that they were adults—or at least making progress. Antismoking activists, in conjunction with key legislators and regulators, realized that an outright ban of cigarettes and other tobacco products would not work, as Prohibition had failed to curtail alcohol use.

The entertainment industry has suffered its share of criticism. Key publics, especially parents, target what they believe to be irresponsible behavior in the electronic game industry. Set in an opinion environment that has become extremely sensitive to acts that ostensibly lead to or sustain violence, congressional review has sought to protect children from being motivated or reinforced to be violent or perhaps just desensitized to violence. Targets of such criticism include stores that sell computer games and companies that create, manufacture, and market them. Games are targeted when they include scantily clad women who act in suggestive ways. Such games not only can be seen as demeaning with women but create desensitized views on violence, including mayhem. Similar criticism centers on contemporary music performers, whose lyrics and music videos motivate activists to acknowledge that even though they may be protected by the First Amendment, they need to be presented in ways that champion rather than offend mature values. The moral outrage of such critics motivates them to chip away at the support for what they believe to be offensive.

Companies ask for trouble when they ignore criticism of potentially powerful groups that can use formal informational means for exerting power resource management. Whereas a win-loss attitude may be the lifeblood of activism, it is the death knell of a corporation. Viewed this way, activism does not arise from misunderstanding but from attacks on some premises and the substitution of others. In this vein, Tichenor, Donohue, and Olien (1977) argued that "community conflicts to an increasing degree involve a contest over information and its interpretation" (p. 107). The interpretation of fact and the contest over information may be part of activists' use of incremental erosion. Similar attacks focus on values that certainly are not static in interpretation or applications but can change incrementally over time.

Incremental change occurs because issue positions emerge and grow slowly. "Usually, issues are born, or make their debuts, in some highly specialized, limited-circulation publication or within some small group of those most interested and involved" (Renfro, 1993, p. 71). Currently, many of these grow strength from sharing the information via social media sites, blogs, and other Web capacities. From narrow discussions (those of interest to a highly involved but relatively small group), they can (but do not necessarily) grow in interest and are reported and discussed by the general media, such as news magazines or television feature programs such as *60 Minutes*. These discussions, Renfro (1993) observed, ripple outward in increasingly broadcast outlets. People have favorite sources of information and opinion. The more cognitively involved people are, the more effort they are willing to expend to obtain important issue-relevant information. They turn from easily accessible stories in the general media to conversations with persons whose opinions they value. Increased involvement is likely to lead people to prefer companies, government agencies, and activists as sources of information (Heath, Liao, & Douglas, 1995).

Activists are strongest, McLaughlin (1969) concluded, when their "ideology is in accord with the Zeitgeist of the era" (p. 349). At other times, they must work to change the premises that form that Zeitgeist. Activist groups survive by associating the interests of their followers with dominant political and moral symbols (Edelman, 1964, 1977). Values such as fairness, equality, environmental quality, and security underpin issue contests. From a corporate point of view, freedom is central—free enterprise is a cultural archetype. In contrast, activists use it to argue for antitrust legislation; the people should be free from the tyranny of monopolies—because restraint of trade is unfair. Labor rights were championed in the name of freedom: Labor should be free from unfair labor practice. Aesthetics, a world of beauty, has been called on to combat pollution. Equality, fairness, and safety underpin social movement persuasion because they are central to the U.S. ideology.

Under attack, institutions struggle to stop the erosion of their authority that is defined by the ideology of society. Basic documents give principles from which control agents draw their authority. According to Edelman (1964),

> The Constitution thereby becomes the concise and hallowed expression of man's complex and ambivalent attitude toward others: his wish to aggrandize his goods and powers at the expense of others: his fears that he may suffer from powerful positions of others and from their predations. (p. 19)

Activists help shift opinions. Typically, such shifts occur slowly, incrementally, during which the principles justifying the corporate view erode and are replaced by principles advocated by activists. For example, child labor was once accepted practice. Through arguments, a power constituency began to believe that children were better off in school than in coal mines or sweat shops. In similar fashion, Louis Brandeis argued that women, because of their weaker constitution, should not be required to work long, hard hours. This view, argued in *Muller v. Oregon* (1908), which seemed enlightened 100 years ago, has in the past 4 decades been opposed by women who argue that many jobs should be open to them because they have the strength to perform the same tasks as men. Each position reflects a different set of beliefs and values. As this section has demonstrated, change occurs incrementally through rhetorical pressures and counterpressures between private- and public-sector organizations and activist groups.

Fostering Mutual Interests Instead of Antagonism

When we think about issues management, we necessarily focus on antagonistic relationships. If the discussion stops there, we are unlikely to have a fully functioning society (Heath, 2006b). One alternative to seeing activists as foes is to view them as allies. They can help companies define product quality, as occurred when the food industry quit fighting mothers who doubted that the food they bought and prepared for their families was sufficiently nutritious. Food group companies created consumer advisory panels to learn what the mothers wanted to serve their families and would buy for them to eat. Combat gave way to a win-win outcome. But such positioning needs to avoid co-optation, the seeming alliance over shared values that ultimately only benefits one party to a controversy.

Chapters 8 (crisis) and 9 (risk) will address in more details the ability of organizations to wisely manage collective risk and avoid the crises that manifest from risk. One innovation increasingly used by petrochemical companies and electric utilities is community (or citizens) advisory committees (CACs). Such committees are sponsored by companies that seek to maximize concerned citizen participation as a means for increasing understanding—perhaps of technical issues—while lessening unconstructive criticism. Companies often hire facilitators who organize a CAC, create its bylaws, set its agendas in cooperation with its members, and conduct its business. CACs serve as sounding boards for companies that strive to create harmony with adjacent communities and solve mutual problems. One example is the use of such groups by Tampa Electric; through the advice of a CAC, a different site was established for the construction of a much needed electricity generating plant. The site was selected because it solved a problem and resulted in the least harm to the community. In the chemical industry, CACs increase understanding of technical issues and operating procedures and help the sponsoring company to adopt emergency response messages that increase understanding while avoiding a sense of condescension (Heath, 1994).

Other industries and governmental organizations have realized the virtue of creating cooperative alliances with critics to bring opinions to bear at a time when they can best be discussed with less moral outrage and toward constructive change. Activists can become stumbling blocks to corporate efforts to execute their business plan on the assumption that lost time is lost dollars. Pressure to increase the cost of doing business is used as an incentive for the company to agree to operate in a manner preferred by the pressure group. Issues managers may ask themselves whether their industry or organization has goals in common with the pressure group, whether their goals can be accomplished only at the expense of that party, or whether their immediate goals are not in conflict but the difference of opinion arises from some other conflict over scarce resources (Blalock, 1989). A basic question for issues managers to address, as the precursor to forming meaningful relationships with critics, is the following: What goals do the entities want to achieve that foster their mutual interests and lay the foundation for collaborative decision making? Thus, we again see the virtue of goal compatibility as a central theme in SIM.

Corporate types, for that reason, accustomed to command and control mentalities are frustrated when they cannot direct the opinions and actions of persons who criticize their business and governmental activities. This kind of mentality can lead to unfortunate and counterproductive strategies and outcomes. One of the most sage advisers for the corporate set is Philip Lesly (1983, 1984, 1992), whose professional experience refined lists of do's and don'ts. Some of them require basic issues monitoring to become informed and able to formulate strong and constructive responses to critics: Know the situation and the climate, know your people, know your adversaries, know what to do, and know how to do it. Although Lesly's approach is firmly committed toward maintaining the self-confidence of management, he acknowledged that the outsiders, the critics, could make valuable and constructive contributions to an improved organization. Thus, he advised, "Listen—they may have something to offer," and he continued, "If a group has legitimate arguments and shows it has a sound approach, enlist its leaders" (Lesly, 1992, p. 330). In other words, Lesly offered advice on how to deal with the unreasonable and unwise critics, but he squarely directed managers to listen, learn, and be able to know what valid criticism was being made. Isn't this the essence of issues management? One essential ingredient for effective SIM is reflective management.

Company or industry personnel often are alarmed at how well activists understand and how firmly and insightfully they disapprove of certain policies and actions. Corporate leaders also feel deep frustration over critics' ignorance concerning their industry. A complex problem may not yield to a simple answer. This fault may rest with critics, but ultimately the responsibility to the community calls for reflective management to be committed to collaboration, willing and able to communicate openly and candidly, and sensitive to strategic options for reducing the legitimacy gap.

Such strategies require sharing control. That has long been a part of the struggles to form and operate industry trade associations but as often as not does not have lasting impact in the development of relationships between business and activists. One effective tool commonly used by organizations that operate in the public policy arena is a coalition. Coalitions are temporary constructs of individuals, groups, and organizations that ban together and advocate for an intended purpose. Coalitions may or may not include corporations or industries. Coalitions derive their power from their size (number of individuals or groups represented, or both) and the credibility attached to both those numbers and the standing of those who comprise the coalition (Tucker & McNerney, 1992). Their power is indicated by their ability to pressure policy makers and affect discourse and behavioral outcomes related to issues and policy decisions.

E. A. Fraser (1982) pointed out two advantages of forming coalitions: Numbers count and coalitions save money. By using coalitions, which may include the critics of corporate behavior, issues managers minimize adversarial relationships. To build coalitions, Fraser recommended that issues managers define issue-related problems and select ones on which to focus. Subsequent steps should identify allies and opponents and decide how participants can be attracted to the coalition and involved in the issues management process. The coalition effort must have budget support. The coalition should monitor its progress and communicate its efforts to constituencies through many channels. Members of a coalition become channels of communication. A coalition must evaluate its results and communicate them to its constituents. "A coalition is effective only when its issue has merit and the coalition members are organized, informed, and conscientious enough to communicate the worthiness of the effort" (p. 194). Pires (1988) offered issues managers steps to follow when working to create coalitions: (a) Define objectives, (b) know the issue, (c) build an alliance, (d) maintain flexibility, (e) treat people decently, and (f) maintain contacts.

As well as dealing with external publics, employee constituencies can be informed and mobilized in issue campaigns. Employees are most likely to participate in a corporate grassroots effort when they experience high cognitive involvement, are committed to the organization, have experienced success in being active on noncompany issues, and recognize that the issue facing their employer concerns their interests (Heath, Douglas, & Russell, 1995).

Conclusion

Proactive, constructive problem solving is preferable to combat. Communication cannot win all battles. Sometimes the only way to solve a problem felt by activists is for industry or government agencies to implement strategic change. A win-win attitude fosters constructive communication and joint problem solving, which leads to mutual interests and harmony. A long-term commitment to inform and cooperate with key stakeholding publics about the challenges facing businesses is a prerequisite for a stable society. All sides in public policy controversy must feel they have prospered from open exchange of ideas and constructive problem-solving negotiation and collaborative decision making.

SIM Challenge: Is Clean Energy an Oxymoron?

In 2006, Texas Utilities (TXU) petitioned the Texas state government to issue permits to build 11 coal-burning electric generating plants. This request was granted by the unusual intervention of the governor by issuing executive orders.

One element of this controversy centered on the role of coal in energy production. The United States has some of the largest coal deposits in the world, sufficient to generate enormous amounts of electricity, but coal is a major contributor to greenhouse emissions and to atmospheric discharge of mercury.

Almost immediately, an advocacy campaign was unleashed to oppose these permits. This advocacy campaign focused both on the environmental impact of coal and the overstated energy need/production ratio report that TXU and the state government issued. In part, it did not include 1,400 megawatts of generating capacity that was available but mothballed. This is a substantial amount of operable production because each megawatt can power approximately 800 homes.

An investment group led by Kohlberg Kravis Roberts & Co. (KKR) (called Texas Energy Future Holding, LP) offered a takeover bid of $32 billion, the largest takeover effort in the history of U.S. business. It got into the fray because it believed the company could be operated in a "greener" fashion while still making excellent profits as a regulated monopoly. KKR and its backers' planning in part relied on the continued and renewed use of natural gas for electric generation. TXU had natural gas (more environmentally sound) plants in marginal operation or mothballed because of natural gas prices. Thus, the move to "environmental responsibility" was buffered by speculation about alternative energy sources, not simply by business ethics.

As a regulated monopoly, TXU can pass energy costs to the customer with normal state government approval. KKR's presentation to state regulators featured the challenge of walking the fine line between meeting energy demand and being environmentally responsible. Such a "line" includes the potential for substantial profit (33% in the fourth quarter of 2006) and depends on honest and candid energy need projections that are typically created by the industry being regulated and used by that industry in rate requests (Fowler, 2007; Steffy, 2007b).

Two of the strongest and best-funded environmental groups (approximately $120 million combined) endorsed the buyout and the proposed terms of operation. These groups, Natural Resources Defense Council and Environmental Defense, extracted a commitment from the holding group to cancel the request for most of the additional coal-burning facilities and to back global warming legislation. Other activist groups complained these activists had settled for too little. (By the way, a substantial amount of this debate occurred on the Internet.) Critics sought to prohibit all new coal-burning facilities. In fact, during the discussion of TXU's plans, it revealed that it was not fully interested in developing all of those facilities, at least not immediately.

Such controversy is predictable as business concerns become more willing to work with activists to make projects and business activities to create higher standards of corporate responsibility. Texas-based activists were particularly concerned by three plants scheduled to be licensed and built. In fact, some of the local activism came from rural conservatives who are inherently pro-business but who also have strong progressive leanings, especially if their interests are harmed. The critics argue that some environmental groups were co-opted to the advantage of the business interests and used to screen them from public criticism. The presence of these distinguished environmental groups could be seen as constituting a front for the buyout, but on the other hand, it could be judged to be wise business practice by bringing critics into the discussion at the planning stage to make it progress more quickly and to higher standards of corporate responsibility (R. Smith & Carlton, 2007).

The voices of the groups varied in important ways but were visible and strong. KKR promised a new energy future for the company and the states where it operates: "To better serve our customers, meet the growing energy needs of Texas, and do our part to ensure a sustainable environmental future, TXU is taking a new approach." The ad promised customer savings/energy cost reduction of 10%, reduction of approved plants from 11 to 3, a new and long-term plan for Texas energy needs, and research to increase environmentally responsible production as well as a move to alternatives to coal (ad published in *Houston Chronicle*, March 1, 2007, p. A19).

The ads by critics were published under the name of the Texas Clean Sky Coalition (created at least in part by the Sierra Club and Lone Star Chapter of Environmental Defense). The print newspaper and online ads featured a variety (ethnic and gender) of "grassroots" spokespersons with smudged faces who voiced the tagline, "Face it, coal is filthy." Each ad featured a factoid, such as "If all of the proposed coal-fired electric plants are built in Texas, Texas will produce as much carbon dioxide as California, New York, and Florida combined" (*Houston Chronicle*, February 12, 2007, p. A9). Another reported, "Texas is already the number-one global warming polluting state in America. If it were a country, Texas would be in the top 10 in the entire world" (*Houston Chronicle*, February 5, 2007, p. A11). Media inquiry asked who sponsored the expensive ad campaign. Was it the natural gas lobby using activists as fronts or the corn/agriculture lobby?

That question was answered in an April 27, 2007, story in *The Wall Street Journal*. In it, Fialka (2007) named the financial and strategic sponsor of this issue ad campaign: Chesapeake Energy, an Oklahoma City natural gas firm. The campaign criticizing coal was not limited to Texas and reached into Washington, D.C.; it targeted federal legislators and regulators. Representative Nick J. Rahall (D–WVA) claimed the ads insulted coal miners (especially in his coal-producing state?). A spokesperson for the National Mining Association claimed the ads provided incorrect or out-of-date information. All of this controversy allowed for more expert testimony, this by John P. Holdren, professor of environmental science at Harvard. He noted that the ads incorrectly called his last name Holden and distorted the number of plants required for the impact he featured in his analysis of the coal industry. Moreover, close analysis found that Jim Marston, director of the Texas office of Environmental Defense, and Ken Kramer, director of the Austin office of the Sierra Club, said their organizations were not cosponsors of the advertisements.

A lesson learned from this case is that a model of public relations is naive and even dysfunctional if it is founded on the assumption that an organization (typically a business) has performed excellent public relations if it listens to a complaining entity and "responds appropriately" to that group's concerns because that group can have an effect on the company. The matrix of players, interests, and issues positions is traditionally far more complex than that view features. The challenge of collaboration is to be reflective, proactive, and willing to work through complex issues, often framed in competing opinions, with groups with different power resources operating out of conflicting interests. We ask SIM to find the "center" and mutual benefits.

Summary Questions

1. What is the moral outrage rationale for activism?

2. How important is power resource management to the understanding of activism?

3. Why is legitimacy gap a focal point for the rise of activism?

4. What is the connection between risk, crisis, and issues as a rationale for the rise of activism?

5. What are the five stages of activism? What does each demand of the activist, and how can the target respond constructively?

6. What is power and how dependent is it on the opinion environment in which activists work to exert power and express moral outrage?

7. Why is advocacy ethically responsible, as is collaborative decision making?

8. What does incremental erosion mean, and how is it a tool used by activists over time when they are the Davids against mammoth Goliath companies, industries, and governmental agencies?

9. How can and why should coalitions be created to achieve mutually beneficial relationships?

6

Issues Communication

Argument Structures and Zones of Meaning

Vignettes
Activists Speak With Many Tools

Throughout the world, animal rights have been a focal point for issue debate and activism. Sensitivity to the well-being of animals has spurred People for the Ethical Treatment of Animals (PETA) to mount and sustain its commitment to protect animals. This is a daunting task because popular culture has created zoos, circuses, and fashion that tend to separate the reality of animals' well-being from public view. Such is even more the case for slaughter, industrial farming, and medical research. The fundamental premise of PETA is that as stewards of the Earth, people must be humane to animals rather than use them for entertainment, food, fashion, and science.

In August 2007, PETA's Web site offered commentary on the Michael Vick case, that of a celebrated professional athlete who was associated with dog fighting, a horrific case of animal abuse for human entertainment. It offered videos of fish and made a case against eating them. It featured celebrities who were fighting various kinds of animal cruelty, including Pamela Anderson versus Kentucky Fried Chicken. It offered video clips of various atrocities, knowing that by featuring atrocities, it brought emotion, empathy, and anger into the debate to raise the involvement of those who shared its zones of meaning.

In addition to Kentucky Fried Chicken, the site has attacked the reputation of Ringling Circus, PetSmart, Burberry, Iams, and the Australian wool industry. It seeks to use shock, provide information, foster identification (including with animals to protect their rights), and promote policies. The policy positions have been a longstanding aspect of PETA,

(Continued)

(Continued)

which argues that animals are not ours to eat, to wear, to experiment on, to use for entertainment, and to abuse in any way.

It offers vegan recipes and fosters alternative shopping. Nudity and sexy models have long been a part of the events to attract media attention and shock people into action and call for increased government restrictions. The site often features a celebrity who announces and proves she would "rather go naked than wear fur."

In the debate, companies respond to PETA, raise their standards of operations, and offer explanations of their policies. PETA is not without its activist critics. As is the case in industry where various companies challenge others to higher standards, the same is true among activists. Critics seek to discredit PETA. One can wonder whether some of the PETA critics are inspired by involved companies as a form of reputation combat.

PETA offers action alerts, breaking news e-mail, factsheets, FAQs, features, literature, multimedia presentations, photos, RSS, videos, and linked Web sites. It also announces victories. It offers a media section and discusses every issue of its concern in hyperbole and often with sexual innuendo. It challenges people to change their behavior to deny markets to those who would exploit fur, but it also strategically makes proposals of public policy such as employing governments to stop various kinds of animal slaughter, especially for fashion and human vanity.

Like the trade association that will be described in the SIM Challenge at the end of the chapter, PETA has its role in issues communication and the overall dialogue of animal rights and welfare. PETA sees itself as a source of information that it believes a variety of stakeholders need to know about, perhaps to understand, and maybe agree with their position. It also turns its reception to understanding what people think about their strategies and tactics and overall mission. It knows that its reputation is crucial to the amount of praise or criticism it receives and the willingness of stakeholders to grant resources to it. It recognizes the responsibility of providing a perspective on such a fundamental concept to society.

Chapter Goals

This chapter begins with an overview of issues communication as ongoing dialogue that occurs in many venues and consists of propositional discourse where statements are made and responded to on the assumption that such discussion can lead to enlightened choices. It consists both of process (including established and counterestablishment infrastructures) and content. It presumes that meaning, as shared and co-created zones of meaning, can achieve sufficient concurrence (if not consensus) that can bridge differences in ways that allow for coordinated collective action—the essence of society. To develop these lines of analysis, the chapter examines the nature of character (reputation, brand) as archetypes. The assumption is that the perceived character of the advocate not only is created by its actions and statements but also is an important factor in how influential it is in the dialogue. Is it a legitimate participant, does it create identification, and does it have a reputation of serving society? The chapter explores the content of issues communication as it focuses on developing premises and platforms of fact, value, and policy. As such, it treats issues communication as argument, the contest of ideas. It also treats issues communication as narrative. Finally, brief attention is given to the campaign elements of issues communication. The illustrations used in this chapter feature the components of issues communication regardless of the kind of organization employing them. This discussion draws examples from issues advertising, not necessarily to advocate the use of that vehicle but to examine the kinds of arguments organizations set forth. In its examination of issues communication, this chapter explains (a) issues communication as argument, (b) organizational persona, (c) issue content, and (d) campaign options, including (e) understanding and targeting stakeholding publics, (f) designing messages, and (g) assessing campaign success. Critics often focus on the nature of a campaign as inherently bad, especially if used by companies in such debate; the truth is that activists (and other nonprofits) create and implement campaigns as do government agencies. A campaign is merely a systematic and focused way of allocating resources in an attempt to achieve some defined outcomes. We emphasize *attempt* because campaign impact is a roll of the dice, a matter of how the issue plays out. It differs from random communication behavior. Some activists actually engage in campaigns of random behavior. All of this fits under the heading of strategic communication, communication that is focused and purposeful.

Whatever type of organization they represent, issues managers recognize the need for using issues communication as tough defense and smart offense (Adams, 1995). Such communication has an issues quality to it because it focuses on enlightened choices. Issue positions can be a part of the organization's brand equity (see Chapter 10). Efforts to define, build, and even repair brand equity or reputation center on the position the organization takes on key issues. Activity over more than the past century has demonstrated that corporations and government agencies have no stranglehold on the formation of opinions that underpin individual and collective decisions (see Chapter 2 for history, Chapter 5 for the role of activists in this dialogue).

Dialogue is foundational to issues communication. According to Burke (1969a), dialogue is narrative, "a process of *transformation* whereby the position at the end transcends the position at the start, so that the position at the start can eventually be seen in terms of the new motivation encountered enroute" (p. 422). Dialectic takes the form of the upward and downward way so that stories take on order because they embody principles of an ultimate *narrative:*

> Beginning with the particulars of the world, and with whatever principle of meaning they are already felt to possess, dialectic "proceeds by stages until some level of generalization is reached that one did not originally envisage, whereupon the particulars of the world itself look different, as seen in terms of this 'higher vision.'" (p. 306)

Stories are dialectical—the act, the reaction, and the thing learned (Burke, 1969a). Their structure is dialectic for working out a principle, an order. Over time, many stories told and retold in a company or one of its subunits establish themes that seem enduring and are treated as such because they are repeated.

Society is a complex of many voices, opinions, and interests within this dialogue. We often like to imagine it as a dialogue that can lead to continually refined policies that collectively manage the risks faced by the people of each society. Some see this as dialogue and look upon it as covered with warts but the best we can get. Others see it as "mere rhetoric" and propaganda. However evaluated, the dialogue consists simply of statement and counterstatement and is the expression of self-interests. Does this process lead to better decisions, a more fully functioning society? As Burke (1946) mused, "How can a world with rhetoric stay decent, how can a world without it exist at all?" Championing the societal value of rhetoric, Lentz (1996) reasoned, "Truth should prevail in a market-like struggle where superior ideas vanquish their inferiors and achieve audience acceptance" (p. 1).

Issues communication also is propositional. It focuses on statements and is expected to justify the advocacy force of the statement. It assumes that people do not agree and are entitled to make enlightened choices. Politicians often do not agree with one another. They take stances that carve out or identify with prevailing opinions. Regional differences can be substantial. Inter-industry and intraindustry differences work against consensus. Media reports and bloggers' commentaries affirm some points and oppose others often in dramatic and hyperbolic style. All of this issue position advocacy can be discordant and chaotic. It certainly is not controlled, and the points of influence shift over time.

Ideas are contested and debated. As Burke (1969b) aptly observed, our society is a marketplace of ideas, facts, values, and policies: "the Scramble, the Wrangle of the Marketplace, the flurries and flare-ups of the Human Barnyard, Give and Take, the wavering line of pressure and counter pressure, the Logomachy, the onus of ownership, the War of Nerves, the War" (p. 23). In this wrangle, private-sector organizations, Sproule (1989) warned, "try to privatize public space by privatizing public opinions; that is, skillfully (one-sidedly) turning opinion in directions favorable to the corporation" (p. 264). Analyzing this hegemonic effort, Dionisopoulos and Crable (1988) concluded that organizations "attempt to secure a desired outcome by aiming their messages toward leading and dominating the terminological parameters of emergent issues" (p. 143). Discourse is important "because of the creative and evocative power of language, the very 'essence' and 'boundaries' of the organization are things to be managed symbolically" (Cheney & Vibbert, 1987, p. 176).

Issues communication entails reaching audiences and publics with vital data, key premises, and conclusions relevant to public policy matters. The goal for all parties in this dialogue is to forge policies that meet the needs and satisfy the values of all stakeholders. In this dialogue, each party presents what it believes to be a compelling argument to support its conclusions. Opinion leader groups contest vital propositions of fact, value, and policy. By listening (issues monitoring and analysis as well as collaborative decision making) to these publics, organizations can decide when they need to agree with or challenge the views of those publics. A public contest of issue positions can increase the chances of all parties becoming more satisfied with the way each issue is resolved.

One guiding assumption behind issues communication is that if individuals and organizations get involved in public discussion before issue positions become fixed in the minds of key publics, communication efforts may have greater impact (Chase, 1984; Crable & Vibbert, 1985; Dionisopoulos, 1986). Early intervention increases the chance of having competing points of view thoroughly discussed while they are malleable (Lesly, 1984; Schmertz, 1986). This set of generalizations highlights the fact that opinions change, develop, and can at least for a while be ossified. In a republic, can we be responsible if we conclude anything other than "let the dialogue continue"?

An array of communication options exist. Communication options range from placed advertisements to news stories, feature articles, books, and published studies, to name only a partial list. Without doubt, the Internet has changed the way issues are discussed. This is perhaps even more true of statements that create crisis, respond to the crisis, and discuss risks (Hallahan, 2009). They range from massive issue advertising campaigns to negotiation and collaborative decision making between leaders of key organizations and critical groups. They include the private communication of the organization. It may entail testimony at legislative and regulatory hearings. It can involve citizen advisory councils and other infrastructure that bring organizations and citizens together to engage in dialogue and work toward mutually beneficial solutions to shared problems. What is important for the discussion in this chapter is not so much the venue of the communication as its structure and content and the process by which the communication and decision making occur. Venues constantly change and evolve, especially with the constant evolution of new information technologies and the latest 2.0, 3.0, and 4.0 of the Web. We want to know about the substance and formation of opinions because ideas count. Issues discussion uses all vehicles to ensure that public policy is best for the relevant parties and establishes a community of shared interest for society at large.

Issues communication is inherently two-way. An issue position favored by one group or organization is likely to suffer varying degrees of opposition from another group or key public. Corporations must be listeners as well as advocates if they are to provide useful "what's-in-it-for-me" information, recommend evaluations, and propose policies about their operating conditions to key stakeholders. They must respond with information each public wants. Businesses and other organizations cannot survive or thrive by telling only what they want audiences to know and not telling what audiences want to know. To this end, senior public relations managers often set as their mission being the first and best source of information on all matters relevant to their organization. They know the virtue of living the motto: Hear it first and best here!

Organizational rhetoric can have what Cheney (1992) called "an individualistic bias" (p. 166). As organizations become larger, they become less personal, and businesses are often seen as being corrupted by the profit motive. Identities of people involved with each business as well as its products or services are caught up in this symbolism. For these reasons, Cheney reasoned that corporate rhetoric is moving beyond individual rhetors to develop an analytic model "that accounts for the corporate, collective nature of much of contemporary rhetoric, while avoiding the danger of reifying the organization (i.e., separating it analytically from its individual contributors)" (p. 178).

A critic of corporate communication practices, Sethi (1977) encouraged issue advocates to narrow the legitimacy gap between business performance and societal expectations. He was outraged by firms that tried to narrow the gap by denigrating societal expectations or by asserting that business performance meets them when such is not the case. He noted that companies that cry the loudest about their inability to gain access to media are often the most irresponsible. Sethi (1981) concluded that "a great number of advocacy campaigns contribute little of anything to the public's information base. Issues are presented with catchy headlines and simple messages that are conclusatory and deterministic. The primary emphasis is on reinforcing the sponsor's position" (p. 12). Despite misgivings, experience has demonstrated that companies cannot manage issues by dominating communication channels even though they ostensibly have the deep pockets needed to drown out voices of opposition. Opinions continue to be at odds with one another.

Publics can be defined by how people communicate and what they communicate about. As such, they are best understood as components of communities having rights and responsibilities to the nature of the community in which they live. For many years, advocates have reasoned that such communication is best seen as occurring in a community and for the collective interest of the community, however narrow (a locale), metaphoric (such as a demographic category like parents seeking child safety), regional, national, and global. By whatever configuration, community is both a context and an incentive to achieve high-quality dialogue (Hallahan, 2004; Kruckeberg & Starck, 1988; Leeper, 2001).

However, as Brummett (1995) warned, the opinions of a community may actually stifle better thought rather than liberate it. People may resist change by arguing that some position, advocated perhaps by an interest group, is contrary to conventional wisdom of the community and therefore wrong. One can recall the rhetoric of abolition encountering such resistance. On such matters, Goodnight (1982) took a constitutive approach suggesting that meaning varies by public. Human communication is a strategic response to some problem. This paradigm centers on reconciling difference and is fraught with consequences for the participants in the dialogue. In this sense, he reasoned, "While public discourse makes open and common collective preference, it also provides an arena where interests conduct controversy and openly struggle for power" (p. 429). Advocacy, in this sense, can be seen as narrow and self-interested or community spirited and a means for collective reflection (Heath, 2006a, 2007a). The challenge is to foster discourse that helps each society to be more fully functioning.

Such discourse traditionally has arisen from recognition of problems collectively or individually encountered. Although some writers believe that problem recognition is a modern twist on communication management, the tendency to address problems and seek solutions is timeless. We can well imagine, particularly with a risk management paradigm in mind, that from the earliest dawning moments of human existence, people have brought problems to one another's attention and sought to determine the best solution.

The Issue of Issues Communication

As has been argued throughout this book, the solution to conflict between two or more entities may not be resolved by communication alone. It may, and often does, require a better strategic business plan, one that incorporates improved standards of corporate social responsibility (CSR). Issues communication, when it occurs, is likely to exhibit varying degrees of planning, as in public policy planning and issues communication planning. It is strategic. At heart in such matters inevitably reside issues of trust and power. Various sides to a controversy may try to bully other sides and force the framing of issues, rather than justify their preferred framing of the controversy. Reporters, news directors, and editorial staff often like to believe they are the independent vetters of issues. However, one reporting style is to point to two opposing points of view and go no farther in the name of "balanced and fair reporting." Or, they invoke frames on issues by what they cover, when they cover it, and who they select to speak on the various sides.

The process and content of issues communication can advance dialogues or frustrate them. In fighting issues, companies have engaged in personal attacks of critics, impugning their motives and character. Companies have engaged spies to infiltrate activist organizations and have sought to cut off the money stream of support to such groups. Companies tell half-truths and have worked to suppress relevant facts. Companies enter Web chat rooms under the cloak of friendship, edit wiki entries to make their company look better, or cover up historical transgressions by the company. They may work to diminish a problem by showing that it is caused by a value such as "progress." Any corporate action, by this logic and no matter how offensive to a community of interest, can be approved in the name of "progress." Corporate strategists have tried to cut activists out of the dialogue. They have tried to drown the opposition in deep-pocket advertising or by strategic philanthropy simply used to paint the organization as being a good citizen. They have created front groups to advocate positions under the cloak of secrecy (see Chapter 7).

By the same token activists, religious organizations, nonprofits, and nongovernmental organizations often use strategic methods that are intended to advance their cause but also may distort the dialogue. Some activists use extreme stunts or events to call attention to problems. They have damaged property and engaged in trespass. They have lied and used a few anecdotal cases as the norm. They have engaged in shock events designed to grab headlines and embarrass those who have created government or corporate activities and policies. The ethics of engagement need to be judged by how well they advance rather than distort the quality of the dialogue used to collectively manage risks.

Rhetoric fosters truth as best as can be done; it serves to solve problems that confront the public. To support this claim, Bitzer (1987) featured principles drawn from the rhetorical heritage. One principle is that "*public communication . . . depends on its subject matter and its function: its subject matter is constituted of problems, questions, information, proposals, and the like that are related to the public's business or affairs; the function of public communication is consideration and conduct of that business*" (p. 425). People experience and respond to problems with personal concern and constraint, which is the classic rhetorical context.

A public can be an advocate as well as the target of others' appeals. The second principle, as Bitzer (1987) reasoned, advocates that sides contend with one another as representatives of the public in the public interest; "*their messages and judgments are shaped significantly by their perception (whether purposeful or not) that their values, interests, and premises accord with—and, as it were, derive authority from—the public*" (p. 425). Each public advocate stands in for others who are silent but intellectually interested in the debate. A third principle of public communication, Bitzer contended, centers on norms of excellence: This practice reflects decisions in statement and principle that are "*as excellent as they can be in probable and contingent circumstances*" (p. 426).

The fourth characteristic of public communication realizes that "*communicator and audience are participants, both are centers of intelligence, both are obliged to weigh evidence and reason soundly, and both must be prepared to express information, objections, and arguments to the end that, in the contest of ideas, the probable truths and the most reliable decisions will emerge*" (Bitzer, 1987, p. 426). Interests and wills of the participants are both explicit and implicit to the process but never independent of it. In all, "The functions of discourse are to portray or argumentatively establish the truth and reveal and correct the false" (p. 427).

Issues management is not merely communication, opinion surveying, or corporate planning. If these activities are integrated at the executive level, an organization can participate as a citizen in a rapidly changing political and social environment. What is required is getting messages to appropriate audiences and working to satisfy the needs of key publics to understand and appreciate the organization's point of view. Such efforts are best when the organization seeking to communicate listens, respects, and responds thoughtfully to the claims proposed by others. Advocacy, in this way, can turn inward as well as outward. The essence of issues communication is best captured by the rhetorical heritage whereby each advocate seeks to make honest and candid contributions to the dialogue in ways that foster mutual knowledge, understanding, evaluation, policy positions, and identity. This is best conceived as a collective process rather than one dominated by one voice. It needs to be multivoice. To the extent that one voice seeks to mute the felt interests of others, it is likely that such efforts increase the heat in the dialogue rather than turn it down or make it more constructive. Classically, activism and even terrorism are more likely when interested, cognitively involved persons are cut out of the process. For that reason, issues communicators need to be attentive to the process, infrastructure, and content of the conversation. Communication cannot fix problems that require improved operations. Organizations must listen to and adopt well-reasoned points of view advocated by other opinion leaders and key publics. The wisest response by an organization is to change its policies and operations because it cannot defend them.

Before turning to more specific aspects of issues communication, a few generalizations will help frame that discussion:

- Issues communication is strategic; the audiences may be a more general population or a highly targeted organization or population. Sources of messages seek to influence specific or general audiences and achieve definable outcomes.

- The kind of organization is likely to predict the kind of communication. Entrepreneurial organizations, especially companies, will tend to be more proactive and even seek stances that create new premises and perspectives. More stable and bureaucratic organizations, especially traditional companies, are likely to present their image and frame arguments in ways that maintain a stable operating environment, even support the status quo or a return "to the good old days." This latter perspective is even more the tendency for organizations or industries in a period of decline.

- Organizations that raise and attack issues tend to do so by focusing on problems and introducing key facts that may be less well known or underused in planning, while relying on a higher order of values to change the playing field.

- Organizations tend to couple their issue position with their mission/ vision and strategic business plan, whether raising issues or defending against criticism. Thus, the issue position reflects a management perception of the organization and perhaps its sense of power resource management. The stance also reflects a perception of the relationship between the organization and the target of criticism.

- How issues are raised and addressed reflects the culture and the ways decisions are made in each society.

- The fundamental rationale for framing, supporting, and resolving issues rests on the assumption that society is formed and managed for the collective management of risks (see Douglas, 1992).

- Issue positions necessarily reflect positively or negatively the political economy where they occur. In one way or another, they create, reflect, refine, or seek to refute narratives that create the terministic screens that guide policy and action in each culture and society.

At the core of issues of issues communication is narrative theory, which can ultimately help the good organization communicate well.

Narrative Theory

One interpretative frame for evaluating an organization's performance is the narrative of events enacted by this organization, set in the frame of responsible and concerned operations and appropriate behavior. Events occur in context. That context exhibits the key aspects of a narrative, a story. How the story is resolved determines whether the crisis goes away or leads to an issue having public policy importance.

No issue develops or is maintained in a vacuum. Reporters frame news events in terms of past events (including the history of each organization and its reputation for managing, suffering, or avoiding issues or crises) that are similar and relevant. People ask themselves whether an immediate event is a continuation of a story—a narrative—they have come to expect as they think about an organization or industry. Or they may ask whether this event is a dramatic shift in narrative—a new story.

People think of events that occur in their world in narrative terms, including archetypes. Interpretation of the events treats them as acts by characters that have a past, present, and future. Events are meaningful because they are part of a larger plot and have a plot of their own. Each plot can demonstrate some theme, some relevant point of view. The life of an organization is a narrative, a sequence of events played out by an arrangement of people (characters having various personae) over time (according to a plot that exhibits a coherent theme). Stories also have order. As enacted by organizations, they must lead to order, through the dialectic of what happened surrounding an issue, what is learned from what happened, and what will be done in the future based on what was learned.

Narrative functions represent "a universal medium of human consciousness" (Lucaites & Condit, 1985). White (1981) described narrative as a "meta-code" for transactional transmission of "messages about shared reality" (p. 2). Narrative theory, devised by Fisher (1984, 1985a, 1985b, 1987, 1989), adds depth to the view that people enact their lives as actors in an undirected play (Cronen, Pearce, & Harris, 1982; Pearce & Cronen, 1980). Narratives are a way of ordering the events of the world that would otherwise seem unpredictable or incoherent. Through narratives, people structure their experiences and actions. Narratives express a set of preferences, the values of the persons who ascribe to those narratives, and the ability to create and share a variety of social realities.

Narratives have substantial rhetorical potency because they are a natural means for understanding the theme that runs throughout a series of events. The primary purpose of rhetorical narrative is to advocate something beyond itself, demonstrating the value for exploring narrative in the evolution of social and political consequences (Fisher, 1985b).

Aristotle pointed out that people do not necessarily experience organizations; rather, they experience the communication that organizations use to explain their actions and the communication about organizations (Elwood, 1995). People, especially in more economic-based countries, have become accustomed to companies speaking as individuals, sharing their thoughts and perspectives on a range of issues and not just those pertaining particularly to the company's or industry's core job functions. For example, chemical companies often voice their opinions about community affairs in which their manufacturing or electrical generating plants are situated. Knowing the common narratives of a group, organization, or society allows strategic issues management (SIM) managers the framework for scanning, analyzing, identifying, and monitoring stakeholders' and stakeseekers' perceptions, as well as participating in shared dialogue and decision making (Palenchar & Heath, 2007).

Two important forms of narrative, in relation to understanding social consequences of particular narrative forms and functions, are unity of direction and unity of purpose. Rhetorical contexts inherently include oppositionality or advocates taking one side or another in dialogue. Since the rhetorical function of narrative advocates a particular understanding of the facts to a particular point of view, it must be voiced and couched in terms of unity and single purposefulness. Quintilian (1966) noted, "For we must state our facts like advocates, not witnesses" (p. 109). Fisher (1987) argued that the unities of direction and purpose combine to form discourse dependency. In this sense, rhetorical narrative is not complete and self-sufficient textually. The claim supported by rhetorical narrative must be articulated outside of the narration as part of a whole and changing world:

> Because the speaker in a rhetorical situation always seeks material gain in some measure, he or she is literally invested in the outcome of the rhetorical process and is therefore expected by an audience to assert and accept responsibility for the power and veracity of the narratives that are featured in discourse. (p. 100)

This view essentially supports Aristotle's (1932) contention that investigation of public discourse cannot be separated from the role of discourse in society. Within society discourse, power is exercised by the groups that are able to frame their interests as those of other groups. Narratives are used to create, maintain, and continue the interpretation and stabilize the distribution of power within a society. In the marketplace of ideas, there are many different stories interpreting any one event. The acceptance of one narrative or interpretation leads to the elimination or muting of the alternatives. This in turn also leads to the conclusion that a group can rise to power when its interpretations or narratives are accepted in the wrangle on the marketplace of ideas (Heath, 1992). Narratives allow people to identify with and understand one another as participating in similar events and having had comparable experiences. Thus, people achieve a shared understanding that helps them to predict the direction that events and actions will and should take. Narrative theory is also fundamental to the good organization communicating well under the direction of SIM.

The Good Organization Communicating Well

In ancient Rome (1st century A.D.), Quintilian set the good person speaking well as the standard of rhetorical excellence. That standard asked people to be morally sound and to learn to communicate in ways that enhanced the likelihood that their influence would prevail against persons of inferior moral character and inadequate rhetorical ability. Today, in this age of the large organization, the corporate rhetor, we may adopt Quintilian's challenge to be this: the good organization speaking well. As Coombs (1992) reasoned, "Members of publics will not support the position of an organization unless they believe that the issue is a legitimate one and that the issue management and the organization's policy proposal also are legitimate" (p. 101).

Character is the persona created by what organizations say and do and how they present their issue position and go about their activities. One of the important dimensions of character is the legitimacy of the various entities communicating, the voices contending over issues. Character is not only what the organization asserts or hopes audiences will attribute to it, but it is also, in final analysis, the traits that the audiences attribute to the organization that define its legitimacy to speak and act on each issue. A persona can affect how key publics react to the organization's public policy stance, and its public policy stance helps establish its persona. As well as being vital to its public policy plan, the persona becomes a factor in how well the organization is received in the marketplace. Advocacy communication, for instance, can advance or harm the organization's interests in the public policy and marketplace arenas. In doing so, does it harm others while favoring some? Do that choice and action demonstrate good character or narrow self-interest?

These functions should not be thought of as separate and independent but interdependent. The attributes that become associated with an organization may differentiate it from others; that point could be contestable, as in the case of one activist group being more conservative or outraged on environmental issues. These associations and differentiations merge to establish identity in the minds of key publics (and lead them to identify with it). This identity may exhibit goodwill for the interests and identity of the targeted audiences—the persona of the organization being one that takes stands and acts in ways that are in the interests of its stakeholders. Combined, these factors constitute the persona of each organization.

To advance the topic of the good organization speaking well, we address three more specific topics: (a) What is the interconnection between image and issue, (b) what cultural archetypes define image and character, and (c) how do the voices establish their legitimacy to speak on each issue? How an organization frames an argument and responds to an issue (including raising it) reflects its character, might enhance or harm that character, and is likely to help or harm the cause.

Images and Issues: Complements and Counterparts

Again we remind ourselves that SIM concerns might not be solved by communication alone but require improved standards of CSR. One proactive issue response is to clean up the organization and bring it to a higher standard of CSR. Once the job of cleaning house is thoroughly enacted though never finished, the organization can benefit by putting its image forward to the judgment of stakeholders. In that sense, issues management could be conceptualized as image management or what some call *reputation management.* An organization that is viewed favorably—is more legitimate and meets key publics' expectations—is likely to suffer less criticism, have a more acceptable voice in such matters, and suffer less public policy constraint than is its less favored counterparts. Thus, issues and image complement one another.

One way to think of organizational image is as the attitude key publics hold regarding the organization. An attitude is an expression of the belief that an attitude object—that about which an attitude is formed—is associated with key traits that are perceived to be positive or negative. That about which people hold a positive attitude is associated with favorable outcomes. An object that generates a negative attitude is believed to lead to unfavorable outcomes (Fishbein & Ajzen, 1975). Thus, if the audience assumes that pollution is bad, an organization that pollutes will generate a negative attitude and is believed to lead to unfavorable outcomes, such as harm to health or a threat to a plant or animal species. Conversely, if an organization claims and demonstrates the accuracy of the claim that it reduces pollution, it is likely to generate a positive attitude and lead to favorable outcomes.

Factors that key stakeholders use to assess a company's image may not be controversial. If controversy exists regarding an organization's image, it may be less of a matter of which criteria should be used to judge it than concerns about whether the organization meets those criteria. Considering ingredients relevant to the attitudes that constitute corporate image, Garbett (1981) defined corporate image advertising by stressing its unique outcomes:

- To educate, inform, or impress the public with regard to the company's policies, functions, facilities, objectives, ideals, and standards.

- To build favorable opinion about the company by stressing the competence of the company's management, its scientific know-how, manufacturing skills, technological progress, product improvements, and contribution to social advancement and public welfare, and, on the other hand, to offset unfavorable publicity and negative attitudes.

- To build up the investment qualities of the company's securities or to improve its financial structure.

- To sell the company as a good place in which to work, often in a way designed to appeal to college graduates or to people with certain skills. (p. 13)

How an organization's image is interpreted demonstrates the close connection between image or reputation (even brand equity) and sociopolitical issues. Sometimes attributes that key publics use to form the image (think attitude) regarding a company, product, service, or industry seem relatively uncontroversial and innocuous. However, critics of business behavior may not see these attributes as supporters do. However long, for instance, an anticorporate set of attitudes has prevailed among some publics, the case is easily made that the very nature of a corporation is viewed as a negative image.

Such distinction or blurring is discussed in Chapter 7 as a part of how, when, and why corporate communication should be regulated. Such efforts often focus on distinctions between commercial and political communication. A marketing mentality, by this logic, sees organizations through marketing terministic screens.

Their virtue is the ability to sell products and services. Critics of companies, especially, see them more as political than as commercial entities construing public policy to private ends—the corruption of the profit motive. Trying to distinguish between commercial and political communication, business critic Meadow (1981) advised differentiating between product and nonproduct advertising. The first falls into what some call commercial communication, and the latter is political, the result of contests between critics whose values differ. Nonproduct ads include a range of statements from those that support company images to those encouraging public support of political candidates and issues. Meadow reasoned that political communication results when controversy exists over the criteria by which organizations, products, or services are evaluated. Writers, such as Parenti (1986) and Gandy (1982), reasoned that premises that guide organizational choices and behaviors, as well as acceptable products and services, are in fact political. They challenge companies, as well as their supporters and critics, to examine political and hegemonic implications basic to the rationale for corporate activities. (As will be seen in Chapter 7, such logics would reduce the likelihood that corporate speech would be regulated because traditionally, political speech is not regulated, whereas commercial speech is.)

Sethi (1977) asserted that issues advertising is a type of corporate image advertising. It is, he reasoned, "part of that genre of advertising known as corporate image or institutional advertising. It is concerned with the propagation of ideas and the elucidation of controversial social issues deemed important by its sponsor in terms of public policy" (1987, p. 281). If one view of corporate activity or policy is preferred, it is a matter of image. Issues advertising typically results from the desire to defend or promote a socioeconomic point of view and establish a platform of fact as well as a platform of evaluation on which to judge and resolve issues, create identifications, and reduce risks.

Issues communication may mobilize or reinforce supporters rather than convert opponents. A substantial portion of issue advertising targets readers of specialty publications and of editorial sections of major newspapers and news magazines. The Internet has increasingly become a venue for issues communication. It is a cheap venue for issues communication, and rather than the shot across the bow nature of traditional mass communication, the Internet makes arguments available as desired and on a 24/7 schedule.

Thoughtful consideration of issues communication options is not designed to help issues communicators solve idle riddles but to challenge them to think through their objectives and the attendant communication requirements and societal benefits—their service to the community of interest. Thinking about communication options is brought into sharp focus by considering how the money spent on such campaigns creates, restores, or maintains stakeholder relationships in ways that foster harmony and a fair exchange of stakes.

As this section demonstrated, the content and role of the communication in ongoing discourse help define its character and the character of the participants. Knowing the kind of communication and seeing it positioned into an array of options can help issues communicators to decide what needs to be said and how the message should be tailored to specific needs. One can reason that the most positive engagement occurs to advance the issue and the community of interest rather than the narrow self-interest of one of the participants. Such observations do not, and cannot deny, the importance of self-interest in issues controversy. But self-interest can become dysfunctional to the ability to be of high character and worthy of influence.

ARCHETYPAL IMAGES AND CHARACTER

One way to view character and image draws on a robust literature that features the prevalent role of archetypal characters. Mitroff (1983) suggested that managers can be analyzed as archetypal characters whose roles are variously constructive or destructive to the climate and culture, the shared meaning required for any organization to operate effectively. By extension, archetypal analysis gives insights into the charter and image of organizations as issues communicators. Who they are and how they work for or against the quality of the ongoing dialogue is instructive, evaluative, and open to strategic options by issues communicators. The dialogue is carried by "characters" in a drama, a narrative. Who the characters are (and the character they exhibit) is a vital component in the co-created meaning.

Advocates of issue positions exhibit personae that are vital to the campaign they are waging. These archetypes in various ways work toward outcomes that include the following: differentiation, association, identity, and goodwill. *Differentiation* results when products, services, issue discussions, procedures, and policy positions advocated by the sponsoring organization make it unique. *Associations* result from attributions that come to mind as a result of the actions, values, and traits that typify the company or industry such as being pro-environmental. *Identity* is the metaphoric residue of the archetype characteristic of the organization's bold advocate, technical expert-adviser, 800-pound gorilla, or defender of national security. *Goodwill* results when policies and actions of the organization benefit others and advance community interests: those of stakeseekers and stakeholders. Such goodwill leads to the granting rather than withholding of stakes.

Issues ads are likely to increase the awareness, readership, and impact if they increase or capture targeted audiences' cognitive involvement by demonstrating how the issue affects the self-interests or altruistic concerns of these audiences. One way to do that is through graphics as the U.S. Council for Energy Awareness (USCEA) did when it pictured Middle East characters, such as Saddam Hussein, as villains who could control the supply of oil to the United States. These 1990 ads depicted a cobra-headed snake with a body made up of barrels of foreign oil that is poised to strike U.S. citizens. Emphasizing the point that 40% of all oil used in the United States comes from abroad, the ad alleged that "excessive dependence on foreign oil could poison America's economy and our national security if our supply were ever disrupted." In another ad in1989, the USCEA used graphics to depict foreign oil as bait in a bear trap ready to spring shut on the United States.

Based on this overview of the elements of issues communication, the remainder of this section will explicate them. This discussion begins with an examination of organizational personae: differentiation, association, identity, and goodwill.

DIFFERENTIATION

Activists perhaps more than businesses seek differentiating archetypes. Greenpeace works to differentiate itself by using a strident attack dog archetype in contrast to its more staid and centrist counterpart, the Audubon Society. In differentiating its voice, PETA balances a wry sense of irony with a pointed challenge to protect animals. It has engaged top models to pose in calendars in which they claim to be willing to wear nothing rather than dress in the fur of animals raised and cruelly killed for vanity. The differentiation of activists includes the World Wildlife Fund, which positions itself as a community action and research organization rather than an activist organization known for engaging in protest. Nature Conservancy buys land and receives it through donations. Then it stewards the land for the community interest. It takes policy stands on conservation issues, engages in education, and promotes the value of the wise steward of the land as its archetype.

Differentiation not only works to give uniqueness to the voice and perspective advocated, but it can result from and foster brand equity—organizational reputation. Brand equity can have commercial benefits for businesses and fund-raising benefits for nonprofits, including activists, and government agencies that specialize in solving certain public policy needs.

Recently, Chevron has engaged in an advertising campaign to instantiate the archetype of technical adviser on matters of energy policy. One 2006 ad posed the claim that "Americans spend over one million dollars on energy every minute." Then, it asked, "So who has the power to change that?" In another ad, the company reasoned that the countries of the world all are energy dependent and therefore energy interdependent. Here is the archetype of the technical adviser. The messages, positioned in venues such as advertising but also placed at Chevron's Web site, raise tantalizing questions that focus on an issue relevant to oil and gas consumption. Thus, one ad made the point that "Russia, Iran and Qatar have 58% of the world's natural gas reserves. The U.S. has 3%." That fact is highly relevant to energy policy since natural gas is one of the most energy-friendly kinds of fuel. Another ad made a claim and then asked a question: "It took us 125 years to use the first trillion barrels of oil. We'll use the next trillion in 30. So why should you care?"

ASSOCIATION

Archetypes are selected, featured, and used in issues campaigns to create associations that establish the campaign sponsor as a worthy, legitimate participant in the issues dialogue. The nuclear generating industry in the United States has worked to feature safety, security, and environmental responsibility. Fear and mystique have surrounded the use of nuclear energy, which, during the 1980s and 1990s, was a top-of-mind issue. Today, a robust policy debate focuses on whether more nuclear generating facilities should be built to reduce U.S. domestic dependency on coal, which contributes to global warming and foreign energy sources. Safety is an attribute associated with the use of this fuel to generate electricity. There is concern that a catastrophic event could kill or seriously harm millions of people who live near nuclear generating facilities. In years of issues communication, the nuclear generating industry reasoned that its technology is widely accepted because it meets energy requirements as well as high safety standards, and now its differentiation relates to a green power source that does not cause global warning, though this ignores other issues and risks related to nuclear energy generation and wastes.

The campaign began when survey results by Opinion Research Corporation (1981) revealed that nearly the entire sample (99%) believed control of radioactive wastes was important. Almost as many respondents (94%) wanted close federal supervision of nuclear reactors. Eighty-five percent thought the

government should "require companies to give public notice of toxic substances they are making or handling." Ecology won out over energy; people
wanted solutions to technical problems and shortages while not abandoning
environmental protection.

The nuclear accident at the Soviet Chernobyl site drew international outcry and prompted legitimate concerns in the United States. The USCEA
responded with an ad to explain factually the differences in design between the
plant in Chernobyl and that at Three Mile Island. The question posed, "Why
what happened at Chernobyl didn't happen at Three Mile Island" (1986). The
answer associated U.S. plant design with safe design criteria. Using graphics as
well as text to explain, the ad indicated that radiation was unlikely to escape in
the event of an accident because it would be contained by a steel-reinforced
concrete containment structure with walls 4 feet thick. Additional concrete and
steel walls existed. The concrete floor was 11 feet thick. The ad stressed the following point: "One important part of 'defense in depth' is that America's commercial nuclear power plants (and most nuclear plants throughout the world)
have multiple protective barriers to contain the effects of an accident." The ad
associated the concept of nuclear generation with the attribute of safe operation, even in the event of an accident.

Activists seek associations typically drawn from their cause. One example
is the traditional shrimp harvesting methods, which drown turtles that must
surface to breath. Trawling methods keep them below the surface so long that
the turtles drown. These activists associate themselves with those turtles, which
they work to imbue with human characteristics. Similar positioning occurs in
those dedicated to protect old growth trees and gorillas. The World Wildlife
Fund uses the logos of the giant panda, one of the most familiar of the endangered species. Environmental groups feature stuffed animals and other means
for humanizing animals to raise awareness of the spirit of species, a strategy
targeted at reaching children in their formative years. They associate themselves with life and survival of huggable beings.

IDENTITY

Identity is one of those top-of-the-mind attributions that audiences assign
to issues communicators based on the association that group or differentiate
them as a class. Some of the class grouping leads them to positive or negative
archetypes.

Liar, Liar, Pants on Fire. Lying to the public is fatal. One incident involved a coal
producer's association advertisement in *The Wall Street Journal* featuring a "coal
miner" as the "man of the year." Rather than being a real miner, the spokesman
was later revealed to be a vice president in the association's advertising agency.

When this fact became known, the coal producer's image dropped dramatically (Stridsberg, 1977).

Technical Adviser. Organizations take aggressive stances to establish their voice as bold advocates or technically expert advisers. One of several industry public information organizations, the USCEA undertook an issue campaign to help the public understand and accept the technology and economic benefits of nuclear generation. Magazine and television ads used pastel colors and lively graphics to attract audience attention and highlight the issue position being set forth.

Activist leaders strive to position themselves as experts, advising key publics and audiences on the perils of not seeing problems and seeking solutions featured by the activists. Their expertise depends on their ability to define problems and craft socially viable and useful solutions.

Pity Party Cry Babies. Many of the archetypes used to create identity are positive, especially those that work to position the organization as an agent for responsible change. Wal-Mart, at times, has assumed a contrasting persona, even as it asks for passage of increased minimum wage to give its shoppers more expendable income. Wal-Mart speaks, as they say, with forked tongue since it sounds both self-interested and has been vilified for its poor treatment of most of its labor force.

Hammers. Long ago, companies and even federal agencies learned the perils of having an identity as a hammer, the voice that pounds the table for concurrence and says, "You are either with us or against us." Activists have lost voice when they attempt such divisive positioning as the archetype of their issue. They may, at least for a while, attract media attention and gain followers and donors, but the pounding can lose voice when the organization is seen merely as a rabble-rouser and the reasonable policy advocate as exhibiting common sense.

Competing archetypes can be seen at play in iconic issue contests such as that surrounding the policy development to determine what should be done to retire Shell's Brent Spar, a terminal buoy use to store crude oil gathered from production wells in the North Sea. Many such terminals have been used to store crude oil in a way that it can be loaded onto tankers to be taken to refineries. As the buoys near retirement, they need to be handled, as Shell proposed in its mission statement on this project, in ways that are scientifically sound, environmentally responsible, and financially solid. Those three concepts define the archetype of Shell and the collaborative decision-making consortium of respected scientific and engineering bodies and governmental agencies teamed to solve the problem. The solution was to scuttle the Brent Spar based on carefully assessed data and collective values. Greenpeace enacted the archetype of savior of the environment from becoming a "cesspool" and scuttled the effort to scuttle the Spar.

Rabble-rouser, steward of the land, champion of civil rights, bringer of energy, creator of sound financial markets: The list of archetypes is long and reads thoughtfully as dramatis personae in the various issues narratives that occur and recur as dialogue. Such dialogue can even become stale and scripted. It often is couched in the goodwill of some interest or cause other than its own, but such matters themselves are contestable.

GOODWILL

Issues advocates adopt the persona of speaking to the goodwill of society. In the midst of the auto safety controversy in the 1980s, General Motors sought to demonstrate its public service commitment by discussing drunk driving and the use of seat belts to help the public cope with the perils of driving. Today, insurance companies work to foster goodwill by asking parents to "have that talk" with teenagers, including discussion about driving safety. Likewise, environmental activists position themselves as goodwill advocates for the focal point of their cause. They fight for endangered species, virgin redwood forests slated for harvesting, or humane treatment of laboratory and farm animals. Goodwill is the lifeblood of activism.

BATTLE FOR LEGITIMACY

Since at least the late 1970s and Sethi's (1977) concern for the legitimacy gap, this topic has received substantial attention. It is a key aspect of persona and brand equity. It is created as meaning and responds to as well as is evaluated by standards reflected in the expectations held by other discussants and audiences (stakeholder/stakeseeker publics). It is a matter of meaning, an independent and dependent variable, in the contest to create and enact shared meaning. As Vaara, Tienari, and Laurila (2006) have argued, "*Legitimacy means a discursively created sense of acceptance in specific discourses or orders of discourse*" (p. 793). These authors reason that there are five discursive legitimation strategies: normalization, authorization, rationalization, moralization, and narrativization.

Normalization is founded on what is expected or normal. Thus, for instance, chemical manufacturing or toy manufacturing companies are being legitimate voices on matters related to emission levels and design safety of toys. Also, we would expect the voices of regulatory agencies and environmental activists and consumer/child safety activists. Normalization in part exists simply by the natural order of who has and therefore who should be speaking. As new voices emerge, they may replace or merely join the chorus.

If normal voices fail to meet the expectations others hold for the continuation of a substantive and reflective discourse, they may be marginalized or ignored.

Authorization results from appeals to authority. Scientists become authorities on matters of risk. Elected officials have authority to speak. So do members of the legal profession and jurists. By election and appointment, as well as special training, these voices become legitimate to speak because of their authorized position in society and as those positions are relevant to each issue.

Rationalization depends on some variation of instrumental or functional justification. People whose interests are affected or at least appear to be affected by an organization are legitimate voices regarding what it does and whether it meets their expectations. Customers, therefore, can speak to product safety, the fairness of business practices, the equality of how they are treated, and even to matters of environmental responsibility. The ideology of various political economies gives rise to rational legitimacy, simply defined as having a rational reason for voicing support or opposition on each issue.

Moralization focuses on value expectations. Activists tend to frame issues in higher moral standards, voicing expectations above those that they believe guide the target organization's policies and practices: strategic business plan and standards of corporate responsibility. Targets of such challenges may discursively respond that the level of action and policy indeed is sufficient or that they have the moral agency to achieve higher standards because of the virtue of such choices.

Narrativization finds a parallel in archetypes, as discussed above. The larger rationale for appeals to legitimacy arises from the dominant and competing narratives that define the role and performance expectations in each situation (Heath, 1994). The assumption of this aspect of legitimacy is that each society and various parts of each society (or community) have operating narratives that define which actions and voices are legitimate. To cause one archetype/persona to be less legitimate or more legitimate requires a change in the narratives that are relative to the discussion.

Discursive efforts to battle legitimacy correspond to the recurring themes of fact, value, and policy. Facts can support or contradict actions and expectations relevant to the legitimacy of various voices. Moral challenges are vital to battles over legitimacy. Policy is the enactment by the voices that are legitimate, enacting standards and plans on behalf of the community.

This section has discussed the value of organizational image and reputation management. Key elements seem central to any organization's persona: differentiation, association, identity, and goodwill. These factors become featured in what each organization does and says. They are essential rhetorical components in the efforts of businesses, industries, activists, and governmental agencies. They guide the organization's efforts to manage its reputation.

Framing: Giving Issues Argumentative Context

Throughout this book, we have featured the essential role of co-created meaning, fact, value, policy, identification, and reputation. By implication, at least, one can assume that all of these matters are not given but subject to competing interpretations. Stressing the reality that issues are framed and the framing of an issue is part of the advocacy battle, Campbell (1996) compared scientists for whom "the most important concern is the discovery and testing of certain kinds of truths" with "rhetoricians (who study rhetoric and take a rhetorical perspective) who would say, 'Truths cannot walk on their own legs. They must be carried by people to other people. They must be explained, defended, and spread through language, argument, and appeal'" (p. 3). From this foundation, Campbell reasoned, rhetoricians take the position "that unacknowledged and unaccepted truths are of no use at all" (p. 3). The rhetorical tradition is founded in facts because since the age of Aristotle, rhetors have been required to assert and demonstrate their propositions by producing fact.

Even the logic of risk as a scientific matter is captured in the following question: "How safe is safe enough?" That scientific question is challenged by a cultural interpretation framed in this question: "How fair is safe enough?" (Tansey & Rayner, 2009). The logic of that question contrasts the scientist's ability to calculate risk, which then is challenged by those who may, have, or will suffer the risk. Framing, at least in part, depends in part on wrestling with questions relevant to how information and argument should be interpreted, evaluated, and joined. In matters of risk, for instance, some have advocated the use of the precautionary principle as a means for causing no harm by adopting untried technologies. Some see that principle as appropriately cautious, for instance, when dealing with matters of the potentially dreadful harms of unknown or unpredictable outcomes of biotechnology. Others see the principle as overly conservative, producing harm by not adopting a technology that could serve humankind (Maguire & Ellis, 2009).

From a media perspective, framing discordant news events is a dominant fact in the contemporary practice of journalism (McCombs, Einsiedel, & Weaver, 1991). In part, this is a result of the common use of the story or narrative in telling an event: "Central to the genre of journalism is the story" (p. 35). As such, framing plays a crucial role in public relations (Hallahan, 1999) and SIM. If the product of communication is viewed not as information but as the quality of the social relationship it supports, then understanding who and what media frame within the coverage of issues is an important message element of the social relationship.

Uncertainty and risk (conflicts) are often attractive issues for media. Framing theories can help explain the influence the resulting media coverage has on issue developments related to SIM. As such, according to Bridges and

Nelson (2000), "Framing theorists suggest that the way an issue is presented—the frame—especially through the media, can affect public perceptions of the issue" (p. 100). Framing concepts related to public relations suggest that what is stated or omitted can define issues such as risk events for audiences. As a result, media build a framework of expectations regarding risks associated with various technologies (e.g., manufacturing of chemicals) by making risks visible, providing a context for evaluation, and shaping expectations about similar or related risks (Nelkin, 1989).

Framing involves a combination of selection and salience. According to Entman (1993), "To frame is to select some aspects of a perceived reality and make them more salient in a communicating text, in such a way as to promote a particular problem definition, causal interpretation, moral evaluation and/or treatment recommendation" (p. 52). He also suggested that media frames could define problems, diagnose causes, make ethical judgments, and suggest solutions. Goffman (1974) conducted some of the earliest work related to understanding the concept of framing and how receivers process information. He argued that people need a way to organize their thoughts and the related discourse. As a result, they form frames or a "schemata of interpretation" (p. 21).

As Entman (1993) described, frames can also be used to describe how communicators build messages. In this context, text contains frames that are manifested in the presence or absence of key linguistic, syntactic, lexical, and semantic elements that "provide thematically reinforcing clusters of facts or judgments" (p. 52). The way that media frame an issue can be significantly influenced by their use of sources. This can depend on several variables, including the journalist's trust in the source, familiarity with the source, and the ability of the source to gain the attention of the reporter, all affecting the amount and type of coverage (Einsiedel & Thorne, 1999).

Entman (1993) identified frames in four locations within the communication process: communicators, text, receivers, and culture. "The text contains frames, which are manifested by the presence or absence of certain key words, stock phrases, stereotypical images, source of information, and sentences that provide thematically reinforcing clusters of facts or judgments" (p. 52). As a result, the language selected by issues managers influences perceptions of those events. As Edelman (1988) argued, "It is language about political events, not the events in any other sense, that people experience; even developments that are close by take their meaning from the language that depicts them" (p. 104).

Framing can ultimately help public relations practitioners and issues managers better understand how key stakeholders navigate the information environment by providing a means to deconstruct the media narratives and information that frame risk communication. This is important, as Einsiedel and Thorne (1999) noted that a significant source of public information is mass media. As a result, people can be influenced by its content, "but simply that, over time, the media can be an important—if not the only—source of information for various publics on many issues" (p. 52). As suggested by Hallahan (1999), one of framing's inherent strengths might lie in the concept's "emphasis on providing context within which information presented and processed allows framing to be applied across a broad spectrum of communication situations" (p. 209).

Framing occurs as various issues combatants apply a premise they prefer to use to interpret, mount, and respond to each issue argument. For instance, in matters of business or private-sector controversy, critics start by framing such issues as "profit corrupts." Thus, if the argument focuses on mine safety, the critics reason that all of what the mining companies say is tainted by their desire for profits above safety.

How an issue is framed is contestable because the framing can influence its strength or weakness in the dialogue. So, issues are framed in ways that position them and those who advocate for and against various positions so that they focus on public relations field dynamics "of multipublic formation, evolution, and interaction" (Springston & Keyton, 2001, p. 117). A vital part of issues monitoring and analysis, as discussed in Chapter 3, is to determine how each issue is being framed, by whom, and to what consequence to the quality of the dialogue about the issue. Thus, framing is neither an idle matter nor the matter of only one party in the discourse. It is co-created through the engagement.

Relying on the theory of social construction of reality (parallel to Burke's theory of terministic screens), Hallahan (1999) reasoned that issues debate is enacted by framing and responding to competing frames. As he concluded, "A *frame* limits or defines the message's meaning by shaping the inferences that individuals make about the message" (p. 207). Such frames are influenced by the overarching interpretive narratives that support and constrain various interpretations. As such, frames depend on syntactical structures, script structures, and various rhetorical structures. These structures affect the cognitive interpretations the combatants use. "Framing's emphasis on *providing context* within which information is presented and processed allows framing to be applied across a broad spectrum of communication situations" (p. 209).

To refine the understanding of framing, Hallahan (1999) reasoned that at least seven frame types exist. Recall the introduction of this topic in Chapter 3, as part of the discussion of issues analysis. *Situation as frame features time and space.* The nature of national security, as well as the debate of relevant measures, changed dramatically in the United States on September 11, 2001, when terrorists hijacked planes and used them as weapons against targets. Advocacy regarding global warming works to impose various situational frames on a common set of facts. Some see the situation as caused by human activity. That argumentative frame is used by religious conservatives who believe the Book of Genesis requires that humans be good stewards of the Earth. Their religious opponents believe all acts are the Will of God, and nothing humans can do will affect that will, even if it means having to accommodate to global warming.

Framing of attributes focuses on standard means for characterizing objects, events, and people. Thus, companies are tainted by profit, governmental agencies are tainted by the politics of influences, and activists are "tree huggers." Following 9/11, the Bush administration framed virtually every policy position as being central to the War on Terrorism, designed to "keep Americans safe." Safety became a defining attribute of each policy, despite the fact that 40,000 U.S. residents die in automobile accidents each year, far more than the 3,100 who died in the terrorist attack. Such framing is also quite relevant to matters of reputation and brand equity.

Framing of choices addresses the issue as offering alternatives that are variously risky or safe, rewarding or harmful. If we define issues as contestable matters, an essential part of that contest focuses on which choices are most enlightened.

Framing of actions draws on interpretations of which acts lead to rewards and avoid harms—to achieve some desirable goal. Actions result from choices, and therefore, framing of choices is vital to ferreting out the actions that might be taken and the rewards or harms from the various ones. Of this frame, Hallahan (1999) wrote,

> Whereas the framing of attributes involves focusing attention on inherent qualities of an object, and whereas the framing of risk choices focuses on willingness of individuals to take risks, framing of actions focuses on persuasive attempts to maximize cooperation in which no independent options or choices are involved. (p. 215)

Framing of issues centers, as we have suggested above, on efforts by cooperating, competing, and even conflicting voices to "examine alternative interpretations of social reality" (Hallahan, 1999, p. 217).

Framing of responsibility addresses who or what is responsible for the problem and its solution that are being considered. Such contests are often fundamental to issues leading to and emerging from crises. Attribution of responsibility might be as broad as religious narrative interpretation, Will of God, constant evolution, and change of the global environment or as narrow as individual corporate and personal acts to reduce carbon emissions. So, we find these conflicting frames at play in the global warming debate.

Framing of news brings into the equation the editorial positions taken by various media companies. It also results from the preferences of reporters, editors, news directors, and executives. During the reporting on Katrina, those who wanted to criticize the federal and local government framed the news to draw adverse attention to the incompetence of those governmental agencies. Those reporters who favored the federal administration pointed to facts that attributed responsibility for failure at the local or state level. Regional and economic narratives predict the framing. Houston media are likely to frame energy policy different from California or Massachusetts media. Midwest media portray agricultural themes different from urban locations. Note also that media tend to report and focus on the risk manifested: car accidents, product recall, mine collapses, murders, sexual predators, and out-of-control entertainers. The theme seems to be that focusing on harm is a useful aspect of the collective management of risk.

How issues are framed is often very controversial. It is contestable. One can imagine that the richness of the dialogue on all-important issues depends on how many involved voices share their opinions on the ways the issues are framed and how they can best be settled through collaborative decision making. It is important to realize that activists serve a valuable role because their unique frames must be considered, respected, and treated for what they can bring to each issue (Reber & Berger, 2005).

Media Effects in a Multitiered Society

SIM recognizes that issues are discussed in various ways, especially with bias and in varying degrees of depth. Popular culture reflects as well as creates and disseminates various interpretive themes and premises that work their way into and reflect issue debates. It is part of the rhetorical mix of voices that reflect and shape issue dialogues. Such dialogues exhibit the characteristic of statement and counterstatement (Burke, 1969b; Heath, 2001).

Dialectic, the cooperative use of competition, progresses from division through merger to identification. "A rhetorician, I take it, is like one voice in a dialogue. Put several such voices together, with each voicing its own special assertion, let them act upon one another in cooperative competition, and you get a dialectic that, properly developed can lead to views transcending the limitations of each" (Burke, 1951, p. 203). The dialogue moves from act, through counteract, to the lesson learned. In issues debate, an organization or spokesperson suffers opposition based on what it does or says: "The dialectical (agonistic) approach to knowledge is through the act of assertion, whereby one 'suffers' the kind of knowledge that is the reciprocal of this act" (Burke, 1969a, pp. 39–40).

In the societal dialogue, rhetors of every kind apply, refine, and reapply warrants or premises that subsequently serve the basis for interpretation and evaluation of facts, evaluations, policies, and identifications. Featuring culture theory, Leichty and Warner (2001) reasoned, "*A way of life* consists of a preferred pattern of *social relations* and a *cultural bias* or set of shared values and beliefs about human society and the natural world" (p. 63). Such biases constitute cultural topoi, the foundations that people share that allow them to make decisions, reconcile differences, and engage in divisive and irreconcilable debates over many matters, framed as private and public policy issues.

Another way to understand the logic of that conclusion is to draw on a robust body of literature that examines how issues come about, who owns them, and how they evolve, devolve, or disappear. This perplexity can best be understood by examining media effects in a multitiered society where media, politicians, activists, and others compete to define, prime, make salient, and support issues as they are discussed within various zones of meaning. These zones form tiers whereby those at "the top" of an issue know more about it, help frame it, prime others to become attentive to it, and otherwise own the issue. SIM is a struggle for issue ownership in the media and other communication venues because how an issue is resolved and in what communication context, including collaborative decision making, depends on how it survives in society itself. As much as we might like for all issues to be resolved through collaborative decision making among the key players, we also know that how an issue plays out in such sessions is never separate from how that issue is surviving in popular discussion. Although some lines of analysis focus their attention on the tug of war between politicians and media for issue ownership, others expand this dialogue to include the entirety of individual opinion makers and organizational voices that join in a wrangle of preferences and ideals.

Tiers can easily be distinguished by imagining how different people (based on degree of being informed or knowledge of a topic) share and even add to a zone of meaning. For some persons in the top tier of an issue, they might be able to craft a substantial statement based on what they know: their knowledge of facts, the richness of their evaluations, and the depth and detail of what they know about policy options. Others at a lower level might know something but less. Perhaps at the lowest level, individuals might only know the topic or a few key words on the topic. For instance, those concerned about illegal immigration in 2007 (but at the lowest level of the tier) might merely think, "Send them home, build a wall, deny them work, and implement current laws." Any or all of those brief, slogan-like positions could be evidence of a heartfelt position but lack much in detail with which to clearly and firmly discuss the topic and make a truly informed decision and recommendation. We even call such opinions a "knee-jerk reaction." This characterization does not deny the feeling and motivational quality of what the person holds as belief and attitude; it merely suggests a paucity of information and a depth of analysis that others at a higher tier would have on the topic and its many issues.

Long ago, professionals and academics realized the confusing and conflicting nature of public opinion. Also understood in varying degrees of acuity is the fact that what issues some in society might understand in detail, others might not know at all. We have tiers of influence and knowledge on many issues. In one sense, the old and new media foster these tiers but often do so by pandering to opinions and reinforcing them rather than taking a leadership role to form opinions that might in some sense actually achieve consensus. As Noelle-Neumann (1983) noted, "Most researchers assume that the mass media have a decisive effect on people's conceptions of reality" (p. 157). However, media often reflect sentiments that form in the minds of publics, some of which are closely identified with issue activism. Television programming and Internet chatter and other media presentations probably reflect, follow, and reinforce rather than lead in ways that create opinion. If a sizable segment of the public were not convinced that corporations are acting against public interests, negative broadcast portrayals of business on entertainment and information programming could not maintain their ratings with such programming. Although in times of issue crisis, people turn to government agencies and activist groups, that does not mean that they do not doubt the objectivity, sincerity, and efficacy of such organizations.

Such discussions have at least two dimensions. One is the salience of an object or actor, such as a company or other type of organization. The second dimension is the salience of the attributes of the object or actor (McCombs, Llamas, Lopez-Escobar, & Rey, 1997). An organization may itself have salience, as might the attributes used to judge it as good or bad, effective or ineffective, responsible or irresponsible. This logic links to issue ownership theory (Petrocik, Benoit, & Hansen, 2003). How well a political party might do, depending on the issue position associated with it, depends on the evaluative criteria, for instance, that exist with large blocks of the voting public. Either discussion of evaluative criteria or of organizations that are associated with the criteria bring those criteria to mind and lead key publics to use them in making various kinds of judgments, including assessments of organizations' reputations (Meijer & Kleinnijenhuis, 2006).

Media appear to have a dominant impact because the points they express seem to correspond to opinions of their audiences. In actuality, people may have formed or are in the process of creating opinions that they avoid discussing in public until those issues are presented in the media; once the topics are discussed in the media, people feel they can legitimately express opinions they had formed quite independently of media reporting and commentary (Noelle-Neumann, 1984).

Because media follow publics' opinions as well as reinforce them, the extrapolation of this analysis is that if groups of people receive different information from different media and interpersonal contact, they develop different conceptions of reality, a multitiered society of different and conflicting zones of meaning. Instead of the media playing a singular role in the formation of opinions on key issues, media and social interaction conversations among people influence key publics' issue priorities (Zhu, Watt, Snyder, Yan, & Jiang, 1993, p. 8).

Another perspective of this problem was provided by Burke (1969b), who contended that one of the most powerful social forces involves living a shared view of reality, what he calls identification. If reporters take their leads from the same sources of other media reports, the trend would seem to be to reinforce the mediated reports on business topics instead of looking for nonconfirming or disconfirming evidence. Reinforcing the danger of media-based reality, researchers discovered that network claims of momentum shifts in candidate popularity during the 1976 presidential election were often based not on poll data but on subjective opinions and feelings of the reporters. Such shifts, as reported, could lead viewers to believe a contrived social "truth" (Meyers, Newhouse, & Garrett, 1978).

This analysis of media impact brings us squarely to the topic of how issue and policy agendas become set in this country and how they become visible and adopted, whether because media personnel decide an issue is important and raise it to invite responses from politicians, corporate spokespersons, or activists or because pressures exerted by these key players motivate reporters to cover stories and take editorial positions (McCombs, 1977; McCombs & Shaw, 1972; Scheufele & Tewksbury, 2007; D. H. Weaver, 2007). Reflecting on this theme, McCombs (1992) acknowledged that even if people do not acquire much of their information or opinion from the media, they do use media to decide what and how to think about the information they acquire. This line of reasoning suggests how various players in public policy development can prime others, make issues salient, and frame the relevant criteria that are used to judge organizations of public interest. Thus, issue agendas are formed by the kinds of issues discussed, the kind of media discussing them, and the sort of coverage given to them (Walgrave & Van Aeist, 2006).

Key organizations, such as businesses, enter into communication with some peril. Their identity as a discussant is likely to evoke a frame that various listeners and viewers use to interpret what is said, why it is said, and how it prospers or harms the issue's status. Forty years ago, corporations began to realize that their communication practices could prove quite damaging (Steckmest, 1982). They are often damned if they seek to communicate but always damned if they don't. Focusing criticism where it was due, Ronald Rhody (1983), former vice president of public relations for the Bank of America, observed,

> Most of the misimpressions, or errors, or unfairness that so many are concerned about is business's own fault. We, in our institutions, (just like the media and government) have been guilty of ignorance, arrogance, bad judgment and negligence. Silence, evasiveness, the lack of candor, the unwillingness to respond, have been like lead weights pulling business down lower and lower in public esteem. The fact that the public may be misinformed on key economic or business issues, may be misled about our respective operations and intentions, is largely our own doing. We have permitted this because, out of fear of either criticism or controversy, we have failed to take the initiative. (p. 46)

Rhody (1983) challenged business leaders to "stop grousing about the media and really learn how to work with it" (p. 47).

Sage prescription was voiced by Kevin Phillips (1981), speaking as president of the American Political Research Corporation:

> The battleground of business-media relations is changing. Television network news is still simplistic, inflammatory and more than occasionally biased, yet it is a problem corporations have begun to take seriously. The larger context of press coverage of business-economic issues is one of improvement, however, and in the growing area of corporate-related First Amendment interpretation, press groups are now frequently emerging as allies of the business community. (p. 60)

Frustrated by lack of access to the mainstream media, private-sector organizations, government, activists, and labor groups have created alternative sources of communication that they can control and shape to their purpose, much of this based around the Internet. These sources of communication have supplied substantial amounts of information and opinions. Although the media may lead on some issues, they likely follow and confirm the growth of key publics' concern that problems exist that need remediation. The media may be a mainstream beacon of the point at which an issue, discussed by several publics, has achieved visibility.

If that model of the role of the media obtains, then it offers additional support for the concept of a multitiered society, which consists of many overlapping and conflicting zones of meaning. Key publics with various opinions, rather than a single public opinion, are the accurate model. In addition, these publics are likely to have a different sense of the importance and content of an issue and the priority of values by which it should be judged and solved. Viewing opinions of public and media influence in this way suggests that issues managers engage in balancing acts between many key stakeholders and stake-seekers, each of whom may not agree with and interpret issues in the same way as the others. They may have their own media preferences and are likely to view the same media stories in idiosyncratic ways.

Issues communicators seek to reach each audience or public at its own level of knowledge, awareness, and concern—including how it evaluates issues by content and priority. The daunting task facing issues communicators is to put out (listen to and appreciate) as much information and opinion as they can so that people who want it can obtain it. Even if the clutter seems turbulent and daunting, it privileges audiences and fosters public debate, discussion, and dialogue.

Communication Technology and Issues Communication

A multitiered society sharply contrasts with Marshall McLuhan's (1969) prediction that advancing communication technology will congeal "the entire human family into a single global tribe" (p. 17). Writing at a time when networks dominated television, McLuhan argued that the media consumption rubric allowed millions of people to view the same event or news item at the same time; this pattern, thereby, led (or would lead) them to form similar opinions. McLuhan's prediction assumed that viewers not only would see, hear, and read the same material but also interpret it in the same way. If his prediction ever was likely to become reality, it is probably less true today.

One of the liabilities of the channel and satellite television era is that viewing choices abound; people avoid and yet also expose themselves to entertainment, news, and commentary in a selective way. Such selection is increased by varied and segmented programming on radio (including a gamut of talk/opinion formats) and diverse voices on the Internet. The abundant availability of information and opinion sources privileges audiences to learn and evaluate, but it can also lead them to dissimilar rather than conforming points of view. New communication technologies privilege less wealthy organizations because the cost of reaching vast global audiences can be quite low, thereby balancing the economic dynamics of the opinion playing field.

The purpose of this section is to review the balance, tug of war, and open combat for the attention of readers, viewers, listeners, and users who are increasingly sovereign given the vastness of the Internet and the power of search engines. A vast array of competing voices, as well as issues, crises, and risks, are not only reported and discussed in cyberspace but are also created there (Hallahan, 2009). For all of the facts that appear in cyberspace, much is hyperbole and smear (Casarez, 2002). The Internet can lead to challenges of the legitimacy of corporate and government organizations that fail to monitor issues there and do not respond quickly, candidly, and directly to issues raised in that venue (Roper, 2002). The Internet makes it easier for publics to form and raise issues, share information, and challenge issue positions as well as the legitimacy of establishment organizations (Coombs, 2002).

Ahead-of-the-curve writers such as Patrick R. Williams (1982) encouraged corporate communicators to become proficient in using new technologies more than a quarter century ago. Bleecker and Lento (1982) challenged public relations practitioners: "As people who manage and disseminate information, we should be in the vanguard of the information revolution. To play out our role in the transformation of our jobs, we must keep up with the technology" (p. 11). Taking this advice to heart, practitioners in the 1990s engaged in a substantial dialogue exploring the possibilities and challenging each other to push the envelope on the use of new technological means to reach ever more narrowcast audiences. Through new technologies, the era of mass narrowcasting is firmly established. In this way, issues discussants can communicate with one another without network intrusion.

As alternatives to the standard media, companies, trade associations, nonprofits, governmental agencies, and activist groups have made available interactive computer-CD systems. These allow an interactive environment for students or concerned members of a community to engage in issues management activities such as trying their skills at managing a forest profitably and in ways that are environmentally responsible. Increasingly, what has been offered via CDs can be accessed through home page Web sites. Using either venue, interested parties might use these tools to solve problems related to community air or water quality standards and regulation of the source of those pollutants. Coalitions with stakeholder groups can be used through their communication channels to reach persons who are interested in their opinions.

New communication technologies offer options that increase the response rate to concerned persons and narrowcasting, with the personal touch of quick response to questions by concerned citizens. Companies, governmental offices, trade associations, and environmental groups can establish electronic bulletin boards and discussion groups that allow concerned influence leaders to ask questions and receive speedy responses and engage in issue discussion.

Unlike any previous time in history, viewers and readers have a plethora of mediated sources of information and opinions. With e-mail and computer-assisted bulletin boards and discussion groups, interpersonal influence is electronic, nearly instantaneous, and global. Society is becoming demassified and more interactive. The dialogue is electronic but not necessarily on network television or radio. Multitudes of discussions and arguments occur each day on new communication technologies, especially those that are computer assisted.

Substantial segmentation arises from cable television, such as C-SPAN programming that includes hearings, forums, and in-depth book reviews of policy discussants. Nonmainstream channels allow the discussion of topics unpopular to major networks, such as programming by the Audubon Society that periodically ran on TBS and environmentally slanted programs on the Discovery channel. Hours of public policy, business, and financial programming go out each week through Cable News Network (CNN), Public Broadcasting Service, and syndication.

Internal communication can be supplied to employees and activist group members by closed-circuit television and by videos that play continuously in kiosks or migrate among departments throughout an organization. Internal corporate-institutional (or business) video is a multibillion dollar industry. Quickly replacing such technologies, Web site home pages and organizational intranets supply such information routinely, allowing for such materials to be archived and searched electronically.

For several years, videos were as cost-effective as a narrowcasting device that environmental groups, for instance, used them. *Making a World of Difference* and *Saving Life on Earth* were sent by the World Wildlife Fund to thank contributors to its environmental projects. These videos reminded viewers of the beauty of nature, the ravaging effects humans have on nature, the success that has been accomplished by the environmental group, and the problems that remain to be solved. These videos reinforce environmentalism and encourage contributions to be spent on that cause. Now similar materials are available at home pages. With weekly, monthly, and quarterly reports (as well as when special issues arise), activist groups can use regular mail and e-mail to alert members to issues and invite them to visit the home page for additional information. If sent by e-mail, the Web page is no more than a mouse click away. Video streaming is replacing standard videos as a means for informing, reinforcing, and convincing members to become engaged in some specific issue.

The U.S. Chamber of Commerce fostered the creation of the American Business Network (BizNet), a business-oriented, closed-circuit private television subscription service transmitted via satellite from the chamber's studios in Washington, D.C., to its members (local chambers, companies, associations, and law firms) and nonmembers (colleges, hotels, and cable companies). BizNet supplied a teleconferencing interactive online network with receiver sites throughout the country for private use. It has been used to bring political action committee (PAC) managers together by video to coordinate lobbying efforts. BizNet has matured, as have other previously conventional communication tools. Today it offers a plethora of business e-tools, as well as Web design consulting.

Under the mission statement–driven theme of "fighting for your business," the U.S. Chamber of Commerce's home page in late 2007 listed a variety of services, including an issues center. It offers updates on elections and provides grassroots alerts. It indexes issues and provides content-driven issues position papers. It supplies letters for Congress, shares business policy priorities, and even provides weekly commentary. It links interested parties to other sites that can be used for additional information and issue documentation and position papers. It monitors legislatures, provides working issue alerts for various bills, and tracks issue debate on key topics of interest to the business community.

The old technologies have a lasting power. However much the print side of the equation has changed, it remains as a staple. News stories in all media types continue to be a vital part of the dialogue. News can be driven by issues, crisis, and exposé. Media reports, however shallow or in-depth, seek various angles and voices on the story. Newspapers may be losing print circulation, but online versions supply information and commentary, as well as news alerts and updates for subscribers. Magazines continue to run feature stories, provide editorial comments, and offer pictures to make stories more "real." Books continue to be published on topics relevant to key issues and by key figures on various issues and political philosophies. Reporters and commentators continue their traditional gatekeeping functions. They determine what facts get published, how they are interpreted, and what conclusions are drawn. They also provide contrasting points of view. Many of the leading voices in the print media also have found an outlet on the electronic side and vice versa. Sunday morning television, for instance, often brings reporters of various media and points of view together to share their perspectives on news development, issue positions, trends, and crises.

Print has taken a new twist with the Internet. Now it is no longer the sort of venue where reporters make weekly or daily comments and reports, only to have that material fleet away into the garbage or recycling bin. It now is available 24/7 and searchable. A news junky or issues monitor can access old stories or earlier versions of current stories by using search engines and by pursuing links between sites. Major organizations not only issue press releases but also archive them for retrieval by interested readers and viewers. This ability gives news a very long life. It also encourages major organizations to see their home pages as a "publication outlet." They not only can give full details of their side of a story but do so framed as they prefer. Such electronic capabilities not only *allow* them to be responsive but also *force* them to be responsive. An interested reader can quickly compare a set of facts and various interpretations. This should lead organizations to live, with the Internet as their power engine, to be the first and best source of information on all matters relevant to themselves and issues that they want and need to address.

Blogging has become a blend of old and new technologies. How important bloggers are in the big picture is still to be established, but beyond doubt, they have and will play a role. A blog may be the first source of a fact that leads to a crisis. How objective and well vetted that source is may pose real ethical problems for established and fair journalists. It also can be a daunting challenge to corporate issue monitors and communicators. That is especially true when the facts are incorrect and yet take on a life of their own because once into cyberspace, they circulate quickly and lose the sense of source responsibility usually associated with professional and fair journalists. As much as we can find lots of good information readily available in print and through video on the Web, we can find a lot of bunk as well.

The Web allows for organizations to have pages hidden that can be activated in the event of a crisis. Messages and other materials (such as pictures and schematics of operational processes) can be held in reserve. Once a relevant crisis occurs (if one does), that Web page can be activated with some changes and adaptations on the theme as originally composed. Such response can provide more quickly details that often take days or weeks to accumulate. And some of those details require management and general counsel approval. Getting those inputs well before a crisis can save valuable response time in a 24/7 world. Such pages can be posted for reporters who want news and may not prefer to ask additional questions. Even if they do prefer to ask questions as follow-up to such prepared statements, they have this information as backgrounders. This information can save response time because it can be updated as some reporters raise questions, and it can be posted, with answers, as FAQs (see Hallahan, 2009).

New communication technologies allow for the use of interactive means for delivering public policy-related information in interesting ways that can be rapidly changed as issue development demands. Technical innovation has added many communication tools to be used by issues managers whether on behalf of businesses, government agencies, activist groups, or media programmers. This list contains electronic mail, electronic bulletin boards, listservs, discussion groups, computerized mailings targeted at key constituencies, and electronic billboards.

Consumer 1-800 numbers can be useful for assisting customers in the proper use of a service or product and in fielding as well as monitoring complaints and diffusing issues. Those numbers provide access for individuals who want to complain about products or services, and this is potentially useful information for issue scanning and analysis. Such insights could foster other research strategies, such as surveys and focus groups. These numbers and Web addresses can be used to alert customers and others to problems and to discuss recalls and proper use of a product or service.

For more than a decade, companies have been setting up online Web sites and Internet equivalents, as well as 1-800 numbers, to field and respond to consumer inquiries and comments. These venues can also be used to debate issues and foster dialogue that is open to Web users. As long ago as 1996, McNeil Consumer Products took out a series of print ads in publications such as *The Wall Street Journal* to engage in dialogue with its concerned customers, supporters, and potential regulators. The issue was the effect of alcohol on pain relievers. The ads began with the cognitively involving advice that if the reader consumed three or more alcohol-containing drinks per day, he or she was advised to discuss this matter with a physician before taking over-the-counter pain relievers. Of special interest were those medications that contain acetaminophen, aspirin, ibuprofen, ketoprofen, and naproxen sodium. Run to the medicine cabinet and read the ingredients!

This response tool has become commonplace in an era where product recalls and challenges to product safety are top-of-the-hour/front-page news. If there is lead in children's toys (as was a recurring story in 2007), what should parents do? The companies in that industry and the companies identified in news reports need to be responsive with information to help parents, friends, and family to manage risks of children's safety. It is not only a matter of corporate responsibility but sound policy for companies, trade associations, regulators, and watchdog activists to do this. A fully functioning society is one where people can obtain information they need to manage risks. If the information is only supplied by the standard media or by some of the voices in a dialogue, the interested stakeholders cannot get the information they need to assess the stakes they are seeking. Conditions of that kind are societally dysfunctional. Realizing that, critics are often the first to post information, voice

evaluations, propose policies, and challenge reputations (legitimacy and identification). Truly responsive and responsible companies and other key organizations are foolish if they don't follow quickly. Knowing that, various
companies and other organizations have "black" sites on key matters prepared
but not made available to Internet users. In the event or when the event occurs
and seems to be on a crisis trajectory, the sites can be quickly reviewed and
tailored; they can be launched quickly to supply needed information and
policy/action recommendations.

Government agencies that are responsive to the public interest have
learned to use the Internet as a source of accessible information. They also
can use telephone and computer alerts to warn, motivate, and actuate key
publics in times of emergencies. The same sorts of alert/warning and action
systems are routinely used by high-risk industries such as chemical manufacturers, which might need to provide a shelter in the event of a major
chemical release. The Federal Emergency Management Agency has improved
in its ability to provide warning/alerts in the event of storms and other major
public health and safety emergencies. It also supplies 24/7 information that
community residents can use idiosyncratically. For instance, it constitutes
alerts specifically tailored to community residents who need continual electricity because of their medical condition. The elderly and infirm can arrange
for special alerts and protocols to use in the case of emergency response.
During a major storm warning, owners of pets, large and small, can quickly
obtain recommendations on precautions and response actions needed in the
event of evacuation.

Activists have taken data gathered by the Environmental Protection
Agency and state regulatory agencies, amalgamated those data by access code
(such as ZIP codes), and have provided them to concerned citizens. Scorecard
is a Web site that allows Internet users to enter their ZIP code to determine
levels of toxics and other hazards in their community. It lists "who's polluting,"
"what pollutants do the most harm," and where the "worst pollution" is. It
allows comparisons by community and states, and it offers the ability to search
numerous companies and chemicals.

Related to that site are others interested in activism on environmental issues.
One is Environmental Defense, which started the practice of amalgamating
and reporting environmental release and impact data. It seeks to foster activist/
industry projects and works for the private sector, as well as economically
feasible solutions to environmental problems. It lists its joint activist/industry
projects as examples. These examples can foster other favorable attention
through coalition building and collaborative decision making. It listed in late
2007 that it worked with chemicals and manufacturing, consumer goods,
financial services, food and beverage, media and IT, retail, and transportation.
It listed its "partners'" corporate logos, such as Wegmans, DuPont, and FedEx.

It listed suggestions for increased environmental responsibility. Its site included an opportunity to meet its experts online and offered a list of its publications.

Instead of relying on mainstream outlets, alternative channels play powerful roles in the generation and exchange of ideas that constitute a public dialogue. Substantial concern was voiced about these alternative sources of information following the bomb attack on the federal building in Oklahoma City in 1995, when it was made public that militia groups could share information regarding how to manufacture bombs via computer networks. Issues management is launching into cyberspace. Mainstream organizations routinely employ communication technologies, including computerized databases that are available to subscribers to use, in scanning issues and creating legislative alerts. One of the earliest and most successful systems was NAMnet, created by the National Association of Manufacturers (NAM). With it, subscribers could obtain legislative and regulatory alerts and issue updates. It included business, financial, and economic news.

By late 2007, the major trade association had developed a wonderfully rich Web site. It even noted the videos that were available to the user via YouTube. The site provided white papers, a continuing staple type of issue communication tool. Instead, however, of wondering how to place these documents into the hands of interested readers—a standard problem of the old media environment—the NAM made them available in downloadable files. The site listed two major types of information services for business users: policy issue information and court cases affecting manufacturing. The site included NAM testimony and statements on the policies and cases. If in the "old" media environment, an organization such as this (and activists as well) would have issued a standard press release or an executive would have appeared on a talk show, and the coverage might have been limited to a brief comment, passing reference, or sound bite. The Web site, in contrast, provided commodified information, including Manufacts that could be included in messages used by its members and friends in their discussion of manufacturing issues. It supplied all of the available information it wanted to place into the public arena on a topic. This could be accessed by friend, ally, foe, and interested neutral parties.

In this "information commons" (Holman, 1998), information is put into play. Dialogue occurs. Although standard old media gatekeepers play a vital role, so too do the organizations that want to participate in the discussion at various levels of detail and engagement. Traditional interpretations of issue agendas have investigated the roles played by standard media outlets (including their framing and priming) and that of politicians. To this array of voices, especially in the new media environment, we add the voices of businesses, key individuals, opinion leaders, activists, other nonprofits, trade associations, and unions—just for a start. Instead of a news story or article in a popular magazine being all of the information and opinion an interested reader might receive on the topic, now that person can easily go to new media for more voices and fuller stories. Activists are much more on par with businesses, no matter how rich and powerful, because they can supply information via a Web site to interested users, including standard media reporters (print and electronic).

Burgeoning consulting and placement services are adding dimensions to issues communicators' access to technologies. Niche agencies and services have grown in response to the burgeoning new communication technologies. News Broadcast Network is a Canadian company that specializes in helping organizations place radio or video news releases. Interactive setups enable specialized users immediate, "face-to-face" access to communication experts and corporate executives. Other companies offer the same or similar services.

The era of the online database and search engine is truly remarkable, especially because they give virtually instantaneous access to individual publications, as well as those of key organizations (businesses, trade associations, and institutes), activists and other nonprofits, and governmental organizations. Whether articles, reports, and white pages are published in old media or online at home pages, they take on additional importance once they have made their way into some of these most well-established databases that are searchable. If this is the age of information, it is also the age of information overload. The new communication technologies make "publishing" results and accessing them increasingly expedient.

We have a society that treats Google as a verb. Web sites offer text and visual images. Listservs and Web discussion pages exist. Some are provided by environmental groups such as Greenpeace and the Aubudon Society. Others are created by other interested parties. Web pages often provide search engines to locate relevant databases and discussion groups. Companies as well provide issue pages and discussion sites. For instance, in 1996, Shell prepared a page that explained its stance on the Nigerian controversy. Shell made available a discussion room for those who wanted to participate in the dialogue. ExxonMobil places its issue ads at its Web site and invites commentary. By looking at its site and then at Greenpeace's home page, one could witness the debate between these two organizations over the fate of the Brent Spar in a format not unlike a virtual town hall meeting (Heath, 1998).

This brief review of communication technologies glimpses the burgeoning and quickly changing array of options that issues communicators (and monitors) have to supply and receive information and issue commentary. Some of these, especially the Web, allow for interactive dialogue, collaborative decision making, and negotiation. Perhaps the most synthesizing conclusion from this review is to observe that we have not yet seen the future of innovation that will give individuals and organizations more immediate and personal access to one another for debate, discussion, and negotiation. Narrowcasting and dialogue rather than mass dissemination of information and opinion is the paradigm of the future.

Issues Communication as Argument

An argument is inherently two-way. It takes two parties to disagree; it consists of statements and counterstatements. Parties disagree because facts often are subjected to different evaluations and interpretations. Predictions frequently are based on uncertainties, subjective probabilities, and even scientific estimates of what will occur. Concerns that argument is not symmetrical can derive from disparity in the ability of one organization (a large corporation) to spend more on its effort than another (a small environmental group). Other factors than money enter this equation. Reportage can balance the equation, at least to a degree. Certainly the Internet has leveled the playing field because it is a means by which information, evaluation, and recommendation can be placed into the public dialogue without having cleared editorial newsworthiness.

Reality demonstrates that goliaths do not always win but are often defeated. The best advocates are those who listen to the views of others and know when to agree, disagree, and supply information and opinion to continue a mutually beneficial discussion. We should not be alarmed by the terms *advocate, argue, debate, assert, agree, defer,* or *capitulate*. Those terms are used to dissect and analyze issues communication. They characterize the rhetorical issues of all public policy segments, including perhaps especially activists (Wallack et al., 1993).

Issues managers do not want to go forward with a strategic business plan, a public policy plan, or a communication plan without having a firm sense of the facts of the case, knowing the premises and values that are used to reason about the facts, and understanding the policy positions that are being advocated. A wise organization uses sound argument to support its own decisions and those of its stakeholders.

Opinions relevant to strategic business planning and operations of organizations exist at macrosocial, community, and personal levels. Macrosocial opinions, interpreted as societal narratives, are unlikely to yield to efforts by a single company, industry, activist group, media commentator, or governmental agency. Formation of macrosocial opinions requires years, even decades. The glacial movement of such opinions is the result of concerted and sustained efforts by activists, industries, and political parties. At microsocial levels, communication efforts can be more successful as the persons involved use macrosocial opinions to make localized decisions.

Under consideration are relevant facts, values, and policies. Propositions of fact are objectively verifiable. Value judgments center on principles regarding right and wrong, better or worse. Propositions of policy are "ought" statements basic to choices, the most rewarding or beneficial of which are preferred. These argument components are valuable for analyzing what advocates should and do say when considering the public policy stance they choose to take.

Advantage can be gained by contesting or adapting principles to performance options and image components of companies and industries. The contest will decide what principles are applicable, in what ways, and to what conclusions, thereby creating a zone of meaning shared by stakeholders and stakeseekers.

In this argument, issues communication uses widely accepted premises, defends contested premises, advocates new premises, and challenges or champions policies. Issue stances enlist audiences to take actions in support of policies; they stress the reward-cost basis for supporting or opposing those policies and the actions that result from them. The outcome of joint or collaborative effort is to create a variety of platforms on which collective decisions can be made. The following review suggests the platform of fact that companies, activists, and governmental officials consider as part of public policy decision making.

PLATFORMS OF FACT: INFORMATION AS THE BASIS OF ISSUE ARGUMENTS

Campaigns should provide information because publics want to understand key aspects of business operations and policies. People pay attention to and carefully consider information when it helps them make sound and rewarding decisions on choices that are confronting them (Atkin, 1973; Heath, Liao, & Douglas, 1995; Petty & Cacioppo, 1986). Company spokespersons complain that they cannot get audiences to listen to what they have to say. Perhaps what they have to say is deemed irrelevant by the audiences. Mendelsohn (1973) found that information campaigns are effective when they (a) provide information in a neutral fashion, (b) show people that they know less than they thought they knew, and (c) give information that the audience perceives to be valuable.

Facts are facts as long as they can be used to make sound decisions. Facts are interpretations of reality. How accurate they are is contestable, as is their relevance to some matter. They deserve to be treated as such as long as the dialogue cannot deny them or does not produce better facts.

VALUES AS THE BASIS OF ISSUE ARGUMENTS

According to Wallace (1963), rhetorical statements raise ethical considerations and address the choices that confront people and organizations: "When we justify, we praise or blame; we use terms like right and wrong, good and bad; in general we appraise" (p. 243). Through public debate, people contest the "goodness" of reasons. As Johannsen, Strickland, and Eubanks (1970) reasoned, "Rhetoric is advisory; it has the office of advising men [and women] with reference to an independent order of goods and with reference to their particular situation as it relates to these" (p. 211).

PLATFORM OF POLICY

Policy statements are contestable recommendations that if specific steps are taken, desired outcomes will be achieved or undesirable consequences will be avoided. Making a policy argument, the Asphalt Institute appealed to readers to let "your lawmakers know where you stand on preserving our streets and highways. The deterioration of the nation's road system must be stopped, before it stops us" (Garbett, 1981, p. 21). The objective of policy arguments is to assert the wisdom of preferred choices and create a zone of meaning with key stakeholders.

On the basis of the interaction of fact and value, issues communicators contest the wisdom, advisability, and expedience of policy. Policy recommendations are characterized by "oughts" or "shoulds." The logic is this: If specific facts are true and if certain values prevail, a policy should be created (defeated) because it is reasonable (unreasonable). The overlap between fact and value gets us squarely at the importance of propositions of policy.

Policy deliberations feature discussions of fact, interpretations of evaluative premises, and considerations of policies. These three focal points constitute the similarities and dissimilarities in the zones of meaning used by issues communicators. They are the key aspects of advocacy, opinion formation and change, and negotiation.

As this section concludes, it is worth noting that campaigns work to create legitimacy for competing organizations, by justifying the positions they take and the usefulness of those positions to the total dialogue. Organizations not only argue for the legitimacy of their positions but also work to demonstrate their legitimacy as discussants. They seek support and work to create identifications that draw supporters together. At the heart of such efforts is the need to attract and use power resources. One of the major power resources is to be considered a productive, useful, and even vital voice on specific issues the organization is seeking to advance.

As such, efforts to participate in the dialogue exhibit characteristics typical of campaigns. Some critics of the process believe that corporations dominate the dialogue because of their superior resources. Others believe all voices must be heard, but doing that requires that they engage in the activists of attention and legitimacy building. A number of traditional public relations tactics and tools are an essential part of such efforts, but any or all campaigns need to be understood as participating in a dialogue. The campaigns, any or each, are merely a strategic use of voice.

Conclusion

Rather than McLuhan's (1969) vision of one global village, society may be inexorably drifting toward polarized "global villages" where consubstantiation and identification on many serious issues are impossible. Assuming the need for a common platform of fact and a shared evaluation of the activities by business and other large organizations, some constructive alternative is necessary so that society can forge supportive rather than contradictory and inharmonious zones of meaning. Arenas of open public debate and collaborative decision making are vital.

The future? Issues communicators may create interactive computer-assisted communication options that allow them to challenge communicants to download informational games. Activists may make available games that allow persons to test their ability to manage solid waste or regulate air and water quality. Chemical companies might challenge communicants to operate a chemical plant in ways that make money, protect employees and area residents' health and safety, and generate jobs and tax revenue for the community. Timber companies can offer their own versions adapted by age of how to operate timber resources as a renewable and sustainable resource. Who knows where the human imagination will lead?

Recognizing that no organization can dominate the course an issue takes, this chapter addressed issues communication as dialogue argument reflecting and forming competing and compatible zones of meaning. The substance of that debate leads to policy formation. Although no organization can dominate the debate, each one as a steward of the democratic process is obligated to assert its point of view, offering support and reason for its conclusions. In public, each position is debated and policy moves forward.

SIM Challenge: Voice of a Trade Association

Trade associations are important links in the SIM process. They serve many purposes. They often are maligned as a way for individual companies to avoid participating in constructive SIM. They are even thought of and often called fronts. This analysis may be true or might have been more true in an earlier era, but one can make the case that they serve a variety of key purposes. First, they can be a means by which leading companies create and impose higher standards of CSR on "the bad apples in the barrel." They serve as one key voice or the voice for an industry. That helps those engaged in the public policy arena to know "an entire industry" opinion on some matter. It gives the individual members of an industry the opportunity to get their "stories straight" before engaging in public policy debate.

The American Petroleum Institute (API) is a trade association for the oil and gas industry. In a couple of words, it is the association for "big oil." This chapter features not only the kinds of arguments made in issues communication but also the tools that are employed. Just a simple review of API's Web site demonstrates their issues communication strategies and tactics, whether one supports their industry or not.

Its stated mission is to serve the interests of the oil and gas industry in many ways, one of which is to foster dialogue among the companies, as well as between them and their stakeholders. It engages in advocacy, speaking for the industry to all branches of government and the media. It engages in issues scanning by conducting or sponsoring research ranging from economic analyses to toxicological testing. For more than 75 years, it has led efforts to develop petroleum and petrochemical equipment and operating standards. These standards often translate into legislation and regulation.

The API has created a series of collaborative decision-making meetings, which in various venues call together national, state, and local leaders. It also engages its activist critics in similar forums. In all of the relevant legislative and regulatory settings, it takes policy issue positions on environmental issues, exploration practices and policies, fuels, taxes, trade, homeland security, and much more. It seeks to educate, although it will in such matters be seen as propagandizing on matters of the cost of fuel, standards of fuel quality, issues of supply and demand, costs of exploration, international politics, and activist effects on production, supply, and cost.

It employs a variety of communication tools: material on safety standards, a media center and media archives, testimony and other policy statements, a petroleum museum, and a variety of teaching materials. It periodically engages in print and television advertising. Its Web page serves as a clearinghouse for such materials.

Summary Questions

1. In what sense can issues communication be characterized accurately as tough defense and smart offense? If we think of it as advocacy, debate, dialogue, argumentation, or a wrangle in the marketplace of ideas, how does it progress in a responsible manner to serve society and not merely consist of propaganda and manipulation?

2. Debate as public contest of ideas is the paradigm for issues communication. This heritage is timeless but has been carefully studied in Western society since the Golden Age of Greece. What is a rhetorical problem, and how does that concept help issues communicators to focus their efforts and progress responsibly?

3. How can issues communication be strategically utilized as narratives to help stakeholders structure their experiences and actions with an organization or industry?

4. How does character count in issues communication? How is character used to differentiate, associate, create identity as archetypes, and produce goodwill? Do you subscribe to the classic principle that an organization needs to be good to be an effective communicator?

5. Issues communication seeks, through dialogue, to establish, refine, and build on platforms of fact, evaluation, and policy. Explain that observation and indicate how premises guide issue discussions and therefore often are a highly contested part of the dialogue.

6. How is issue framing part of the advocacy struggle and battle for issues managers and public relations practitioners?

7. How is the innovation of new media technologies changing old technologies and affecting positively and negatively the ability of people and organizations to communicate on mutually involving issues?

8. If the old media continue to play a role in society, how are the new communication technologies, more specifically the Internet, shaping or reshaping mediated communication?

9. In this regard, are people's views likely to become more similar or more diverse because of reading, listening, viewing, and Internet use patterns?

7

Obligations and Constraints on Issues Communication

Vignette:
Corporate Speech—Free, Free for Some, or Not at All?

One of the most sensational cases dealing with the right and responsibility of companies to engage in speech (commercial or noncommercial) came out of a critique of Nike's business practices. Nike is one of the world's largest sellers of sports apparel. Like many companies, especially those that sell apparel, they buy manufactured goods rather than operate their own manufacturing facilities. For more than a century, apparel and other types of manufacturing have migrated to geographical locations where labor is abundant and cheap. Costs, which often predict a sizable segment of the apparel market, can be reduced through productivity measures such as machine operations, logistics, and proximity of manufacturing and raw materials. In such businesses, however, one of the primary predictors of cost is employees' wages. This business plan has traditionally led to questionable business practices. One of the labels of some of these practices is sweatshops.

A sweatshop is a work location where people are paid low wages and forced to work long, hard hours under daunting conditions. Sweatshops were part of the industrial model in the United States during the late 19th century that continues today. Impoverished seamstresses worked in tenement sweatshops located in many cities where recent immigrants converted small apartments into contract shops that doubled as living quarters, which were common in the late 19th and early 20th centuries (Liebhold & Rubenstein, 1998). "A combination of forces at home and abroad contributed to their reappearance: changes in the retail industry, a growing global economy, increased reliance on contracting, and a large pool of immigrant labor in the U.S." (p. 1).

(Continued)

(Continued)

The term *sweatshop* is loaded with heavy emotional and value-laden baggage. Some of the strides toward increased quality in the workplace promoted by unions during the late 19th century and early 20th century brought an end to such practices, although they still exist in America, especially when illegal aliens can be worked in harsh conditions. President Clinton formed the White House Apparel Industry Partnership, in 1996, to pursue nonregulatory solutions. The group is made up of representatives from industry, labor, government, and public interest groups. Although reform is one solution, another is to continually move the manufacturing facilities to areas where there is supplied cheap labor with little regulation or indifferent authority in the face of the regulation.

The Nike crisis reaches back to the mid to late 1990s. At that time, Nike, like its competitors and other kinds of companies, routinely contracted with companies owned and located in countries such as Korea, Vietnam, Taiwan, China, Thailand, and Indonesia. The workers in such facilities often were women, especially young women younger than age 24. Over the years, such manufacturers were required to sign a Memorandum of Understanding. This agreement commits the purchasing company to work to ensure compliance on the part of the manufacturing companies to prevent sweatshop conditions. The offensive conditions, however clearly or ambiguously stated, include such standards as minimum wage, overtime, child labor, holiday, vacations, insurance benefits, and general working and living conditions, including comfort and safety. Such conditions include sexual abuse, physical abuse, and improper medical attention. In 1991, Levi Strauss & Co., one of the world's largest clothing manufacturers, instituted the first corporate code of responsible contracting. Since then, the practice has become more common in the garment industry. Workplace monitoring is one way to ensure that contractors abide by manufacturers' codes of conduct. Whether these inspections should be performed by manufacturers' representatives or by independent monitors remains highly controversial (Liebhold & Rubenstein, 1998).

Out of this business practice arose a recent legal controversy. It threatens to both actively constrain corporate speech (all forms of communication) and give managements an incentive to not communicate despite the continuing advice of public relations and issues communication specialists that "nature hates a vacuum." Into a communication (fact, value, and policy) vacuum created by the absence of corporate speech, a great deal of misinformation and unsound opinion may prevail simply because of the absence of the corporate side. Indeed, many have argued that it is not a privilege but an obligation on the part of large organizations to communicate on all matters of public interest.

Beginning in 1996, there were numerous allegations that Nike was mistreating and underpaying workers at foreign facilities, including a feature published by *Mother Jones*. Nike responded to these charges in numerous ways, such as by sending out press releases, writing letters to the editors of various newspapers around the country, and mailing letters to university presidents and athletic directors. In April 1998, a California resident named Marc Kasky sued Nike for unfair and deceptive practices under California's Unfair Competition Law and False Advertising Law, asserting that "in order to maintain and/or increase its sales," Nike made a number of "false statements and/or material omissions of fact" concerning the working conditions under which Nike products are manufactured (*Nike v. Kasky*, 2003, pp. 1–2; the Supreme Court version reversed the order of the names from *Kasky v. Nike*). The Supreme Court case constituted an appeal of an April 2002 California Supreme Court ruling that centered on the constitutionality of a California law allowing citizens to complain about the intent and factuality of statements made by companies on matters of public policy. One part of that appeal focused on whether companies are persons and therefore included as such in the First Amendment of the U.S. Constitution.

Provisions in the discussion of this case relate to those concerning the Federal Trade Commission (FTC) arguments in the *National Commission on Egg Nutrition v. FTC* (1978) case. This case allowed the FTC to rule against an ad placed by sponsors who claimed that no scientific evidence supported the conclusion that eating eggs increased the risk of heart disease. The logic of that case was later applied to allow the FTC to rule that R. J. Reynolds' "Mr. Fit" ad was commercial rather than issues communication. By that ruling, the FTC could regulate the content and actual presentation of the ad. As framed by critics of specific company statements and even by the general right of companies to speak on public policy issues, this ruling is often captured as the principle of "the corporate right to lie." This principle presumes that all speech by companies is self-serving and so distorted as to be inherently untrue and, that like individuals, companies have the right to lie.

Kasky v. Nike involved Nike's appeal of an April 2002 California Supreme Court ruling that rejected claims by Nike's lawyers that the First Amendment immunized the company from being sued for an allegedly deceptive public relations campaign. A trial on the merits was precluded by the parties' settlement following the U.S. Supreme Court's decision to send the case back to a lower court. At heart in the Nike case was the need on its part to create and maintain brand image and its related equity. That means, as follows: If a company is seen to be good and good in a particular way, that perception can motivate buyers to prefer that company's products as a category and as a type in preference to those of competitors. If Nike, in this case, is associated with sweatshop labor conditions and its competitors are not, that fact, once known by customers, would harm Nike's brand equity and competitiveness in the sports apparel industry. To advance its brand

(Continued)

(Continued)

equity, the company engaged in various forms of strategic philanthropy. Included in that effort is the offering of grants to create playgrounds, primarily basketball courts. To support its apparel business, it requires products manufactured by 300,000 to 500,000 workers employed by foreign companies operating in foreign countries. The complaint specified that most of these employees are women younger than age 24.

In response to challenges to its business practices, Nike created a committee to investigate the charges and to create and monitor a set of standards intended to preclude offensive business practices. In addition, in 1997, Nike commissioned a report by former ambassador to the United Nations Andrew Young on the labor conditions at Nike production facilities. After visiting 12 factories, "Young issued a report that commented favorably on working conditions in the factories and found no evidence of widespread abuse or mistreatment of workers" (*Nike v. Kasky*, 2003, p. 1). Once this report was available, it was made public. Nike spoke out in its defense.

At the same time, many reports generated by other bodies reported facts on working conditions that differed from the facts reported and the conclusions drawn in the Nike report. The facts included a sense of desperation on the part of workers that they were being held in captivity, suffered respiratory illnesses, were required to work compulsory overtime (11- to 12-hour days), and were aware of workers as young as 16 years of age. In part, these facts were interpreted as evidence of global imperialism caused by powerful companies feeding products into wealthy nations. These reports were based on whistle-blower facts and the judgment of humanitarian groups.

Again, Nike spoke in its defense. It responded to these allegations in press releases and letters to key stakeholder groups. In this way, it engaged in a battle of facts and interpretations in the media and among stakeholders. The key elements of the case centered on whether Nike was a responsible company and whether reports, its and others, were true and unbiased. In its campaign, it declared working conditions it found offensive and stated what it was doing to prevent these conditions.

In the face of Nike's defense, a complaint was filed in California under its corporate communication restrictions, under the Business and Professions Code, which prohibits intentional or reckless misrepresentation. Two provisions of the code are particularly interesting. One would require the offending company to disgorge all moneys made through the offensive business practices, and the second would require the company to engage in a public communication campaign to remedy the misinformation disseminated by its false advertising and unfair practices.

What are the implications and conditions provoked by this case? Is fact and the careful interpretation or reinterpretation of fact allowable and even acceptable corporate speech? What speech is prohibited; for instance, is commercial speech different from noncommercial or issue communication? Is rebuttal allowed? We know that warranties about products can provoke claims of misleading or false advertising. What about statements about the business practices that produce goods and services? Are those statements commercial speech (unprotected) or noncommercial/issue communication (protected)? On one hand, commercial speech has traditionally been treated as unprotected because customers often cannot independently verify the accuracy of details and claims that might motivate their purchase. In contrast, noncommercial speech (issue communication) is such that each side of the controversy can present its case for the public to decide, even if the public does not or would not purchase a product based on the claims. To this end, commercial speech is defined as that which directly or indirectly proposes a commercial transaction.

Thus, the courts of appeal were asked whether the debate over the working conditions was commercial speech or noncommercial speech, or what might be called public debate or issue communication. When pressed on this issue, the California Supreme Court ruled 4–3 that such statements by Nike constituted commercial speech. Thus, they were not protected, and the company could be punished for the public statements it had been making on this topic. Observers of the case believe that it demonstrates a double standard. Critics who do not have a direct commercial interest can speak and make statements that might even be incorrect and not rebutted. By the same token, Nike would be prohibited from speaking even though its statements were true and useful to audiences in their efforts to form an opinion on the case.

The U.S. Supreme Court agreed to hear the case but then refused to issue an opinion. Those who wanted to judge the case argued that it was not protected because the message mixed commercial and political speech but did so to discuss the issue, not make a recommendation on the purchase of a product. In essence, the issue was whether Nike supported sweatshop conditions and had misrepresented that fact rather than whether it had alleged that a product purchase depended on the fact that Nike did not support those business practices. None of Nike's advertisements addressed the connection. Instead, that issue was debated as an issue.

Nike and any other company whose business practices might be questioned would have to be cautious in how it addressed the issue because the California Supreme Court left open the question of whether a voice might express an opinion on business practices unrelated to his or her specific decision on a project. Such voice need not be true or accurate but simply public to constrain the speech of a corporate entity and deny it the right of participation in public issue communication if the plaintiff found that debate offensive.

(Continued)

(Continued)

As part of its settlement of the California case, Nike agreed to pay $1.5 million to the Washington, D.C.–based Fair Labor Association (FLA) for "program operations and worker development programs focused on education and economic opportunity." This settlement, however, did nothing to resolve the much more fundamental question of the limits and responsibilities of corporate speech, as well as the blend or chasm between commercial and issue communication.

Whether in fact they do, companies have reason to believe that they must either be extremely cautious or not speak at all on matters of commercial activities that would be assumed according to tradition to fall in the category of political or noncommercial speech. The current decision, therefore, is likely to have a predictable chilling effect on corporate speech, which some feel limits companies' ability to make society more fully functioning. The logic of the supporters of the California law reason that the only incentive companies have to speak on public policy issues is for commercial advantage; therefore, all of that speech is not protected. Thus, for instance, energy and chemical companies could be constrained from discussions on environmental issues because, the logic would apply, the only reason they do so is to achieve favorable business practices at the potential and, by implication, likely detriment of environmental quality and public health.

Such interpretations clearly instantiate the principle that corporations are inherently bad and business arrangements can dominate public discourse to the disadvantage of the public interest. Nothing such organizations could say, the logic follows, could serve the public interest because it is inherently at odds with the corporate interest. Thus, the principle in the case as it stands in fact might not mute companies and governmental officials but merely give them the rationale to do the public business outside of the public venue. That position would seem to contradict the very principle underpinning the case of the party (parties) offended in the case of Nike's speech. It might also lead companies to be wary or unwilling to state their corporate responsibility standards, which in turn could reduce the likelihood that they would be properly attentive to those standards. The principle of the case as it stands could also lead trade associations and front groups to become the primary spokespersons for industry-specific or general issues. Individual companies might mask their incentives and identities behind such groups as a way of protecting their "right to speak" and commercial interests.

Chapter Goals

This chapter offers principles and guidelines that can be used to determine how and when organizations can engage in issues communication. Although the First Amendment of the U.S. Constitution seems to guarantee unfettered rights of communication, in reality, organizations are constrained in various ways. The chapter opens with an overview of the rights and privileges, as well as responsibilities. It focuses on the Federal Communications Commission, Internal Revenue Service, and Federal Trade Commission. It makes passing observations about restrictions on new communication technologies. It closes with a brief examination of the principles introduced in the opening case, *Kasky v. Nike*. The central theme of the chapter is that commercial speech is constrained, whereas issues communication is less so. Over the years, however, the definition of issues communication has moved this form of discourse closer to the guidelines of commercial speech. Those guidelines apply to businesses, do not apply to nonprofits, and apply less if at all to government agencies. If the communication playing field unduly constrains businesses' voice in public policy discussions, that could mute one of the useful forms of issues communication. By the end of this chapter, the reader should have a better understanding of the rights and responsibilities of issues communication as well as a rationale for advocating the role of businesses in issues communication.

Throughout this book, the authors have featured Quintilian's advice that the effective speaker must first be good—a person or, in this case, an organization of high character. With that principle in mind and the opening vignette in our memory, we look with interest on Nike's (2007) *Innovate for a Better World: Nike FY05–06 Corporate Responsibility Report.* "We see corporate responsibility as a catalyst for growth and innovation," said Mark Parker, Nike, Inc.'s president and CEO. "It is an integral part of how we can use the power of our brand, the energy and passion of our people, and the scale of our business to create meaningful change" (p. 4). Noting the inseparability of sound business practices and high standards of corporate responsibility, Nike reported that it set benchmarks to improve labor conditions in contract factories, create a climate-neutral company, drive sustainable product design and innovation, and unleash potential by giving youth greater access to the benefits of sport, which feature the theme that strategic issues management (SIM) requires four carefully connected pillars. In more detail:

- Improve labor conditions by eliminating excessive overtime in Nike brand contract factories by 2011. Excessive overtime is one of the most serious ongoing labor compliance issues the company and the industry face. Nike's priority continues to be improving conditions for the almost 800,000 contract factory workers who make the company's products.

- Make all Nike brand facilities, retail, and business travel climate neutral by 2011. Nike has exceeded its reduction targets for CO_2 emissions over the past 2 years through the World Wildlife Fund's Climate Savers program. The company also eliminated fluorinated gases (F-gases) across all Nike brand products following 14 years of research and development in the company's Nike Air cushioning system.

- Design all Nike brand footwear (more than 225 million pairs per year) to meet baseline targets by 2011 for waste reduction in product design and packaging, elimination of volatile organic compounds, and increased use of environmentally preferred materials. All Nike brand apparel is targeted to meet baseline standards by 2015 and equipment by 2020. Nike is designing sustainable innovation solutions into its products that the company anticipates will create benefits throughout its supply chain and support achievement of its targets.

- Invest in community-based initiatives that use the power of sport to unleash potential and improve the lives of youth. Over the past 2 years, Nike has invested $100 million in community-based sport initiatives. The company is targeting a minimum investment of $315 million through 2011.

In addition to setting business targets, Nike continues its commitment to supply-chain transparency by updating public disclosure of the more than 700 contract factories worldwide producing Nike products. In 2005, Nike was the first company in its industry to disclose its factory base to encourage industry transparency and collaboration. For the first time, Nike also has posted on its Web site the company's contract factory auditing tools. The tools help to provide further transparency and insight into how the company evaluates and monitors its contract factories for compliance with company standards.

It should be noted that numerous activist organizations remain vocal critics of Nike's business practices, suggesting that not much has changed since Kasky's lawsuit. Web sites such as BoycottNike and Global Exchange have argued that Nike's labor and business practices remain unethical. However, according to A. Bernstein's (2004) piece in *Business Week,* "when most human rights groups and even student protesters find a problem at a Nike factory, they now deal with the company directly instead of pounding it with public demonstrations. That's one reason why you don't see Nike getting hit with ugly sweatshop publicity so much these days" (p. 1). Bernstein quoted Maria S. Eitel, Nike's vice president for corporate responsibility, stating, "You haven't heard about us recently because we've had our head down doing it the hard way. Now, we have a system to deal with the labor issue, not a crisis mentality" (p. 1).

Many advocates of the importance of corporate speech on matters of public policy reason that if companies are expected to achieve ever more daunting standards of corporate responsibility, one of the pillars of that effort is to communicate about important issues. That challenge extends to the companies' need to communicate on what principles define corporate responsibility, how well or badly they meet those standards, and what they say in response to critics on such matters. Since corporate critics often have unlimited speech opportunities, muting or chilling companies can lead to a lopsided dialogue that does disservice to the key publics who want and expect to know corporate positions.

A central principle in this discussion is the "citizenship" status of organizations, including companies. Another is the problem that deep pockets can distort the dialogue to the advantage of companies.

Legislative, Judicial, and Regulatory Constraints on Issues Communication

Courts and legislatures recognize that organizations, businesses, and nonprofits are "artificial" or "unnatural" persons. As a "person" in the eyes of the law, these entities have rights, privileges, and responsibilities. Among those is the right to speak responsibly in public to make statements on issues of public interest for public policy formation. To "speak" takes many forms, whether paid or unpaid; for instance, advertising whether using television, a billboard, a newspaper, or radio is a form of paid speech. Speech can include making financial contributions; to spend money for or against public policy issue positions or political candidates is a form of corporate speech.

Speech can also occur on the Internet, especially through home pages and blogs. As artificial citizens, organizations have certain rights and responsibilities under the First Amendment of the Constitution. For example, *Reno v. American Civil Liberties Union*, a 1997 Supreme Court decision, made it clear that speech on the Internet was fully protected by the First Amendment. This decision overturned Congress's Communications Decency Act of 1996, which was created to regulate indecency on the Internet by controlling who could operate certain Web sites, but the Children's Internet Protection Act of 2000 has remained.

Critics of business practices often seek to constrain corporate communication primarily because they worry that the ability to spend substantial sums of money to buy time and space as well as use professional communicators distorts the public dialogue. This deep-pockets effect, some worry, results from the ability to make financial contributions for and against ballot positions, thereby increasing the chances that the corporate interest can prevail over what the public interest otherwise would have been. If businesses have disproportionate impacts on issues and if the stance they take is incorrect, ordinary persons or poorly funded activist groups may have limited ability to properly balance the public policy dialogue. The result can be an incorrect and unwise public policy stance, one that is not based on all of the relevant facts or does not give fair hearing to all of the information and opinion that should be brought to bear. Critics of business speech seek to (a) prohibit or limit the amount of money spent on issue campaigns, (b) require all advertising and public relations claims be factual, and (c) bar issue communicators access to the electronic.

Defenders of business speech reason that hearing multiple opinions, including those of business, is important in a society that prizes freedom of speech. The rationale for this position is not simply the iconic virtue of freedom of speech but much more fundamentally the virtue of interested parties having access to the opinions of all parties interested in taking a position on various issues—the logic of the town meeting as a marketplace for the interchange of ideas. Kerr (2007) offered a detailed analysis of the legal status of this challenging interpretation of the First Amendment and its impact on business speech. He sees the continuing tension between a laissez-faire interpretation, as reflected in *First National Bank of Boston v. Bellotti* (1978), and one that more carefully achieves a balanced dialogue that is not corrupted by the ability of one voice to dominate, perhaps because of its ability to spend.

Despite problems, government officials acknowledge the right, indeed the responsibility, of corporate entities to speak on issues that affect their well-being, especially when that interest is tied to the public interest. This principle recognizes that public policy decisions can be wise and informed only if the interested parties put their ideas and information out for public scrutiny. As collectivities of persons acting for a shared interest, organizations are designed to express interests that people cannot make individually. People are allowed to create and join corporate entities on the assumption that such membership is a useful form of financial or public policy power.

For several decades, observers have acknowledged that interested publics must have the opportunity to obtain accurate, balanced views as to the faults and strengths of corporate behavior, operating requirements, and corporate responsibility (Lukasik, 1981). The question is how to balance that dialogue and limit those players who have the potential of undue influence. On this point, Sethi (1987) reasoned,

> In order for society to operate in a reasonable, socially equitable and politically acceptable manner, some restrictions are inevitable to curb the excesses of one group while facilitating greater expression for other groups that would otherwise be squeezed out of the market-place of ideas. (p. 281)

Rather than accept this dire view, a more positive one is that by allowing maximum communication by those who have vested interests in each issue's outcome, the dialogue is enriched rather than corrupted. If corporations or activist groups, for instance, place paid advertising asserting their preferred view on an issue, reporters and news commentators become aware of issues they might otherwise not notice or ignore. Alerted to the issue, their reporting of competing points of view can enrich the public policy dialogue, increasing the likelihood that key publics will obtain relevant information and create wise policy conclusions. In the past several years, the growth of the Internet as a key medium for issues communication has increased the likelihood that interested parties and key publics can have fair and full access to the dialogue without the corrupting influence of deep pockets.

Government control of corporate speech is problematic to implement under the best circumstances. American Civil Liberties Union Executive Director Ira Glasser (1983) argued that supporters of restrictions "see the free flow of information as a threat, and seek increasingly to insulate governmental decisions from public debate" (p. 2). Issues managers who do not know and appreciate these restraints are likely to make mistakes regarding the advice they give senior management regarding the design and execution of communication campaigns.

The real power of the First Amendment, adopted in 1791, relates to government restriction of five separate rights, including assembly, petition, presses, religion, and speech. Four clauses from the First Amendment, Cutlip, Center, and Broom (2006) suggested, relate to the core of public relations: (a) *speech rights,* including ideological and symbolic, and the right to hear and the right to remain silent; (b) *press rights* and the dissemination of information, which belongs to all citizens and not just media; (c) *assembly rights* to gather for any purposes related to governmental policies and ideas; and (d) *petition rights* that allow people to question their governmental representatives without fear of reprisal. A quick recap of the book argues that these concepts and rights are fundamental to the practice of public relations and SIM.

While overall there is no such category as "public relations" in the courts or with First Amendment scholars (Cutlip et al., 2006; Fitzpatrick & Palenchar, 2006), Petersen and Lang's (2000) review of the U.S. Supreme Court decisions from 1766 to 1999 suggests that there is a strong link among public relations and the lobbying of government for redress of grievances, tactics such as publicity campaigns, and the marketplace of ideas. Fitzpatrick and Palenchar's (2006) review of Court decisions in relationship to public relations' third-party techniques and front groups demonstrated a Court that was willing to listen to aspects of public relations in relationship to free speech, lobbying, and monopolies.

The Rationale for Organizations Speaking as Citizens

As persons in the eyes of the law, what privileges and responsibilities do organizations enjoy? That question addresses the right or privilege companies and other organizations have to communicate in public. Central to this analysis is the awareness that the courts feel strongly committed to protect natural citizens' rights to receive information and ideas.

Supreme Court decisions grant corporations limited protected rights to speak on issues of public interest (*Consolidated Edison Company of New York v. Public Service Commission,* 1980; *First National Bank of Boston v. Bellotti,* 1978).

The basic premise in these decisions is the public value of having companies supply information and argument on public policy issues. The key in such decisions is public interest, the right to know. That principle, often championed as a rationale for risk communication, rests on the reasoning that people have a right to information relevant to risks and corrective actions that affect their well-being.

The *Bellotti* case asked whether companies could make financial contributions in support of or in opposition to state referendum questions that did not materially affect their property or business activities. The state of Massachusetts had prohibited such expenditures. First National Bank of Boston and four other corporations wanted to spend money to defeat a referendum item that would have created a graduated personal income tax. The majority view of members of the Supreme Court on this case was that the discussion of public policy issues is central to the First Amendment, the right of persons whether natural or artificial to address public issues to inform public policy. If the public's interest is served, the speech is protected. The issue of whether the speaker is materially affected is not relevant to the right of the individual to speak. The larger issue is the value of enlightened public opinion. The public interest is the vital criterion in deciding whether to protect speech. To prohibit companies and other organizations from speaking on referendum issues even when they do not have a direct interest in that issue, the state needs to demonstrate a compelling state interest.

The Supreme Court considered the potential contamination of deep pockets on the political process and concluded that unlike unlimited spending to support political candidates, corruption would not necessarily occur merely because one side could spend more on an issue position than its opponents. Politicians can be "bought" with indebtedness gained through campaign contributions. But issue positions cannot be similarly bought. Ideas are put forth for public consideration without inherent bias that they will play a disproportionately large role, despite the amount of advertising purchased. If a state wishes to limit spending on ballot issues, it must demonstrate a compelling public interest for that restraint.

Even if the advertising purchased by large organizations can influence election outcomes, that does not mean that the influence is inherently contrary to the public interest. Concern about balanced public discussion was addressed by the Court, with the majority view pointing out that *Buckley v. Valeo* (1976) rejected the concept of "equalization" of speech. *Buckley,* however, affirmed the conclusion that to spend is to speak: If a company contributes or uses money for or against some issue position, the expenditure is speech. The importance of the *Bellotti* case is its affirmation that public discussion of issues is valuable and any restriction on such speech must be founded on a compelling argument that such restriction enhanced the political dialogue.

In *Consolidated Edison of New York v. Public Service Commission* (1980), the justices ruled that Con Edison had a First Amendment right to send out bill stuffers advocating the use of nuclear fuel to generate electricity without giv-ing equal time to opponents of the use of nuclear fuel. Nuclear generation, although controversial as an energy source and, therefore, ostensibly political, has substantial commercial importance. Likewise, increased use of electricity has "political" implications. Opponents of the use of nuclear fuel to generate electricity sought to force Con Edison to include their position on the bill stuffers, a kind of balanced discussion of the issue of nuclear generation. Citing *Bellotti*, the Court justified its verdict by reaffirming the public's right to acquire information and downplayed the fear that a captive audience, the per-sons who received the bills, are likely to be easily and decisively swayed by Con Edison's communication campaign. One issue in this case was the eco-nomic incentive the company had for conducting its advocacy campaign. The *Consolidated Edison* ruling found that the bill stuffers were political speech due to the controversy surrounding the use of nuclear fuel and not commercial. One reality is that companies can indeed create a boomerang effect. As it advo-cates some position, key publics are likely to attribute profit motive for the rea-son for the position taken. That motive can harm the character of the speaker and weaken the credibility of the position taken.

In *California Medical Association v. FEC* (1981), the Supreme Court began to be more cognizant of issues that had been raised by minority justices in the previous cases. They questioned whether deep-pockets spending skewed the ballot campaign process. Evidence was entered into the case that indicated that large contributions weakened the individual's influence in the ballot process and skewed the results. Justices writing for the minority applauded the efforts of the election commission to define limits on corporate participation in the ballot campaign process. To spend was to spoil: That was the minority position.

The *Austin v. Michigan Chamber of Commerce* (1990) decision reexamined principles basic to the *Bellotti* decision and laid a foundation for subsequent prohibition or at least restrictions on the rights of organizations to speak on issues of public policy. The chamber sought to fulfill its organizational mission by spending money from its treasury to buy newspaper advertising space to promote a specific candidate running for office in the Michigan House of Representatives. The chamber's message was that this candidate would work to foster jobs and strengthen the economy. A Michigan election statute prohibited such expenditures. The Supreme Court upheld the election statute, based on the public's need and right to know the issues in public policy debates, includ-ing those central to political campaigns.

The theme that survived in this case was one that had been raised before. Does the power to spend more money lead to greater political influence? The Court's answer was yes. The Court wanted to distinguish between the value of placing ads and engaging in other forms of communication as compared with spending money on behalf of a specific candidate. Stressing the desire to main-tain or achieve a level playing field so that all ideas have an equal play in the public policy debate, the Court was willing to allow limitations on corporate speech, thereby suggesting that "state-created" (artificial) individuals could be limited in their political communication and that this limitation could include restrictions on spending. In this regard, the Court weakened the *Buckley* prohibition on equalization. (For an extensive review of this case, see Casarez, 1991.)

The cases reviewed in this section deal with the constitutionality of limiting corporate political speech. Of related interest are court decisions that have clarified or blurred the distinctions between political (noncommercial) and commercial communication. In *New York Times Co. v. Sullivan* (1964), the Supreme Court ruled that advertising that is valuable to public opinion may be protected even if it is commercial. First Amendment protections were extended to commercial speech in *Bigelow v. Virginia* (1975). Commercial speech, said the Supreme Court, is protected when it discusses issues of value to society, in this case, the availability of abortions. Over the years, especially with the Kasky controversy, the distinction between commercial and political speech is blurred. Thus, the previous protection of commercial speech when it discusses policy may in fact be reversed so that all speech is commercial and not protected, especially when it discusses controversial matters.

In such matters, the prevailing interest scrutinized by the Court is not so much the right of the organization to speak but the right of the public to hear what is said. Similarly, the Court protected individuals' right to receive information in *Virginia State Board of Pharmacy v. Virginia Citizens Consumer Council* (1976). In *William F. Bolger et al. v. Young Drug Products Corp.* (1981), the issue was whether a company could advertise a birth control product (commercial speech) and discuss venereal disease and family planning (political speech). The Court ruled that discussion of family planning and venereal disease made the mailing of sufficient public value to extend First Amendment protection to commercial speech.

Because the right of commercial speech under the First Amendment is not absolute, the Supreme Court has followed the premise that truth and the value of information to the public are the essential criteria for regulating communication. A four-part analysis set forth in *Central Hudson Gas & Electric Corp. v. Public Service Commission of New York* (1980) held that (a) advertising that concerns lawful activity and is not misleading is eligible for First Amendment protection, (b) the state government must demonstrate a compelling interest to restrict advertising content, (c) regulation must directly advance the government's stated interest, and (d) regulations may not exceed the boundaries necessary to serve that interest. In striking down a blanket ban forbidding utilities from advertising to stimulate the use of electricity, the Court concluded that even though the state was correct in wanting to conserve energy and, therefore, sought to prohibit speech that advocated the use of energy, the state could not justify its legislative action by merely wanting to suppress information about electric devices or services even when that advertising would cause no net increase in total energy use. This case defined commercial speech as that which is in the economic interests of the speaker and its audience and which proposes a commercial transaction.

Commercial speech proposes and promotes a commercial transaction (*Board of Trustees v. Fox,* 1989; *Edge Broadcasting,* 1989). It is relevant to the exchange of goods and services for pay: price, quality, location, and availability. Commercial speech relates to the economic interest of the sponsor and is used by consumers to make better buys. Not so easily included in this definition are discussions of attributes of the company, its image, or reputation. Some image components do not directly suggest commercial outcomes but are related to public policy issues, such as safety of plant operation. As will be seen in the following section on the FTC, statements that have public policy implications but are made to protect the public policy integrity of a product, such as cigarettes, can be considered to be commercial speech. The key to this analysis is that commercial speech is less protected by the First Amendment.

These cases suggest that corporate entities have a protected right to speak on issues of public interest as long as their influence does not corrupt the public policy process. The rationale for that opinion is not merely the entity's right to speak but the public's right to receive information and opinion in its effort to form thoughtful opinions. Commercial speech is not protected unless it is accompanied with messages that are vital to the community's need for information and opinion and presented in ways that are candid, honest, and verifiable.

Federal Constraint

While the remainder of this chapter considers the influence of the Federal Communications Commission (FCC) and the Federal Trade Commission (FTC) over corporate communication, numerous legal areas and federal agencies are both a guideline and a constraint on the practice of SIM and public relations: legal issues such as tort law (libel and privacy issues); "food slander" laws; copyright law, including copyright issues on the Internet; litigation public relations; and trademark law. The Freedom of Information Act of 1966 relates to disclosure of governmental activities, and the 1996 Electronic Freedom of Information Act added access to digital information held by those federal government agencies.

In relationship to lobbying, which is a fundamental part of public policy dialogue and SIM, the Regulation of Lobbying Act of 1946 was enacted "to provide for increased efficiency in the legislative branch of the government" (S. 2177, 79th Cong., 2d Sess., Public Law No. 601: 2 U.S.C. 261–272). The legislation required the disclosure of expenditures made by or on behalf of any person (defined to include organizations) with the purpose of influencing federal legislation. Those covered were persons whose "principal purpose" was to aid in the "passage or defeat of any legislation by the Congress of the United States" or "to influence, directly or indirectly, the passage or defeat of any legislation by the Congress of the United States" (S. 2177, 79th Cong., 2d Sess., Public Law No. 601: 2 U.S.C. 261–272, 1946).

Primarily because of its vague and confusing language, this act had limited effect. For example, the "principle purpose" phrase effectively exempted many organizations and individuals whose principal purpose was not related to lobbying activities but who became involved in policy matters only when a particular piece of legislation affected them. According to Kuntz (1994), the act was "widely ignored for decades" because of the "patchwork of loopholes" (p. 103). In 1983, the Department of Justice deemed the law "unenforceable" (Kuntz, 1994, p. 104).

In 1995, new legislation addressed perceived flaws and loopholes in the 1946 act. After several failed attempts at lobby reform, Congress passed the Lobbying Disclosure Act of 1995 (104th Cong., Public Law No. 104–65; 21 U.S.C. 1601), which tightened lobbying disclosure requirements both internationally and domestically. Public relations practitioners, among others, who focus on "lobbying activities" on behalf of domestic and foreign interests are required to register under this law. The Foreign Agents Registration Act of 1938 (FARA) (H.R. 1591, 75th Cong., 1938) requires the registration of agents of foreign principals, including those related to lobbying and public relations activities.

Federal commissions also can play a large role in the dialogue of public policy advocated in the principles of SIM. The Securities and Exchange Commission primarily involves investor relations issues such as the Sarbanes-Oxley Act of 2002 (officially the Public Company Accounting Reform and Investor Protection Act), which is supposed to increase investor confidence in a company's accounting procedures by having CEOs (chief executive officers) and CFOs (chief financial officers) who are subject to criminal prosecution for misrepresentations or inaccuracies, certify the accuracy of financial reports. Other federal regulatory agencies include the Food and Drug Administration; the Bureau of Alcohol, Tobacco, and Firearms; and, in a little more detail, the Internal Revenue Service and the Federal Trade Commission.

INTERNAL REVENUE SERVICE

Another federal agency is the Internal Revenue Service (IRS). As was reasoned in the *Bellotti* and *Austin* cases, to spend is to speak. That principle was affirmed by the U.S. Supreme Court in 2007, which also said that laws infringe on corporate speech if they incorrectly constrain spending. Business critics and some governmental officials assert that if an entity can spend more, it speaks more with greater impact. Such arguments are at least 30 years old. A 1978 House of Representatives hearing brought forth persons who advocated using a broad interpretation of what kinds of advertisements should not be deductible under IRS Regulation 162–20 as necessary and ordinary operating expenses (U.S. Congress, 1978a, 1978b). Business critics sought to use IRS guidelines to force companies to decide not to use paid advocacy communication because the impact on their budgets would be too great. Activists who oppose corporate speech try to make it costly, rather than deductible. Therein lies the role of the IRS in issues communication.

The IRS can affect how and when you communicate by its ability to determine which expenditures are legitimate business expenses and thus affecting your SIM efforts. For example, if corporate dollars are not deducted, executives are reluctant to participate in communication campaigns. For nonprofits, their 501(c)(3) status affects their cost of doing business as well. Fund-raising activities receive special tax code status because they are conducted by nonprofit organizations.

How tax code provisions regarding business deductions are interpreted affects companies' participation in public discussion of issues because corporate communicators are reluctant to allocate nondeductible advertising dollars. For instance, during the energy debates of the early 1980s, Shell decided not to engage in the windfall profits tax debate because advertisement costs on the pending piece of legislation were nondeductible. Participating in this campaign would have meant that "half of Shell's advertising budget would go for taxes" (Iverson, 1982, p. 18). Willing to spend such funds, Mobil took a conservative stance regarding the tax deductibility of its campaign expenses. Mobil pioneered issue advocacy as we know it today, but at a cost. Mobil Tax Legislative Counsel Thomas J. DuBos (1982) observed, "If in doubt we would decline to deduct the expenses. This position was conscientiously taken to reduce the public criticism that large companies, particularly Mobil, receive from time to time from the media and even elected officials."

A substantial advantage of proactive issues management accrues from the ability to monitor issues and communicate about them before they progress to the stage where they become pending legislation. If a company incurs costs in its efforts to enhance its ability to meet corporate responsibility expectations, it can deduct those expenses. If a communication campaign is undertaken to prove the company is acting responsibly and should not be punished as is being threatened by legislation or regulation, the costs might not be deductible but still a solid return on investment. One might speculate that an advertising campaign under this circumstance might be treated differently than corporate participation in public hearings, for instance. If corporations are unwisely constrained, the public may lose a valuable and often unique source of information, thereby defeating a well-established principle of court review of communication policy: the right of the public to receive valuable information on policy issues.

FEDERAL TRADE COMMISSION

The FTC's predecessor, the Bureau of Corporations, was created in 1903, and the FTC Act became law in 1914. You are most likely familiar with the FTC in relationship to advertising and product promotion. When you refer to care labels in clothes, product warranties, or stickers showing the energy costs of home appliances, you are using information required by the FTC. SIM managers and public relations practitioners must be familiar with the laws requiring truthful advertising or prohibiting price fixing. When the FTC was created in 1914, its purpose was to prevent unfair methods of competition in commerce as part of the battle to "bust the trusts." Over the years, Congress passed additional laws giving the agency greater authority to police anticompetitive practices. In 1938, Congress passed the Wheeler-Lea Amendment, which included a broad prohibition against "unfair and deceptive acts or practices." In 1975, Congress passed the Magnuson-Moss Act, which gave the FTC the authority to adopt trade regulation rules that define unfair or deceptive acts in particular industries. Since then, the commission also has been directed to administer a wide variety of other consumer protection laws, including the Telemarketing Sales Rule, the Pay-Per-Call Rule, and the Equal Credit Opportunity Act (FTC, n.d.).

The FTC is empowered to regulate the substance of commercial communication and retains broad power to define and regulate unfair or deceptive advertising claims (T. L. Carson, Wokutch, & Cox, 1985; Cohen, 1982; Section 5 of the FTC Act as amended, 15 USCS Section 45). Former FTC attorney H. Robert Ronick (1983) observed that even a "cursory reading of the FTC's implementing statute will show that the agency has enormous latitude and can literally use its imagination in deciding what is and what is not unfair, deceptive, or unlawful" (p. 38). The FTC's substantiation program requires factual support for advertised claims regarding a product's safety, performance, efficacy, quality, or comparative price.

From a public relations perspective, the FTC has jurisdiction over product news releases and other forms of product publicity, such as videos and brochures. Recent issues the FTC has dealt with include product promotion endorsements and testimonials by movie studios and entertainment companies, guidelines for green marketing, and publicity for "healthy" food products such as "low-carb" (Cutlip et al., 2006).

The nature of issues advertising is such that traditional FTC guidelines on factual verifiability are extremely difficult to apply. Issues ads involve arguable interpretations of fact, value, and policy. As Sethi (1977) wrote 30 years ago and still remains true today, "It is well nigh impossible to develop reasonably objective measures of proof of accuracy for most advocacy advertising without making them so onerous as to be unimplementable, or ad hoc and therefore capricious" (p. 258). In fact, it is easier to determine whether claims are unsubstantiated than to determine whether they are true, and establishing criteria to operationalize verifiability often lags behind the need to apply them ("Perspectives on Current Developments," 1983). For 3 decades, in various federal administrations, FTC staff members have taken steps to regulate image advertisements and differentiate between them and issues advertising. SIM practitioners need to stay abreast of the latest changes in regulations in the FTC and other federal agencies.

As is evident in the *Kasky v. Nike* battleground, which stands today without clear Supreme Court opinion, support exists for FTC interpretation that ostensible issue advertising is commercial speech when it is used to defend a product, service, or company against allegations, even when fact can be used in judging the issue. At issue in such decisions is the extent to which the information put out for public consideration is of value to the public or only expressed in the interest of the advocate. Such interpretation has been provided by Cutler and Muehling (1989), who stressed the potential benefits of the advertisement: to the sponsor, the industry, the business community, or society as a whole. The farther the ad moves from the narrow interest of the sponsor to the concerns and well-being of others, the more likely it is not to require FTC intervention. In this sense, the telling distinction between commercial and political speech is the degree to which the resolution of the issue has a competitive impact favoring the sponsoring organization. If the advocated position benefits the industry and the society, it is political rather than commercial.

The FTC guidelines regarding what is regulatable speech seem to be narrowing the latitudes available to organizational spokespersons. *Kasky v. Nike* also suggests limits on when, where, and how companies can speak. The apparent attempt is to assist the public in its efforts to obtain honestly developed and fairly presented fact and information that serve an interest beyond that of the sponsoring company. Such provision, however, seems to apply only to companies since nonprofits are regulated by different standards. Many nonprofits are political to the extent that they take positions on factual, social, economic, and moral issues. If they want to maintain their tax-exempt status, they are cautious in taking issue position. However, many nongovernmental organizations (NGOs) are designed to spend all of their revenue, and doing so to promote issues is a fundable part of their mission.

In this critique, be mindful of the peril posed by Knight and Greenberg (2002), who noted that Nike was targeted because it had successfully integrated commercial and social concerns in its promotion and brand equity claims: "Nike has become a major target [of activists] because it has successfully integrated different forms of corporate communication into the promotion of a high-profile corporate identity" (p. 542). That theme addresses points throughout the book but alerts us to key ideas discussed in Chapter 10, which addresses the connection between promotional efforts (as well as crisis response) to build brand equity and SIM.

Long before Kasky's criticism of Nike, business critics had attempted to politicize corporate communication. The historical review of the FCC will help to provide a clearer picture of the process and role of federal agencies on issues communication constraint. The guiding principle of all these constraints relates back to the concept that issues communication should foster the good of the community (Kruckeberg & Starck, 1988).

FEDERAL COMMUNICATIONS COMMISSION

The Federal Communications Commission was created by the Communications Act of 1934 and is charged with regulating interstate and international communications by radio, television, wire, satellite, and cable. Communication technology has evolved, and so has the role of the FCC. Its responsibilities: educates and informs consumers about telecommunications goods and services; enforces the Communications Act; regulates AM radio, FM radio, and television broadcast stations, as well as cable television and satellite services; oversees cellular and PCS phones, pagers, and two-way radios and regulates the use of radio spectrum; addresses public safety, homeland security, national security, emergency management and preparedness, and disaster management; and is responsible for rules and policies concerning telephone companies that provide interstate and, under certain circumstances, intrastate telecommunications services to the public through the use of wire-based transmission facilities (FCC, n.d.).

Two decades ago, the FCC played a dominant role in determining what issues communication made its way through the electronic airways. It might someday again play a major role on such matters. For instance, in 2007, the federal Congress discussed the apparent conservative bias in television and radio talk shows. The question asked was whether such bias violated the spirit of the FCC, which for years protected and promoted balanced coverage of issues. The motive was to ensure that both or more sides of an issue were covered in electronic media so the general public could make an informed decision among the competing points of view. If it only errs on one side or has one side presented as substantially superior to any alternative, then a decision based on balanced coverage would be impossible.

Another area that the FCC has become more aggressive in is indecency, partially as a result of Janet Jackson's infamous "wardrobe malfunction" during the halftime show of the 2004 Super Bowl and because of the political climate.

According to Cutlip et al. (2006), "Public relations personnel also are feeling the heat as broadcasters express more caution booking talk show guests who discuss sexual and reproductive health" (p. 318). They noted a public relations agency that had to cancel interviews related to topics such as female sexual dysfunction while another client, a clinical psychologist, had her syndicated show dropped in three markets. The decisions and actions by the FCC can have a positive or negative effect on SIM and public discourse of issues and public policy.

The FCC has been roundly criticized for its leadership or, as some would say, lack of leadership in relationship to media ownership. For example, in December 2006, the FCC approved new rules that affect ownership of the nation's media companies. One rule change gave newspaper owners more leeway to buy radio and television stations in their markets. Recent FCC regulations have created a climate of large media ownership concentration, and some argue this stifles discourse, differing opinions, the dialectic of rhetoric, and other fundamental aspects related to SIM in relationship to making sound public policy decisions.

The FCC has also been widely criticized for doing virtually nothing to prepare the country for the conversion to digital TV in 2009 to free up valuable space in the airwaves. In fact, no federal agency has taken the lead on the transition. In fact, it is the Commerce Department that created the almost $1 billion coupon program by providing two $40 coupons that could be used toward the purchase of a digital-to-analog converter box . Consumer advocates believe that absence of leadership by the FCC has created a public dialogue based on profit led by the consumer electronic companies and the National Association of Broadcasters. Those organizations argue that the failure of the FCC to take a lead in educating the U.S. population, as well as the failure to provide financial support for national education about the conversion to digital television, left them with the responsibility. According to Joel Kelsey (2007), grassroots coordinator for Consumers Union, the nonprofit publisher of *Consumer Reports Consumers Union,* said during an interview on National Public Radio, "You see the federal government relying a lot on manufacturers, broadcasters, cable companies, satellite companies, non-profits, to get the word out and because there are so many different people that come at the transition with so many different types of agenda; consumers are very confused about whether they are affected, what they need to do to prepare for the digital transition."

However, today, the FCC plays much less of an active role. The creation of the Internet alone may reduce that potential role. However, the advent and spread of ideologically oriented (if not politically oriented) radio talk show formats has motivated some to call again for FCC scrutiny of the airwaves to ensure balance where bias is not masked by marketing. Under these conditions, a brief understanding of the past can be instructive regarding the kinds of practices that would prevent the return of this regulatory control. While a review of FCC laws and regulations is beyond the scope of this chapter, all FCC rules and regulations are codified in Title 47 of the Code of Federal Regulations (CFR). Reflections on past policies of the FCC may shed light onto what could become its new stance on public policy discussions.

Section 326 of the Communications Act of 1934, as amended, forbade the FCC from censoring broadcast programming; however, Section 307 directed the commission to grant and renew licenses "based on its assessment of the licensee's ability to serve the public convenience, interest, or necessity." Contained in Section 315(a) of the act, as amended, the fairness doctrine charged station licensees "to devote a reasonable amount of broadcast time to the discussion of controversial issues" and "to do so fairly, in order to afford reasonable opportunity for opposing viewpoints" (*Fairness Doctrine and the Public Interest Standards,* 1974; *Report on the Handling of Public Issues,* 1974).

The fairness doctrine expected broadcasters to seek balanced and contrasting views on controversial issues. In practice, as Henry Geller, former FCC general counsel (1964–1970), observed, "In its post-1962 reach for perfect fairness, the Commission has lost sight of the real goal: robust, wide open debate. However well-intentioned, its actions now thwart or tend to discourage such debate" (Friendly, 1977, p. 223).

In the late 1980s, through a series of decisions by the FCC, federal Congress, and President Reagan, the fairness doctrine was abandoned and has been replaced with the principle that the marketplace of ideas will take care of the public's need and right to become informed. Once this FCC requirement was abandoned, persons seeking to place advertisements on the electronic media or wanting to respond to conclusions made by issue opponents or media reports could follow this principle: Electronic media outlets are not required to accept issue advertising, under any principle, including the need to balance the record being made available to the public.

Part of the rationale for the current status of the fairness doctrine grew out of the Supreme Court ruling that the First Amendment rights of advocacy advertisers are not abridged if they are denied access to electronic or print media. This means that no news director is required by law to air any particular organization's issue advertisement. For electronic media, this principle was established in a complex of cases, including but not limited to *Columbia Broadcasting System, Inc. v. Democratic National Committee* (1973); *Business Executives Move for Vietnam Peace v. FCC* (1973); and *Democratic National Committee v. FCC* (1973). Basing its decision on broadcast media's special status, the Court majority expressed its desire to avoid making electronic media common carriers.

Because the electronic media constitute a special public resource, said the Supreme Court, their regulation is best left to government and the journalistic discretion of those who prepare the programs. The justices supported the need for the public to be informed fully and fairly, arguing that if those forces with more money to spend on advocacy advertising were also allowed to demand time, the broadcast media could become their tools. The majority opinion concluded that financial differences could be diminished if stations provided free time for one group to respond to the editorial advertisement paid for by another group. As laudable as that strategy is, it offends the concept that journalists should have the say over the broadcast coverage of public issues. Any change in policy would shift that responsibility from the journalists who are accountable to the public for their editorial policy to private citizens who are not similarly accountable.

Siding with corporate and special interest commitment to inform the public, Justices Brennan and Marshall dissented. They acknowledged the usefulness of the fairness doctrine to regulate the broadcast industry by forcing balanced airing of controversial issues. Citing *Grosjean v. American Press Co.* (1936), these justices emphasized the need for policy that at least partially corrected the imbalance of issue presentation. Groups should not dominate public policy discussions because of their superior ability to spend. With these arguments, the decision pitted the fairness of journalistic discretion of licensees as regulated by the FCC against the imbalance that could result from deep-pocket spending by advocacy advertisers. The decision blocked private access to the broadcast media.

Little over a year later, in *The Miami Herald Publishing Company v. Pat L. Tornillo* (1974), the Supreme Court granted newspapers the privilege of rejecting advocacy advertising. At issue was a Florida statute that required newspapers to print replies. The Court decided that the statute was contrary to the principles of the First Amendment because it interfered with the primary function of editors: to determine what news and opinion deserve to be presented to readers. A newspaper is not a passive vessel through which advertisers can supply information and opinion to audiences. Journalists have a right and a responsibility to participate in the editorial decisions regarding what should be made available to readers.

The changes in FCC doctrine resulted in part because managers of electronic media argued that the public is best served by choices broadcasters make in regard to regular news and public affairs programming and not by companies seeking to spread "partisan viewpoints on the basis of who is first in line . . . because of their ability to pay" (Kaiser Aluminum & Chemical Corporation, 1980, p. 19). Under fairness doctrine guidelines, judgment to accept issue ads was a personal call made by network or station "standards and practices" executives along with their legal counsel.

The FCC is charged with the obligation implied in the right of the public to be informed. In *Red Lion Broadcasting Co. v. FCC* (1969), the Supreme Court narrowed the rights of broadcasters when it affirmed the right of the public to receive suitable access to social, political, environmental, moral, and other ideas and experiences. Over the years, the FCC has adhered to this principle:

> The sole function of the fairness doctrine is to maintain broadcasting as a medium of free speech not just for a relatively few licensees, but for all of the American people. As such it is not only consistent with the First Amendment, it promotes the underlying concept of the Amendment. (*American Broadcasting Co.,* 1969)

In one of its most seminal statements of its regulatory philosophy, the FCC interpreted the Supreme Court as requiring the fairness doctrine "to promote robust discussion of controversial issues." As a consequence, the FCC accepted a broad mandate for its activities:

> There is no conceivable legal reason why views should not be expressed, notwithstanding that they be distasteful, incorrect or even absurd. The burden of the licensee is to give opposing views a chance for utterance and to protect persons who might have been attacked by giving them a chance to reply. (*Brandywine-Main Line Radio, Inc.,* 1968)

Appeals for airtime have led in interesting directions. One of these directions was explored by special interest advocates who have contended that they should be allowed airtime to respond to product advertising because it was associated with larger political topics. An interest group, for example, that opposes slaughter of animals might ask for airtime to discuss the "horror" of slaughter. An environmental group might request time to blast oil companies' ads or timber and building materials ads. Efforts such as these evidenced the impossibility of drawing neat lines between commercial and political advertising. Uncertainty as well as the desire to not anger product advertisers has led station managers to refuse such controversial issue advertising.

The FCC said the fairness doctrine normally applied "to ballot propositions, such as referenda, initiative or recall propositions, bond proposals and constitutional amendments" (*Fairness Doctrine,* 1974). But whereas political campaigns were considered "to be controversial issues of public importance within the meaning of the fairness doctrine" (*Radio Station KKHI,* 1980), there was a loophole. The FCC ruled that although changing the Virginia constitution was prima facie evidence of a controversy, a broadcaster could talk about the revision's constitutionality without inviting a response because the discussion did not touch on the controversy of the issue itself (*George R. Walker,* 1970).

Once stations allowed corporations or political action committees (PACs) to purchase advertorial advertising on ballot issues, the fairness doctrine prescribed that free airtime must be made available to responsible representatives of the opposing view. Clarifying the FCC's stance was a case involving the 1982

Proposition 11 statewide bottle-recycling campaign favored by Californians Against Waste (CAW). Because of the heavy bottler-canner advertising blitz to defeat the measure, CAW was able to invoke the doctrine to gain access. Its own ads featured actor Eddie Albert as a spokesman explaining how the proposition, if adopted, would lessen litter. These were run throughout California at no expense to CAW (Waz, 1983). Efforts have been made but fail to get much legislative traction to limit or balance issue ads or "character" ads used by special interest groups during political campaigns.

Exercising its mandate on electronic broadcasting, the FCC ruled that an issue did not require response or balanced coverage unless it centered on a controversy. In an attempt to assist broadcasters and other interested parties, the FCC broadly distinguished between controversial and newsworthy topics. The FCC stated that even if an issue was newsworthy, it might not be "a controversial issue of public importance" (*National Football League Players Association*, 1973). Likewise, the FCC consistently ruled that a licensee's freedom of speech would be infringed if the commission prescribed what persons were invited to provide the views that balanced the coverage (*WCMP Broadcasting Co.*, 1973). The fairness doctrine did not quantify the amount of coverage and did not involve equal time requirements. No attempt was made to support those who would seek equal time because the coverage was biased.

Network programmers seemed particularly sensitive to ads that criticize the government. Fear of government reaction, even retribution, perhaps more than the potential clash of contestants, led to the frustration W. R. Grace Company experienced when it attempted to air its ad, "The Deficit Trials, 2017 A.D." This advertisement criticized government spending and the seeming unwillingness of federal legislators to curtail the growth of the national budget deficit, a public policy stance that Grace feared would leave a legacy of financial ruin for subsequent generations. For this reason, national television networks were reluctant to air the ad.

Setting and applying guidelines to offer oversight of issues communication is problematic. McCoy (1989) reasoned that "the development of the technologically more sophisticated marketplace rendered the very constitutionality of the fairness doctrine questionable, then obsolete" (p. 70). Guidelines are best used proactively while issues communicators breathe a sigh of relief and apply these rulings as they propose advertising that could prompt reimplementation of the fairness doctrine (Hazlett, 1989; McCoy, 1989). The good news: As issues communicators seek to place issues advertising with television and radio stations, they no longer need to worry that network affiliates will reject the advertising to avoid the intrusion of the FCC into news reporting and commentary programming prerogatives. The bad news: This breath of freedom is offset with the ruling in the Columbia Broadcasting System case that news directors are not required to sell time to any entity that wants to communicate about issues.

Although for the moment a benign policy, the issue of fairness could reemerge. Discussion that occurred during the 1996 debate over new telecommunications policy raised the question that led to the fairness doctrine. What must those broadcasters who are granted control of broadcast frequencies do to demonstrate their public responsibility in balanced broadcasting? How do they demonstrate their efforts to ascertain the problems and issues prevalent in the community of license? That underpinning concern sustains interest in a doctrine of fairness (Holsinger & Dilts, 1997; Schneider, 1996). Deploring the move by the federal courts to end the fairness doctrine, Lentz (1996) claimed that action violates a crucial principle: "Truth should prevail in a market-like struggle where superior ideas vanquish their inferiors and achieve audience acceptance" (p. 1). To this end, broadcasters are now allowed a fair amount of latitude in terms of how they air issues. Some are comfortable in the option of self-selection. People can get the news and editorial opinion they want, is one mantra, because the total spectrum of electronic outlets allows people to pick and choose. No single corporate, advocacy, or media outlet can dominate discussion and deny the general public access to an array of opinions. The media richness of the American society is the strongest argument for limited control over the right of broadcasters' editorial policy. The Internet has added substantially to this richness.

Public relations approaches to issues communication are more likely to find their way into general media discussion than is issue advertising. The latter is too dependent on the willingness of news directors and others to accept the ads, with all of the baggage that can entail. In contrast, participating in government hearings, for instance, can gain media attention and offer more information than is likely to occur in an ad. Such information and evaluation can also be placed on the sponsor's home page and is likely to be a useful backgrounder for reporters working the issue.

Conclusion

Sponsors of issues communication are likely to be more successful if they frame the content of their messages and the purposes of their campaigns in terms of the demonstrable need and desire of key stakeholding publics to obtain information relevant to public policy discussions and decisions. Beyond this rubric, guidelines are specific to the particular regulatory agency. Although key organizations can be faulted for speaking in ways that are self-serving of their own interests and preferences, by putting ideas into the public arena for scrutiny by others, they meet their stewardship responsibility. In such matters, the courts have preferred to center their interpretations on the right of citizens to have access to information and opinion rather than organizations' right to express such opinion, especially in ways that are obviously construed to be in their self-interests.

SIM Challenge: Looking to the Future

Based on what you have read and knowing the implications of the *Kasky v. Nike* case, what position do you take on that controversy and why? How would it affect how you seek to design issues communication for a company?

Summary Questions

1. What is the different between a natural citizen and an artificial citizen? Why is that distinction important in terms of discussing the communication rights and constraints of companies and nonprofits?

2. Why is the right of citizens to know and receive information on matters of public interest an important principle? Is it more or less important than the right of companies to speak?

3. How does the Federal Trade Commission work to regulate commercial and issues communication? Under its interpretation, are the guidelines differentiating the two kinds of speech clear, and can they be used by issues communicators in ways that predict whether their speech will be regulated or protected?

4. Traditionally, the Federal Communications Commission was given the mission of ensuring that all sides of an issue could be obtained by citizens. Why is that charge to the FCC different today than when it was created decades ago?

5. Do you agree or disagree with this statement from Sethi (1987): "In order for society to operate in reasonable, socially equitable and politically acceptable manner, some restrictions are inevitable to curb the excesses of one group while facilitating greater expression for other groups that would otherwise be squeezed out of the market-place of ideas" (p. 281). Why or why not?

8

Issues Management and Crisis Communication

Vignette:
It Takes Two to Tango

If two organizations experience a crisis, both suffer various amounts of fault. In terms of organizational crisis, the two parties can make matters worse for stakeholders by blaming the crisis on each other. Such is the case for brand equity and product safety crises in 2008. One party is one or more major international toy manufacturers, most notably Mattel. The other is the country of China, which hosts multinational manufacturing facilities, Chinese manu- facturing facilities, and subcontractors for parts and elements of finished products. Although for some product problems, the consuming public is tolerant of some errors in manufacturing, consumers are intolerant when the products can result in the ingestion of lead by children and infants. Standards are well known, and purchasing as well as manufacturing standards are well defined and implementable. So, why do tainted products get into the hands and mouths of children and infants? Is this a crisis? If so, for whom? Does the crisis bring up an issue, or is it part of some issue? How can sound strategic issues management (SIM) practices help bring control and maintain brand equity?

It's a bit difficult to determine exactly how many toys required recall. In September 2007 (only 3 months until Christmas), Casey, Zamiska, and Pasztor (2007) offered one partial list: about 2.8 million toys recalled due to lead paint and 18.2 million toys recalled due to design flaws involving tiny magnets that could become ingested. The theme of this news story was not only the magnitude of recall but the fact that Mattel, one of the world's largest manufacturers of toys, was offering "a public apology to China for damage to the country's reputation stemming from a spate of toy recalls"

(Continued)

(Continued)

(p. A1). Instead of blaming China, Mattel accepted responsibility for the design flaw. Would that recall staunch another aspect of the crisis, such as lawsuits by Chinese companies or by the Chinese government? China had prompted this apology by attacking Mattel and U.S. regulators for lax standards in product design. The company had quietly put out an olive branch to those responsible for China's quality control agency. It voiced a strong commitment to cooperation to reduce the likelihood that similar events would happen again.

The Chinese government was concerned about not only the specific product but also the brand equity of "Made in China." China is keenly sensitive about its reputation as host of the 2008 Summer Olympic Games in their country. Attention to that issue had been voiced by Chinese officials. Debate over responsibility for toy safety followed other product safety challenges—namely, tainted pet food and tainted toothpaste. Mattel's charges led to various collateral damages. Some of the manufacturing facilities in China closed. Cheun Shnu-hung, owner of Hong Kong–based Lee Der Industrial Company, one of Mattel's major manufacturers, killed himself because of accusations. At issue was the specificity of manufacturing details. The crisis raised an issue in the U.S. Congress: Were more laws, regulations, and regulators needed to oversee importation of toys into the United States? Recalls hurt Mattel's stock market value, one indicator of its brand equity (Casey & Lloyd, 2007).

Mattel was not alone. Around Halloween, military toys and gag teeth were determined to have unsafe lead levels. This recall affected manufacturers of specific products as well as toy retail giant Toys "R" Us. Stories continued to emerge. Casey and Zimmerman (2007) reported on November 9 that three more toys were recalled: (a) Fisher-Price's Laugh & Learn brand was discovered to have pieces that posed a choking risk to children; (b) the Consumer Product Safety Commission recalled approximately 4 million Aqua Dots arts and crafts kits, which contained a chemical that in stomachs became a disorienting and potentially deadly chemical; and (c) Curious George by Marvel Toys had lead on the toys' faces.

As the holiday season neared, brand-name manufacturers and retailers moved to calm public concern. They loudly proclaimed they had received the message. They would oversee products under their label. The buying and gift-giving public could rest assured that products sold would be safe. This is a classic case that demonstrates how a crisis is a risk manifested. As toys are manufactured and sold, the buying public can worry whether they are safe. Such matters often are made salient near holidays by watchdog activist groups that list poorly manufactured toys. Traditional and nontraditional media keep such matters on the front page and at the top-of-the-hour news coverage. A search on any of several search engines can bring reports and lists of products recalled to the attention of parents and grandparents.

The stark realization is that policing from the inside is essential, as it is along the entire product line. Vigilance counts. The best-managed crisis is the one that does not happen. This vignette demonstrates how SIM theory stresses that crisis management not only is a communication activity but also starts with sound business strategic planning that is reflective, employs high standards of corporate responsibility committed to zero tolerance, and employs issues monitoring to keep abreast of issues and trends that can signal crisis. The efforts are holistic and reflective if they are going to be effective.

Chapter Goals

Chapter 8 defines crisis in the context of strategic issues management (SIM) as risk manifested. It takes a holistic approach to crisis that discusses various communication tactics but goes beyond them to look closely at business planning and corporate responsibility options that may reduce crises or mitigate their damage as they occur. Indeed, crisis response often requires a lesson learned that specifies the strategic business planning/implementation or corporate responsibility changes that are required as a positive response to the crisis. Crisis management is an issues management function that entails issues monitoring, strategic business planning, and getting the house in order, to try to avoid events that trigger outrage and uncertainty and have the potential of maturing into public policy issues. If all of these management pieces are in place, then crisis communication, especially media relations, is easier to manage. After reading this chapter, you will better understand the circumstances that can lead to a crisis event and what its consequences and challenges are. The chapter stresses the need for crisis prevention to maximize the sense of control the organization exerts over its affairs and the mutually beneficial relationships it should create and maintain with its stakeholders. Based on an issues management approach to crisis management, discussion centers on the precrisis efforts as well as the communication options that are available during and in the wake of a crisis or at least during what seems to be a crisis.

Individuals and organizations need to prepare for the worst. It takes only a short list to highlight some quintessential crises and the issues motivator each made salient.

- *Consumer safety:* Sixty-five milligrams of deadly cyanide was intentionally introduced into Johnson & Johnson's Tylenol capsules, killing eight people and costing Johnson & Johnson more than $250 million, in 1982. Most crisis communication researchers have argued that throughout the crisis,

Johnson & Johnson was viewed as an innocent company that worked to protect public safety despite financial losses and that this case study is an excellent example of ethical behavior that proved to be good for Tylenol's business and customer loyalty.

• *Environmental quality:* The Exxon (now ExxonMobil) *Valdez* oil tanker ran aground, spilling 250,000 barrels, an amount equal to more than 10 million gallons, of oil into Alaska's Prince William Sound on March 24, 1989. This environmental disaster would go down in crisis management history as a textbook case of how not to handle or communicate during a crisis, and "by the time the media was finished, the Exxon name was synonymous with environmental catastrophe" (Haddock, 2000).

• *Fairness:* Fairness to customers and a possible crisis to the brand occurred at Chrysler Corp. in the late 1980s when a group of senior executives at Chrysler were taking cars off the assembly line, up to 60,000 total, driving them a couple of months, turning back the odometers, and selling them as new. Brian Delaney, president of Clarke & Co. Public Relations in Boston, said that "the reason you may have missed this crisis was because Lee Iacocca, then chairman, got on television and said in essence, 'We found this out, we reported it. I promise it will never happen again. Those who did it will pay for it'" (Widmer, 2000, para. 16).

• *National security:* President John F. Kennedy was assassinated on November 22, 1963.

• *Student safety:* Thirty-three people were killed April 16, 2007, on the campus of Virginia Tech in what is one of the deadliest shooting rampages in American history.

• *Worker safety:* Irving J. Selikoff's studies showed the greatly increased mortality of insulation workers exposed to asbestos and made clear that an epidemic of occupational and environmental cancer was under way (Selikoff, Churg, & Hammond, 1964). According to LaDou (2004), the asbestos cancer epidemic would have been largely preventable if the World Health Organization (WHO) and the International Labor Organization (ILO) had responded early and responsibly, especially at the global level. "Part of the problem is that the WHO and the ILO have allowed organizations such as the International Commission on Occupational Health (ICOH) and other asbestos industry advocates to manipulate them and to distort scientific evidence. The global asbestos cancer epidemic is a story of monumental failure to protect the public health" (para. 1).

While there are many more historical crises than those listed above, these crises have become iconic, a part of the popular culture of U.S. society. They define the types of events that academics and practitioners think of as crises and the responses expected or not expected in their aftermath. One of the major outcomes of these events was a keen practitioner and academic interest in the nature, causes, responses, and preventions of crisis—a cottage industry.

The industrial and information ages have created a whole new range of risk, crises, and issues, while advances in communication and information technologies have increased people's awareness of these risk, crises, and issues, as well as increasing the opportunities for dialogue and shared decision making based on SIM and associated political and social discussions. Risk, crisis, and ultimately disaster are the definitive challenge to SIM and public relations practitioners who research about or work for organizations, as well as their related stakeholders and stakeseekers, whose business, political, or social missions involve managing health, safety, and environmental risks (Palenchar, 2009). As Erikson (1994) stated, modern disasters challenge humans with a new species of trouble.

Analysis over the years has revealed a close connection between crises, issues, and risks. Palenchar's (2009) review suggested that crises and risk can and should be viewed together within strategic public relations and SIM literature and are historically linked. Crises come in all kinds and exhibit degrees of severity. Some become issues because key publics debate facts relevant to the crisis and evaluate whether the organization was willing and able to implement proper standards of corporate responsibility—to exert proper control over its activities.

A crisis can cause concerned individuals and organizations to work issues to change policies and procedures. Issues can create crises; perhaps no better example is the strain on the tobacco industry after years of debate about tobacco safety. Some are the products of what others do, as in the case of a terrorist attack on an airliner. We are surrounded with many risks. We can work up emergency response protocols and put legislation and regulation into place. Regulation and legislation may not prevent a Hurricane Katrina from happening, but will they mitigate the damage and maximize the response effort to put everything right? Will emergency management reduce the likelihood that wild fires will destroy homes in places such as California or merely help in response to fight the fire and reduce loss of property and life?

Crisis management and issues management are also linked. A crisis doesn't necessarily become an issue and often does not. At other times, however, such as health and safety concerns over toys produced in manufacturing facilities in China, a crisis leads to dialogue related to fact, values, and policies that spur national and international regulations and public policies as a response to the slow actions by manufacturers to improve production and labor qualities. Some crises have the potential for becoming issues if they create or add to a key public's sense that a problem exists that needs public policy remedy. Some issues may become crises as key publics press organizations and industries to achieve higher standards of performance. In rare cases, the issue can threaten the existence of the company or industry. A crisis can be an event that creates an issue, keeps it alive, or gives it strength.

Discussion of crisis communication and issues management might open by posing a hypothesis: If an organization has a reflective management that works hard to act responsibly and engages in the fundamentals of issues management, it will not be surprised; it will not suffer the unsettling experience of a crisis. That statement is fraught with wishful thinking. A more accurate prediction of the connection between crisis and issues management is this: If an organization is engaged in issues management before, during, and after a crisis, it can mitigate and perhaps prevent the crisis from becoming an issue by working quickly and responsibly to establish or reestablish the level of control desired by relevant stakeholders.

By this logic, those who examine crises closely have defined strategies over the years by stages: precrisis, crisis event, and postcrisis. When crisis is assessed from an organizational perspective, one of the primary goals is to decrease damage inflicted by the crisis. For example, Ulmer, Sellnow, and Seeger's (2007) work comprises several phases, including a precrisis stage, before the crisis actually begins; an acute crisis stage, immediately following a dramatic event; and a postcrisis stage, when an organization must respond to the crisis (see also Coombs, 2007). What can be done before a crisis to prevent its occurrence and mitigate its impact? What is the best precrisis management and communication planning? What must be done and said during a crisis? What can be done and said postcrisis to restore the organization and put it on a track for recovery? Can the crisis response actually not only restore but also enhance its brand equity because of its responsiveness to the lessons learned from the crisis? These questions reveal the link between SIM and crisis. Effective SIM can increase the likelihood that the organization knows and can exert proper control to prevent and mitigate a crisis. Such logic suggests that crisis is not merely a matter of effective communication but, more important, a holistic approach to effective management.

Crisis Management: The Search for Control

The number and severity of crises are rising with the complexity of society and technology. Overall, the increasing media coverage of hazardous incidents and related risks has increased the prominence of crisis management.

From an American perspective, crisis communication was originally applied to political situations, following the Cuban missile conflict in the early 1960s, using a series of hypothetical situations with strategic applications measuring the cost and/or benefits of preventing crises. When Tylenol capsules were replaced with cyanide capsules in the 1980s, it sparked the beginning of research in organizational crisis communication. The Exxon *Valdez* oil spill in 1989 furthered this practice by lending validity to corporate crisis communication and helping to serve as the foundation for widespread research in the 1990s (Fishman, 1999). For the environmental community, the 1962 release of Rachael Carson's *Silent Spring* was an iconic publishing event that alerted scientists, emerging environmentalists, and the general public to the prospect that chemicals and nature were on a collision course, making people think about the environment in a way they had never done before (M. B. Smith, 2001).

Probably more than any other incident and federal response to a crisis, the 9/11 terrorist attacks on the United States spurred the creation of the Department of Homeland Security (DHS) and put crisis management and communication to the front of the line for federal government resources and research dollars. Based on the Homeland Security Act of 2002, the new department was tasked with providing federal assistance to state and local governments that responded to natural or accidental disastrous events. The Federal Emergency Management Agency, the department that coordinates all federal assistance for natural and nonnatural crisis events, became the central component of the DHS. The new department was charged with the development of an all-hazards approach to crisis response (Abbott & Hetzel, 2005).

Large, eclectic arrays of federal agencies play a role in risk and crisis communication in the United States. The Centers for Disease Control and Prevention is the lead federal agency for protecting the health and safety of people and providing credible information to enhance health decisions. The Federal Bureau of Investigation (FBI), on the other hand, has final authority over the release of information about an incident related to terrorism and bioterrorism. The Department of Justice, along with the FBI, has principle objectives to ensure that health information be provided promptly and accurately during a terrorist or suspected terrorist incident.

So what is a crisis? Not all newsworthy events are crises. Nor must the definition of crisis be limited to that which threatens the existence of an organization. For example, the *Valdez* oil spill previously mentioned did not threaten Exxon's existence, but it has been widely considered to be an archetypal crisis. Whereas the magnitude of the Exxon spill and poor management decisions might have destroyed many companies, Exxon had sufficient financial and technical reserves to weather that storm. Framed in this manner, this section defines crises and suggests that they occur in degrees of severity and threaten the integrity of the organization. It views crisis management and response as a search for control, either by the offending organization or by society. SIM is a search for order for control.

The inability of Enron management to exert proper control over its strategic business plan not only led to many people suffering criminal and civil charges but dramatically harmed the future and nature of the company. Finally, the veneer came off the management team, as well as that of consultants and other companies. Massive debt had been hidden. In that sense, management was cooking the books to make the company appear stronger than it actually was.

This example indicates an important point. We often think only about the crisis suffered by an organization, an organizational bias to crisis management and communication. In the case of Enron, these management decisions created a crisis for innocent investors, employees, and many nonprofits that had come to depend on Enron's goodwill efforts.

What, then, is a crisis? It is an untimely event that can be anticipated to occur (a risk manifested), which may prevent management from accomplishing its efforts to create the understanding and mutually beneficial relationship with interested parties needed to negotiate the mutually beneficial exchange of stakes. If unattended or poorly managed, the crisis can prevent the organization from making satisfactory progress toward achieving its mission and vision. According to Fink (1986),

> A crisis is an unstable time or state of affairs in which a decisive change is impending either one with the distinct possibility of a highly undesirable outcome or one with the distinct possibility of a highly desirable and extremely positive outcome. (p. 15)

Lerbinger (1997) defined a crisis as "an event that brings, or has the potential for bringing, an organization into disrepute and imperils its future profitability, growth, and possibly, its very survival" (p. 4) while noting three classes of crises—of the physical world, of the human climate, and of management failure. Coombs (1999) added technical breakdowns to his typology of crisis types.

Fearn-Banks (2001) incorporated threat in her latter definition of crisis when she defined it as a "major occurrence with a potentially negative outcome affecting an organization as well as its publics, services, products, and/or good name. It interrupts normal business transactions and can, at its worst, threaten the existence of the organization" (p. 480).

Weick (1988) concluded that "crises are characterized by low probability of high consequence events that threaten the most fundamental goal of an organization" (p. 305). A crisis threatens the physical system of the organization as well as "its basic assumptions, its subjective sense of self, its existential core" (Pauchant & Mitroff, 1992, p. 12). Coombs (2007) synthesized common traits others have used to define and describe a crisis, including that a crisis is perceptual, unpredictable, but not unexpected; violates expectations of stakeholders about how organizations should act; has a serious impact; has the potential to create negative or undesirable outcomes; and causes environmental damage as an outcome of the accident.

A clear, denotative definition of crisis may be easier to come by than connotative meanings held by researchers, journalists, and other stakeholders. According to Fishman (1999), the term *crisis* is field or context dependent; "one individual's crisis may be another's incident . . . with no attempt to delineate the scope or severity of a given problem" (p. 347). A definition of *crises*, however, must include an awareness that they come in degrees, therefore requiring different kinds and amounts of response. For instance, a crisis event can be characterized in terms of its potential impact on the health of an organization:

- Bed rest: an event that receives front-page, top-of-the-hour coverage. It attracts public attention but is unlikely to threaten the existence of the organization, even if it fails to make a strategic response.

- Medication: an event that requires the organization to respond to media inquiry and may demand changes in operations to prevent or lessen the likelihood of recurrence; explanation and sympathetic response as well as modest change are likely to suffice as crisis responses.

- Chronic: an event that demands that the organization communicate with the media and formulate changes that are implemented to prevent recurrence of this event. Without such response, confidence is likely to be lost in regard to the organization's operations and key personnel. People will see reason to allocate their resources to other organizations.

- Fatal: an event that ends the existence of the organization because it lacked the technical, financial, human, and communicative resources to restore faith with its stakeholders. The organization is so badly damaged that it cannot generate the resources it needs to sustain itself.

The first two conditions are more likely to be a crisis only in the sense that they create unfavorable press rather than challenge the organization's ability to operate. They may be manageable largely with communication, although they may require acknowledgment that lessons have been learned because the crises revealed mistakes. These types of events often can be corrected by routine actions of the organization working to put its house in order. The second two are more serious—true crises that pose major operational and policy changes for the organization. They may even lead to public policy action, even if the organization does not survive the crisis. The tendency is to create regulation or legislation to prevent incidents from recurring.

Although this list addresses crises in terms of a hierarchy of health concern metaphors, it might feature concepts related to the integrity of materials: tension, strain, stress, and failure. Similar lists could be proposed to suggest a progression from the point where an organization is under extra pressure through a series of stages where its integrity fails. For instance, Coombs (2007) suggested that while crises have different characteristics, there is an identifiable typology of crisis types, which he developed from a variety of researchers. This includes (a) *natural disasters,* (b) *workplace violence,* (c) *rumors,* (d) *malevolence* (when an external person uses extreme measures such as product tampering or computer hacking), (e) *challenge* (stakeholders challenge an organization with claims that it is inappropriately operating), (f) *technical error accidents* (when technology used or supplied by an organization causes an industrial accident), (g) *technical error product harm* (when technology used or supplied by an organization produces a defective or potentially harmful product), (h) *human error product harm* (product defect with potential harm is caused by human error), (i) *human error accidents,* and (j) *organizational misdeeds* (management decisions and behaviors that knowingly put stakeholders at risk or violate law) (for more details, see Coombs, 2007, p. 65).

The locus of responsibility could be internal (poor operational procedures) or external (act of God or terrorism). Set against these options are considerations of whether the crisis resulted from intentional (transgressions of corporate responsibility) or unintentional (act of God) reasons. As external and unintentional factors come together, we have a faux pas. When unintentional and internal factors occur, they produce an accident. Terrorism is one product of intentional motives and external acts. Transgressions result from intentional motives and internal acts. However, in recent years, organizations have found it difficult to shake responsibility for transgressions and acts of God. Should the federal government and the airline industry have been more vigilant prior to the calamity on 9/11? Should the persons and organizations responsible for weather prediction, the integrity of the levees in New Orleans, and emergency response (regional, state, and federal) have been more vigilant before and during Hurricane Katrina?

The objective of crisis management is to exert control over activities in ways that ensure stakeholders and stakeseekers that their interests are cared for and fostered by the organization. That is a best-case scenario. Even the best, most vigilant organization can suffer events that, even when foreseen and planned for, cannot be prevented. Effective planning and the exertion of corporate responsibility as well as informed and responsive communication are the tools an organization, even an industry, can use to avoid the imposition of external control.

Crisis response is likely to be better if it follows planning that includes all relevant specialists. Issues managers and public relations practitioners seem to benefit from the size of their organization and whether it has experienced a serious crisis; however, many organizations still do not have a crisis plan. Of the respondents in a national survey of communication practitioners in 1995, only 36.3% reported that they worked in an organization that both had a plan and practiced it (Guth, 1995). In 2002, according to a survey by the American

Management Association (2003), 64% of executives said their companies have a crisis management plan, up from 49%. Sixty-two percent of the companies have designated a crisis management team compared with 54% in 2001, while 42% have conducted crisis drills or simulations, up from 39% in 2002. And these numbers keep increasing. Once a crisis is encountered by an employer, communication practitioners find themselves more included in the creation and practice of crisis response plans.

At the core of planning is control, and crisis is about control. People want control of that which affects their self-interest and altruistic interests. Control springs from their desire to lessen the uncertainty that actions of some entity may adversely affect their health, safety, aesthetics, and well-being as well as that of animals or other aspects of the environment. Uncertainty is uncomfortable. As a personal trait, it is the perception of one's degree of certainty in a social situation (C. R. Berger & Calabrese, 1975). The concept can be viewed as "a lack of sure knowledge about the course of past, present, future or hypothetical events" (Driskill & Goldstein, 1986, p. 41). As Albrecht (1988) concluded, uncertainty is "the lack of attributional confidence about cause-effect patterns" (p. 387). According to this approach to crisis and risk (a topic expanded in Chapter 10), people believe either that circumstances are so random and unpredictable, due to the crisis, that no favorable outcome can be predicted, or they compensate for that discomfort by predicting that dire rather than favorable outcomes will occur. People tend to assume that dire consequences will outweigh positive ones; therefore, they engage in self-protective thinking and behavior.

If actions of an organization actually or even seemingly interfere with an individual's effort for control, he or she is likely to seek to achieve or reassert control. One means for achieving control is to support activist criticism of an organization or industry, seeking to browbeat it into submission. Another means for exerting control is to call on government to intervene on behalf of the public and against the organization. Courts provide avenues for exerting control.

Although control can have a negative connotation, in reality no stakeholder or stakeseeker wants to engage in stake exchanges with organizations that are unwilling or unable to establish and maintain proper amounts of control over their activities as defined by resource dependency theory. Crisis occurs when an organization actually or seemingly loses control of its operations, and the consequences of that action appear or actually do have dire consequences. Crisis strains the appearance and actuality of control. Crisis response is the enactment of control in the face of high uncertainty in an effort to win or restore audiences' and publics' confidences.

Given the need to assist organizations' efforts to achieve proper control, issues managers should have two major game plans, one for long-range objectives and one for crises. Many crises seem to involve an issue such as the

Johnson & Johnson's Tylenol capsule-tampering case. If Johnson & Johnson had not proactively undertaken measures (partly to avoid liability and partly as a marketing strategy) to provide tamperproof packaging and adopt the use of caplets in place of capsules, legislation would have been likely. Capsules could be opened and toxic substances, such as cyanide, could be placed inside in place of the proper ingredients. Because of the responsible behavior evidenced by the company and the industry in this situation, the issue was not defined as a problem that would not be corrected voluntarily.

Some crises prove that an issue needs attention. For instance, the Three Mile Island nuclear generating plant incident increased national concern over the safety of such facilities. Public pressure focused on the Nuclear Regulatory Commission. This incident produced a domino effect of increased regulation of existing plants as well as those under construction. Some safety features were retrofitted to bring existing plants to new levels of safe operation.

Issues management entails strategic business planning and management with sensitivity to the public policy arena of the organization: issues monitoring, efforts to define and implement standards of corporate responsibility needed to meet key publics' expectations, and issues communication. Any company or other organization may suffer a crisis because what it did does not satisfy stakeholder expectations; it may be dead wrong, doing the wrong things, and stupid given the circumstances of the organization vis-à-vis its key publics' expectations. Actions that prompt the crisis may be illegal. Thus, crisis management must consider the total array of activities engaged in by the organization, set in the context of expectations held by its publics and observed from their point of view.

Circumstances of a crisis may be, but do not necessarily constitute, an issue. An issue is a contestable matter of fact, value, or policy that results in conflict between concerned parties and entails the distribution of resources, either as threat or opportunities for the organization. The events of a crisis may be contestable, requiring and even expecting informed persuasion to set the record straight. Beyond that circumstance, a crisis is likely to be best defined in terms of the organization's strategic business and public policy planning. Either the organization brings the crisis to an end by exerting proper control to resolve it, or a public policy issue has the potential of maturing into a regulatory or legislative change or an adverse court decision.

If strategic business planning uses issues management to calculate and navigate threats and opportunities, the crisis may require expenditure of moneys, which, if wisely allocated, can restore or build a mutually beneficial relationship between the organization and its stakeholders. Failing that effort, which may entail implementation of higher standards of corporate responsibility, key stakeholding publics may try in the marketplace or the public policy arena to force higher standards of performance on any organization that suffers a crisis and does not make responses needed to control its activities in the interest of concerned publics. These responses may require communication. They may require improved strategic planning or higher standards of corporate responsibility. They may mature into public policy battles. They are not merely terminological.

Crisis response has become that aspect of issues management that entails imagining events that could become crises, leading to issues and planning for the eventuality that an event will occur, which has immediate negative consequences for the organization and its constituents that its products are unsafe, its procedures are unsafe, its values are corrupt, or its management is callous, uncaring, or incompetent. Given the paradigm that issues management is a discipline that is central to society's search for order, a crisis can become an issue when the offending organization seems unable or unwilling to exert sufficient control to create and maintain the mutually beneficial relationships its stakeholders expect.

Prevent a Crisis From Becoming an Issue

One prerequisite for effective crisis management is a watchful concern that certain actions and policies could constitute a crisis. As emphasized throughout this book, SIM is a strategic planning and response option that organizations can use to create and maintain mutually beneficial relationships with key stakeholders and stakeseekers. If monitoring of issues and activities is sufficiently rigorous and if the house is in order (meeting high standards of corporate responsibility), then the organization is more likely to avoid suffering a crisis. If one occurs, these strategic options decrease the likelihood that the trajectory of a crisis will become an issue of public policy concern. This section addresses strategies that organizations may use to prevent crises and lessen their long-term effects.

Wise crisis management begins before a crisis occurs—crisis prevention through effective reflectiveness and response to early warning signs. Effective crisis elimination and mitigation requires an organizational culture that promotes detection and problem solution rather than denial or indifference. It entails (a) wise strategic business planning; (b) issues monitoring in support of crisis management (see Chapter 3); (c) having key personnel coordinated and trained to communicate honestly, clearly, factually, and candidly with minimal interference from legal counsel who understand court procedures better than they comprehend media relations and the consequences of being tried in the court of public opinion; and (d) working to ascertain and implement high standards of corporate responsibility (not discussed here but discussed in Chapter 4).

First, *strategic business planning* entails wise expenditures to ensure a level of performance high enough to control the activities that can affect the financial well-being of the organization and the health, safety, and environmental quality of entities it affects. Strategic planning consists of allocating resources to achieve the mission of the organization. Crises can frustrate that effort. Executives can cut financial corners to such a degree that they increase the chances that a crisis could damage the organization. On the other hand, careful balance is required between making expenditures that are sufficient to minimize crises by meeting expected operating standards while not devoting so many financial and human resources to crisis prevention that, at least in competition with others, the organization becomes unable to generate income needed to profit and meet its obligations. To prevent such outcomes requires contingency planning, which is designed to manage risk, minimize loss, and ensure business continuity (Myers, 1993).

Contingency planning requires defining problem areas where crisis could occur. The organization needs to audit what actions and policies might lead to a crisis and determine how well it would respond to a crisis. Strategic planning requires preventive measures to minimize the likelihood of a crisis, to develop an organized response if one should occur, and to formulate an operating plan for maintaining business continuity in that event. Strategic planning entails budgeting that can, for instance, include allocations for training personnel to increase the likelihood that they can work at a level that reduces the chance of a crisis event. Strategic business planning can require expenditures to establish manufacturing processes that reduce the probability that a piece of equipment could fail unexpectedly. Expenditure on research and development can increase the likelihood that the safety processes in manufacturing and high product standards can lessen the probability that the product will be found wanting in the court of public opinion.

Strategic business planning can include choosing to create or abandon products or services, depending on the degree of risk associated with them—for instance, their manufacture or use. Strategic budgeting may be needed to ensure that manufacturing processes are monitored with such precision that all parties who handle a product, such as Tylenol, can be screened, trained, and overseen so that the company can quickly ascertain where tampering might have occurred and by whom. Allocations may be needed to create a company fire department and emergency response team in the event that a crisis occurs, such as at a chemical manufacturing plant. Strategic business planning options should be guided by issues management to look for opportunities and avoid threats associated with predicted events that could outrage the media or key publics.

Second, *issues monitoring in support of crisis management* is two-pronged. One prong results from the need to ascertain the status of sentiments that will surface if an action of the organization becomes a crisis. Research can ascertain, even second-guess, performance expectations held by key publics regarding the impact of the organization on people, animals, and environment. The second prong requires internal surveillance to monitor the quality of personnel, service, and manufacturing processes. This process may require, for example, knowing how headache remedy capsules are manufactured, stored, and provided to retail outlets. It may entail using focus groups of employees to obtain their opinions regarding the high-risk processes and weak links in the manufacturing system. Quality assurance and internal security can be vital when determining why events occurred that raised stakeholders' concerns and a sense of uncertainty and resulted in intense media scrutiny.

As a monitoring tool, a crisis audit looks for the points in the organization's operations where, if a problem were to occur, it would generate public outrage and uncertainty. If a chemical vessel malfunctions, media, concerned citizens, and government officials want to know what chemical(s) was in the vessel, how it was designed and operated, what its construction and maintenance specifications were, how well trained the personnel were who handled it, and how much of the material escaped. Inquiries can be endless. The company or other organization has to know its business intimately, have excellent records of its activities, and know what persons are responsible for assessing the nature of the crisis and for predicting how quickly activities will return to normal or be improved to a level whereby a similar crisis will not occur.

Monitoring is vital at various stages in the crisis process. The first stage, *prodromal,* exists when warnings first appear, as warning clouds form on the horizon. This crisis phase is similar to an emerging issue. The second stage is *acute,* when some event has occurred and damage has been done. The *chronic* stage is only reached when responsible parties lose control of the crisis and, as Fink (1986) said, "the carcass gets picked clean" (p. 23). As crisis events play out, monitoring should ascertain whether the crisis is moving toward the chronic or fatal stages or whether events are settling down to a precrisis norm.

Coombs (2007) suggested a crisis-sensing mechanism built on three aspects: (a) locating the source of the crisis or risk information; (b) developing a management and communication system to move that information to where it needs to be, including a central location; and (c) making sure the information is analyzed so it turns into knowledge that is useful and useable.

At a media relations level, the crisis can be monitored by the frequency of reporter inquiries, the amount of time-space devoted to the crisis, and the degree of outrage expressed by reporters and persons affected by the crisis, the number of hits on your opposition's Web sites, and the level of Web chatter on blogs and social media sites. A second line of monitoring is specific to the policy issues that may arise from the crisis. Here the question is whether voluntary efforts of the organization or industry are sufficient to calm fears, reduce outrage, or lessen uncertainty on the part of affected parties or whether those parties are keeping the issue alive by commenting on it to their family and acquaintances, followers, reporters, and members of regulatory or legislative bodies.

One or more key publics, as well as media reporters and governmental officials, have a legitimate right to hold expectations regarding the performance of each private-sector firm. A similar expectation can be assumed to exist in regard to the performance of governmental agencies that are accountable to concerned citizens and corporate entities that can be affected by agency performance. A crisis occurs when an event or action introduces uncertainty into how well the organization manages its affairs so that they do not adversely affect persons who come into contact with them. The public does not, for example, expect a company to manufacture breast implants that can have adverse health consequences. Investors do not expect a company to irresponsibly invest and manage their investment dollars. A company does not expect a governmental agency to make gross errors in its judgment of financial or foreign affairs.

The list of examples is endless and contains sensor points that an issues manager wants to understand and monitor to be ready for crisis response. If the company did not meet public expectations, the crisis communication team will need to explain why flawed judgment or performance occurred. Perhaps the company could not foresee what is routinely called an act of God, one excuse for a crisis. If human error due to faulty training and the attribution of corporate greed are available to explain the cause of the crisis, the crisis response team has little moral ground on which to stand. If the crisis occurred despite reasonable and responsible efforts on the part of the organization, which voluntarily agrees to set and meet even higher standards in the future, the crisis response is likely to have more favorable outcomes. When an organization's activities can spark concerned public outburst, the monitoring and management efforts to know and meet standards of corporate responsibility must be high.

By knowing how the organization creates and executes its strategic business plan, the crisis communication response plan can be formulated in a candid, honest, and informed manner. If the organization has wisely and thoroughly monitored to ascertain the expectations key publics hold in regard to its efforts, the response team is more likely to be prepared. If the organization has worked to set and maintain sufficient performance standards so that the affected groups are not shocked and therefore charge the organization with moral malfeasance, the response can be positive, and uncertainty can be quickly lessened. In this way, crisis communication is a planning, preventative, and emergency response activity that follows in the footsteps of careful strategic business planning, issues monitoring, and moral foresight.

Third is to have *key personal coordinated and trained to communicate honestly, clearly, factually, and candidly with minimal interference from legal counsel who understand court procedures better than they comprehend media relations and the consequences of being tried in the court of public opinion.* To achieve the

desired quality of response, crisis teams need to be vigilant and engage in training, especially the enactment of decision-making processes and the formulation of messages. The quality of the decisions made under strain depends on
the crisis team's ability to analyze the problem, establish or rely on preestab-
lished goals and objectives, and evaluate the positive and negative qualities and
consequences of available choices in message responses.

Early in a crisis, spokespersons who meet the press and regulatory agents
may not know the facts. In terms of finding vital facts, regulatory agents, such
as those from the Department of Transportation, may become the crucial fact-
finding body. Their judgment of the fact may be final. The company, for better
or worse, can rely on them and use their investigative time frame in responding to media inquiries. If the legitimate interest of media is getting the story,
they must wait until that story can be known. Months and even years may be
devoted to learning the facts. In some crises, facts are never fully forthcoming
because of the nature of the event. In those instances, the methodology used to
find the truth may be the story that captures media attention.

At least for crisis marketing, the first stage in the effort to recover markets
lost or potentially lost due to a crisis is to publicly acknowledge what went
wrong. More than making an apology, the response requires reporting investigative findings. A final step is crucial: "Present and maintain the positioning
of the company in a larger context than the problem" (Marconi, 1992, p. 30).

In the investigative process, organizations under pressure are wise to be
cautious, precise, open, honest, and scientific in finding the relevant facts. They
should be collaborative in that effort. They do not serve themselves well if they
work to be the only source of information. The quality of information as a scientific product and in terms of public acceptance increases as it is subjected to
independent review. Organizational spokespersons who venture beyond what
is known or knowable in their reports are fools.

This observation brings us to one of the disciplinary battles that needs to
be resolved prior to a crisis event: that between legal counsel and public relations. Typical counsel from lawyers is to say nothing that can be used in a court
of law, which is quite different from the court of public opinion. The court of
public scrutiny plays by different ethical and evidentiary standards than does a
court of law. The public no longer believes there is such a thing as an industrial
accident. Faith in engineering and operating expertise abounds. Accidents are
blamed on carelessness and cutbacks, smacking of corporate irresponsibility
along with its dire implications for corporate and industry reputations and
images. Unwillingness to make statements is admission of guilt.

The training of lawyers is to put the burden of proof on the adversary and
to operate on the principle that an organization (or individual) is innocent
until proven guilty. Experience has taught savvy communication counselors
that the world outside the courtroom works on the opposite heuristic. During

a crisis, an organization is guilty until it proves itself innocent, and what it does not say can and will be held against it. A collaborative effort, in advance of and during the event, is likely to win a more favorable public and media response toward the organization in the event that it does end up in court (Fitzpatrick & Rubin, 1995; Heath, Lee, & Jares, 1999).

This section has attempted to establish the point that good crisis managers and communicators have the inclinations and mental discipline of the scientist while maintaining a genuine ethical commitment to resolve the issue in the interest of the relevant stakeholders. The goal of prevention and response is to understand operations, take the best available preventative measures, and be scrupulous in the pursuit of understanding why a crisis could or did occur.

CRISIS COMMUNICATION OPTIONS

Practitioner and scholarly publications are replete with advice on how to communicate during a crisis. A typical list might advise some or all of the following. Develop a strategic crisis communication plan. Plan how to communicate with reporters to give them details such as the names and phone numbers of crisis team members, command center location, emergency responses, procedures to avert additional crises, and policies to display open and honest concern for persons affected by the crisis. Assign key spokespersons and train them for media response. Practice the plan. During a crisis, make senior management and other key spokespersons available to reporters during a crisis. If the crisis is one that could endanger lives, such as an explosion in a chemical plant, have places available where the press can meet and work in safety away from the flow of hazardous or toxic materials. Tell what you know and what you don't know. Be candid, honest, and truthful.

Perhaps these prescriptions are sufficient; perhaps not. This section reasons that regardless of such prescriptions, crisis communication needs to be driven by a central theme: Address the interests of persons affected by the crisis and downplay its effects on the offending or at least ostensibly offending organization. Birch (1994) captured this theme: "Crisis management teaching stresses the need to show that the company cares and feels concern when something has gone wrong" (p. 32). This section addresses crisis communication approaches, crisis communication plans, and communication styles from a SIM perspective.

There are an abundance of *crisis communication approaches*. Planning and actions typically occur at three stages: precrisis, event response, and postcrisis (Coombs, 1999; Millar & Heath, 2004; Seeger, Sellnow, & Ulmer, 2003). Management activities serve preventative and mitigation objectives if properly implemented in the precrisis stage. Effective actions and policies can mitigate and even prevent a crisis. Communication can serve useful purposes prior to an event. Employees as well as external stakeholders can benefit from information and action plans. For instance, emergency managers/responders need to receive information on how to mitigate and communicate about a crisis before one occurs (Rowan, Botan, Kreps, Samoilenko, & Farnsworth, 2009). In a review of crisis management literature, Coombs (2007) identified three influential approaches to crisis management that have guided a preponderance of the literature. These three are Fink's (1986) four-stage model, Mitroff's (1994) five-stage model, and a general three-stage model previously mentioned.

Fink's (1986) four-stage model is one of the earliest models based on stages in the crisis life cycle, including the prodromal stage, which hints that a potential crisis is emerging; acute triggering crisis event stage; chronic stage based on the lingering effects of the crisis event; and resolution stage. Mitroff (1994) suggested five crisis management stages, including signal detection, probing and prevention, damage containment, recovery, and learning and evaluation.

Mitroff (1994) went a step further by addressing what steps should be taken during each phase in a crisis. He divided crisis management into five stages: signal detection, when an organization detects new crisis by identifying and acting to prevent it; probing and prevention, working to reduce the potential for harm; damage containment, attempting to prevent the spread of a crisis once it has occurred; recovery, attempting to return to normal business operations; and learning, evaluating crisis response and use of information gained to improve future plans. Mitroff organized crisis responses, placing primary emphasis on containing the effects of the crisis, based on the best preventive actions for each phase.

Within the organizational perspective lies a large area of research dominated by the development and analysis of *crisis communication plans*. Much of the traditional crisis management literature descriptively highlights the value of developing, implementing, and maintaining a crisis management plan (Penrose, 2000). Crisis management plans are advocated to guide organizations during times of crisis. The crisis management plan and crisis communication plan are both considered primary tools of the field to prepare for or follow when a crisis occurs. Fearn-Banks (1996) described a crisis communication plan as "providing a functionally collective brain for all persons involved in a crisis, persons who may not operate at normal capacity due to the shock or emotions or the crisis event" (p. 7). (While a detailed discussion of crisis communication management and plans is beyond the focus of this text, see Coombs [2007] and Ulmer et al. [2007] for more information.)

A common theme among crisis communication literature is the need for a crisis management plan (Quarantelli, 1988), including clear, tested crisis communication. Penrose (2000) posited the four most common elements of a crisis plan: the plan, the management team, communication, and postcrisis evaluation.

However, an unlimited amount and variety of crisis situations makes a specific or paradigmatic guiding principle of crisis management nearly impossible (Burnett, 1998). Several problems persist in the development of these manuals: They provide a false sense of security, living documents are updated rarely, they lack a temporal context, and they are filled with irrelevant information (C. M. Pearson, Clair, Misra, & Mitroff, 1997). Ostrow (1991) presented a negative side of crisis planning as he claimed that as organizations prepare for crisis, they begin to "assume that crises will evolve to defined scenarios" (p. 24).

Marra (2004) also found crisis plan shortcomings when he questioned the usefulness of simply creating instructions, suggestions, and checklists. He claimed that the value of crisis communication plans may be overrated as organizations with comprehensive plans often manage crises poorly while those with no plan often manage crises well. Marra argued that this is a result of crisis communication research primarily focusing on the technical aspect of managing crises.

The organizational perspective, though dominant, is not the only crisis communication perspective in crisis planning. Martin and Boynton (2005) pointed out that now the focus of crisis communication has shifted from the organization to those with an interest in the organization, reflecting stakeholder theory literature. At the core of stakeholder theory is that stakeholders are affected by corporations and other organizations, but these organizations also are affected by stakeholders.

Other researchers have moved away from quantitative, categorized, prediction-oriented research in their study of crisis communication. For example, Tyler (2005) suggested that crisis communication should be explored from a postmodern perspective. She used postmodern theory to criticize the emphasis on current research on crisis plans and regaining order and control. Tyler wrote that instead of focusing on the impossibility of crisis control and protecting those in power, crisis communication should be used to alleviate stakeholder suffering—that the voices of management should not be the only ones heard and that postmodern perspectives to crisis communication are a more humane way to communicate. SIM's control focus supports this postmodern perspective.

Numerous elements of postmodern research are starting to be discussed in relationship to risk and crisis communication, including but not limited to concepts such as resistance to positivism and certainty, realization of chaos, resistance to metanarratives, and differences in power disparities in relationships. For example, chaos theory looks at the underlying reasons for a system to appear to be in a chaotic state. According to Sellnow, Seeger, and Ulmer (2002), "Chaos theory may elucidate how communicators characterize the behavior of such systems in their descriptions and predictions of outcomes. It may also point to the ways in which communication processes relate to systems moving in and out of chaos and order" (p. 269).

Regardless of theoretical perspective, preparation includes not only careful planning, drills, and a cautious approach to high-risk operations but also the formation of a reputation that can help sustain an organization in times of crisis (Coombs, 1999). An organization with a reputation for truth, openness, candor, safety, fairness, environmental concern, and honesty brings that persona with it to the first press conferences after the crisis event has occurred. An organization with the opposite reputation begins with media reporters and other participants doubting its accounts. Such doubt gives publics the incentive to look for sources of information that disconfirm rather than confirm the organization's version of the crisis event. Standard logics of public relations reason that if an organization has a good relationship with its stakeholders, it is less likely to suffer a crisis. And, if one occurs, the crisis is likely to be shorter and less damaging.

Crisis communication style as a crisis response philosophy is augmented by Chase's (1984) insights into communication styles that help people prepare for and engage in issues response. Communicators can adopt a reactive-style stonewalling that involves denial, avoidance, and postponement. An adaptive style voices "openness to change, a recognition of its inevitability" (p. 58). Adaptive style assumes that the errors of judgment and performance that led to the crisis will be corrected largely as prescribed by outside forces, such as activists or governmental officials. The third style, dynamic, can respond aggressively to critics who do not understand the circumstances that led to the crisis. It can include refutation of claims and charges made about the performance of the organization. It can state what changes are pending or being implemented to decrease the likelihood that the event will be repeated. This stance includes comments about the proactive and collaborative decision-making measures the organization has taken or is initiating to improve its operations.

The key to these three styles is the locus of control. The reactive style ignores the desire for control on the part of parties affected by the crisis; this can be a saddening, even startling mistake to the management of the offending organization. The adaptive style evidences so much willingness to accommodate others' expectations that it yields all of the control to them. The dynamic style assumes a shared sense of control, the outcome of which contains the best performance and management options to be exerted by the organization on behalf of all parties concerned with the crisis. The dynamic style assumes the organization is responsible for constructing appropriate corrections and making decisions, if necessary, in conjunction with other relevant parties. It seeks win-win outcomes and willingly takes crisis situations as opportunities to demonstrate the quality of operations and planning that is characteristic of the organization. It uses the crisis as an opportunity for collaborative improvement.

Failure to have designated persons to meet the media during a crisis will allow reporters to select the spokespersons based on those who make the most quotable statements or are easiest to contact or both. Even when a communication plan calls for executives and skilled public relations practitioners to act as spokespersons, reporters do not limit themselves to those sources.

Operations personnel may understand technical processes and be able to explain them and answer technical questions more credibly than can executives or professional communicators. Even after a crisis, operations people are likely to be contacted by reporters because they were eyewitnesses and may be able to give newsworthy details about events and operations. They often give a narrative of events that seems to be authentic rather than manufactured by slick communication personnel, executives, and lawyers. Regardless of whether the CEO goes to the scene of the crisis, he or she is responsible for enacting the company's response (Small, 1991).

Employees and other constituencies need information, particularly if safety is a factor. Customers require information if product safety or reliability is at issue. Crises often resist neat and tidy explanations where the information is decisive and readily available (Finch & Welker, 2004). Crises, by definition, are risk manifested. They require explanation in terms and with facts that sustain themselves under scrutiny.

At times, a crisis response calls for the assigning of blame. *Dateline NBC* alleged that General Motors pickups were unsafely designed because their gasoline tanks could ignite on side impact. They demonstrated the problem. However, their demonstration was contrived. They had rigged the test vehicles with incendiary devices to make a more vivid dramatization. To correct the record, GM counterattacked in search for the truth and demonstrated that the story was fabrication and hyperbole (Hearit, 1996).

Audiences are often more attentive to organizations' messages during a crisis. This situation can offer opportunities to communicate and demonstrate a corporation's commitment to responsible behavior and the measures it has taken and is taking to be responsible. Stephenson (1982) demonstrated how Dow Chemical turned a crisis to its advantage. Two train derailments (Mississauga, Ontario, in November 1979 and MacGregor, Manitoba, in March 1980) brought attention to Dow products that were being transported by rail. Dow took the opportunity to explain some of the properties of these products along with the safety procedures that were designed to ensure that no one was harmed. Such events, especially in industries with high outrage potential, offer the chance to explain how emergency response teams are trained and how they act to minimize harm to people and damage to the environment.

Organizations that suffer a crisis are often criticized for being unresponsive to media inquiry. This prescription assumes that not only do crisis managers and communicators need to understand the standard media, but they also must think beyond them to new communication technologies. Birch (1994) advised crisis communicators to be prepared to respond to a daunting list of challenges posed by new communication technologies. One challenge is the number of news channels looking for stories—CNN, for example. Another challenge is the enormous amount of detail that is available to reporters through online databases. In a bit more than the blink of an eye, reporters who have learned of a crisis event can go online and call up stories and retrieve data about a company or other organization from vast databases. In a few moments, this wealth of information can be compressed into stories that frame whatever detail becomes available to the reporters regarding the crisis. Such databases can contain and make continuously available false or deceptive information that reporters may rely on perhaps without ever contacting the company for verification. For this reason, someone in the organization suffering a crisis (or an agency assisting the organization) needs to monitor the databases to look for incorrect information that can be recirculated in an infinite variety of inaccurate news stories. Online communication has taken on a life of its own, not only creating crises but also offering many channels for critics to provide information and evaluation to which organizations are often challenged to respond (Hallahan, 2009).

This section has examined prescriptions that routinely guide crisis planning, management, and communication. These response options add to an organization's ability to enact a coherent voice and trustworthy persona. An organizational culture of being wisely cautious and proactive lays a foundation for looking for problems that could result in crises and prepares employees and executives to enact a persona of candor and caring if a crisis occurs. These response options can be enhanced by an understanding of narrative, apologia, and other crisis response strategies.

NARRATIVE

As noted previously (see Chapter 6), people think of events that occur in their world in narrative terms, as element of a constructed story. Interpretation of the events treats them as acts by characters that have a past, present, and future; events are meaningful because they are part of a larger plot and have a plot of their own.

Companies and most other organizations work hard to enact the persona that they are in charge of their destinies and aware of the interests and concerns of the other characters in the narrative (key publics which are deserving of resources on which they depend for success). Crises strain the appearance of control. When a crisis occurs, a spokesperson is expected to explain publicly and quickly why it happened and what will be done to correct operations and protect people from further harm as well as repay and comfort those who have been harmed. Crisis communication is the enactment of the narrative of control (or at least its appearance) in the face of high uncertainty in an effort to win external audiences' confidence in ways that are ethical.

Control is a dominant cultural archetype. The performance of an organization through the enactment of its personnel or members is expected to meet publics' sense of an organization that is in control, one that can develop and implement policies and procedures that allow it to properly manage the balance of its interests with those of its key stakeholders and stakeseekers. Narrative interpretations of crisis ask audiences to consider whether the acts that were committed are consistent with the characters in the case and constitute a reasonable theme. This theme has to meet standards of fidelity and probability. Audiences use those standards to understand and judge whether the account as given is plausible and justified under the circumstances.

Narrative is also a dialectic, Burke (1969a) observed, "a process of *transformation* whereby the position at the end transcends the position at the start, so that the position at the start can eventually be seen in terms of the new motivation encountered enroute" (p. 422). Part of the transformation of an organization during a crisis is to learn from it and make appropriate corrections. Concerned publics expect the organization to have learned how to exert control more appropriately, to become better at meeting public expectations (Gold, 1982).

Viewed from a narrative perspective, a crisis is either a break (a dramatic interruption) or a shift in plot from one narrative (normal operations) to a crisis or emerging issue narrative. This analytic approach allows us to think of a crisis narrative as a subnarrative in the plot of the larger narrative of routine operations. It can even entail competing narratives. As subnarrative analysis, the larger narrative forms a framework or point of view that concerned publics use to interpret and evaluate each unique event and decide whether it is a crisis. The dominant narrative gives continuity to the past, present, and future of the organization and other organizations of the same type. For instance, a plane crash is a subnarrative of years and millions of miles of safe operations. Or it may be viewed as a continuing narrative of unsafe operations by an uncaring industry indifferent to passenger safety.

Narrative frames people's understanding of the past, knows what is occurring in the present, and projects events into the future. A crisis is best framed in terms of what happened, what response is being made, and where that effort leads. "Time is critical because transactions have no meaning outside of their historical contexts: the expectations attendant upon an interaction moment are crucial for understanding the meaning of that interaction" (Eisenberg, 1986, p. 89). Through their efforts to help create and enact narratives relevant to their activities and missions, businesses engage in symbolic processes by which they represent themselves and define their boundaries (Cheney, 1992; Cheney & Dionisopoulos, 1989; Cheney & Vibbert, 1987).

So do reporters. For instance, Nimmo and Combs (1982) identified three narratives used by reporters in comments on the nuclear generating plant crisis at Three Mile Island: human interest, fact finding—big picture, and educational. Treating war as crisis management, communication regards that military effort as narrative: the mighty and just good folks against their evil adversaries (Hiebert, 1991).

The company suffering a crisis must be able to tell a credible story, one that has factual fidelity that can withstand the scrutiny of reporters, governmental investigators, and concerned citizens. Stories provided by company spokespersons, for instance, shape details in ways that portray the company as favorably as possible. This response is strongest when it is sincere and probable, given the characters involved and the theme relevant to the crisis. Subsequent accounts of crisis events must be consonant with early accounts if crisis communication is to have the desired narrative impact (Hobbs, 1991). Inconsistencies in stories suggest the presence of deceit and falsehood and a lack of control by the organization under scrutiny.

Within this dialogue and contest, words have propositional values (Burke, 1966), and the selection of those terms affects how information is considered, accepted, acted upon, or altered—fundamental roles of risk communication. For example, the Texas City explosion on April 16, 1947, is an iconic narrative for residents along the Houston Ship Channel. Mention "the explosion" and everyone knows exactly what you are talking about—the loss of life, the community and industry destruction, the changes in legislation and enforcement of transportation codes, and the sense of risk that still resides in the local communities. Deconstructing risk narratives ultimately can help public relations practitioners understand how stakeholders and stakeseekers navigate through the information and public policy environment.

Narratives that lead only to positive outcomes for the ostensibly offending organization may leave concerned publics dissatisfied. Policy statements appear to be most persuasive and satisfying when they consider the self-interest of the public as well as the organization. Activist groups build their cases by arguing that corporate behavior conflicts with the public interest.

APOLOGIA

Can words put a crisis right? Crisis communication may include strategies for saying, "We are sorry," making an apology to harmed or concerned publics. This section examines apologia as a communication response to a crisis. It acknowledges that performance outweighs communication in the long run. That means that an apology is typically insufficient to set things right, but it can help if it is a demonstration that the organization has recognized its failure to respond responsibly to the needs and expectations of its stakeholder and stakeseeking publics (Hearit, 2006).

Public relations and crisis communication scholars have focused much more on the organizational perspective of crisis. Dionisopolous and Vibbert (1988) extended Ware and Linkugel's (1973) examination to the use of apologia to defend reputations. In the event that an organization's image cannot be protected from crisis, Benoit (1997) provided an argument for using image restoration theory as an attempt to repair it. He focused on message options, or what an organization can say when faced with a reputational crisis. The image repair line of research, building on apologia, includes five primary aspects of image restoration: denials as a course of action, evasion of responsibility, reduction of the perceived offensiveness of that act, corrective action, and finally mortification.

Crisis communication may employ the rhetoric of apologia, the use of terms to define and redefine events to give what the company or other organization postulates to be the accurate interpretation of events that led to and resulted from the crisis. As Hearit (1994) concluded,

> An "apologia" is not an apology (although it may contain one), but a defense that seeks to present a compelling, counter description of organizational actions. It functions to situate alleged organizational wrongdoing in a more favorable context than the initial charges suggest. This is done in an effort to neutralize the argumentative force of the initial charges of wrongdoing. The tone of most apologia is that once key publics understand a corporation's explanation, then they will be unable to condemn the corporation. (p. 115)

A key strategy of apologia is to provide a different descriptive and interpretative (evaluative) name for the event than the one offered by the media or the critics. One common response is that an action (which seems to violate the expectations of key stakeholders) is not illegal.

An apologia is likely to carry an expression of regret; it may have more rhetorical impact if it is expected because an organization has made a mistake in judgment for which it is expected to express moral atonement. The veracity of this claim is less likely to depend on the assertion by the subject organization than it is to be based on the presentation of evidence to demonstrate its regret. Of related importance is the quality of the prior relationship. If the organization has had an honest, candid, and mutually beneficial relationship with the concerned publics, then reputation is likely to lend credence to its current expression of regret.

One potential communicative benefit of a statement of regret is this: It implies that the problem that precipitated the wrongdoing has been isolated and resolved. This may explain why a strong denial does not necessarily resolve doubts about organizational wrongdoing; the organization may still have a problem that it simply has not located (Hearit, 1994, p. 118).

Cultural differences offer marked contrast on how companies—airlines, for instance—demonstrate their personae under crisis. The president of

Japanese Airline was publicly active in his airline's ceremonies to apologize to victims and survivors after one of its planes crashed in 1985. A senior maintenance technician with the company committed suicide, an act not unlikely for personnel in a Japanese company. In contrast, airline executives did not personally appear at the scenes of crashes such as the Pan Am catastrophe in Lockerbie, Scotland, or United's crash near Sioux City, Iowa (Pinsdorf, 1991).

Events are subject to definition and redefintion; in this regard, crisis response is never separable from the challenges of framing (Hallahan, 1999). Knowing that terms used to define an event shape perceptions of it, spokespersons may propose the defining words for a crisis. In doing so, they divert responsibility from themselves or explain why key publics' concerns are justified. Ordinary words, such as *mistake,* are offered as an explanation when, for instance, *moral malfeasance* is a more accurate term. A spokesperson may attempt to assuage concerned publics by indicating that the circumstances that led to the crisis are not illegal. Companies often confuse in their minds or attempt to assume that the public does not distinguish between that which is legal and that which is ethical.

Without doubt, events that constitute a crisis are subject to interpretation. However, the standard by which crisis management is judged seems quite simple. Affected and concerned publics expect the organization that has created or experienced the crisis to exert control and to put matters right. For that reason, blame placing can be a tricky strategy, as likely to backfire as it is to succeed. Management does not serve the integrity of the organization and the persona of being in charge when blame is placed on subordinates. If mortification, then correction and eventually bolstering. The organization can bolster its position as a reputation restorative or maintenance strategy by demonstrating its acumen, which at least momentarily failed. Placing blame and apologizing is usually an insufficient response (Benoit & Brinson, 1994). What is needed is evidence of the organization's concern and desire to restore appropriate control in the interest of its stakeholders. And apologies, like all statements, must meet key standards: Be truthful, sincere, timely, and voluntary. Make statements that address the interests and needs of all stakeholders, not just the interests of the organization. Be sure the statement is made in the appropriate context (Hearit, 2006).

Crisis communication seems best when it is framed in terms of what concerned publics want to know and how they make decisions. Facts evaluated in terms of established premises are valuable. Crises are likely to make established premises salient as decision heuristics; people want to interpret events according to established expectations. Crisis response is likely to be value laden. As judgments of preference, values assist individuals in establishing priorities and making evaluations. Image and reputation seem strongest when organizations demonstrate as well as state that they share the values of the relevant community of interests and act in ways that affirm those values. Policy is a means for demonstrating reflective and responsive control. If an organization, as well as related organizations, can demonstrate that it can manage its affairs in ways that meet or exceed community expectations, it is likely to suffer no additional burden from having policy imposed from the outside.

This section examines how a crisis is a test of an organization's ability to understand, accept, and respond to the appropriate standards of corporate responsibility. It assumes that failure to respond to these standards is one cause of a crisis. Mere apology is likely to be insufficient response, but it helps to demonstrate the organization's goodwill and willingness to understand and meet key publics' performance expectations.

SITUATIONAL CRISIS COMMUNICATION THEORY (SCCT)

Coombs (2007), building off some of the work in apologia, developed the situational crisis communication theory (SCCT) as part of a growing body of research built from attribution theory to crisis management (e.g., Ahluwalia, Burnkrant, & Unnava, 2000). Coombs's (1998) symbolic approach perspective emphasizes how communication can be used as a symbolic resource to protect the organization's image. Crisis communication provides attributes of responsibility, and in turn these attributes shape how a stakeholder feels and behaves toward an organization. SCCT organizes crisis response strategies by determining if the intent of the strategy is to change perceptions of the crisis or of the organization in crisis (Coombs, 2007).

SCCT embraces influences from management, psychology, public relations, and rhetorical theory to advance logic to guide crisis planning and response beyond a tradition of relying on best practices (Coombs, 2008; Heath & Coombs, 2006). As such, crisis communication is a subdiscipline of crisis management (as SIM embraces but consists of more than issues communication). One of the primary motives behind the development of SCCT is to better understand how to protect the reputational resources of one or more spotlighted organizations.

SCCT focuses on planning and communicating during three phases of crisis: precrisis, event, and postcrisis. Both internal to an organization and externally, various messages can prepare stakeholders for a crisis, if it occurs, and provides advice as to what to do to mitigate the impact of the event should it occur. This theory draws upon attribution theory for its rationale; it assumes that individuals need (and therefore bring to bear) explanation of events as part of a causal rationale. Depending on their attributional frames and others' interpretations of a crisis, they will assign cause to explain what happened, why it happened, and who or what is to blame. Worth noting, one of the key variables in attribution is the crisis history of the organization and its relationship to its various stakeholders/stakeseekers.

Reasoning that crisis attribution and response is multidimensional, the theory argues that ethical crisis response can deny current attributions, diminish them, or acknowledge them. In the latter case, the target organization may need to engage in ingratiation, express concern for victims, offer compensation, express regret, and offer an apology. Effective "deal responses" assume the ability (and target's willingness) to accept expressions of compassion. In fact, relationship histories as well as crisis history are key to the rhetorical potency of that response.

Coombs (2007), building on the work of Benoit and others, developed a comprehensive list of crisis response strategies grouped by postures an organization takes toward the response. The first posture is *denial,* which includes (a) attacking the accuser by confronting the accuser or the organization that claims a crisis exists (sometimes with the threat of a lawsuit), (b) *denial* that the crisis even exists, and (c) *scapegoating,* which entails blaming some other individual or group. The second posture is *diminishing,* which includes (d) *excusing* and (e) *justification. Rebuilding* is the third organizational posture in crisis response strategies, which includes (f) *compensation* and (g) *apology.* The fourth posture is *bolstering,* which includes (h) *reminding* (when the organization informs stakeholders about its past corporate social responsibility efforts and good work), (i) *ingratiation* or praising stakeholders, and (j) *victimage,* which is when the organization shares how it is a victim in the crisis.

According to Wan and Pfau (2004), both Coombs's (1998) and Benoit's (1997) approaches center on postcrisis communication skills that are helpful for organizations after crises have occurred. However, the need for proactive strategy focusing on the prevention of crisis in the first place is stated as their ideal orientation to crisis communication. Their results revealed that "inoculation, as well as the traditional bolstering approach, work to protect people's attitude slippage when encountering a negative occurrence" (p. 324). Their recommendation is to be well prepared in advance for organizations that have maintained positive images (and no prior crises) to consider including both supportive and inoculation approaches in their crisis communication plans.

As contestable matters (issues), explanations of the event, as well as its causes and effects, are of particular concern. As such, the SIM concern focuses on whether key publics believe the organization is appropriately responsive; willing to engage in fair, factual interpretations; and able to exert controls that minimize the likelihood of crisis recurrence. To the extent that such conditions are met, the crisis is less likely to mature into an issue of public policy relevance. If doubt exists on the part of one or more stakeholders, they are likely to use their stakes to force (resource dependency) more corrective behaviors either by the organization or through the public policy process.

Conclusion

Crisis management gives issues managers the opportunity to engage in planning and foresight that can lessen the likelihood of a crisis event. Such effort can lessen the loss of control and negative consequences in the event that a crisis occurs. For this reason, thoughtful preparation is a major part of preventing crises from maturing into issues.

Each crisis is a rhetorical exigency; it requires responsible parties to enact control in the face of uncertainty, with the objective of winning audiences' confidence and meeting their ethical standards. A crisis is an event that threatens lives or the well-being of stakeholders and stakeseekers and the ability of the organization to enact the narrative of responsible change and continuity. Control assumes order, and people desire a sense of order and predictability that leads to positive rather than negative outcomes. Crisis narratives feature mistakes and dreaded outcomes. The goal of issues management before, during, and after a crisis is to restore and strengthen the relationship between the entity suffering a crisis and its stakeholders and stakeseekers.

To the extent that we only focus on one organization as the focal point in crisis communication, we are suffering a managerial bias. What the organization has done and does is likely to affect others. In fact, the crisis is often defined not by the damage done to the organization but the damage it does to various stakeholders. In light of such damage, if the organization is not appropriately reflective and responsive, crisis is sure to mature into an issue and become a matter of concern in the public policy arena.

SIM Challenge: Can a Crisis Be Prevented From Exploding Into an Issue?

One of the most horrific modern industrial crisis events occurred on December 3, 1984, by the release of methyl isocyanate (MIC) at the Union Carbide plant in Bhopal, India, which caused more than 3,000 deaths and over 200,000 major injuries (Shrivastava, 1987). According to Union Carbide (2004), the release caused more than 3,800 deaths while several other thousands suffered permanent or partial disabilities. The loss of human life, the end of a major American company that employed thousands of people around the world, the callous disregard for health and safety by management, and the environmental impact cannot be underscored enough, but there are lessons to be learned from this crisis.

The catastrophe fostered international interest in risk management and risk communication. This is a paradigm case of a crisis becoming an issue as society sought control over the chemical industry, which continually violated stakeholders' expectations. The focal organization in this case, Union Carbide, generated such concern and outrage that legislators and Environmental Protection Agency (EPA) regulators imposed new, stringent requirements on the chemical industry in the United States.

Immediately after the Bhopal tragedy, Rosenblatt (1984) observed, "If the world felt especially close to Bhopal last week, it may be because the world is Bhopal, a place where the occupational hazard is modern life" (p. 20). Worry generated activist concern, which prompted passage of the Emergency Planning and Community Right-to-Know Act, Section Three of the Superfund Amendments and Reauthorization Act of 1986 (SARA Title III). It mandated each governor to appoint members to a State Emergency Response Commission, which in turn created local emergency planning committees. This was one step toward the Clean Air Act of 1990, which was projected to cost approximately $166 billion over 2 decades for chemical plant improvement (Sullivan, 1993).

Normally, a story about India would receive minor play in the U.S. press. Helping fuel interest in Bhopal was not only the magnitude and severity of the tragedy but also the fact that it involved a U.S. firm that was manufacturing the same lethal chemical in this country. After Bhopal, the media recalled prior instances of disaster, including Texas City, Texas, in 1947; Saveso, Italy, in 1976; Biers, France, in 1977; and the BASF factory failures in 1921 and 1979. Discussions of classic cases of a crisis make an issue so salient that the likelihood of government intervention substantially increases.

Newspapers speculated that because of Bhopal, the chemical industry might face a fresh wave of legislation. Editorials debated the value of chemicals to protect lives and promote food production (Boffey, 1984) versus their safety and that of the facilities where they are manufactured (Beck, Greenberg, Hager, Harrison, & Underwood, 1984; Grier, 1984).

Activists demanded stricter regulation as they pointed out that the manufacture of dangerous substances in populated areas is common. At the time of the Bhopal incident, approximately 6,000 facilities were making toxic and hazardous chemicals, with 180,000 shipments occurring by rail and truck each day in the United States. A *Newsweek* article acknowledged that

> the U.S. chemical industry can boast of a strong safety record. But with more than 60,000 chemicals produced and stored in America, government regulators and watchdog groups can't even tell where potential time bombs are let alone guarantee that they won't go off. (Whitaker, Mazumdar, Gibney, & Behr, 1984, p. 28)

The Wall Street Journal writers similarly observed, "On the inside, the chemical and refining industries maintain the most exemplary safety record in U.S. manufacturing. But outside the plants, community ignorance of chemical risk remains widespread, and preparedness for the unlikely calamity remains spotty" (Petzinger & Burrough, 1984, p. 1).

A complicating factor—authorities did not know much about the dangers posed by the chemicals in use and under manufacture. The Toxic Substances Control Act, passed in 1976, required that new chemicals be studied before they go on the market, but that requirement had been applied to only about 20% of all products by the mid-1980s. Chemical companies developed internal safety rules, created their own extraordinarily competent fire departments, and established precautions to protect workers, forestall regulation, and maintain proprietary control over various chemical products (Loddeke, 1984).

Henry A. Waxman (D–CA), House subcommittee chairman, held hearings on this issue. He was asked on ABC-TV's *This Week With David Brinkley* whether "we let the industry continue to police itself or does the government step in?" In addition to measures designed to increase safety from toxic leaks, Waxman was concerned with the long-term effects of chemical exposure, particularly cancer. Underscoring his worry, the California Democrat recalled a 1981 study by Union Carbide that depicted periodic leakage of MIC and other chemicals during manufacturing and handling processes. In the midst of this controversy, Union Carbide was fined $55,000 for nine environmental violations it had reported having occurred since 1982 at its South Charleston Technical Center ("Carbide's U.S. Plant," 1984).

One of the most damaging pieces of information surrounding the disaster was Carbide's claim that it knew a runaway disaster was possible at least three months prior to the Bhopal accident. A warning memo had been prepared by a Carbide safety inspection team and was received by the manager of the Institute, West Virginia, plant on September 19, 1984. This memo was made public by Rep. Waxman, who indicated that he did not know whether corrective actions had been taken at any plants ("Carbide Was Warned," 1985).

Later, Carbide reported that it had revised its operating procedures several weeks before the Bhopal incident. Jackson B. Browning, director of Health, Safety, and Environmental Affairs for Carbide, stated that the changes implemented in the operations at the Institute plant were irrelevant to Bhopal because the two plants were designed differently. Browning noted that the company had undertaken increased safety measures at the Institute plant to detect the presence of water and other contaminants in the process for manufacturing and storing MIC. Training procedures were revised (Winslow, 1985a). The industry tried to play down the 28 leaks, whereas activists and governmental regulators charged that any leaks were unsettling. Carbide also operated an MIC facility in France, where residents asserted they were caught between working in possibly hazardous conditions and suffering unemployment (Kamm, 1984).

After the Bhopal catastrophe, Carbide ceased MIC production at the Institute plant. By mid-February 1985, it was ready to resume producing the chemical there because corrective actions had been taken. One change was the addition of a computerized system to monitor weather and wind conditions and predict how they would disperse chemicals in the event of a leak. In opposition to this announcement by Carbide, Waxman claimed that starting up production was "premature." Rep. Robert E. Wise (D–WVA), whose district included the Institute, welcomed the plant restarting (Winslow, 1985b).

Such publicity added fervor to those seeking to impose stringent national and even international standards. Activist groups, including the Environmental Action Foundation, Washington Fair Share, and Public Citizen Health Research Group, used this opportunity to voice their opinions (J. B. Solomon & Russell, 1984). Several cities and states passed or at least considered legislation to require companies to inform workers of any hazardous chemicals they were handling. An EPA study reported that current law then may be inadequate to protect people who live near such facilities (Meier, 1985).

Just how effective was Carbide in dealing with the press, government, and the public at large? That's hard to answer, given the considerable national and international attention to the incident and mixed news coverage Carbide received. It appears that the corporate players in this crisis believed that a low-key effort was best because they were slow to mount a crisis response campaign. Union Carbide made itself available to the press and showed signs that it was interested in safety. It issued media releases on legal developments, scientific findings, new safety measures, and operating changes. The company provided funds for medical care and established a research program at a university hospital in Bhopal.

A 1985 opinion survey conducted by the Media Institute of 20 major daily newspaper and weekly news magazine editors and 20 major chemical corporation public relations executives found that Union Carbide scored above average in its responsiveness to media requests. Editors and executives virtually agreed that the overall tone of media coverage toward the company had been neutral (*Chemical Risks,* 1985). Demonstrating the limits to communication as a crisis response, however, today what once was Union Carbide, a freestanding corporation, is part of Dow Chemical Company.

In their contacts with the media, company representatives were not always well prepared. In the face of initial questioning by reporters, for example, Carbide admitted there were no emergency evacuation plans for Bhopal, nor did the company understand the circumstances of the accident well enough to be able to explain how it happened and thus how it could have been prevented (Marbach, Gibney, Gander, Tsuruoka, & Greenburg, 1984). Even a month later, Union Carbide still was unable to account for the operating procedures that led to the release of MIC. Such information gaps raised uncertainty and assisted activists by sustaining audience interest in their policy agenda.

Despite Union Carbide's statement that it would pursue a total communication program as part of its 1985 marketing strategy, company spokespersons agreed that the program was slow to emerge because of continuing uncertainty over how to approach a post-Bhopal information and opinion climate ("Leading 100 business/industrial advertisers spend $420 million," 1985). Much more could have been said publicly if not for liability claims so large they threatened the financial future of the company. At some point in every crisis, executives must listen to legal counsel; perhaps they listen too much and too soon to counselors trained to think only of court proceedings and not the court of public scrutiny.

The Bhopal incident harmed the image of chemical manufacturers and their operating environment. Aftershocks were not confined to Carbide. The industry had limited impact in playing down the seriousness of leaks, whereas activists and governmental regulators proved effective in charging that any leak is unsettling because of immediate safety concerns or long-term health reasons. Demonstrating a strong sense of corporate responsibility and a prudent sensitivity to community outrage, many companies decided to enhance their operating standards.

Concern and rage continued. *The Wall Street Journal* noted that "the idea of applying criminal laws to corporate executives is getting increased attention worldwide" because of the mass poisoning in India. The "tragedy," the *Journal* reported, "is generating demands for tougher corporate-responsibility laws." Quoted was 19th-century English judge Edward Baron Thurlow's lament: "'Did you ever expect a corporation to have a conscience when it has no soul to be damned and no body to be kicked?' Then . . . 'By God, it ought to have both'" (Trost, 1985, p. 14). This story pointed to the iceberg tip of the controversy, which suggests that what we often see as a crisis is actually only a part of the story. Over time, a larger narrative emerges. One key SIM question is the extent to which the organization adds to the narrative that emerges or offers a counternarrative that simply does not hold up over time.

In response to calls for criminal actions against chemical company executives, the National Association of Manufacturers claimed that civil court is the proper place for remedies. Quoted in opposition was Timothy Smith, director of the Interfaith Center on Corporate Responsibility, a coalition of church investors, who said, "Let's send people to jail" (Trost, 1985, p. 14). In this opinion atmosphere, the chemical industry decided to change operating procedures and communicate quietly if at all.

Summary Questions

1. What is a crisis? How can crises differ by degree of severity? What difference does the degree of severity mean for management and communication?

2. How can effective SIM responses to severe crises prevent them from becoming issues?

3. Why do badly managed crises lead to public policy changes? What communication strategies can and should be used?

4. Explain how crisis communication is the enactment of the narrative of control (or at least its appearance) in the face of high uncertainty?

5. What is apologia, and what are its strengths and limits for crisis communication?

6. What is situational crisis communication theory (SCCT)? What are its theoretical underpinnings? How can it serve the organization under scrutiny?

7. How does strategic business planning interact with issues management and crisis management in relationship to the health, safety, and environmental quality of entities it affects?

8. How and why should crisis be interpreted as a community challenge, rather than merely a challenge of management?

9

Issues Management and Risk Communication

Balancing Public Well-Being With Technology

Vignette:
Risk, Risk Everywhere

Once again, instead of a specific vignette, let's look at a range of risks that required the attention of society and strategic issues management (SIM) managers of all types of organizations. Broadly, these range from health, safety, and environmental concerns, including political and ecological destruction, human health and safety impacts, poverty and corruption, security arrangements, and human rights abuses.

Factors that have a propensity to increase risk and crises proliferate, and headlines and blogs shout out newsworthy crises such as increasing population density, increased settlement in high-risk areas, increased technological risk, aging U.S. population, emerging infectious diseases and antimicrobial resistance, increased international travel, and increased terrorism (Auf def Heida, 1996).

What specific risks do people face daily? The list is endless. Automobile and traffic safety. Medical treatment. Financial investments. Pesticides on food and in living and work locations. Herbicides in agricultural and residential locations. Food additives that increase the color and the shelf life of products. Electromagnetic fields associated with the transmission and use of electricity power lines, computer screens, backyard transformers, and household appliances. Automobile transportation. Releases of toxic and hazardous chemicals during manufacturing processes as well as the transportation of those materials by truck, railroad car, and pipeline. Crimes

(Continued)

(Continued)

against people and property. Terrorism. Harmful chemicals in water supplies. Airline safety. Recreation. Exposure to chemicals and addictive components in cigarette smoke and other tobacco products. Fat in foods. A long list of carcinogens that seems to be associated with all of what people eat and with all the things they come in contact with. Toys poorly designed so small parts can choke children and that are contaminated with lead, for instance. Natural hazards, such as earthquakes, fires, hurricanes, floods, tsunamis, blizzards, and tornadoes. Occupational safety, particularly in farming, mining, fire suppression, and police patrol. Safety in the home.

This illustrative list features an array of choices people face each day and year while engaging in routine activities. Part of the overall challenge of this book is to consider how organizations can help to strategically manage and communicate about those decisions and actions, the routine and the nonroutine risks of society.

Chapter Goals

The primary goal of this chapter is to further develop the relationship between issues, crisis, and risk. By the end of the chapter, you should be able to define risk, risk management, and risk communication and have a basic understanding of the concept of community right to know. Central to this discussion is the role of the societal approach to risk, which reasons that the people of a society, however unsophisticated in their understanding of science, have a role in risk democracy. You should become able to explain several dominant themes regarding risk: the mental models approach to risk, perceptual themes, cultural concerns, and infrastructural or dialogic approaches. In this discussion, you should come to appreciate why and how ordinary citizens express concern and worry, as well as their need to struggle to understand and appreciate risks and appropriate responses to them. The chapter focuses on perceptual themes and reviews key concepts to develop a list of guidelines for fostering dialogue that helps risk bearers participate in ways that either reduce the issues debate or take it in truly collaborative directions.

Few issues management challenges loom as ominously as those that arise from risks people suffer or fear they suffer in their places of work, residence, and daily activities. History is a drama of people assessing, communicating about, and creatively preventing or adapting to risks (Plough & Krimsky, 1987). In fact, society may exist essentially for the collective management of risks (Douglas, 1992). In essence, the production and consumption of risks have become as equally important as, if not more so than, the production and consumption of goods and services (Beck, 1992). The societies that manage risks best may suffer less and benefit more in the march of history.

Identifying or pointing to a specific date or event that launched the modern era of risk communication is impossible, as the movements grew organically out of a variety of perspectives and initiatives, whether they are community-based activism, government response, or industry initiated. Certain incidents, events, and research streams, however, loom large in the direction of risk communication research and practice and their relationship with strategic issues management (SIM).

The history of risk management and risk assessment can be traced back beyond Greek and Roman times (Covello & Mumpower, 1985). The origins of risk analysis have been traced to the Babylonians in 3200 BC, where myths, metaphors, and rituals were used to predict risks and to communicate knowledge about avoiding hazards; risk communication was embedded in folk discourse (Krimsky & Plough, 1988).

Modern risk analysis was developed in the early part of the 20th century by engineers, epidemiologists, actuaries, and industrial hygienists, among others, who looked at hazards associated with technology that was rapidly developing from and during the Industrial Revolution (Kates & Kasperson, 1983). The development of probability theory during the 17th century in Europe brought explicit formulations of risk concepts. U.S. federal legislation in the 1970s, including the formation of the Environmental Protection Agency (EPA), elevated the role of formal risk assessment. Interest in risk communication was considered "quite recent" during the late 1980s (Krimsky & Plough, 1988). According to the National Research Council (NRC, 1989), the motivating sources and goals for this direction in risk communication were a requirement for or desire by government and industry officials to inform, to overcome opposition to decisions, to share decision-making power, and to develop effective alternatives to direct regulatory control. Overall, according to Krimsky and Golding (1992), the field of risk studies, including risk communication, developed from the practical needs of industrialized societies to regulate technology and protect its citizens from natural and manmade technological hazards.

If exposure to risk is not new, then why was there and why does there continue today a renaissance in risk communication research and communication? Peters, Covello, and McCallum (1997) suggested that there has been a long-term decline in public confidence and trust in traditional social institutions, especially government and industry, that has paralleled the growth in environmental risk communication legislation. At the same time, as noted by Laird (1989) more than 2 decades ago, there has been a dramatic growth in the rise of citizen environmental groups, which is a major institutional shift in society moving from trust in public institutions to trust in citizens groups. Fischhoff (1990) argued a similar perspective, that stakeholders and other publics have insisted on a role in deciding how health, safety, and environmental risks will be managed. According to Macauley (2006), "Perhaps what is different today is the widespread attention throughout all echelons of modern society—the public at large; governments at the federal, state and local levels; industry; and universities and other nongovernmental organizations—to questioning the limits and applications of risk analyses" (p. 1).

Today, techniques for assessing and responding to risks may have matured little beyond those of the ancients (Douglas, 1992), even though science has opened minds collectively to data never analyzed before. The challenge to be managed is how to understand and control risks as well as how to gain acceptance for risk mitigation measures in ways that foster the wisest outcomes in any community of interests (Freudenberg, 1984). In their struggle to control risks, people seek and contest facts, evaluative premises, and draw policy conclusions to be derived from those facts and premises. They also create identifications, whether they are professional, organizational, or of other kinds, including issue-oriented activists.

Residents of every community, culture, and country have legitimate reasons to be concerned for their own and others' health, safety, and environmental quality, especially since there are no absolute standards or, as some would argue, no objective standards. For example, alarm and outrage can result when people believe they are exposed to manufacturing processes and other technologies that distress or harm them, whether they live, labor or are temporarily near the risk, or encounter it while using or consuming a product.

A primary motivator of personal mitigation and community involvement related to community health and safety risk is residents' desire to be safe and healthy, coupled with their vigilance. When organizations are perceived, rightly or wrongly, as abusing the privileges given to them by their constituencies and other stakeholders who affect and are affected by them, individual and community responses and governmental controls and regulations can and should sanction the capacity of organizations to continue to operate (Palenchar & Heath, 2006). This evolution of powerful and influential consumers, heavily involved community residents, and overall a critical public is "not coincidental but a symptom of the emergence of the risk society" (R. Jones, 2002, p. 49).

Safety, fairness, equality, and aesthetics are among the numerous motivators that community residents, who bear health and safety risks due to living near chemical manufacturing facilities, use when deciding whether a problem exists that affects them and deserves their attention, including the option of making personal responses or collaboratively seeking collective solutions by engaging in public policy struggles. Concerns also include threats of nature such as hurricanes (e.g., Katrina) or tsunamis like the one that struck several countries in Southeast Asia in 2004. These motivators, among others, have been at the forefront of public debates regarding risks over the past 3 decades.

As emphasized in Chapter 8, a crisis results when publics are confronted with events that lead them to feel uncertainty, concern, and even outrage regarding some condition that threatens their well-being and violates their expectations of responsible organizational performance. Thus, a crisis is a risk manifested, which is foundational to SIM. Paramount in the thinking of persons in the past century are the hazards they encounter as they seek the benefits of technology. Science has dramatically improved the quality of life, but key publics are convinced that innovation is not without dire consequences. As chemicals, for instance, have added to the safety of large segments of society, people have also become chemophobic. Such worry is not new. As Chapter 2 stressed, the concerns publics had regarding railroad and product safety led to major pieces of legislation around the turn of the 20th century. A review of the plethora of legislative enactments in the past 3 decades of that century reveals how heightened concern translates into legislative and regulatory reform all aimed to increase publics' ability to control technology and lessen the risks they suffer.

Despite the exposure they suffer, people find that their life is better because of the risks they incur. Risks are offset by benefits, some of which people accept and even gladly seek, such as gambling or engaging in recreation, including various extreme sports. People earn their living by working in occupations with high risk exposure: chemical workers, power line workers, miners, timber cutters, urban commuters, air commuters, and farmers.

Risk is a dialectic of benefit and harm. We engage in games of chance, such as buying a lottery ticket on the prospect of financial gain while being cognizant that we will likely lose our dollar. We have a trained technician spray our homes to reduce the presence of undesirable insects. We fertilize our lawns and gardens to feel satisfaction and meet or exceed the expectations of our neighbors. We believe that seeing friends, relatives, business associates, and recreational sites offset the risk of traveling by air, car, bus, foot, water, or rail. Farmers work with dangerous equipment, hazardous chemicals, and powerful animals, all in the name of income and personal freedom. In such dialectical balances, what is a body to do? Families undertake the risk of having and raising children.

Whether individually or as members of groups, people make decisions when risks, especially those controlled by someone else, conflict with their self-interests and the interests of others. For instance, do residents have to choose between tolerating a chemical plant operating in their community or lose it as a source of wages and taxes? A homemaker must balance the risk of serving foods that contain preservatives against the risk of serving dangerous spoiled food. Each person, whether a member of the public or an executive of a company, has to weigh competing beliefs and evaluations to estimate rewards and losses. In this sense, beliefs (degrees of certainty that one or more attributes are associated with an object or situation) interact with evaluations (positive or negative judgments).

Reviewing accomplishments in risk communication research achieved from 1995 to 2005, McComas (2006) concluded that notable achievements had occurred in understanding the role of mass media, social trust, science, and effect. She pointed to advances in strategically designing messages by using risk comparison, narratives, and visualization. She reasoned that key advances were continuing in the understanding of risk severity, social norms, and response efficacy because foundations for improving risk communication can lead to productive outcomes for the benefit of society and those concerned about and affected by risks. She believed that one of the major communication contexts, public outreach, was also improving in design and execution. In all, risk communication advances best in practice and through research when it is seen as multidisciplinary and multidimensional and when trust is emphasized in risk management.

Risk communication and issues management merge at the point where key publics feel deeply that companies and governmental organizations (and even nonprofits, including activists) create or allow risks to occur that will affect the health, safety, environmental quality, and economic well-being of community residents and users of products. Of related importance is the emerging concern that the placement of manufacturing companies, waste disposal facilities, and hazardous occupations does not equitably expose rich persons to risks as often or as severely as poor persons and those of color, an argument at the heart of environmental equity and environmental racism charges. The challenge of issues management has many aspects: ascertaining the degree to which a risk exists, learning to manage that risk within tolerable limits, ascertaining those limits, and communicating with key publics about those risks. This communication is a means to receive information and expressions of concern from key publics, to learn scientific opinions, and to express facts and opinions that enrich the community decision-making process. At the core of discussions and research about risk communication and SIM is the concept of community right to know.

Community Right to Know

Citizen participation in environmental regulation is a relatively new development, although since the mid-1970s, it has been viewed as a standard feature of public policy (Szasz, 1994). The legacy of today's philosophy of community right to know began to change dramatically in the mid-1980s. This change was influenced by a series of industrial accidents, with numerous researchers suggesting that the Union Carbide plant explosion in Bhopal, India, was the main triggering event for increased regulations (see Chapter 8 for more details of this tragedy). Community right to know policies following Bhopal became one of the benchmarks of responsible organizational communication in the United States.

Within 2 years of the disaster, after 145 lawsuits against Union Carbide and after the occurrence of other incidents on American soil—among smaller incidents, a Union Carbide plant in West Virginia leaked a different toxic gas in 1985, injuring 135 people ("Averting More Chemical Tragedies," 1985)—the U.S. Congress heeded advice from a federal government-sponsored research project that showed more than 7,000 accidents of the kind between 1980 and 1985 (Falkenberry, 1995) and developed and passed numerous provisions and legislations.

One common element of these provisions and legal instruments, regulatory mechanisms, and epistemological approaches to risk management is communication based on community right-to-know initiatives. As described by EPA (1997), "Empowering the public with information helps assure [industry] compliance with existing laws and encourages companies to take additional measures to reduce industrial chemical releases" (p. 3). These laws and regulations, which were created by the U.S. Congress along with an array of city, county, state, and federal governmental agencies as well as private industry and industry associations, are intended to minimize the likelihood and consequences of chemical and other manufacturing accidents. They are in part a response to a lack of oversight and a series of large chemical accidents in the United States and India during the 1980s (Belke, 2000).

Most notably, the Comprehensive Environmental Response, Compensation, and Liability Act (CERCLA), or Superfund, and its reauthorization (Superfund Amendment and Reauthorization Act [SARA] of 1986) require that specific procedures be implemented to assess the release of hazardous substances. Specifically focused on risk communication, SARA requires public participation provision and the community right-to-know requirements of the Emergency Planning and Community Right-to-Know Act of 1986 (EPCRA). SARA requires companies to provide public information concerning chemical emissions; in so doing, this act gave a new scope and purpose to risk communication. According to Peters et al. (1997), "In a period of barely ten years, environmental risk communication has evolved from a management concept to codified legislation" (p. 43).

For risk communication, the key part of SARA is EPCRA, which gives EPA oversight of risk communication efforts related to the formation of local emergency planning committees (LEPCs). SARA also mandated each state's governor to appoint members to a State Emergency Response Commission (SERC), which in turn created LEPCs. Each SERC is responsible for implementing EPCRA provisions within each state, including the 3,500 local emergency planning districts and appointed LEPCs for each district.

Codifying environmental risk communication, SARA and other federal policies require companies to inform citizens regarding the kinds and quantities of chemicals that are manufactured, stored, transported, and emitted in each community. SARA's underpinning assumption is that as companies report the toxicity about the materials they produce, transport, and store, people could become more informed of the level of risk in their neighborhood. Among other outcomes, this federal initiative was intended to increase the flow of various kinds of technical information from experts to community residents and to open channels of commentary between them. It is also likely that some of the motive for the legislation was to pressure the industry to adopt and implement even higher standards of community and employee safety.

By 1986, 30 states or cities had some form of community right-to-know requirements (Hearne, 1996), and every state presently has some community right-to-know requirements, whether industry or government mandated. Within EPCRA's (1986) guidelines, the burden of informing the population belongs to organizations that work with, manufacture, refine, or store hazardous materials, with a unique responsibility for the strategic communication of health, safety, and environmental risks falling on the shoulders of corporate communicators, particularly public relations practitioners specializing in risk and environmental communication.

EPCRA is a document divided in two parts. The first regulates the emergency planning requirements for the states, and the second "provides for public access to mandatory reports filed by industries concerning their chemical releases and general chemical inventories" (Falkenberry, 1995, p. 4). The regulation passed by the U.S. Congress in 1986 limited this right to know to a list of 400 extremely hazardous substances out of 60,000 chemicals in commercial use in the United States at the time (EPCRA, 1986). In this way, the right to know observed in the Environmental Impact Statement carries a duty to inform that falls only on risk-generating organizations with their obligation to provide complete, truthful, and accurate reports to the local governments (EPCRA) but not on the government, which, according to Hadden (1989a), should "ensure that the other parties can exercise their rights and fulfill their responsibilities . . . [by] designing and, if necessary, redesigning public policies" (p. 217).

EPCRA also allows citizens to enforce the law (Bass & MacLean, 1993; EPCRA, 1986). However, to be able to enforce the law, citizens first need to be able to access, understand, and process the information into action (Bass & MacLean, 1993; O'Rourke & Macey, 2003; Shapiro, 2005). According to the agency's own regulations, EPA has an affirmative responsibility to collect and disseminate information that furthers public health and environmental goals (Bass & MacLean, 1993). According to EPA (1997), "Empowering the public with information helps assure [industry] compliance with existing laws and encourages companies to take additional measures to reduce industrial chemical releases" (p. 3).

Reviewing the Right-to-Know provision for the Public Relations Society of America, Newman (1988) concluded, "The theory behind these toxic laws is that this information will not only help answer citizen questions about [chemical] releases, but will also assist them in pressuring government and industry to correct practices that threaten their health and environment" (p. 8). Understanding the nature and impact of a source of risk is not the only factor involved in risk assessment, management, and communication. Another factor is the power resource within the rhetorical struggle by parties engaged in negotiating levels of risk and standards of regulative or legislative control.

According to Hadden (1989b), the numbers of citizens who are able to use the law effectively can be increased with the use of communicative educational practices that translate technical information into useful and empowering knowledge to communities. The regulation by itself is useful but not enough to avoid accidents such as the one in Bhopal (Hadden, 1989a). Crude technical information about the proximity of hazardous materials alone does not empower citizens to control or prevent disasters in industrial facilities.

Lewis (2005) argued that those practices are more than a legal requirement; they are also a moral duty because access to quality information can effectively prevent disasters and help combat environmental discrimination. According to recent research (Jacobson, 2003; S. M. Johnson, 2005; Palenchar, Heath, & Dunn, 2005), knowledge about the presence and risks of hazardous and toxic chemicals in nearby facilities can even help to diminish the fear of the risk of terrorist attacks.

Hadden (1989a) concluded that, although there are many approaches to the concept of right to know, they are not "entirely distinct, blurring into each other on the edges. Thus, a more appropriate image would be that of a continuum of rights to know, with the four points marking transitions" (p. 203). The four points, according to Hadden, are basic right to know, right to know for risk reduction, participatory right to know (decision making), and right to know for changing the balance of power.

In this way, the literature in the field reaches a rare consensus about the importance of right to know. Researchers have found that access to quality of information is essential to empower communities to be able to discuss with corporations and governments in a balanced position of power (e.g., Branch & Bradbury, 2006; Bullard, 2004; Helfand & Peyton, 1999; Lewis, 2005; O'Rourke & Macey, 2003; Shapiro, 2005). Moreover, the quality of information has to meaningfully build the community's capacity to use it to improve participation in the decision-making process (e.g., Branch & Bradbury, 2006; Shapiro, 2005; Webler & Tuler, 2006). Finally, once the access to meaningful information is provided, the ability of the community to process it and turn it into action is one of the most important factors in risk and pollution prevention and in the development of sound and equalitarian environmental regulation (e.g., O'Rourke & Macey, 2003; Shapiro, 2005). For example, two key community right-to-know initiatives in a little bit more detail are EPA's SARA Title III (specifically, the formation of LEPCs), and the chemical industry's Responsible Care Program.

SARA Title III requires the formation of LEPCs, which are designed to plan for manufacturing emergencies and to serve as monthly community forums where nearby residents, government officials, industry representatives, health and safety officials, and any other concerned individuals and organizations could request information and voice concerns. EPCRA and LEPCs have four major provisions: emergency planning (Sections 301–303), emergency release notification (Section 304), hazardous chemical storage reporting requirements (Sections 311–312), and the Toxic Release Inventory (TRI; Section 313), which requires a publicly available EPA database that contains information on toxic chemical releases and other waste management activities reported annually by certain covered industry groups as well as federal facilities.

EPA (SARA, 1995) has argued that the TRI is one of the most successful environmental laws in the United States. Critics, however, have argued that the TRI is simply a pollution accounting system and makes no attempt other than, through the power of information, to control how pollution is managed or market incentives to minimize pollution (Hearne, 1996) and that it does not cover all toxic chemicals or require reporting from numerous significant sources of pollution releases (Environmental Defense Fund, 2003).

The Responsible Care Program, developed by the American Chemistry Council (formerly the Chemical Manufacturing Association), is an industry initiative that functions to meet the requirements of SARA Title III. Responsible Care works to achieve improvements in environmental, health, and safety performance, as well as developing industry risk communication tools related to community emergency response preparation. According to the American Chemistry Council (2003), the guiding principles of Responsible Care include (a) to operate facilities and develop processes and products in a manner that protects health, safety, and environment; (b) to lead in the development of responsible laws, regulations, and standards; (c) to work with customers, carriers, suppliers, distributors, and contractors to foster the safe use, transport, and disposal of chemicals; and (d) to seek and incorporate public input regarding our products and operations. The Responsible Care Program established industry standards in six different areas: community awareness and emergency response, process safety, distribution, pollution prevention, employee health and safety, and product stewardship.

Part of the Responsible Care Program includes the formation of community advisory committees or panels (CAC/Ps) that serve as a forum for public dialogue related to manufacturing concerns and risks. CAC/Ps are composed of individuals, with membership drawn from a cross section of the community, who provide a link between the public and various organizations that operate in the region by providing counsel and recommendations on matters of public policy. According to the American Chemistry Council (2003), CAC/Ps provide a level of accountability by opening up decision-making and policy formation processes to concerned citizens while providing resources for citizens to participate in the public policy process.

The effectiveness and value of CAC/Ps have been questioned. Heath, Bradshaw, and Lee (2002) found a lack of awareness of their existence and low use, while at the same time, more than two thirds of the residents surveyed approved of their intended functions.

A recent addition to Responsible Care is the 2002 Responsible Care Security Code, developed in response to 9/11, the focus of which is to safeguard against potential terrorist attacks, expand industry relationships with law enforcement, and provide a model for chemical site protection. The Security Code uses a risk-based approach to identify, assess, and address vulnerabilities; prevent or mitigate incidents; enhance training and response capabilities; and maintain and improve relationships with key stakeholders. Some specific examples include companies using tools to analyze the security of products sales, distribution, and cyber security, as well as maintaining open and effective lines of communication, including steps such as sharing effective security practices with others throughout industry and communities and maintaining interaction with law enforcement officials.

The Difficulties of Risk Assessment

Risk forces individuals, companies, activists, communities, and governmental agencies to balance many interests and to consider all of the dynamics that shape communities where risks exist. This section features those difficulties and challenges as a foundation for discussing response options in sections that follow.

Decades of related risk management and communication research argue for an infrastructural, community-based approach (Palenchar & Heath, 2007). A fully functioning society knows and acknowledges risks and develops plans tailored to community conditions. These messages need to survive the experiences and the conversations of people in each community:

> An organizational culture of transparency acknowledges and respects the information, communication and decision-making expectations and demands of all its stakeholders and stakeseekers, and does not stage-manage them by limiting access to, propagandizing information about or manipulating decision-making regarding risk. (Palenchar & Heath, 2007, p. 124)

Several concepts predict effective risk communication, emergency management planning, and execution: social accountability, knowledge/understanding, cognitive involvement, harms/benefits, control, trust, narrative enactment, and identification (Heath & Abel, 1996a, 1996b; Heath et al., 2002; McComas, 2003; Palenchar & Heath, 2002).

Uncertainty is central to each risk because, by definition, people experience doubt as they decide whether a risk exists and whether it is tolerable. Risk is by definition a matter of uncertainty. For instance, the routine of driving changes dramatically when uncertainty occurs. It might be as simple as seeing a parked patrol car as one comes over a slight hill. It might be the sensation of suddenly driving on ice. It could include a dramatic swerve as a tire blows out. Similar feelings come to mind as people consider who to trust and how much trust is warranted on matters of health and safety. As a technical concept, risk is conventionally defined as something that can be given a numerical value by multiplying the probability of an outcome, typically one with negative consequences, with its severity. This expectancy value is used to estimate and compare risks (Hansson, 1989) that are perceived differently depending on the heuristics and biases each person uses to judge them (Tversky & Kahneman, 1986).

These decision models offer approaches to understand beliefs and values that underlie public judgments of risk acceptability and predict people's personal and public policy responses, as does Fishbein and Ajzen's (1975) expectancy value theory (Ajzen & Fishbein, 1980). Risk judgments are affected by persons' attitudes toward the risk, attitudes toward the individual or collective measures to be taken to mitigate the risk, and the desire to conform to the social norms of a community (R. J. Griffin, Neuwirth, & Dunwoody, 1995). Attitudes toward risks and their harm are likely to be affected by the sociopolitical roles of individuals engaged in the assessment (K. Thomas, Swaton, Fishbein, & Otway, 1980).

Sizable numbers of people distrust the operations and spokesperson reports regarding the safety and health implications of many business and government activities. Hyperbolic reports in newspapers, books, and magazines, as well as on television and radio, heighten apprehensions and foster distrust of business or governmental activities. These reports, framed as they are, often lead people to doubt the technical competence and fairness of reporters to obtain and provide valid and valuable information. Part of the lack of trust in risk communication comes from the uncertainty that is inherent in scientific processes that deal in probabilities and not certainties. Scientists tell people that 1 in 100,000 persons (or some other probability) will suffer the health or safety effects of exposure to something, but they cannot predict who that person will be. Scientists disagree. Politicians disagree. Scientists use technical terms and concepts that, in the judgment of laypersons, obscure truth rather than reveal it. Using dramatic frames, reporters sensationalize, overgeneralize, and oversimplify rather than explain risks and their consequences (Cohn, 1990; Covello, 1992; M. Moore, 1989).

People look to government and other sources of sociopolitical power to help discover risks, assess their severity, solve them by reducing their chances of occurring, or mitigate their negative consequences. Grave sociopolitical implications lead to public policy discussions, whereby harmed parties seek to regulate those entities that are liable for the risks. No single, universally accepted standard of risk estimate is available to help people know whether they should be concerned, for instance, about the presence of toxic materials in their neighborhoods and workplaces. Thus, government often becomes an unwilling and even inexpert arbiter.

Considerations of risk acknowledge that not all members of a community have the same tolerance for a particular risk, as they may have different information and opinions regarding it. What is a tolerable risk for some is intolerable for others. What some think is a risk that is intolerable, deserving to be subjected to greater control, perhaps through legislation or regulation, to others may be a trivial, inconsequential risk not deserving the burden of governmental intervention. Even when members of a public perceive a risk to exist, they may conclude that its benefits are worth the risk. In this way, many of them form key publics and become active toward various outcomes, all of which have the potential of becoming major controversies.

Two major overlapping scenarios of risk exist. In one, organizations such as public health agencies attempt to alert and inform people about health or safety risks over which they have personal control, such as driving with fastened seatbelts, eating low-cholesterol foods, immunizing children against diseases, or having safe sex. A second scenario involves responses by industries and government agencies to help people understand and agree to regulated (controlled) levels of risk such as those created by chemical or biotechnology companies. In this mix of voices are reporters and activists, both of whom have self-interested reasons to treat simplistically and with hyperbole the conceivably harmful aspects of risks and the avarice of businesses coupled with the ignorance or co-optation of governmental regulators—the wolves sent to guard the henhouse!

Companies have a different choice to make in risk assessments than do other parties, such as whether or not to upgrade operations to lessen public criticism that may increase operating costs and lower the ability to compete and attract investors unless all members of an industry adopt the same standards. In today's economy, governmental agencies are caught between competing stakeholder interests, which include the costs of regulation, safety of citizens, and the ability of domestic companies to compete in global markets where other countries do not impose the levels of constraint typical of the United States. Government agencies become the playing field for tugs of war between legislators, members of the executive cadre of government, business spokespersons, and citizens who are convinced that specific intolerable health, safety, or environmental quality risks exist.

This section has provided insights into these variables as a preamble to considering the community-based decision processes that aim to assess and control risks. Issues management enters this process to consider the strategic business planning options and communication approaches, issues monitoring, efforts to properly achieve corporate responsibility, and risk communication.

Risk Management and Communication Approaches

Several theories and models have developed as unique options for the research and practice of risk communication. The four most useful approaches are mental models, cultural theory, perception theory, and infrastructure theory. Included within this discussion is the concept of power dynamics and control over risk, as well as the interaction of control within risk communication.

MENTAL MODELS

An important line of research is the mental models approach to risk communication that is based on the concept of how people understand and view various phenomena grounded in cognitive psychology and artificial intelligence research (Geuter & Stevens, 1983). The mental models approach, as applied to risk communication, is built on the work of researchers from Carnegie-Mellon University, including Baruch Fischhoff, Granger Morgan, Ann Bostrom, and associates (M. G. Morgan, Fischhoff, Bostrom, & Atman, 2002).

The mental models approach fits solidly with the scientific approach to risk discovery, awareness, management, and communication. Scientists help people discover risks and worry about when and whether a risk is safe enough (Fischhoff, Slovic, Lictenstein, Read, & Combs, 1978). Three decades ago, keen thinkers realized that risks lent themselves to probabilistic assessments and scientific methods. The communication aspect of this approach reasons that scientists have substantial responsibility of getting the science correct and then communicating to narrow the gap between what scientists know and believe and what target audiences and key publics know and believe (M. G. Morgan et al., 2002).

Out of this line of reasoning has come the precautionary principle. This principle has often been captured in various cultural truisms. "Look before you leap." "Two wrongs do not make a right." "Better safe than sorry." "An ounce of prevention is worth a pound of cure." Colloquialisms such as these can be challenged by other familiar sayings. "The early bird gets the worm" suggests that the bird willing to judge the risks of daylight or springtime is more likely to get the reward than will the more cautious one. We might add this one: "Nothing ventured, nothing gained."

The key assumption in the very complex debate over ways to systematically make risk decisions or decisions about risk is to be cautious but, in doing so, do no or less harm. Maguire and Ellis (2009) offer the following insight:

> Contradicting a popular accusation against it, however, we have shown that the precautionary principle does not politicize decisions about risk; rather, it renders the inherently political nature of risk management more explicit, highlighting the distributive consequences of both action *and* inaction. (p. 135)

The question forged by critics of a purely sound science approach is this: How can we truly make assessments and communicate recommendations that best serve society, not some interest to the disadvantage of others?

CULTURAL THEORY

Cultural theory has been advanced through Mary Douglas (1992; see also Beck, 2004) and others who have argued that risk decisions are more than the product of scientific investigation. They are political, sensitive to the vagaries of the societal institutions that arise to address, challenge, and accommodate risks. Risk decisions are invariably associated with the legitimacy of power relations and resources (Tansey & Rayner, 2009).

Part of the rationale for this approach to risk management and communication grows from the premise that the underpinning rationale for society is the collective management of risk. Science plays a role, but the theory assumes that each individual of society is not a rational decision-making machine that necessarily and easily makes decisions based on probabilistic scientific assessments of risks and their reward-benefit ratios. In fact, risk assessment, collectively constructed, may be simply and singularly rational and functional. That means that rather than merely acknowledging and acceding to functional interpretations of risk, members of society may prefer alternative interpretations and institutions. They may also literally re-create the risk relationships and interpretations to frustrate the authority of functional science.

One of the leading frameworks within risk communication studies that has been widely debated among sociologists and public relations theorists, among others, during the past 20 years within cultural theory and other related theories is "risk society." Beck (1992) argued that the evolution of Western societies is more and more characterized by the pervasiveness of risk—uncertainties, insecurities, and hazards. Central elements to risk society include uncertain personal identity that is subject to flux and choice, environmental hazards posed by new technologies, and "self-endangerment" of industrial societies as their environmental choices and consequences become increasingly large and uncontrollable.

According to Beck (1992), one of the unique differences with Chernobyl in respect to risk is that the accident destroyed any concept of geographical boundaries for risk. The risk was not tied to a local community, physical location, and governmental boundary. Hazardous materials and their effects not only affected citizens in Belarus and the Ukraine but went beyond borders, including no temporal limitations, with unknown long-term effects (Beck, 1992; Wynne, 1996). "The injured of Chernobyl are today, years after the catastrophe, not even all born yet" (Beck, 1996, p. 31). According to Beck (1995), incidents such as Chernobyl reformulate social understanding of risk.

Evidence abounds that risk perceptions and estimates are affected by decision heuristics that reflect the cultures of key groups, based largely on their roles in society. Krimsky (1992) believed risk assessments based on science must be couched in the social reality zone of meaning of the communities that are assessing the risks. Such is the case because "when faced with complex problems involving probability estimates or estimates of the frequency of events, people apply certain discernible rules of judgment called heuristics to simplify the problem. The use of heuristics often leads to judgment bias" (p. 17). Companies and governmental agencies can communicate to improve faulty heuristics, but they cannot dismiss or ignore them without dire consequences. The upshot of this line of reasoning is that assessments of risk require matrixed decisions that are sensitive to prevailing cultural preferences and institutions, no matter how frustrating that may be for strict functionalists. Thus, participants are empowered and appreciated rather than marginalized because risk is a societal phenomenon, not merely the purview of sound science.

PERCEPTION (PSYCHOMETRIC) THEORY

An interest in how people perceive and respond to crises became institutionalized in the United States primarily following the crisis at the Three Mile Island nuclear generating facility (this line of analysis is advanced more in detail below in the sections on risk communication options and the dynamics of the management of risk issues). Here we want to lay out the more fundamental rather than functional approach to this theory.

Leiss (1996) determined that the term *risk communication* was coined in 1984, according to references listed in the fourth edition of Rohrmann, Wiedemann, and Stegelmann's (1990) *Risk Communication: An Interdisciplinary Bibliography*. According to Leiss, risk communication has always from the onset had a practical intent based on the differences between risk assessments by experts and how they are perceived and understood by those who are affected.

While some suggest that these streams developed separately, risk assessment (including perceptions) and risk management research have never been separate streams of the risk research branch. A 1989 NRC report, known as the

Red Book and titled *Improving Risk Communication,* as well as other early risk research by EPA argued that risk assessment and management, including communication, was a common theme. Goldstein's (2005) review of advances in risk assessment and communication suggested that "a common theme by those involved in assessing and managing risks has been the need to integrate risk assessment and risk communication" (p. 142).

One of the proponents of this approach features cognitive explanation of risk decisions. By this logic (one not at odds with logics that run throughout this book), decisions are based on knowledge (K), attitudes (A), and behavior (B). The assumption is that given knowledge, individuals assess risks by using the evaluative and predisposing aspect of attitudes to determine what behaviors they believe to be rewarding or less harmful. Now, anyone engaged in risk analysis knows that this equation is not simple. In fact, it does not even invariably follow the KAB sequence or logic. Valente, Paredes, and Poppe (1998) documented how people idiosyncratically in the same society may approach risk assessment and risk communication processes and messages with any of many alternative configurations: KAB, AKB, BAK, ABK, KBA, and such.

Looking at the underlying logic beneath this line of analysis, Sjoberg (2000) reasoned, "Risk perception is hard to understand" (p. 9). Considering perception of nuclear energy, Sjoberg shared these insights:

> The fact that attitude plays such a prominent role in the models is interesting. It suggests that risk perception is to a large extent a question of ideology in a very specific sense, not in the general sense, that is posited by Cultural Theory. People who, for some reason, are strongly in favor of nuclear power tend to see it is risk free, and vice versa. (p. 9)

For these reasons, advocates of the perceptual theory approach and risk communicators must understand and adapt to the logics applied by various individuals and key stakeholder publics if the design of messages is to be effective. Such analysis seems to feature the role of the risk assessor-communicator, whose responsibility it is to understand audiences and tailor messages to them. There is, then, some of the mental models approach underpinning this approach since it assumes that sound science determines what the message should be. Proponents of this logic, then, believe they offer insights on how to communicate effectively based on the psychometrics at play.

INFRASTRUCTURAL THEORY

Infrastructural theory combines themes from the previous three theories and offers insights intended to draw on the best of each and avoid the pitfalls of all. The assumption of infrastructural theory is that even though sound science is important, the multiple voices will offer various interpretations and instantiations of their interpretations of that science. For instance, in the current debate over global warming, competing evangelicals in the United States draw from the Book of Genesis. Some say that God created the Heavens and Earth, and thus, if there is global warming, it is the will of God and beyond the impact of humans. The alternative interpretation read in the Book of Genesis is that man was given dominion to believe that humans must act to protect and husband that which was given to them.

This illustration suggests that the rationale for infrastructural theory works to embrace the need for voices to produce facts, engage in evaluations, foster identifications, and develop policies that work best within each society to define, control, accommodate, and otherwise manage risks or risk responses. The list of guidelines offered at the end of this chapter grows from the research-driven best practices for those whose work brings them to be analysts of and voices for organizations that are charged with risk assessment and policy development. The challenge is to participate in and even create infrastructures that allow multiple voices to speak on risks and develop culturally sensitive approaches that evolve through dialogue rather than are prescribed by the assumed authority of one or more individual organizations or institutions.

Infrastructural theory is central to our understanding of risk democracy, which reasons that in association with various experts, individual voices of risk bearers must be brought together to create systems and shared perspectives that appropriately assess, mitigate, and respond to risks that may be unevenly borne throughout any community or larger society. The logics explored in this chapter parallel the analysis by numerous researchers, such as Scherer and Cho (2003), who have reasoned that an individual cognitive approach to risk perception ignores a myriad of social influences. Preferring to feature network contagion theory, they found "that social linkages in communities may play an important role in focusing risk perceptions" (p. 261). Decades of interpersonal communication research have also confirmed this community view of knowledge, attitudes, and behaviors. Ultimately, better managed risk and crisis communication is likely to result in less financial and social capital damage.

While the study of risk and crisis communication, strategies, models, and theories is important and helpful, we are reminded that these fields of study also have human implications, and a critical examination must be included in the research stream. For example, McKie and Munshi (2007), in a critical reflection on the 1984 Union Carbide crisis in Bhopal, India, suggested that postcrisis research in public relations publications "continue[s] to treat Bhopal as a source of data to help frame guidelines for Western centres, without much concern for the fate of the victims of the tragedy" (p. 67).

As one could easily argue from the variety of risk communication orientations and models and typologies that have developed over the past 3-plus decades, there has been a tremendous and eclectic growth in risk communication research.

Pidgeon, Kasperson, and Slovic (2003) charged that despite substantial progress, the risk perception and risk communication literature remains "seriously fragmented: between the psychometric paradigm and cultural theories of risk perception; between post-modernist and discourse-centered approaches and behavioral studies of risk; between economic/utility-maximization and economic-justice approaches; and between communications and empowerment strategies for risk communication" (p. 2). McComas (2006) suggested that while a strength of risk communication is the interdisciplinary nature of the research, the knowledge is not centralized; "risk communication research presently is characterized by many, sometimes overlapping, variable analytic studies but few integrative theoretical frameworks" (p. 85), noting exceptions such as the social amplification of risk (Kasperson et al., 1988) and risk information-seeking and processing models (R. J. Griffin, Dunwoody, & Neuwirth, 1999).

ISSUES MANAGEMENT OF RISK: DECISION MAKING AIMED AT CONTROL

Within SIM and risk communication, another key factor is the differences between one's own perception of ability to control a risk relevant to one's own interest as opposed to the perception of how capable others are to control risks relevant to their behavior. Parents, for instance, worry that their children are likely to encounter (and even willfully bring onto themselves) risks greater than their ability to control. Although various populations, for various psychometric reasons, may believe they are able to exert sufficient control and even more control than others can over a risk, it is likely that if they worry about others' deficiencies in this regard, they will support increased control (either by the source of the risk or by government). That logic, for instance, has been central to the antitobacco campaigns, even including reducing youth access to cigarettes. The logic is that children/young teens cannot control their urge to engage in such risky behavior and therefore must be protected by eliminating cigarette vending machines, banning sales to minors, and even keeping cigarettes beyond easy access by locking them into storage areas in places where they are sold to persons above a certain age. That same logic applies to access to alcohol.

The central worry in community risk perception studies is the tendency of potential risk bearers, risk generators and policy makers to be inaccurate in their ability to assess properly the likelihood that certain risk events will occur and, if they occur, whether they will lead to negative or positive outcomes. The issue to be managed is how to understand and control risks, as well as gain acceptance for these measures in ways that foster the wisest outcomes in any community of interest (Freudenberg, 1984). Krimsky (1992) noted that the field of risk studies grew out of the practical needs of industrialized societies to regulate technology and to protect people from natural and technological hazards. "From its inception the study of risk was positioned at the intersection of academic, governmental, and industrial interests" (p. 8).

An issues management approach to risk assessment and communication argues that these activities are more likely to be successful when they increase the control that key publics have over the technical information, risk assessment process, and regulation of any threatening product as well as its manufacture or transportation. Control is perceived to work best when it arises from a constructive partnership between organizations that create risk and local government that champions the interests of citizens (Heath et al., 2002). It seems that community members favor the intervention of an activist group, to increase their control, only when government fails in this role. Activists may pose a challenge for community members who have no "control" over them, whereas they at least can work to replace local government officials. That theme guides the analysis in this section.

Groups that assess risks try to control not only risk decisions but also the availability and interpretation of relevant information. These can either be scientists employing a mental models approach (M. G. Morgan et al., 2002) or the development of institutions that exert cultural evaluation and sanctions on sources of risk (Tansey & Rayner, 2009). Experience led Ellen Silbergeld, speaking as senior scientist with the Environmental Defense Fund, to conclude, "Equal access to resources is needed to understand the issues, to go behind the presentation being made by the communicator to reassess the risks, if you will, to reevaluate the grounds for decisions and discussions" (qtd. in Davies, Covello, & Allen, 1987, p. 34).

Concerned publics realize that if they accept risk experts' assessments of risk, they are obliged to concur with the consequent recommendations, including the decision that a specific level of risk exposure is tolerable. When publics worry that they are at the mercy of risk assessors, their recourse is to refuse to accept those expert evaluations. Reflecting on this quandary, Covello, Sandman, and Slovic (1988) claimed,

> A risk that the parties at risk have some control over is more acceptable than a risk that is beyond their control. A risk that the parties at risk assess and decide to accept is more acceptable than a risk that is imposed on them. (p. 6)

In the face of unknown, poorly controlled, or unacceptably high risks, noncompliance by key publics forces risk assessors to strive toward zero risk or to "bravely" and "resolutely" bear the burden of justifying any level higher. In this feeding ground, activists are likely to enter and attempt to force companies and government agencies to prove that no harm exists or to implement measures to reduce risks or increase effective responses to them. That rhetorical stance contrasts with the assumption that concerned citizens must prove that a risk is intolerable. Many who have studied risk, for better or worse, believe in the spirit of risk democracy that people are entitled to their concerns no matter how unfounded they are. Addressing those concerns is the centerpiece of effective and ethical efforts to help citizens feel that sufficient control is being brought to bear.

In this battle, concern about risks matures into power politics, a realization of issues managers. Such insight is warranted, William Ruckelshaus reasoned, because our adversarial form of government features advocacy:

> Ours is a government of the people in this country, and it derives, as we have been told since we were children, its just powers from the consent of the governed. If the governed withhold that consent or take a portion of it back, it simply means that the government has been forced to once again share the power to govern with those who had earlier given their consent. (qtd. in Davies et al., 1987, p. 4)

Any public that is unwilling to tolerate a risk is likely to work for its control. Activism results from detection of a problem, perception that minimal constraints are likely to be encountered during protest, and belief that the problem affects them (J. E. Grunig, 1989). A constructive issues management response to concerned people is to encourage them to participate in decision making. Otherwise, they may assert that right. Scrutinizing the politics of risk assessment, EPA administrator Lee Thomas recognized that

> we will never return to the days when we were content to let people in white coats make soothing noises. Citizens must share directly in decisions that affect them, and we must ensure that they do so with a fuller understanding of the inevitable trade-offs involved in the management of risk. (qtd. in Davies et al., 1987, p. 25)

Expectations are subjective as well as scientific and are capable of being influenced through communication. The rhetorical struggle balances the degree of risk, the benefits that offset it, the ability to control it, and the collaborative participation of all stakeholders and stakeseekers. This section has featured those challenges as a prelude to considering what risk communication options are viable.

SIM's Approach to Risk Communication

EPA established risk communication as a means to open, responsible, informed, and reasonable scientific and value-laden discussion of risks associated with personal health and safety practices involved in living and working in proximity to harmful activities and toxic substances (NRC, 1989). Defined this way, risk management, including communication, is successful to the extent that people who fear that they may be or are demonstrably harmed by a risk can become more knowledgeable about and confident that sufficient control is imposed by the sources of the risk and by government or other external sources that are responsible for monitoring the risk generators.

Persons who design risk communication have at times reduced it to a list of simplistic prescriptions. One such list, EPA's (1988) "seven cardinal rules of risk communication," advised risk communicators to tailor their messages to audiences and to use

> simple, non-technical language. Be sensitive to local norms, such as speech and dress. Use vivid, concrete images that communicate on a personal level. Use examples and anecdotes that make technical risk data come alive. Avoid distant, abstract, unfeeling language about deaths, injuries, and illnesses. (p. 4)

This advice assumes that "if people are sufficiently motivated, they are quite capable of understanding complex information, even if they may not agree with you" (p. 5). Such lists tend to miss the dynamics of technical ignorance, power, and controversy that frustrate the risk communication process. These lists can assume incorrectly that merely supplying information to people leads them to be educated, calmed, and risk tolerant.

This approach to risk communication predicts that if people receive credible and clear information regarding scientifically assessed risk levels, they will accept the conclusions and policy recommendations of risk assessors. This model overassumes the power of information and does not acknowledge the power resources that concerned publics employ to exert political pressure in their efforts to impose higher operating standards on the source of the ostensibly intolerable risk. The view assumes that "if people are given the facts, their subjective perceptions will begin to align with scientific judgments" (Liu & Smith, 1990, p. 332). That perspective reasons that if laypeople understand the company's or government's side of the story, then confidence about risk will increase and complaints will go away (Gaudino, Fritsch, & Haynes, 1989).

Numerous other risk communication scholars, in their review of the literature, have suggested various typologies or evolutions of the field. Rowan (1994) suggested that risk communication literature contains three kinds of work that could provide a foundation for future risk communication. These include a technical versus democratic research perspective; the technical perspective compares and contrasts a more organizational management perspective that tends to privilege scientific and technical information to persuade the lay public, whereas a more democratic perspective is concerned more with matters of justice and fairness. The second perspective includes phenomenological analyses of people's everyday experience and notions of environmental risk, and the third perspective builds on broad philosophical principles for what constitutes good risk communication.

Fischhoff (1995) summarized the first 20 years of risk communication research into the developmental stages in risk management, moving through the various developmental stages characterized by the primary communication strategy: All we have to do is get the numbers right, all we have to do is tell them the numbers, all we have to do is explain what we mean by the numbers, all we have to do is show them they've accepted similar risks before, all we have to do is show them that it's a good deal for them, all we have to do is treat them nice, all we have to do is make them partners, and, finally, all we have to do is all of the above.

Witte, Meyer, and Martel (2000) noted that risk communication is most closely aligned with research focused on fear appeals as persuasive models, presenting a threat and then subsequently providing and describing a behavior that may alleviate the threat. Sandman's (e.g., 1993) work on risk as a function of hazard (technical assessment) and outrage (cultural, personal view) has provided a framework and reference for much of the work in risk communication and health communication.

So what's to be done? If zones of meaning—facts, value premises, identifications, and behavioral/policy conclusions—in communities differ, then risk responses must be tailored to each public, and convergence must be achieved. Decide on what information is valuable, provide it, decide on what decision heuristics are appropriate, and apply them. Organizations that are seeking to act in the mutual interests of themselves and their stakeholders work to make institutions yield to these changes. Organizations that are likely to be thought inadequate in their standards of corporate responsibility use bureaucracy to maintain barriers instead of removing them.

The preferred risk communication model assumes that publics are active rather than passive information receivers and processors. Risk communication entails institutions trying to reach individuals in various states of collective behavior and engaging in collaborative decision making. Developing shared points of view may result from linear communication, but dialogue seems to be required because cultural relativism assumes "that the validity of public knowledge depends on its relation to the context of its creation through social activities such as science, technology, religion, and even magic" (Rayner, 1992, p. 93).

We miss the point and, therefore, generate useless research and professional prescriptions when we approach risk communication as information exchange about risks while failing to acknowledge that people compete through persuasive exchanges to achieve greater control over the risks they believe to exist. Control is the motive behind efforts to define, estimate, and understand risks. For this reason, industry shares key publics' desire for control over risks, although their means may differ. Does industry sufficiently control its operations and employ proper research to understand risks it may create? Does the company or government agency share this information and foster dialogue and criticism so that people interact and form relationships with members of the industry in a collaborative fashion, seeking to maximize the safety of all parties involved? Is industry ethical and responsive to the needs of its key publics and committed to building mutually beneficial relationships? Herein lies the essence of risk communication as conceptualized through the principles of issues management.

An issues management approach to health and safety risks requires a view that embraces several key variables. Ongoing research has yet to define these terms and their relationships satisfactorily; however, enough is known that we can lay out some conclusions and frame a philosophy of risk communication. Current research assumes that people's support or opposition for an organization that ostensibly creates or allows a risk to exist depends on whether they believe the organization subjects them (or relevant others) to a likely and harmful risk over which they have limited individual or collective control. Rather than a linear communication relationship, whereby information and opinion influence flow from the firm to key publics, an issues management approach to risk views laypeople as a vital part of a complex communication, opinion formation, and decision-making infrastructure.

The primary outcome of the management of risk issues is not understanding or agreement, as some approaches argue. Rather, the outcome is control. Even to the extent that understanding and agreement are dependent variables, they in turn become independent variables affecting other dependent variables. This reasoning does not discount the importance of understanding or agreement. Rather, it acknowledges that they are often difficult or impossible to achieve due to the fact that corporate or governmental spokespersons often are not trusted sources of information, opinions, and advice. In addition, concerned publics typically lack the technical expertise needed to make independent judgments of complex risk issues, especially those requiring knowledge of scientific concepts and research methodologies.

Even if they do not have the scientific expertise to rely on their own knowledge and judgment but do not trust company spokespersons, they may conclude that a risk is tolerable if its benefits outweigh its harms. They may be assuaged in their apprehensions by knowing that mechanisms exist by which a dialogue can occur that considers their opinions and treats their concerns seriously. That last point stresses the importance of open, candid, honest, and responsive community dialogue as the basis for creating a harmonious, mutual-interest relationship between the key players when a risk may exist. For these reasons and as noted previously, *risk communication seeks to increase concerned publics' sense of control over the risks they believe can affect them.*

Drawing on his own research as well as that of others, Covello (1992) featured several variables to predict how people respond to risks. This list includes catastrophic potential, familiarity, understanding, uncertainty, controllability, voluntariness of exposure, effects on children, effects on manifestation, effects on future generations, victim identity, dread, trust in institutions, media attention, accident history, equity, benefits, reversibility, personal stake, and origin.

Given these factors, how do we progress to comprehend and create proactive responses to publics' concerns about the risks they believe they encounter? An issues management approach to risk assessment and problem solving begins by acknowledging the rhetorical nature of the dialogue and related power struggle that surround the assessment and control of risks (Heath & Nathan, 1991; Rowan, 1994). This view requires that issues communication allow for *rhetorical and political influence from community members.* It embraces the *uncertainty* people have regarding whether a risk exists and whether it can be controlled; *evaluation* regarding what is equitable, fair, safe, and environmentally sound; and *cognitive involvement,* which results from people's self-interest or altruistic concern for others. It should acknowledge the problematic role of *knowledge* and focus on people's estimation of whether the risk *harms or benefits* them. In this analysis, *control* and *trust* are outcomes desired by the relevant parties, even though the definition and sociopolitical means for accomplishing them may differ. The outcome sought is public support for the risks—their sources, rewards, and controls.

This review of risk assessment and the communication of those assessments recognizes how important trust is, not only as an attribute of communication sources but also as part of each key public's awareness of and confidence in communication processes and business operations over time. This approach to risk communication assumes that narratives change and organizational activities both create risk narratives and must conform to narratives preferred by concerned citizens, especially activist publics. Because risk assessment is public policy resource based, efforts to alter risk perception and behaviors entail the evaluation, weighing, and negotiation of stakes. To allay key publics' concerns, companies or government entities that create risks may have to spend money to improve operations to reduce those risks. As part of each company's or industry's public policy plan, efforts may be made to set standards that are required by law to lessen the effect of the so-called bad apples, the least responsible members of an industry. Community support is the fundamental outcome to be derived from the process of identifying risks as well as assessing their causes, magnitudes, and solutions and engaging in appropriate remediation.

The analysis and response to risk requires insights into the variables discussed here and throughout the book. As an outcome variable, the concept of organizational support is the ultimate objective of managing the organization's response to the concern on the part of key publics, and this needs further discussion. Either a risk exists or it does not. It is controllable in various ways and degrees or it is not. It is controllable by collective, community, or public policy actions; self-regulation of the potential source of risk; or persons who believe they suffer the risk and its consequences. The public policy contest (activist, company, and government agency) is to gain the support of key players. Companies desire to solve the problem through self-regulation without having regulation imposed through governmental actions as an expression of public will. Issues management of risks seeks to displace opposition with support by (a) making appropriate strategic business plans, (b) engaging in effective issues monitoring and analysis, (c) using public policy planning in the mutual interest of stakeholders, (d) seeking to meet key publics' expectations of corporate responsibility, and (e) communicating in ways that maximize the control people feel is reasonable to achieve harmony and foster multiple stakeholders' mutual interests.

People support that which benefits them and oppose that which harms them. That equation underpins issues management. One study of a town highly economically dependent on chemical manufacturing facilities discovered that perceived economic advantages correlated with support, whereas economic harms correlated with opposition. Advantages included personal income, business opportunities, community income, community tax base, real estate values, and job opportunities. In contrast, opposition correlated with personal medical insurance costs and environmental cleanup costs (Heath, Liao, & Douglas, 1995).

What rationale exists for this issues management approach to risk assessment and communication? For one, Nathan and Heath (1992) found that opposition correlated with the opinion that risks are intolerable. When considering whether they would tolerate the potential discharge of harmful substances—particularly lead—into coastal waters, nonsupporters were more likely to believe potential risks from a chemical manufacturing facility would be greater than did supporters.

In a similar fashion, persons who oppose or do not support the presence of a chemical plant in their community tend to think that harm from the plant outweighs its benefits—such as jobs, business income, and taxes (Heath, Liao, & Douglas, 1995). Persons who oppose such a plant experience higher levels of cognitive involvement than supporters do; opponents believe that they need to be attentive to plant operations and information about them because of the likelihood that those operations adversely affect their self-interests. The longer people live near a chemical plant or similar facility, the more accommodating they become to it. Likewise, they become more willing to support its presence in their community (Nathan & Heath, 1992).

Heath and Palenchar, through many of their studies (Heath & Palenchar, 2000; Palenchar & Heath, 2002), have demonstrated positive relationships between organizational support and trust, knowledge, reduced uncertainty, and personal and organizational control. For example, they have demonstrated increased support related to awareness of steps community residents can take during an emergency related to a chemical accident, increased support related to the simple act of communicating about risks and benefits, and increased organizational support in relationship to conducting worst-case scenario research. Overall, this section has demonstrated how issues managers can enhance risk communication and increase support for their organizations when they help key publics become a part of the decision and information-sharing and interpreting processes, cater to the needs (information, advice, decision heuristics) people want and use, and deliver information and advice as well as help shape interpretative heuristics people think are useful, ulti-mately making an argument that risk communication is most effective when it manages issues through dialogue.

RISK COMMUNICATION: MANAGING ISSUES THROUGH DIALOGUE

As discussed previously in this chapter, risk-relevant publics exist because people have different interpretive heuristics as well as conflicting understand-ings of whether something creates risk, whether that risk should be tolerated, and whether avoidance strategies or control measures are warranted. Publics arise because information and opinion regarding each risk do not uniformly exist throughout society. Pockets of concern become fertile ground for employing government to intervene between the public and the source of the risk. They constitute key zones of meaning, sometimes compatible and some-times at odds.

Risk communicators realize that each key public makes an idiosyncratic response to each risk based on its unique decision heuristic. Each concerned public has a proclivity to engage in or at least support activism to exert public policy solutions onto intolerable risks. That point was central to the discussion of the power resource dynamics in the previous section of this chapter. This sec-tion builds on that analysis to consider how communication can bring about the proper level of control and allay concerns on the part of citizens regarding the degree to which they are at risk as they go about their daily activities.

The past 30-plus years have seen a continued maturation of the field of risk communication based on the fundamental principle of dialogue. During this period, at least three theoretical options have guided the way in which risks are calculated, evaluated, and controlled, which has dramatically affected the evolution of risk communicators managing issues through dia-logue: (a) scientific positivism, whereby data and methodologies of scientists dominate efforts to ascertain the degree of risk—once the decision has been reached, an elite manages and communicates about the risk on behalf of the community; (b) constructivism-relativism, which assumes that everyone's opinions have equal value so that no opinion is better or worse than anyone else's; and (c) dialogue—through collaborative decision-making processes, scientific opinion becomes integrated into opinions that are vetted by key publics' values (McComas, Arvai, & Besley, 2009; Renn, 1992a; 2009).

Scientists and some members of risk-producing industries scoff at any risk assessment and decision-making approach other than the first, but proactive issues managers acknowledge that community-based relativism should not be dismissed. Reflecting on the difficulties of incorporating risk assessments into policy, the NRC (1989) concluded, "To remain democratic, a society must find ways to put specialized knowledge into the service of public choice and keep it from becoming the basis of power for an elite" (p. 15). Resolution of risk controversies requires more than clear, candid, and honest information.

> At the scientific-positivism end of the risk assessment and policy formation continuum, scientists, actuaries, and epidemiologists determine the extent to which people, as a community, are at risk. This risk assessment is driven by the scientific use of health and safety patterns and incidence of disease and harm, a macroassessment. Such analysis calculates the advantages of the risk in balance with community health patterns (Starr, 1969). At the other end of the theoretical spectrum (relativism), each key public expresses its opinions and insists on the integrity of its views, no matter how ill-informed they may be.

Comparing these choices, Renn (1992b) observed that a positivistic-objective approach fails to account for cultural differences, whereas the relativism of constructivism leaves the decision-making process "with no anchor for baseline comparison" (p. 179). Relying on the data at hand, which they believe and which confirm their predilection to support or oppose the source of risk, "social groups in a political arena try to maximize their opportunity to influence the outcome of the collective decision process by mobilizing social resources" (p. 180). If they opt for political activism, rather than a purely scientific approach to risk assessment and abatement, "individuals and organizations can influence the policy process only if they have sufficient resources available to pursue their goals" (p. 181). Community groups seek to have rules accepted and promulgated based on their values. In the absence of self-regulation by the ostensible source of risk, people turn to enforcement agencies to enforce the rules. "To be successful in a social arena, it is necessary to mobilize social resources" (p. 184). This is true both for responsible companies seeking community support and for activists working to wield their influence.

Social movements grow from people's concerns about health and safety as well as environmental quality. Concern is expressed rhetorically as the strain they feel between what is and should be the level of safety in their community. Believing that collective action can lead to increased safety, activists use rhetorical efforts to gather and mobilize power resources. With this power, they work to force confrontation over data and their interpretation relevant to the degree of risk: its potential, its likely severity, and the best means for abating or mitigating it. Through confrontation, the combatants seek means by which to negotiate and resolve their differences. If that occurs, the final stage in this protest scenario is the enforcement of appropriate standards and communication efforts to explain why that solution is appropriate.

Activists often go to great pains to define and explain the stakes various players have to use in social conflict. They battle over the degree to which risk exists and whether benefits outweigh harms. Typically, activists attribute negative motives to companies and other organizations that create or allow risks to occur, such as greed, laxness in operations, failure to care about people or the environment, stupidity, racial bias, or corruption. Public debate can get out of hand and truly decrease the potential for constructive outcomes especially if risk-related evidence is poorly defined and members of a community experience evidence gaps and, therefore, rely on scanty evidence from their own experience.

Even authorities cannot be free from such gaps. For instance, people are prone to exhibit risk intolerance and lack of trust for science and its use in risk predictions and abatement; evidence of such intolerance is captured in demands voiced as, "Can you assure the members of this community that they are not at risk?" Community members often rely on evidence and reasoning such as this: If a mother worries about the health of her children, who have moved with the family to a place where she or her spouse can work in an industry that potentially harms persons' health, is she going to rely on or dismiss the evidence she generates on her own of the incidence of health problems such as colds or rashes? She is likely to use the data she experiences to confirm rather than disconfirm her fears.

This evaluation and evolution is confirmed by Krimsky's (2007) and Leiss's (1996) historical analysis of risk communication. At its inception, risk communication took on a source-oriented, linear approach that privileged the expert as the key participant in the process. Leiss called this the technical risk assessment period. In this period, industrial spokespersons were advised to appease or assuage the publics' apprehension by being credible and clear; it featured the role and work of experts who conducted epidemiological studies to ascertain whether risks exist. Part of the technical risk assessment period was the original work done by the NRC (1989) that emphasized the dissemination of information and featured potential outcomes. It treated risk communication as successful only to the extent that it raises the level of understanding and satisfies those involved that they are adequately informed within the limits of available knowledge.

Risk communication progressed through a period during which experts advised organizations that pose health, safety, or environmental risks to assuage employees' and community members' apprehensions by being credible and telling the truth. The truth was to be based on the known likelihood of each risk's occurrence and the magnitude of its effect. The second phase of risk communication featured a more interactive approach: "We see risk communication as the interactive process of exchange of information and opinion among individuals, groups, and institutions" (NRC, 1989, p. 2).

This interactive approach to risk communication is characterized by the fundamental notion that if people receive trustworthy, consistent, and clear messages regarding scientifically assessed risk levels, they are more likely to agree and accept the findings and policy recommendations of risk management experts. This era of risk communication, as noted previously, over-assumes the power of information and underassumes other forms of power such as social capital and the power of rhetoric that concerned publics and activists utilize to exert political pressure in their effort to impose higher operating and community standards. A better understanding of information in relationship to power regarding risk assessment, decision making, and communication helps to move forward risk communication research.

Continuing his summary of the discipline's history, Leiss (1996) identified a third phase, the current version of risk communication that features social relations. Risk communication based on a shared, social relations, community infrastructural approach works to achieve a level of discourse that can treat the content issues of the risk—technical assessment—and the quality of the relationships along with the political dynamics of the participants. Krimsky (2007) succinctly suggested three stages to the evolution of risk communication that also lead to a focus on dialogue. Stage 1 is a linear communication process of delivering messages to a potentially unrealistic and irrational lay audience. Stage 2 was founded on the scientific uncertainty as well as subjective and cultural aspects of risk, while Stage 3 is tied to postmodernist and social constructionist views of risk.

Hadden (1989b) observed crucial differences between what she defined as the old and new versions of risk communication. In the old approach, "experts tried to persuade laymen of the validity of their risk assessments or risk decisions." This option is "impeded by lay risk perception, difficulties in understanding probabilities, and the sheer technical difficulty of the subject matter" (p. 301). In contrast, the new approach is based on dialogue and participation. According to Otway (1992), "Risk communication requirements are a political response to popular demands. . . . The main product of risk communication is not information, but the quality of the social relationship it supports. Risk communication is not an end in itself; it is an enabling agent to facilitate the continual evolution of relationships." (p. 227). This and other more recent approaches to risk communication highlight the importance of a dialogic, relationship-building approach to dealing with the concerns and perceptions of community residents and employees.

The new form of risk communication, however, is often impeded by the lack of institutions that are responsive to the needs, interests, and level of understanding of the publics affected by the potential or ostensible risk. Hadden (1989b) found that institutional barriers stand in the way of meaningful dialogue in communities where people experience risks that they worry are intolerable. Such barriers result, at least in part, from statutes that do not specify what technical data are crucial and, therefore, should be collected. People often encounter a maze of agencies, do not know where to acquire information, and suffer data dumps that provide huge amounts of information in ways that make it difficult to interpret.

Favoring an approach to risk that takes into consideration key publics' concern, Fischhoff, Slovic, and Lichtenstein (Fischhoff et al., 1978; Slovic, 1979, 1987; Slovic, Fischhoff, & Lichtenstein, 1987) initiated "expressed preference" research, which involves measuring a wider array of attitudes than merely weighing the benefits in the effort to ascertain tolerable risk levels. These researchers found that laypeople's risk ratings, unlike those of experts, are not just influenced by fatality estimates but also by their judgments of several "qualitative" factors. Of particular note, the public evaluates an activity or technology as more risky if it is involuntary, unfamiliar, unknown, uncontrollable, controlled by others, unfair, memorable, dreaded, acute, focused in time and space, fatal, delayed, artificial, and undetectable as well as if individual mitigation is impossible.

Dialogic, rhetorical community risk assessment assumes, as Slovic (1992) did in his psychometric paradigm, "that risk is subjectively defined by individuals who may be influenced by a wide array of psychological, social, institutional, and cultural factors" (p. 120). The underpinning theory, "the social amplification of risk, addresses the fact that the adverse effects of a risk event often extend far beyond the direct damages to victims, property, and environment and may result in massive indirect impacts" (p. 141).

Rather than a purely scientific and actuarial approach, a dialogic view stresses the likelihood that people's fears as well as their expressed desires for the benefits accrued from risks become part of a community of thought, the culture of a neighborhood, or even a profession. For instance, persons who farm, serve as law enforcement officers, fight fires, cut timber, and mine ores are subjected to higher than average job-related risks. To cope with such risks, each culture weighs the benefits, costs, and strategic behavior needed to reduce or accept their likelihood.

Given such interpretations and personal choices, people either come to think positively or negatively about the risks they suffer. One factor that can influence that outcome is the likelihood that a stigma will result from the risks (Slovic, 1992). As they experience risks, people may become stigmatized. One aspect of a stigma is its concealability, whether it is hidden or open to public view. If people think they are likely to suffer a stigma that will become known to others, they are likely to oppose the risk. A stigma may involve aesthetics, whereby the person who suffers a risk becomes unattractive. Because of the possibility of stigma, people discuss and evaluate the effects of a risk. Discussion does not rely solely on empirical assessment but also on values. For this reason,

> whereas experts define risk in a narrow, technical way, the public has a richer, more complex view that incorporates value-laden considerations such as equity, catastrophic potential, and controllability. The issue is not whether these are legitimate, rational considerations, but how they integrate them into risk analyses and policy decisions. (p. 150)

Unless scientists and managers of organizations that create risks take factors such as stigmas into account, they fail to properly monitor public expectations and track the evolution of issues. For these reasons, they become less able to formulate the appropriate sense of corporate responsibility and may miss the emergence of activism calling for the creation or change of public policy.

Because scientific data are hard to interpret and risk decisions are value laden, differences of opinion are not easily reconciled. Policy often is not the product of shared points of view but negotiated resolution of conflicting opinions. Such communication is likely to be disproportionately shaped by key players, industry, government, media, and activists. Although no group actually represents the public—because there are many publics—each of the dominant groups strives to speak and act as though it were the advocate and champion of the public interest. Such outcomes may leave all parties dissatisfied. Conflicting interests and epistemologies unique to the battlefield of risk often prevent communicators from finding "common ground between the social world of risk perceptions guided by human experience and the scientists' rational ideal of decision making based on probabilistic thinking" (Plough & Krimsky, 1987, p. 5; see also Fischhoff, 1985).

Communities that are concerned about risks are not passive, waiting for scientists and corporate managers to define and assess risks. Rather, such communities, whether through media or activist leadership, tend to raise issues, even if flawed by lack of relevant and sound information or scientific methodology. For this reason, Otway (1992) emphasized a crucial point: "Policy decisions about hazardous technologies have the paradoxical quality that they are likely to be most urgent just where scientific knowledge is most uncertain" (p. 220). He too is aware that "what is commonly thought of as objective risk has a large subjective component, which may be based on one's experience of being at risk" (p. 220). These factors, coupled with the disparity in risk estimates by experts examining the same risks, lead communities to learn self-reliance and to formulate opinions and expectations, however crude, through dialogue. The outcome of this process is not orderly science but "political negotiations among stakeholders, informed by expert advice" (p. 222). Rather than immediately seeing that their interests match those of the source of risk, community leaders who recognize a problem—or at least its potential—ask and even demand "more democratic control of technology" (p. 226). "Risk communication is not an end in itself; it is an enabling agent to facilitate the continual evolution of relationships" (p. 227). The outcome of that process is a set of policies, whether self-imposed by the source of risk or through public policy planning, that results from a power resource and rhetorical struggle over standards, locus of responsibility, and the formulation of public expectations.

To enhance this decision-making process, Rowan (1994; see also Rowan et al., 2009) reduced the sequence of steps to the acronym CAUSE: credibility, awareness, understanding, satisfaction, and enactment. The first step calls on leaders to establish credibility with key publics. *Credibility* can increase or decrease, depending on how well the subsequent steps progress. The second step is to create or become *aware* of the likelihood or occurrence of the risk and its severity as well as measures for a constructive response to it. This requires *understanding*, becoming scientifically insightful to the risk and its consequences. The linear risk communication (scientific-positivistic) model assumes that scientists become satisfied by the assessment and management of a risk and seek public concurrence. According to Rowan's scheme of things, *satisfaction* is community based. The last step, *enactment*, requires that appropriate measures—by the individual, by the risk entity, or by a government agency—be put into place so that the decision is derived through the rhetorical processes of community dialogue.

An issues management approach to risks reasons "that the defining of risk is essentially a political act" (Kasperson, 1992, p. 155). Concern ripples move outward as from a rock thrown into a pond. Concerns expressed by some foster expressions of others' concerns. This leads to outcry for governmental intervention. Social amplification produces increased and extensive amounts of communication about the risk and its consequences. This dynamic process leads to opinion formation. In this community of discussion, people act as they do in part because of role-related considerations. Membership in social groups shapes the selection of information that each individual regards as significant.

Once amplification has begun, interpretations or comments that are inconsistent with previous beliefs or that contradict the person's values are often ignored or attenuated. They are intensified if the opposite is true. People evaluate risks through their own opinions—heuristics—and those recommended by significant groups. In this model, media reports contribute the basic step for the rippling effect to occur. Perhaps for this reason, as well as the limited ability of many reporters to understand and report objectively on risks, media reports are not trusted by scientists and managers of the organizations that create risks. Often, media reporters do little more than to quote persons from opposing sides of a risk controversy without making any effort to decide and inform readers, listeners, or televiewers what point of view is correct. For this reason, the media at best are likely only to fan the fires of outrage. But even hyperbolic stories do not always lead to that end (Cohn, 1990; M. Moore, 1989).

Risk assessment that does not consider the dynamics—communication and opinion formation—of each community is likely to lead to frustrating outcomes for the persons making the risk assessment and for the laypeople of the community. Information and the premises by which it is judged arise through a constant dialogue within a community. For this reason, persons who create risks—at least those that some people believe to exist—are savvy when they acknowledge rather than dismiss the existing communication infrastructure and opinion formation processes. Such responsible individuals are wise to work with that infrastructure and opinion formation process rather than to dominate it. If trust leads to control, people are prone to trust those entities that listen to them and acknowledge their concerns. People like to believe their concerns and cultures have been given credence. If risks are acknowledged and people are armed with the means for mitigating the consequences of those risks, they feel empowered (Juanillo & Scherer, 1995).

Based on the reasoning and research data presented in this chapter, several conclusions seem worth stating as guidelines for issues managers who deal with risk issues:

- Accept the desire on the part of key publics to exert control over factors they worry affect them and other entities for which they have concern.

- Collaborate with them to engage in information gathering, risk assessment, and risk control.

- Empower community members by demonstrating to them through their participation in decision making that they are a constructive part of the risk assessment and control process.

- Recognize the value-laden personalized decision process they apply, and frame the risk assessment accordingly.

- Build trust over time through community outreach, collaborative decision making, and demonstrations that community expectations are met or exceeded by product design, manufacturing procedures, and emergency response.

- Empower relevant publics by helping them to develop and use emergency responses that can mitigate the severe outcomes in the event of a risk event.

- Acknowledge the uncertainty in risk assessments; do not trivialize this uncertainty, but use it as an incentive for constantly seeking better answers to the questions raised by the members of the community.

- Accept criticism of data and decision processes in a collaborative manner; use objections to define the standards and goals to guide decision making to increase safety, health, environmental quality, and the likelihood that all people suffer risks equally, regardless of color or economic condition.

- Feature legitimate benefits while acknowledging harms, but do not assume that all persons' decision heuristics or values lead them to the same weightings of risk harms and benefits.

- Participate in the risk assessment and communication process; don't attempt to dominate it.

- Frame all questions and concerns in terms of the experiences and values of community members.

- Recognize that harmony can be increased by strategic planning and proactive measures taken to reduce concerned publics' sense that risks exist and are likely to result in harms greater than their benefits.

- Innovate to reduce operating costs and increase customer satisfaction by proactive reduction of risk through strategic business planning.

- Have as your goal the outcome of the members of the community believing that through the risk assessment and decision-making process, they have achieved better conclusions or have been unable to honestly and candidly find fault with the decisions of others.

Building and refining this list, Palenchar and Heath (2006) suggested that a combination of public partnership, shared control, uncertainty environment, community decision making, trust and collaboration, individual values, community relativism, and community is at the heart of dialogue about risk issues. Within this structure lies an issues management approach to risk assessment, management, and communication that aims to empower the persons in a community rather than to deny them access to information and processes that they do not have the technical knowledge and expertise to understand and evaluate. Dialogue and decision making may be more important than the ability of people to play constructive roles as participants. If they cannot understand the scientific assessments, they know when they feel that their concerns and interests have been responded to and regarded. Even if they do not know science, people know when they are taken seriously. For this reason, proactive responses to risk concerns see great value in the open, rhetorical, and honest discussion of issues to achieve outcomes that reflect mutual interests.

Risk and Crisis Communication Working Together

Recently, efforts have been made to combine risk and crisis communication into an area of research and practice defined as *crisis and emergency risk communication*

(Reynolds, 2002). According to Reynolds (2002), in conjunction with the Centers for Disease Control and Prevention, crisis and emergency risk communication merge the urgency of disaster communication with the necessity to communicate risks and benefits to stakeholders and the public, especially in response to an era of global health threats. "Crisis and emergency risk communication is the effort by experts to provide information to allow an individual, stakeholder, or an entire community to make the best possible decisions about their well-being within nearly impossible time constraints and help people ultimately to accept the imperfect nature of choices during the crisis" (p. 6). According to the authors, this type of communication differs from risk communication because of the narrow time constraint, decisions may be irreversible, and decision outcomes are uncertain and often made with incomplete or imperfect information, while this type of communication differs from crisis communication because the communicator is not perceived as a participant in the crisis or disaster except as an agent to resolve the situation.

According to Reynolds (2002), within this framework, risk communication is seen within the developmental stages of a crisis. This combination of perspectives is demonstrated in five stages in the crisis and emergency risk communication model: precrisis (risk messages, warnings, preparations), initial event (uncertainty reduction, self-efficacy, reassurance), maintenance (ongoing uncertainty reduction, self-efficacy, reassurance), resolution (updates regarding resolution, discussions about cause and new risks/new understandings of risk), and evaluation (discussions of adequacy of response, consensus about lessons and new understandings of risks).

Environmental risk communication is another merged perspective and definition that has gained attention in recent years. According to Lindell and Perry (2004), *environmental risk communication* is an accurate term to describe risk communication related to technological risks of hazardous facilities and transportation, as well as natural hazards. Abkowitz (2002) described environmental risk as manmade or natural incidents or trends that have the potential to harm human health and ecosystems, including physical assets of organizations or the economy on a broader scale, and suggested that environmental risk communication address such incidents or trends in two distinct categories: events that might occur in the future, where prevention is the focus, and emergency situations that require immediate notification and deployment of mitigation and other response actions.

Oepen (2000) defined *environmental communication* as the "planned and strategic use of communication processes and media products to support effective policy-making, public participation and project implementation geared towards environmental sustainability" (p. 41). According to Oepen, then, to influence the policy-making process is constitutive of environmental communication, as much as to guarantee the implementation of projects that envision the protection of the natural environment through public participation.

Oepen (2000) saw the role of environmental communication as an educative and engaging social interaction process that enables people to "understand key environmental factors and their interdependencies, and to act upon related problems in a competent way" (p. 41). Hence, environmental communication is not only—not even mainly—a tool for disseminating information but a process that aims at producing "a shared vision of a sustainable future and at capacity-building in social groups to solve or prevent environmental problems" (p. 41).

For Cox (2006), a well-informed public is fundamental for good governance, and environmental communication is the right tool for the job for "[i]t educates, alerts, persuades, mobilizes, and helps us to solve environmental problems" (p. 12). Moreover, according to him, it also "helps to compose representations of nature and environmental problems as subjects for our understanding" (p. 12).

Epictetus (1983), the Greek Stoic philosopher, suggested that people are disturbed not by the things themselves but by the view they take of them. As such, risks are embedded within and shaped by social relations and the continual tacit negotiation of our social identities (Wynne, 1992). Such an orientation toward risk and crisis communication adds value to society by increasing organizations' sensitivities regarding how stakeholders create and manage interpretative frames related to issues that define, affect, and ultimately support or oppose organizational activities, such as supporting or imposing limits on business activities that can either be beneficial or harmful.

As this chapter and the previous chapter have demonstrated through the intertwined developments and rapid expansion of both fields, two unfailing philosophies that should guide risk and crisis communication have developed, whether located in the academy, private practice, governmental agencies, or nongovernmental organizations: Better managed risks and crises are likely to result in less financial and social capital damage, and risk- and crisis-generating organizations are required, by regulation, law, or community standards, to demonstrate how and why they are responsible for events that can harm themselves, their employees, and the interests of humans. Underlying these two concepts and running at the core of risk and crisis communication research and practice is that a crisis can be defined as risk manifested (Heath, 2006b). When a risk is manifested, such as occurred with Hurricanes Katrina and Rita in 2005, it is likely to create a crisis and lead to the creation of multiple issues that must be addressed, or the continuation of the risk cycle will result.

At the core of a decade of lessons learned from developing and analyzing risk communication campaigns, Palenchar and Heath (2007) argued that each organization should strive to be moral and communicate to satisfy the interests of key markets, audiences, and publics that strive to manage personal and public resources, make personal and sociopolitical decisions, and form strong and beneficial relationships. A good organization can and should use risk communication and crisis communication to empower relevant publics by helping them to develop and use emergency responses that can mitigate the severe outcomes in the event of a risk event.

Conclusion

Companies engaged in risk communication face obstacles as they work to form, change, or reinforce opinions and behavior regarding risks. Zones of meanings contain themes and principles that reflect competing self-interests of companies, regulatory agencies, and activist publics. Risk assessments and policy formation entail the enactment of control, opinion formation, evaluation, and collaborative decision making. As Rayner (1992) concluded, "Risk behavior is a function of how human beings, individually and in groups, perceive their place in the world and the things that threaten it" (p. 113). The rightness of decisions depends on which version of their self-interest that key audiences believe needs to be advanced (seeking rewards and avoiding losses). Corporate managers and governmental officials make a grave mistake when they miss that point, arguing that some action is legal as though that will satisfy the critic's sense of ethics and security.

SIM Challenge: Reality List

We should adopt the view that risk is a central part of the human experience and that in many relevant matters, one or more organizations are either legitimate to the extent that they responsibly manage a risk for others in society or, if they are the source of risk, they responsibly meet or exceed the expectations of their stakeholders/stakeseekers on the matter. Issues arise in response to the need to access and evaluate risks. They respond to efforts to create identifications where risks are recognized as central problems. They grow from policy debates: What should specific organizations do, what should individuals do, and what should other organizations (as society collectively) do to best assess, manage, and communicate about risks?

Simply stated, issues management is risk management. To that end, a quick review of some of the leading risks implies where they are in the SIM cycle.

Mine safety

Biotechnology

Nuclear generation

Global warming

Societal sanctions of alcohol use

Violent/deadly storms

Sustainable, affordable, and environmentally responsible energy

Public health challenges

To continue the list, consider the following:

"A future for fossil fuel," *The Wall Street Journal,* March 15, 2007, p. A17. Authors: John B. Deutch and Ernest Moniz

"BP cost cuts cited in blast at Texas plant," *The Wall Street Journal,* March 21, 2007, p. A12. Author: Chip Cummins

"Studio executives, directors, producers, screenwriters, & actors: You have the power to reduce teen smoking." Ad in *The Wall Street Journal,* March 15, 2007, p. A13; also online at www.realitycheckny.com

"Unsafe food additives across Asia feed fears," *The Wall Street Journal,* May 9, 2007, pp. B1, B2. Author: Nicholas Zamiska

"J&J stent failure hurts standing in development of heart devices," *The Wall Street Journal,* May 8, 2007, p. A3. Author: Avery Johnson

"Invoice links two Chinese firms to bad pet food," *The Wall Street Journal,* May 7, 2007, p. B13. Author: Nicholas Zamiska

"China confronts crisis over food safety," *The Wall Street Journal,* May 30, 2007. Authors: Nicholas Zamiska, Jason Leow, and Shai Oster

Allstate's advertising campaign in 2007 to encourage parents to discuss safe driving as they may have discussed other dangers to their children

"Toys recalled in the U.S. are still for sale in China," *The Wall Street Journal,* January 3, 2008, pp. B1, B2. Authors: Sky Canaves, Jane Spencer, and Nicholas Casey

"Cloned livestock poised to receive FDA clearance," *The Wall Street Journal,* January 4, 2008, pp. B1, B2. Authors: Jane Zhang, John W. Miller, and Lauren Etter

"China's environmental agency gets teeth," *The Wall Street Journal,* December 18, 2007, p. A4. Author: Yochi J. Dreazen

The list goes on and on, suggesting the reality that there is lots of work to do at the individual, organizational, institutional, and societal levels to manage issues relevant to risks.

Summary Questions

1. Reviewing both Chapters 8 and 9, what is the connection among crisis, issue, and risk? Why is it best to think of them as interconnected? How can SIM help organizations to spot, prevent, mitigate, and respond to crises?

2. Discuss the notion that history is the management of risk and that society is organized for the management of risk.

3. How is risk a dialectic of benefit and harm?

4. What is the relationship between risk, uncertainty, and control?

5. What challenges led to the development of the modern era of risk management and communication?

6. How does collective decision making advance each society's sense of control?

7. Define and differentiate four theories or approaches to risk assessment, management, and communication.

8. Compare the advantages of an interactive to linear approach to risk communication, one that features dialogue versus one centered on monologue.

9. How do perceptions of risks (psychodynamics) affect the ability to assess, manage, and communicate about risks? Is this another argument for a risk democracy approach to risk management?

10. What key variables seem most helpful in risk research and best practices?

11. What are the guidelines of risk communication that foster a commitment to dialogue?

10

Brand Equity and Organizational Reputation

Marketing and SIM

Vignettes:
Proactive Versus Reactive

The connection between brand equity and strategic issues management (SIM) can be illustrated both as an offensive and defensive strategic process. The following vignettes illustrate a variety of options. Unlike previous chapters, several vignettes are offered here to help establish and illustrate the relationship between brand equity and SIM. Organizational reputation is a lynchpin in this relationship. Stressing the relevance of brand equity and SIM, Knight and Greenberg (2002) pointed to the success that Nike Corporation had in using product promotion by emphasizing Nike's stance on social issues to define its brand equity. It was a sports apparel company with a heart. Because it had demonstrated a concern for social issues, it was eventually targeted as being a hypocrite by those who believed its products were made with exploited labor. That attack raised the issue of whether Nike deserved the reputation of being socially aware and responsible.

Proactive/Offensive

Trend data demonstrate that customers, especially women, prefer to purchase foods that are "organic" as opposed to those that are produced by traditional farming, especially those methods that use chemicals to control weeds and insects and promote growth. Capturing this trend trajectory, companies work to enhance the brand equity of "organic" food and then use

(Continued)

(Continued)

those defining criteria to define their brand and organizational equity. The same logic applies to products that are "natural." Which criteria truly define organic or natural products are contestable, as is whether any specific farming and produce handling technique is truly organic or natural.

During the summer of 2007, news reports came out in Austin, Texas, that milk for sale on grocers' shelves was contaminated with perchlorate, an ingredient in rocket fuel that could have negative health implications. Various amounts of this chemical were showing up in milk, including organic milk. The chemical, associated with warfare manufacturing, was apparently getting into milk supplies through water. How does a report of this kind harm the brand equity of traditional or organic farming? Also, especially in the context of risk assessment, how much of the chemical was in the products, and was that amount harmful? Those issues of fact were vital to the brand equity debate.

Brands can be built on equity earned from increased standards of corporate responsibility. This is especially important for nonprofits and governmental agencies. As nonprofits seek to build their brand equity, thereby soliciting higher amounts of stakes from donors, they not only work to enhance the standards of their performance but also strive to report those advances. They might, for instance, demonstrate the positive impact they have on solving some social problem, such as homelessness (see, for instance, Habitat for Humanity). Similarly, companies work to raise their standards and work hard to achieve those standards. This strategy has been employed by the oil and gas industry, as well as chemical companies, over the past few years as they not only worked to abate emissions and work more safely but also use those performance measures to raise their brand equity and foster a positive reputation. Despite severe issue challenges noted in other chapters, British Petroleum continues to communicate how it is becoming a more environmentally responsible company. One can therefore imagine it uses such advertising and promotion to attract investors and customers. Is it coincidence that BP brands itself with a color of green and yellow to symbolize itself as an environmentally responsible company?

Parcel delivery companies, including the U.S. Postal Service, seek to brand the speed, reliability, and trackability of their delivery services. Banks brand themselves by featuring product offerings and customer relationships. Automobile companies work to brand themselves on design and superior function, such as mileage. The hybrids are doing for the latter standard what organic foods are accomplishing in their industry. The software and hardware players in the computer industry and Web/Internet industry fight to demonstrate higher performance standards as the essence of their reputation. They also seek industry and governmental standards that might give some of them more or less brand equity. It would seem ironic, one can speculate, that spam companies actually compete to establish their brand equity for spamming those of us who spend a lot of time and money in preventing and deleting the spam.

Reactive/Defensive

As much as SIM experts can advise management about the potential costs of crisis, inadequate risk management, and ineffective issues management, it is often hard to quantify in advance the value or equity such measures have for a product, service, or organizational brand. However, in the breach of a crisis, risk manifested, or lost issue battle, the cost can be calculated. For instance, one year after the cartoon scandal created by a Danish newspaper, the largest dairy food company in Denmark indicated that it had lost 35% of its market, not because of what it did but because of the Middle East outrage and boycott of all Danish dairy products. And, we might note, the dairy food industry was the victim of actions of another industry, at least one player in that industry. It's ironic that the circulation of the newspaper rose during the months after the publication of the cartoons. Crisis can cost, but the locus of the crisis might not be the victim.

Likewise, in 2007, contaminated (actually illegally altered) food stuffs from China were used for the manufacture of dog and cat foods in Canada and the United States. Pet deaths and severe health concerns led to investigation. Not only had the pet food products been altered with a toxic chemical, but the documentation designed to mitigate such crises had been forged. Lies and fraud hurt the brand equity of key pet food companies in the United States that sold the imported products. The ones first mentioned in news reports might have taken a more serious hit because they were the first mentioned, but others were named as time went on. Without doubt, the brand equity of these companies was dented, but their brand equity also gave them protection and aided their recovery. One can only speculate whether the perpetrators' companies brand equity will be destroyed. The villains might even go to jail. However, in such circumstances, executives have been known to start new businesses and actually benefit from the bad dealing because they are "new." This corporate social responsibility (CSR) violation was one of a series associated with "Made in China." An excessive level of lead in paints on toys was another of the scandals. Name-brand toy companies had to protect their brand equity and reputation by recalling and pointing their fingers at "Made in China."

As companies seek to improve products or produce high-quality products, they work to advance the brand equity by making research known to prove their equity. Such facts (think in terms of software, hardware, automobile tires, automobile engine additives, cleaning products, health care products, and toys)

(Continued)

(Continued)

are often reviewed by experts and/or governmental regulators. Review standards, conclusions, and recommendations can affect brand equity positively or negatively. Proactively, companies promote facts; reactively, they may argue with the review conclusions.

Litigation can affect brand equity. Litigation, such as product safety or environmental compliance, makes fact-based and evaluative claims about the quality of a product or the corporate responsibility of the organization. These claims not only can harm brand equity by associating the product, service, or organization with negative attributes but can also reduce the marketability of the product or service. One can easily sense the potential damage of litigation by monitoring traditional and nontraditional media for promotions, advertisements, and discussions that solicit persons who think their lives have or might have been seriously harmed by the product.

Activist claims can be made in a way intended to intimidate organizations into complying with higher CSR standards. One of the standard brand equity targets is to create a media event that is designed to embarrass the organization's management into compliance with the activist expectations by creating unfavorable publicity. As demonstrated in Chapter 6, People for the Ethical Treatment of Animals (PETA) continues to focus on a variety of organizations that engage in animal cruelty. It attacks the reputation of companies, products, and people associated with animal cruelty.

In sum, each of these vignettes suggests the logic of brand equity and organizational reputation. Proactively, organizations seek to create and promote brand equity by associating themselves and their products/services with unique and positive attributes that become part of stakeholders' thoughts that drive their actions. Those who attack the brand equity of an organization and/or its products or services work to associate them with negative attributes or deny their positive association with unique and differentiating attributes. The rest of this chapter expands on this logic.

Chapter Goals

This chapter links marketing and strategic issues management (SIM) as two interconnected means by which an organization (or its products and services) has brand equity. After this chapter, the reader will understand how marketing and SIM can cooperate to create, protect, and rehabilitate brand equity. We start with an overview of this topic, proceed to discuss the logic of brand equity, and explain how attitude theory supports the logic of brand equity, the connection between corporate responsibility and brand equity, and the relationship between brand equity and crisis communication and risk management.

In sum, the connection between SIM and brand equity focuses attention on how issue discussion (fact, value, and policy), operable standards of corporate responsibility, public policies, crisis response, and risk management can affect the brand equity of a product, service, or organization.

As long ago as the 1960s, academics and practitioners began to refer to an organization's brand equity and reputation. Over the years, that concept has taken on many lives and perhaps even more faces. It endures in the professional and academic literature because it points to a valuable asset of businesses: Each company's reputation and the reputation of its services and products have some "value" that attracts stakes. Although by far most of the discussion has centered (and continues to center) on businesses and their products and services, the concept is quite relevant to nonprofits (even activist groups) and governmental agencies. The most robust discussion of brand equity has occurred in the marketing and advertising literature. There, it is essentially featured as the conceptual and attributional value of an organization's reputation and uniquely defined image or that of its services or products. In short, brand equity features the unique market value of some population's (such as customers, donors, or shareholders) attitudes toward the organization, as well as its products and services. Brand equity distinguishes one organization from all others.

Although the term is widely associated with marketing coupled to advertising and the promotion and publicity aspects of public relations, it can wisely be connected to SIM, risk management, and crisis management. Marketing claims the term, believing that brand equity is the product of skilled advertising and public relations promotion that leads to careful positioning of a company, product, or service. Those who believe in the management connections with SIM are likely to argue that marketing can be supported by SIM in its efforts to create brand equity, even in the sense of promotion and publicity. This is even more likely to be true when we think that brand equity (even its emotional components) is subject to issue analysis and controversy. Such controversy is a substantial potential during a crisis. A crisis can result from or lead to damaged brand equity and harmed reputation. In our time, scandals such as those surrounding Enron, WorldCom, and other businesses engaged in unethical and illegal business activities have demonstrated how brand equity has to be defended and can be squandered in an issues environment rather than, or in addition to, marketing.

As we preview this chapter, for a moment consider all of the linkages between marketing, SIM, and brand equity. From this list, we not only become sensitive to the connections but also lay a foundation for definitions of brand equity that support the remainder of the chapter. The linkage begins with two solid foundations. One is the fact that SIM is inseparable from effective strategic business planning. As the organization plans to define, create, and rehabilitate its brand equity and reputation, the assignment may well rest with marketing, but as each ingredient or attribute of brand equity is contestable, the broad and long shadow of SIM casts itself over this challenge. What an organization's brand equity is and whether it deserves that equity is contestable. Such contest will be launched by competitors, critics, and even activists, legislators, and regulators. It also is inseparable from the organization's CSR. Who and what the organization is essentially address an SIM theme. How deserving it is of that aura is an SIM challenge.

A second connection is the public policy environment or the manner in which a brand is presented to the public, especially markets and shareholders or donors. A public policy advance might require a higher standard of product safety than one or several companies in a group were traditionally achieving. That standard might in fact mean that some products no longer can be sold or must be redesigned. For instance, public policy pressures on the fast-food and big-food industries have focused attention on the health hazards associated with trans fats. Ironically, this is not a problem that can be solved only by the food industry. It requires that a steady and ample supply of food stuffs be produced by farmers to supply the needed healthy ingredients.

This overview sets the scope and purpose of this chapter and connects SIM and brand equity. So let's look at even more specific connections.

1. If an attribute such as maintainability, reliability, or safety is a key part of a brand's equity, if that claim cannot be made with solid fact, its equity will be harmed by that sort of issue debate. Thus, if an automobile company features its product line as being at the cutting edge of safety, automobile reviewers may harm the brand equity by successfully challenging that factual claim. Likewise, if the claims of safety by the company are accepted and then promoted by the reviewers, those statements are likely to add to the product's brand equity.

2. If a new standard, such a product safety, occurs through litigation, regulation, or legislation, it can harm brand equity for those companies that have to spend additional money or might even be unable to achieve the standards. If a utility company is heavily dependent on coal and public policy increases the emission abatement standards, that will harm the company or industry's brand equity and reputation.

3. By changing public policy, a company or industry might shift cost and burden for risk management to another industry, as the insurance industry lobbied for increased automobile safety: design and construction. It might also set higher standards that would please customers. For this reason, either by individual company design or by industry, the credit card industry might proactively increase provisions against fraud, including higher penalties for engaging in fraud. Such efforts suggest how inter- and intraindustry SIM efforts become a vital factor in organizational reputation.

Concepts such as brand knowledge (facts about the brand), brand evaluation (evaluations of the attributes that define the brand), and preferred products and services that deliver rewards and avoid harms (personal buying/investment/contribution choices) all are comfortable with the logic of SIM analysis, tracking, and communication. So is that daunting concept of identification, as well as the relationships that arise as a positive or negative response to a brand and an organization's reputation.

Corporate Branding

So how is the term *branding* defined? According to Frost and Cooke (1999), branding is a process for distinguishing one product from another, identified as brand positioning, and the characteristics that consumers use to choose one product over another, identified as brand personality. At a corporate level, according to Frost and Cooke, features that enable a stakeholder, such as an employee, to identify with one organization include a wide range of factors, from product value and quality to financial security, customer care and an organization's corporate social responsibility record.

A brand is important for individual or corporate personalities because it represents what others outside the organization view or perceive the person or company to be. Brand quality may determine the success or failure of a person or company in a particular field.

One of the key aspects of having a corporate brand is consistency, which helps maintain the same image over a period of time among key target audiences. "Consistency has been widely acknowledged as a core principle of successful brand development" (Knox & Bickerton, 2003, p. 1009). On the other hand, Jevons (2005) stated that a brand "distinguishes a product from its unbranded counterpart through the sum total of consumers' perceptions and feelings about the product's attributes and how they perform" (p. 118).

D. Bernstein (2003) argued that a brand name "associates the physical product with the values of something else" (p. 1139). Accordingly, a brand should stand for more than just the product and must represent more than just the surface of the corporation. For effective brands, the "link between the product or corporation and the association should not be arbitrary. The brand must be rooted—and seen to be rooted—in the product" (p. 1139). The brand identity for the brand "should be about truth: the truth of the product (i.e. physical) and truth-to-oneself (i.e. psychological)" (p. 1139). As Knox and Bickerton (2003) have reasoned about product branding, corporate branding is considered to be "more complex by managers conducting these practices at the level of the organization, rather than the individual product or service, and the requirement to manage interactions with multiple stakeholder audiences" (p. 999).

To better understand corporate branding, we must discuss brand personality. A brand that has a personality can be "a product or service, which a customer perceives to have distinctive benefits beyond price and functional performance" (Knox & Bickerton, 2003, p. 999). All of the branding elements need to be consistent over a period of time to establish the personality for the brand. Effective branding results in a number of advantages. "Consistency between attitudes, beliefs and product category images enhance the potential for brands to transfer these images and personality to a new product" (James, Lyman, & Foreman, 2006, p. 175). Brand personality for a corporation is also an "important measure to include as consumers form relationships and attachments with brands that can be communicated through human personality descriptors" (p. 175). Consistency for a corporation can often determine if it will weather a crisis or not.

An important element that defines a corporate personality and reputation is the company brand. A company brand can be implemented on a corporate personality as well as an individual personality. The impact of an individual personality on a corporation is important to recognize due to fact that the future success or failure for a corporation will rely heavily on this one individual. Basically, a corporate brand is what defines the product or corporate image for the company among its key audiences.

Several characteristics should be kept in mind when looking at a corporate brand. Some of the characteristics determine the reputation and perception for the brand among other products and also among the key audiences for the corporation. Brands can become more like the company than the companies that they are known for on their own—"a devastating transformation that compromises the very viability of an organization. Because when a Brand becomes a company, it loses qualities both tangible and intangible, often permanently" (Edelman Change and Employment Engagement Group, 2006, p. 2).

Some brands that are particularly powerful and influential are considered to be strong brands. Corporations want to have this type of brand because strong brands "have the luxury of being viewed through a different lens by consumers, prospects, suppliers, analysts, media and employees" (Edelman Change and Employment Engagement Group, 2006, p. 2). Another reason why corporations want strong brands is because they are "more heavily evaluated by subjective measures, such as their promise, innovation, personality, history and creativity, all of which are conveyed through product development and commercialization, marketing, communications and the overall interaction between the Brand and its constituents" (p. 2). Some examples of strong brands that are present today would include Nike and Tide.

Six characteristics can define a corporate brand, including brand context, brand conditioning, brand construction, brand consistency, brand continuity, and brand confirmation (Knox & Bickerton, 2003). Out of the points listed, brand consistency and brand continuity are the most important. To have a stable corporate image, corporations have to have a clear and recognizable personality. This will allow them to maintain their publics' awareness of them among their competitors. Also, brand continuity will serve well for corporations that wish to stay in their specific industries, although corporations must be aware that they may have to change their brand in order to adapt to their audience's perspectives and society's technological advances. Each corporation and individual will have their own characteristics of corporate branding, and they will decide what elements are important or not in their particular situations.

Brand Equity: Many Faces and Definitions

Decades ago, the International Association of Advertising took the strategic position that corporate image advertising treats the company as if it were a product, positioning it with care within its industry or industries, giving it a clear differentiation from others resembling it, and basically "selling" it to the audiences selected. The selling objectives are usually financial, legal, and, to a lesser extent, governmental support, to facilitate the company's pursuit of its business objectives (Stridsberg, 1977).

This logic would seem to apply to organizations other than businesses. Their reputations are crafted, and attempts are made to communicate in ways that get targeted audiences to see the organization as its management prefers. Actions, however, are a vital part of this effort, which cannot be left to advertising alone.

Another definition to note is brand equity, which is "a set of brand assets and liabilities linked to a brand, its name and symbol, that add to or subtract from the value provided by a product or service to a firm and/or that firm's consumers" (Aaker, 1991, as cited in Viosca, Bergiel, & Balsmeier, 2005, p. 86). Brand equity is considered to be multidimensional in terms of how it is used—it can be communicated through various channels to many different audiences (Viosca et al., 2005).

Two additional concepts require further explication, including market value or brand value and brand equity. The term *market value* or *brand value* is favored by accountants and financial analysts since it refers to the "hard" assessment of numbers—the value of a brand or the organization as an asset—rather than the more subjective assessments favored by advertising and marketing specialists. What is a business worth based on shareholder confidence? For private-sector organizations, if they are publicly traded, their market value is what they are worth if one multiplies all tradable shares by the daily share value. Market value consists of a composite of book value and the ability to take that book value and generate profit. Thus, *book value* is the worth of the organization if it were sold in parts and pieces—the actual value of its assets. Sometimes the market value is substantially greater than the book value. This relationship assumes that the sum is worth more than the parts. In other cases, the parts are worth more than the sum. This principle was demonstrated during the dot.com era when companies that had never generated a profit were greeted during initial public offerings with extraordinary shareholder enthusiasm. They were often substantially overpriced in market value when in fact they had little book value and less actual ability to make money and show profit, which drives actual market value rather than sheer speculation (for related definitions, see Sowa, 2005; Wood, 2000).

Expanding on the concept of brand value, J. W. Smith (1991) reasoned that it is "the measurable financial value in transactions that accrues to a product or service from successful programs and activities" (p. 43). From this view, scholars estimate the financial value of brand equity, like plant and equipment, for accounting purposes in such occasions as mergers and acquisitions or for divestiture purposes. Mergers and acquisitions, in particular, have led to calculating the value of brands along with the tangible asset of the company such as assembly lines. Such equity relationships were the centerpiece in the successful effort by Rupert Murdock to buy the Dow Jones complex of products, including *The Wall Street Journal*. He paid $5 billion for a company at the time that had $1.7 billion of market value.

Brand equity is a consideration of both market value and book value. As such, it can be "interpreted as a measure of the strength of consumer attachment to a brand," and, it is some combination of "the associations and beliefs the consumer has about a particular brand" (Sowa, 2005, p. 95). Brand equity is an idiosyncratic blend of customer preferences and the related associations and relationships with the product, service, or organization. In the most base terms, it rests on the answer to the question of what is the equity value of the brand, whether a product, service, or the "image or reputation" of the organization. Thus, Coca-Cola has substantial brand equity, as does General Electric. As a nonprofit, so does the National Rifle Association, as well as the Internal Revenue Service, one of the prominent government agencies. In part, the brand equity as the reputation of an organization is its authority to speak on some matter and the power resources it can bring to bear on a market purchase, share value, or a governmental policy. As Aaker (1996) reasoned that brand equity is supported by the associations that consumers make with a brand.

Second, for the purpose of building strategies to strengthen a brand (i.e., company-based perspective), Farquhar (1989) defined brand equity as "the added value to the firm, the trade, or the consumer with which a given brand endows a product" (p. 32). From this approach, a strong brand serves many purposes, including making promotion more effective, helping secure distribution, insulating a product from competition, and facilitating growth and expansion into other product categories (Hoeffler & Keller, 2003). Brand equity becomes an intangible asset to increase profits in the product market through price premiums, decreasing sensitivity to competitors' prices, and securing and maintaining distribution though channels. For example, Starbucks can be successful on supermarket shelves because of its strong brand value from in-store selling.

Third, in the customer-based perspective, consumers perceive a brand's equity as the value added to the functional product or service by associating it with the brand name (Aaker & Biel, 1993). Brand equity is part of the consumer's attraction to a particular product (Keller & Lehmann, 2006). Through understanding customer-based brand equity, firms can build strategies to strengthen a brand. Kapferer (1997) explained that the value of a brand consists of various associations of tangible attributes of the product itself and intangible, psychological, or social attributes. A "strong" brand means that a brand has acquired distribution, awareness, and image. For example, the brand value of Coca-Cola, which is regarded as one of the strongest brands in the world, comes from the association of not only the name and logo but its significance of being popular since 1886 worldwide. Fashion products often have more or less customer-based brand equity. How much of the difference between a $60 pair of shoes and a $1,300 pair is brand equity? Companies in this industry even feature their logos as brand equity prominently on the product.

The concept of brand equity has been studied from an eclectic range of perspectives, resulting in different viewpoints, causing some confusion and dissatisfaction with the term. In other words, the specific approaches to motivating and defining brand equity can vary depending on the perspective and purpose adopted. Among the three perspectives on brand equity, only the customer-based perspective leads researchers and firms to specifically consider public relations (and advertising) roles in the management of brand equity. These roles include increasing brand awareness or making favorable brand attitudes and associations in order to build strong brand equity (Keller, 1993). In advertising, there has been extensive research regarding the relationships between brand equity and advertising (Aaker & Biel, 1993; Hsu & Liu, 2000; Kanetkar, Weinberg, & Weiss, 1992; Kim, 1998; Raj, 1982). For example, a few studies examined a correlation among advertising expenditure, brand equity, and financial returns (e.g., Fombrun & van Riel, 2004; Kim, 1998, 2001). However, there has been little research on brand equity from the public relations discipline (Keller, 1993).

Keller (1998) indicated that the concept of customer-based brand equity stems from strategy-based motivation and is the differential effect of brand knowledge in relationship to the marketing of the brand on consumers. These two functions (i.e., brand awareness and brand image) contribute to customers having strong or weak, favorable or unfavorable, and unique or unremarkable brand associations in their memory. Consequently, a brand is said to have positive (or negative) customer-based brand equity if consumers react more (or less) favorably to an element of the marketing mix for the brand. The rationale behind this framework is to recognize the importance of the customer in the creation and management of brand equity. The basic premise with customer-based brand equity is that the power of a brand lies in the minds of consumers and what they have experienced and learned about the brand over time. By extension, reputation is part of brand equity and the most vulnerable to issue and crisis attacks and missteps.

Wood (2000) reasoned that working toward a standard set of terms, a shared vocabulary, could assist individuals in marketing and accounting in their efforts to build brand and measure it. Such dialogue must include others in management, such as research and development as well as general counsel. And, because of the logic of SIM, factors relevant to brand equity must be central to the matrix arrangements that bring many disciplines and specialists together to support the SIM process, or the SIM process needs to be charged with helping to build, manage, protect, and maintain brand equity and promote as well as protect the organization's reputation.

Many of the tools and the fundamental theory of SIM support this conclusion. It is a way of connecting the organizational mission/vision and what is necessary to accomplish them with the advancement and protection of the means, branded product, service, and reputation.

Following this discussion, it is fair to conclude that one basic connection between SIM theory and brand equity focuses on the concept of a stakeholder/ stakeseeker. Brand equity predicts to an extent which stakeholder is more likely to give (trade) a stake to one organization rather than another in exchange for a product or a service. The extension of this logic features the stakeseeker as one who looks for the brand that is most likely to meet or exceed the needs, wants, and other expectations.

Brand Attributes and Attitude Theory

The logic of brand equity and organizational reputation rests on well-established attitude theory. The logic simply stated is this: Each brand is associated with one or more defining or differentiating attributes. People learn to make these associations through communication and direct experience. The extent to which markets and publics know and believe this association to be true is predictive of the brand's equity and central to the organization's reputation. If the belief is strong, it shapes attitudes that are dispositional; that means they motivate people to support rather than be indifferent to or oppose the organization. By this logic, individuals prefer to support (buy and recommend) the brand with the strongest equity (most favorable and strongest belief strength). Brands are variously supported by brand knowledge, what people know about the brand compared with the brand equity of competing organizations and brand. Brands often enjoy or suffer a subjective evaluative dimension as well. In short, people have "feelings" about brands and identify with them to varying degrees.

One of the strongest theories of attitudes, information integration theory (Fishbein & Azjen, 1975), supports the theory of reasoned action (Azjen & Fishbein, 1980). In short, information integration theory predicts that an attitude is the sum of the strengths of various positive and negative attributes associated with an attitude object (such as product or organization), situation, or behavior. For this reason, this attitude theory, as is the case of attitude theory in general, seeks to understand, explain, and predict why people make judgments and take actions that seek to lead to rewards and minimize negative outcomes.

In this way, a brand and its equity can predict why people (markets or publics) would prefer one brand over others and therefore prefer to buy and otherwise associate with that brand in preference to others. As a simplified way of thinking about preference, we can use the shorthand words: *likes* and *dislikes*. By this logic, people prefer what they like most and seek to avoid what they like less or dislike.

This logic has underpinned discussion in previous chapters and in fact is a rationale for the SIM process. As a management strategy, executives seek to position their organization so that it is liked and therefore granted resources, instead of disliked and therefore singled out to be either avoided or punished. Herein lies one of the strongest logics connecting the marketing of brand equity and issues management.

This connection is carried into the monitoring process. Issue positions (what persons like and dislike, what they believe and don't believe, what they prefer and don't prefer) take on the logic of fact, value, and policy. They can be contestable. Monitoring seeks to know what is liked and disliked, by whom, how strongly, and to what end (such as support and opposition). Attitudes change. That can be a trend. What is the reason for this trend? Does the trend support or harm or limit the organization's ability to enact its strategic business plan? SIM offers tools and systems for monitoring the attitudinal environment, which has implications for brand equity claims: their relevance and believability.

Another explicit connection between SIM, brand equity, and attitude theory focused attention on the standards or expectations of what standards of CSR are prevailing and the degree to which organizations meet or exceed these standards. That logic underpins the discussion in Chapter 4; the logic of getting the house in order is exactly the logic of creating positive and differentiating brand equity. This logic not only focuses on how well the organization operates but also includes the value it adds to society, including its strategic philanthropy, for instance. Such logics are the focal point of activist scrutiny. Activists seek to influence the attitudes that are used to judge corporate responsibility, issue position, and brand equity. This logic is explained in Chapter 5 as the logic of issue position. Attitudes can be changed, and they can be associated with or dissociated from various issue positions. For instance, persons who have a positive attitude toward environmental quality (like) can be motivated to dislike organizations that harm the environment. Such attitudes can be influenced by facts and the shaping of evaluations. As we have argued elsewhere in this book, attitudes are predisposition—predictive of the actions and policies people prefer and support rather than oppose.

Issues communication, like marketing communication, is fraught with making and supporting evaluative claims. Its basic logic is arguing for that which is liked or to be liked and against that which is to be opposed or not supported. It is based on adopting and applying attitude positions that exist. It may seek to change attitudes and replace one attitude for a preferable attitude. And so the logic goes.

This section seeks to combine and apply principles near and dear to the rhetorical heritage to the essence of attitude theory. They are not strangers. The next section applies this logic a bit more in the terms of brand equity scholarship and best practices.

Logics of Brand Equity

Over the years, academics and practitioners have advanced the logics of brand equity by seeking to develop models and theories, as well as define terms for foundational concepts. This section features key terms, their logics, and the implications for connecting SIM and brand equity. The following comments extract conclusions from a solid and growing body of literature about brand equity.

As noted above, Farquhar (1989) defined brand equity as "the added value to the firm, the trade, or the consumer with which a given brand endows a product" (p. 32). Brand equity is part of the consumer's attraction to a particular product (Keller & Lehmann, 2006). The logic of brand equity is founded not only on attitude theory but also on cognitive perception theory. Each of these cognitive decisions can be contested as issues, affected by crises, and is a crucial ingredient in how well organizations manage risks for the good of others.

Product-related attributes are the defining and unique characteristics people associate with a product. Cognition theory suggests that all of what people perceive is similar or different in varying degrees depending on the characteristics of similarity or difference between that which is perceived. For instance, a carrot and a radish are both vegetables (attributes of similarity), but they are different in color and taste (attributes that allow us to tell one type of vegetable from the other). So, we might ask what features distinguish over-the-counter medications from prescription medications. What distinguish those we prefer from those we don't? What attributes would lead us to avoid and perhaps campaign against a medication or support its sale? Thus, we have the logic of product-related attributes that not only feature marketing differentiation but also give the rationale for activism. Keep in mind that some of the activism for or against a medication could come from competitors within an industry or from other industries (intraindustry). For this reason, the automobile insurance industry supports increased automobile safety and highway design safety. Other examples include corporations that support health issue causes such as breast cancer awareness (Lifetime Network) or environmental issues (Starbucks). Corporations want to ensure that the issues that they represent are related to their products and values.

Non-product-related attributes may be highly subjective, such as prestige or thrifty. Think, for instance, about an expensive and stylish watch. Its prestige is supposed to rub off on the user and perhaps even the one who might give it as a gift. Or, the watch might be inexpensive but highly functional, a thrifty purchase, one that is well worth the money. They may include the quality of the relationship that exists, should exist, or once did exist between the organization and its stakeholders. If a company or its brand is acquired by a larger and highly prestigious company, that can add non-product-related brand equity. Likewise, if a company or brand is sold, it can harm its brand equity.

Brand associations are those empirical and subjective attributes (positive and negative) that the targeted persons associate with the product, service, or organization. In addition, associations may be the factors that produce identification among those who prefer and use the product or service. This latter dimension is the birds of a feather flock together sort of additional brand equity. Brand associations are easy to see in the use of celebrities to endorse certain products or issues. The use of Tiger Woods by Buick and Michael Jordan by Hanes has resulted in significant, positive brand associations for these corporations. However, negative associations can also occur when the celebrity endorser's behavior provokes a negative response by audiences. For example, the disgrace of Olympian Marion Jones and football star Michael Vick is likely to lead to negative brand associations for Nike. To avoid these negative outcomes, corporations should evaluate their brand associations using measures of attributes, benefits, and attitudes (Pitta & Katsanis, 1995).

Brand-specific effects include the perceived (empirical or subjective) results of purchasing and using a product, supporting a nonprofit or governmental agency. "Next day" delivery once distinguished delivery services and tended to raise their brand equity above the U.S. Postal Service. Now all present themselves that way and offer trackability, so some brands now feature the "reliability" of such service or the ease of trackability. This brand equity dimension asks essentially whether people can "perceive the differentiating effects" of a specific brand. Corporations can use perceived differences to gain a positive advantage over their competitors. For example, the "Eat Fresh" Subway campaign, featuring spokesperson Jared Fogle, suggests to consumers that if you eat at Subway you can lose weight. It is unlikely that people perceive fast-food restaurants as helping them to lose weight, so this campaign can provide strong differentiation for the Subway brand.

Brand awareness refers to consumer perceptions of and preferences for a brand, as reflected by the various types of brand associations held in consumers' memories. Awareness is a measure of the extent to which anyone, but specifically a target market, knows or is aware of one or more differentiating attributes of a product, service, or organization. We might simply ask, for instance, to what extent a target audience is aware of the unique and defining features of one cell phone over another. Such awareness is a matter of fact. It is a "fact" that people either do or do not know of the brand attribute. This dimension suggests but does not include the possibility that a target might know the alleged attribute but simply not believe it. "Sure, they claim their product is X, but I don't know it is true or I doubt it to be true." Brand awareness is vital for corporations because having a well-known brand can increase sales and the likelihood that a corporation's target audiences will remember its brand and products (Pitta & Katsanis, 1995).

Brand knowledge is described as an association in consumers' memories. It has two components: brand awareness and brand image. Brand awareness is related to the strength of the brand in consumers' memories, as reflected by consumers' ability to recall or recognize the brand under different conditions. Brand image refers to consumer perceptions of and preferences for a brand, as reflected by the various types of brand associations held in consumers' memory. Brand associations come in many forms, although useful distinctions can be made between attributes, benefits, and attitudes. At its basic level, brand knowledge simply is an expression of what people know about a brand. This can be predicated on advertising, comments by friends and family, and personal experience. People make decisions about a company's product based on input from trusted sources. According to the most recent Edelman Trust Barometer (Edelman, 2006), people are more likely to trust sources that they consider to be "like them" rather than hearing directly from the company or other media outlets.

Brand recognition and recall are two ways to achieve and measure brand equity. Recognition depends on simple stimulus and response. As described by cognitive theorists, recognition is what happens during a true/false exam; recall is required to fill in blanks, complete short answers, or write an essay. An ad or the specific brand is likely to spark recognition in a consumer. Such is the case since ads tend to feature, explain, and otherwise give legs to a brand's equity. Recall is more dependent on what is recalled, top of the mind, at the mention of the brand. The most successful brand campaigns are those in which consumers remember not only the advertisement or public relations campaign but also the product (Pitta & Katsanis, 1995). The Nike "Just Do It" commercials and the Gatorade "Is It In You" campaigns are examples of excellent practice. In these cases, people remember the logos and catchphrases as well as the product. Recall or recognition can occur if a brand is damaged or associated with bad attributes. Seeing or thinking about the brand can prompt recognition or recall. In this latter condition, recall is often more likely than recognition. SIM strategies can be used to combat or erase the negative associations to the extent that it possible and ethical.

Strength of brand associations is a measure of the salience or ability to recall and associate attributes with the brand with minimal prompting. It is also a measure of the believability of the attributes. One dimension of strength is likelihood that a person believes the claims about the attributes. If a product is less filling, do targeted customers believe that and use that to differentiate that product from competing products? Strength can be a measure of endurance. How long do people recall or recognize the association between the brand and various attributes that affect its equity, positively or negatively? How likely are they to act on those associated attributes? For example, after the release of the documentary *Super Size Me* in 2004, McDonald's developed a new public relations campaign focusing on new healthy food options on their menu. Unfortunately, for the corporation, McDonald's brand associations with fatty foods are very strong, whereas their associations with "healthy" foods probably remain weak. It is unlikely that consumers would quickly recall and associate "healthy" attributes in response to the McDonald's brand.

Brand benefits are the positive outcomes of using the brand. Does the Department of Homeland Security make Americans safe? Safer? Absolutely safe? Does Social Security make older citizens secure? If one brand of automobile is more energy efficient, is that good, and does it motivate us to buy the product? Does our experience prove that the attribute is true (strength through personal experience)? One can assume that this aspect of brand equity can have negative effects or harms. Such conclusions are in "the mind of the beholder." A motorcycle brand might lead one set of customers to identify with the brand and buy it. Others are simply never going to see or imagine those benefits, probably because they don't see any motorcycle as safe. Does public policy appeal for (even mandatory requirement) wearing safety helmets make the motorcycle (or any motorcycle) seem safer or less safe? Does it add equity to a brand of chainsaws if the company also sells a related (and branded) line of safety equipment to protect the operator? Sometimes benefits are at odds with themselves. In an era of higher gasoline costs, do customers still prefer the SUV because it is "safer"? Do they prefer the hybrid because it is less costly to operate and more environmentally friendly?

Uniqueness of brand refers to the extent that a single brand can differenti-ate itself by one or more unique attributes. Gasoline companies try to differ-entiate themselves by touting how the brand will produce a cleaner engine. Is that attribute "believable" and truly "differentiating"? Detergents are branded by getting whites whiter while protecting colors. Is that unique and truly dif-ferentiating? Because products necessarily are similar and therefore competi-tive, it is hard to imagine any that are truly so unique that they are the "only one of a kind." But one objective of marketing, positioning, and advertising is to work to give a brand more equity by making it more competitive because of its "uniqueness." In this era of pharmaceutical ads, we note that some are "faster acting," "longer lasting," or "more effective." Those adjectives or adverbs suggest uniqueness that is intended to give a "brand ownership" of a market segment. Communication tools, such as a company logo, can become a part of a brand's equity and uniqueness. One liability of such uniqueness is that it can become a lightning rod for activist criticism and even interindustry rivalry. Allegations can focus on the fact that the brand attribute simply is not unique or the company is unique to its detriment.

Brand Equity and Crisis

Interest in crisis management (precrisis, crisis, and postcrisis) has sparked a wide discussion about the role of crisis communication as a means for recov-ering brand equity and image restoration or repair (see Benoit, 2005, 2008). Touting this logic, Benoit (2008) observed,

> A corporation's image, or reputation, is a very important asset. Customers are, and should be, reluctant to do business with companies with tarnished reputations. We must be able to trust that products and services, from pre-scription drugs and food to investment advice and airline travel, are safe and effective. Therefore, when a business's product or service does not live up to expectations, unpleasant consequences can occur for consumers, ranging from death to inconvenience. Obviously, such adverse effects can be expected to make other customers reluctant to do business with that company. Furthermore, a firm's reputation is important for other reasons beyond the need to have consumers willing to purchase its good and services. For exam-ple, a firm's image could influence how closely the government regulates its actions. (p. 244)

Especially since the iconic Johnson & Johnson Tylenol response, scholars and practitioners have asked how and whether appropriate crisis response can protect the brand equity of products, services, and organizations. Crisis prob-ably was a major topic before the Johnson & Johnson case, but afterward it became a cottage industry. As discussed in Chapter 8, crisis is a relevant part of issues management. It is also a substantial part of brand equity management because the "image" of a brand and the organization's reputation can be tarnished by a crisis, which suggests that something damaging occurred and that recovery and restoration are needed. Attention is given to many types of organizations according to this logic. Failure to protect American citizens can hurt the Department of Homeland Security; failure to respond quickly in the case of a hurricane such as Katrina damages the image or reputation of the Federal Emergency Management Agency. A nongovernmental organization such as Red Cross can suffer an image-damaging crisis, as might the United Way, especially when an executive takes advantage of financial gain in the case of the latter. Activists can even engage in behaviors that outrage people whose identification they are courting.

First, no error might have occurred, so defense against what seems to be a crisis and bad news situation requires minimal commentary. The facts can, in this case, speak for themselves unless the reputation of the organization before the crisis event was so bad that its comments are not credible. Such condition would itself constitute a crisis, perhaps further damaging brand equity.

Second, the organization might have made a mistake, violating stakeholder/stakeseeker expectations. In that event, it is easy to imagine that the organization needs a crisis response that includes lessons learned. Such statements indicate what is going to be done to reduce the likelihood of the crisis event's occurrence.

In a proactive sense, precrisis communication and management can mitigate the likelihood that a crisis can occur. Such efforts are effective SIM because they entail the kinds of strategic business planning/management, issues monitoring, and achievement of CSR, which reduce the likelihood that a crisis will occur. Effective efforts along with these strategic options can reduce the amount and duration of damage in the event a crisis occurs.

After a crisis has occurred, engagement is needed to show that changes can and perhaps have restored an organization's brand equity. Postcrisis communication is often neglected because managements want to put the "bad news days" behind them and not remind people about them. In truth, however, such communication can indicate that the organization is of such character that it knows how to respond and work to avoid recurrence of bad news events. Willingness and ability to learn from such events demonstrates care and concern. It can reduce the legitimacy gap between action and expectation.

Brand Equity and Risk

As was argued in Chapter 8, a crisis is a risk manifested. Good and bad events can occur. They can be predicted. The larger challenge is to know when the risk event occurs, who will be harmed, and the amount of damage that occurs.

Over the years, stakeholder/stakeseeker expectations have increased, so the allowable amount of inherent innocence an organization can claim is increasingly limited. In fact, even an act of God, such as a storm, does not excuse organizations from blame and criticism if they did not plan properly, act effectively to prevent a risk, or mitigate its damage should it occur.

We know, for instance, that a vendor might sell tainted or adulterated goods that another manufacturer puts into human or animal food. We know that fraud might be committed so that every effort is made to disguise or hide the presence of the harmful material. Do those actions, however evil, excuse the company that eventually uses the tainted material to manufacture and sell human or animal food or cosmetic items? Engineering and process management standards are sufficiently high that a company deserving of high brand equity can and therefore must protect customers by taking proper precautions and carefully monitoring the quality of the materials that are used in its products that enter the retail market, whether they produce the product or not. Its name, and therefore its brand equity, literally is on the line and the product. Its reputation is at stake. People don't want to do business with an organization that should have the knowledge to protect their interests but is unwilling or unable to do so.

The underpinning theme in this discussion is the principle, discussed in Chapter 9, that the rationale for society is the collective management of risk (Douglas, 1992). A toothpaste company earns its brand equity by its ability to protect teeth from decay, promote healthy gums, reduce bad breath, and whiten teeth. One reason we can make that observation is the recurrence of such marketing and advertising claims by those companies. Automobiles are designed and manufactured to be safe. Nevertheless, we can predict 40,000 to 43,000 deaths from automobiles in the United States annually. So cars are not safe. Some may be safer than others. So, product safety testing is conducted. It can be and is used to make product quality statements as part of the development of brand equity. If automobile tires or specific models of automobiles are found to be unsafe or less safe, such discovery is likely to reduce brand equity.

Similarly, brand equity can be achieved through employee safety standards (and lost through inadequate risk and crisis management). Such standards are often reflected in the mission and vision of organizations. The rationale of effective strategic business planning and management depends on the ability to budget for and achieve the mission and vision of the organization in ways that please stakeholders and stakeseekers demonstrating the organization's ability to effectively manage risks on behalf of customers and others. Offending this standard is likely to lead to activism, regulation, legislation, and judicial actions aimed at forcing standards of behavior higher than the organization is willing and able to achieve voluntarily. That logic is now well demonstrated. It has been a constant theme of this book since page one.

Issues monitoring is needed to know the sorts of changing standards required for brand equity and how well each organization is perceived to be meeting those standards. Communication about risks can help people to understand and perhaps accept them, but such standards depend on the institutionalized cultures of the people who are making the assessment, both as sound science and as value. Standards are debatable, but each organization is by the nature of the beast part of the larger dialogue and community on such matters. Failure to realize this fact and act accordingly is likely to create or widen the legitimacy gap. The consequences of such choices have positive or negative implications for brand equity. Ironically, in such matters, marketing communication can actually lead customers to expect a level of risk management, the principle of the paradox of the positive, that is higher than the organization's ability to achieve.

For that reason, strategic business planning, issues monitoring, corporate responsibility, and issues communication are part of effective individual and collective risk management. However this plays out in each case can have implications for organizations' brand equity.

SIM Challenge: Corporate Responsibility and Long-Term Planning

In previous chapters, we featured extended cases at the beginning and end of the chapter. In this chapter, we offer much shorter vignettes. These are true cases to show the relevance of SIM and brand equity, even though they are not extended ones.

- A major news program alleges that a specific brand of pickup truck is a fire hazard because of where the gas tanks are located. If the story is true, it could lead either to a voluntary design change by the vehicle manufacturer to maintain its brand equity or to damaging regulatory changes. The problem: The network rigged the news story to be able to show dramatic simulated fire. The manufacturer learned that the footage used had been rigged, sued, and won.

- A branded pharmaceutical company/product is hit by successful individual and class action suits. The litigation and decision by the Food and Drug Administration would damage the brand equity.

- Changes in emission standards raise the public expectation, and which can harm the pricing of electricity sold because it is produced with much lower standards of pollution control.

- Imported personal health care products are found to contain ingredients that are prohibited by federal law.

- A company selling products to the construction industry decides to move its operations offshore to avoid import duties into the European Union. Union workers challenge this move because the company has touted its products as "Made in the USA."

- Web sites that attract children and young adults are found to be a "playground" for sexual predators.

- A government agency charged with emergency response is placed under a new federal department. A major emergency calls into question whether this change has reduced its responsiveness because it is encumbered by the parent organization's mission and by funding reductions.

- Executives made significant financial decisions about their companies' business plans that hid debt, give undisclosed financial benefits to executives, and use corporate money for personal purposes of the executives.

- Executives tend to blame "mistakes" on employees rather than take responsibility for the culture that allowed or encouraged/rewarded those employees' actions.

- Actions of celebrities can harm the brand equity of their sponsors. For instance, if a celebrated athlete is involved in illegal and highly offensive acts such as being involved in dog fighting, the sponsor may delay the release of signature product lines, abandon a contract with the person, and even take legal action against the person.

- Actions by another party can hurt the brand equity of a specific industry. In a cartoon case in Denmark, the newspaper that ran the ads offending some persons in the Middle East cost contracts on the part of the agricultural export companies in Denmark. They suffered the actions of others that hurt their brand equity.

- A country that has product exports associated with fraudulent documentation and kickbacks can worry about the brand equity of statements such as "Made in China." If it indicts and executes a major government official for violating statutes, does that help or harm the brand equity of its products and its country, which has a brand equity issue regarding its lack of humanitarianism?

- Major companies arrange tax breaks and direct governmental subsidies at the same time they are reporting record profits.

- Developers seek and obtain governmental variance to build residential and commercial properties in areas where endangered species are known to inhabit.

- Legislation requires warning labels on products. Over time, these become more dramatic. In some countries, the warnings are required to include graphics or pictures highlighting the warning.

A Brand Equity Case Study: Coors Boycott in the 1970s

The Coors boycott case study represents an example of a large corporation whose name and brand are tightly connected and the importance of maintaining brand equity. The Coors Company and family name is intimately associated with the reputation of the company as a whole, and consumers have associated the personality of the family with how they perceive the Coors brand itself.

The Coors boycott case study shows that the characteristics and traits that were attributed to the company during the crisis and were the main concerns of their target audiences originated from the Coors family itself. This crisis began on April 5, 1977, when 1,472 members of Brewery, Bottling, Can and Allied Industrial Union Local No. 366 walked out of the Coors Brewery in Golden, Colorado. The members walked out because of the issue of human rights: All employees at Coors had to participate in a mandatory polygraph test. Coors management claimed that the polygraph tests were used because they felt that it was necessary to detect an applicant's health problems or malicious intent against the company or the family. The boycott continued until 1987, when an agreement was finally reached between the AFL-CIO and Peter Coors (*Coors Boycott*, 1974–1977). The following is the resolution that both the interest groups and Coors agreed upon to end the crisis that was damaging one of the leaders in the beer industry.

As described by internal documentation, Coors leadership believed that a 1982 *60 Minutes* interview was a turning point in the crisis. Shirley Richards, who was the director of corporate communications at Coors, was responsible for preparing Coors representatives for the interview with anchor Mike Wallace. Some of the key message points that they wanted to include in this interview were the following: Coors has fair hiring practices and is a good place to work; the boycott is unfair and is carried on by a few rejected union officials; Coors cares about its employees, its products, its community, and its country; Coors is not anti-union; and Coors makes a unique-quality beer (*Adolph Coors Company (B)*, 1983). By stating that Coors has fair hiring practices, the company also addressed the history of its labor union strikes as well as its policies regarding its employee polygraph tests.

Coors wanted to present its side of the boycott story, and the leaders felt that the more information they gave, the more trusting the public would be. Coors officials also stated that they cared about their employees and their other audiences, and this was appropriate to say because there would be a few employees who might not have participated in the boycott and are still loyal to the Coors Company. The Coors interview on *60 Minutes* was the number two show for the week for CBS (*Adolph Coors Company (B)*, 1983). This interview marked a change in the public's perceptions of the Coors corporate personality, and it changed its personality from a negative one toward a more positive and receptive personality. The impact of this boycott on Coors raised several different obstacles that it will have to continue to address.

The conclusion and key message that Coors will have to realize is that in a crisis situation, no matter how your brand equity is perceived by the public, consistent messages and a clear definition of the personality of a corporation will go a long way to being proactive in a crisis situation. Coors learned that perceptions of the company personality and the personality of the family that started Coors appeared to be one and the same, making it very difficult to determine what Coors the company and its brand really represent.

Summary Questions

1. What is brand equity? What specific concepts combine to create a brand's equity?

2. What is the commercial value of creating, promoting, and defending brand equity?

3. What is the potential for SIM damage to a brand during a crisis?

4. We often associate the concept of brand equity with businesses, as well as their products and services. Can the same logics be applied to nonprofits and governmental organizations? Explain why or why not.

5. What is the connection between crisis management and communication (including crisis prevention) and brand equity? What is the logic of why avoiding or responding properly to crises can help and restore brand equity? Can high brand equity help an organization recover from a crisis?

6. What is the connection between CSR and brand equity? Does brand equity come from demonstrated CSR? Can it? Will failure to know and apply CSR standards help or harm an organization's brand equity?

References

Aaker, D. A. (1996, Spring). Measuring brand equity across products and markets. *California Management Research, 38,* 102–120.

Aaker, D. A., & Biel, A. L. (1993). *Brand equity & advertising: Advertising's role in building strong brands.* Hillsdale, NJ: Lawrence Erlbaum.

Abbott, E., & Hetzel, O. (2005). *A legal guide to homeland security and emergency management for state and local governments.* Chicago: American Bar Association.

Abkowitz, M. D. (2002, March). *Environmental risk communication: What is it and how can it work?* Paper presented at the Environmental Risk Communication Summit, Vanderbilt University, Nashville, TN.

Ackerman, R. W., & Bauer, R. A. (1976). *Corporate social responsiveness: The modern dilemma.* Reston, VA: Reston.

Adams, W. C. (1995). Marrying the functions: The importance of media relations in public affairs planning. *Public Relations Quarterly, 40*(3), 7–11.

Adolph Coors Company. (1983). Retrieved October 2, 2006, from http://www.tuck.dart mouth.edu/faculty/publications/cases.html

Ahluwalia, R., Burnkrant, R. E., & Unnava, H. R. (2000). Consumer response to negative publicity: The moderating role of commitment. *Journal of Marketing Research, 27,* 203–214.

Ajzen, I., & Fishbein, M. (1980). *Understanding attitudes and predicting social behavior.* Englewood Cliffs, NJ: Prentice Hall.

Albrecht, T. L. (1988). Communication and personal control in empowering organizations. In J. A. Anderson (Ed.), *Communication yearbook 11* (pp. 380–390). Newbury Park, CA: Sage.

Alinsky, S. (1971). *Rules for radicals: A practical primer for realistic radicals.* New York: Random House.

American Broadcasting Co., 15 RR 2d 791 (1969).

American Chemistry Council. (2003). *Security code: Responsible Care practitioners' site.* Retrieved April 22, 2003, from http://www.americanchemistry.com/rc.nsf/unid/lgrs5jrmfe?opendocument

American Management Association. (2003, September 3). *More companies have crisis management plans American Management Association survey shows.* Retrieved January 17, 2008, from http://www.amanet.org/press/amanews/crisis_management.htm

Andrews, J. R. (1983). *The practice of rhetorical criticism.* New York: Macmillan.

Ansoff, H. I. (1980). Strategic issue management. *Strategic Management Journal, 1*(2), 131–148.

Apostle, H. G. (1984). *Aristotle's Nichomachean ethics.* Grinnell, IA: Peripatetic Press.

Aristotle. (1932). *Rhetoric* (L. Cooper, Trans.). Englewood Cliffs, NJ: Prentice Hall.

Armour, J. O. (1906, March 10). The packers and the people. *The Saturday Evening Post,* p. 6.

Armstrong, R. A. (1981). The concept and practice of issues management in the United States. *Vital Speeches, 47,* 763–765.

Arrington, C. B., & Sawaya, R. N. (1984). Managing public affairs: Issues management in an uncertain environment. *California Management Review, 26*(4), 148–160.

Arthur W. Page Society. (2007). *The authentic enterprise.* New York: Author.

Associated Press. (2002, May 9). *Public records tougher to view since Sept. 11.* Retrieved July 25, 2007, from http://www.firstamendmentcenter.org/news.aspx?id=3918

Atkin, C. K. (1973). Instrumental utilities and information seeking. In P. Clarke (Ed.), *New models for communication research* (pp. 205–239). Beverly Hills, CA: Sage.

Auf der Heide, E. (1996, May). Disaster planning, part II: Disaster problems, issues and challenges identified in the research literature. *Emergency Medical Clinics of North America, 14,* 453–480.

Austin v. Michigan Chamber of Commerce, 494 U.S. 652 (1990).

Averting more chemical tragedies. (1985, December 4). *New York Times,* p. A30.

Babcock, H. (2007). National security and environmental laws: A clear and present danger? *Virginia Environmental Law Journal, 25*(2), 105–156.

Baglan, T., Lalumia, J., & Bayless, O. L. (1986). Utilization of compliance-gaining strategies: A research note. *Communication Monographs, 53,* 289–293.

Ball, J. (2006, January 10). As Exxon pursues African oil, charity becomes a political issue. *The Wall Street Journal,* pp. A1, A10.

Ball, J. (2007, January 11). Exxon shifts "green" policy. *The Wall Street Journal,* p. A3.

Barnes, B. (1988). *The nature of power.* Urbana: University of Illinois Press.

Barnet, S. M., Jr. (1975). A global look at advocacy. *Public Relations Journal, 31*(11), 17–21.

Barnouw, E. (1978). *The sponsor: Notes on a modern potentate.* New York: Oxford University Press.

Barone, J. J., Miyazaki, A. D., & Taylor, K. A. (2000). The influence of cause related marketing on consumer choice: Does one good turn deserve another? *Journal of Academy of Marketing Science, 29,* 248–262.

Bass, G. D., & MacLean, A. (1993). Enhancing the public's right-to-know about environmental issues. *Villanova Environmental Law Journal, 4,* 287–310.

Bateman, D. N. (1975). Corporate communications of advocacy: Practical perspectives and procedures. *Journal of Business Communication, 13*(1), 3–11.

Beck, B., Greenberg, N. F., Hager, M., Harrison, J., & Underwood, A. (1984, December 17). Could it happen in America? *Newsweek,* pp. 38–44.

Beck, U. (1992). *Risk society towards a new modernity.* London: Sage.

Beck, U. (1995, Fall). Freedom from technology. *Dissent,* pp. 503–507.

Beck, U. (1996). Risk society and the provident state. In S. Lash, B. Szerszynski, & B. Wynne (Eds.), *Risk, environment and modernity: Towards a new ecology* (pp. 27–43). London: Sage.

Beck, U. (2004). Risk society revisited: Theory, politics, and research programmes. In B. Adam, U. Beck, & J. Van Loon (Eds.), *The risk society: Critical issues for social theory* (pp. 211–229). Thousand Oaks, CA: Sage.

Belke, J. C. (2000). *Chemical accident risks in U.S. industry: A preliminary analysis of accident risk data from U.S. hazardous chemical facilities.* Washington, DC: U.S. Environmental Protection Agency.

Benoit, W. L. (1997). Image repair discourse and crisis communication. *Public Relations Review, 23*(2), 177–186.

Benoit, W. L. (2005). Image restoration theory. In R. L. Heath (Ed.), *Encyclopedia of public relations* (pp. 407–410). Thousand Oaks, CA: Sage.

Benoit, W. L. (2008). Crisis communication and image repair discourse. In T. L. Hansen-Horn & B. D. Neff (Eds.), *Public relations: From theory to practice* (pp. 244–261). Boston: Pearson.

Benoit, W. L., & Brinson, S. L. (1994). AT&T: 'Apologies are not enough.' *Communication Quarterly, 42,* 75–88.

Berger, B. K., & Reber, B. H. (2006). *Gaining influence in public relations: The role of resistance in practice.* Mahwah, NJ: Lawrence Erlbaum.

Berger, C. R., & Calabrese, R. J. (1975). Some explorations in initial interaction and beyond: Toward a developmental theory of interpersonal communication. *Human Communication Research, 1,* 99–112.

Bergner, D. (1982). The role of strategic planning in international public affairs. *Public Relations Journal, 38*(6), 32–33, 39.

Berkowitz, D., & Turnmire, K. (1994). Community relations and issues management: An issue orientation approach to segmenting publics. *Journal of Public Relations Research, 6,* 105–123.

Bernays, E. L. (1955). *The engineering of consent.* Norman: University of Oklahoma Press.

Bernstein, A. (2004, September 20). Nike's new game plan for sweatshops. *Business Week,* p. 1.

Bernstein, D. (2003). Executive perspective: 2. Corporate branding—back to basics. *European Journal of Marketing, 37,* 1133–1141.

Bigelow v. Virginia, 421 U.S. 809 (1975).

Birch, J. (1994). New factors in crisis planning and response. *Public Relations Quarterly, 39*(1), 31–34.

Bitzer, L. (1987). Rhetorical public communication. *Critical Studies in Mass Communication, 4,* 425–428.

Bivins, T. H. (1980). Ethical implications of the relationship of purpose to role and function in public relations. *Journal of Business Ethics, 8,* 65–73.

Bivins, T. H. (1992). A systems model for ethical decision making in public relations. *Public Relations Review, 18,* 365–383.

Black, L. D., & Hartel, C. E. J. (2004). The five capabilities of socially responsible companies. *Journal of Public Affairs, 4,* 125–144.

Blalock, H. M., Jr. (1989). *Power and conflict: Toward a general theory.* Newbury Park, CA: Sage.

Bleecker, S. E., & Lento, T. V. (1982). Public relations in a wired society. *Public Relations Quarterly, 27*(1), 6–12.

Board of Trustees v. Fox, 492 U.S. 469 (1989).

Boe, A. R. (1972). The good hands of Allstate: A Spectator exclusive interview with Archie Boe, Allstate's Chairman of the Board. *Spectator, 10,* 1–3.

Boe, A. R. (1979). Fitting the corporation to the future. *Public Relations Quarterly, 24*(4), 4–5.

Boffey, P. M. (1984, December 23). Bhopal: The case for poison factories. *Denver Post,* pp. 1D, 12D.

Bostdorff, D. M. (1992). "The Decision Is Yours" campaign: Planned Parenthood's characteristic argument of moral virtue. In E. L. Toth & R. L. Heath (Eds.), *Rhetorical and critical approaches to public relations* (pp. 301–314). Hillsdale, NJ: Lawrence Erlbaum.

Bourdieu, P. (1986). The forms of capital. In J. G. Richardson (Ed.), *Handbook of theory and research for the sociology of education* (pp. 241–258). New York: Greenwood.

Bowen, S. A., & Heath, R. L. (2005). Issues management, systems, and rhetoric: Exploring the distinction between ethical and legal guidelines at Enron. *Journal of Public Affairs, 5,* 84–98.

Bowman, C. (1990). *The essence of strategic management.* New York: Prentice Hall.

BP settles claim from Texas blast, avoiding trial. (2006, November 10). *The Wall Street Journal,* p. A2.

Branch, K. K., & Bradbury, J, A. (2006). Comparison of DOE and Army advisory boards: Application of a conceptual framework for evaluating public participation in environmental risk decision making. *Policy Studies Journal, 34,* 723–753.

Brandywine-Main Line Radio, Inc., 14 RR 2d 1051 (1968).

Bremner, R. H. (1956). *From the depths: The discovery of poverty in the United States.* New York University Press.

Bridges, J. A., & Nelson, R. A. (2000). Issues management: A relational approach. In J. A. Ledingham & S. D. Bruning (Eds.), *Public relations as relationship management: A relational approach to the study and practice of public relations* (pp. 95–115). Mahwah, NJ: Lawrence Erlbaum.

Brodwin, D. R., & Bourgeois, L. J., III. (1984). Five steps to strategic action. *California Management Review, 26,* 176–190.

Broom, G. M. (1977). Coorientational measurement of public issues. *Public Relations Review, 3*(4), 110–119.

Broom, G. M., Lauzen, M. M., & Tucker, K. (1991). Public relations and marketing: Dividing the conceptual domain and operational turf. *Public Relations Review, 17,* 219–225.

Brown, J. K. (1979). *The business of issues: Coping with the company's environments.* New York: Conference Board.

Brown v. Board of Education of Topeka, 347 U.S. 483 (1954).

Brummett, B. (1995). Scandalous rhetorics. In W. N. Elwood (Ed.), *Public relations inquiry as rhetorical criticism: Case studies of corporate discourse and social influence* (pp. 13–23). Westport, CT: Praeger.

Buchholz, R. A. (1982a). *Business environment and public policy: Implications for management.* Englewood Cliffs, NJ: Prentice Hall.

Buchholz, R. A. (1982b). Education for public issues management: Key insights from a survey of top practitioners. *Public Affairs Review, 3,* 65–76.

Buchholz, R. A. (1985). *The essentials of public policy for management.* Englewood Cliffs, NJ: Prentice Hall.

Buckley v. Valeo, 424 U.S. 1 (1976).

Bullard, R. D. (2004). *Environmental justice in the 21st century.* Retrieved October 12, 2007, from http://www.ejrc.cau.edu/ejinthe21stcentury.htm

Burke, K. (1937, January 20). Synthetic freedom. *New Republic,* p. 365.

Burke, K. (1946, October 22). Letter to Malcolm Cowley, Burke File, Pennsylvania State University Pattee Library, University Park, PA.

Burke, K. (1951). Rhetoric—Old and new. *Journal of General Education, 5,* 202–209.

Burke, K. (1966). *Language as symbolic action.* Berkeley: University of California Press.

Burke, K. (1969a). *A grammar of motives.* Berkeley: University of California Press.

Burke, K. (1969b). *A rhetoric of motives.* Berkeley: University of California Press.

Burke, K. (1973). *The philosophy of literary form* (3rd ed.). Berkeley: University of California Press.

Burnett, J. J. (1998). A strategic approach to managing crises. *Public Relations Review, 24,* 475–488.

Business Executives Move for Vietnam Peace v. FCC, and Democratic National Committee v. FCC, 414 U.S. 94, 93 S.Ct. 2080 (1973).

California Medical Association v. FEC, 453 U.S. (1981).

Campbell, K. K. (1996). *The rhetorical act* (2nd ed.). Belmont, CA: Wadsworth.

Carbide was warned disaster possible. (1985, January 25). *Houston Post,* p. 5A.

Carbide's U.S. plant fined for violations. (1984, December 17). *Houston Post,* p. 3A.

Carroll, A. B. (1991). The pyramid of corporate social responsibility: Toward the moral management of organizational stakeholders. *Business Horizons, 34*(4), 39–48.

Carroll, A. B. (1999). Corporate social responsibility: Evolution of a definitional construct. *Business and Society, 38,* 268–295.

Carson, R. (1962). *Silent spring.* Boston: Houghton Mifflin.

Carson, T. L., Wokutch, R. E., & Cox, J. E., Jr. (1985). An ethical analysis of deception in advertising. *Journal of Business Ethics, 4,* 93–104.

Casarez, N. B. (1991). Corruption, corrosion, and corporate political speech. *Nebraska Law Review, 70,* 689–753.

Casarez, N. B. (2002). Dealing with cybersmears: How to protect your organization from online defamation. *Public Relations Quarterly, 47*(2), 40–45.

Casey, N., & Lloyd, M. E. (2007, October 17). Recall hurts Mattel's profit. *The Wall Street Journal,* p. A12.

Casey, N., Zamiska, N., & Pasztor, A. (2007, September 22–23). Mattel seeks to placate China with apology on toys. *The Wall Street Journal,* pp. A1, A7.

Casey, N., & Zimmerman, A. (2007, November 9). Toy recalls revive worries for industry. *The Wall Street Journal,* p. B4.

Central Hudson Gas & Electric Corp. v. Public Service Commission of New York, 447 U.S. 557 (1980).

Chase, W. H. (1977). Public issue management: The new science. *Public Relations Journal, 32*(10), 25–26.

Chase, W. H. (1982, December 1). Issue management conference: A special report. *Corporate Public Issues and Their Management, 7,* 1–2.

Chase, W. H. (1984). *Issue management: Origins of the future.* Stamford, CT: Issue Action Publications.

Chekouras, K. (2007). Balancing national security with a community's right to know: Maintaining public access to environmental information through EPCRA's non-preemption clause [Electronic version]. *Boston College Environmental Affairs Law Review, 34,* 107.

Chemical risks: Fears, facts, and the media. (1985). Washington, DC: Media Institute.

Cheney, G. (1992). The corporate person (re)presents itself. In E. L. Toth & R. L. Heath (Eds.), *Rhetorical and critical approaches to public relations* (pp. 165–183). Hillsdale, NJ: Lawrence Erlbaum.

Cheney, G., & Dionisopoulos, G. N. (1989). Public relations? No, relations with publics: A rhetorical-organizational approach to contemporary corporate communications. In C. H. Botan & V. Hazleton Jr. (Eds.), *Public relations theory* (pp. 135–157). Hillsdale, NJ: Lawrence Erlbaum.

Cheney, G., & Vibbert, S. L. (1987). Corporate discourse: Public relations and issue management. In F. M. Jablin, L. L. Putnam, K. H. Roberts, & L. W. Porter (Eds.), *Handbook of organizational communication: An interdisciplinary perspective* (pp. 165–194). Newbury Park, CA: Sage.

Chrisman, J. J., & Carroll, A. B. (1984). SMR forum: Corporate responsibility—reconciling economic and social goals. *Sloan Management Review, 25*(4), 59–65.

Cieri, M. (2000). Introduction: You cross that line. In M. Cieri & C. Peeps (Eds.), *Activists speak out: Reflections on the pursuit of change in America* (pp. 1–14). New York: Palgrave.

Coates, J. F., Coates, V. T., Jarratt, J., & Heinz, L. (1986). *Issues management: How you can plan, organize and manage for the future.* Mt. Airy, MD: Lomond.

Cochran, P. L., & Nigh, D. (1990). Illegal corporate behavior and the question of moral agency: An empirical examination. In W. C. Frederick & L. E. Preston (Eds.), *Business ethics: Research issues and empirical studies* (pp. 145–163). Greenwich, CT: JAI.

Cochran, P. L., & Wood, R. A. (1984). Corporate social responsibility and financial performance. *Academy of Management Journal, 27,* 42–56.

Cohen, D. (1982). Unfairness in advertising revisited. *Journal of Marketing, 46*(4), 73–80.

Cohn, V. (1990). *Reporting on risk: Getting it right in an age of risk.* Washington, DC: Media Institute.

Collins, E. L., Zoch, L. M., & McDonald, C. S. (2004). When professional worlds collide: Implications of *Kasky v. Nike* for corporate reputation management. *Public Relations Review, 30,* 411–417.

Columbia Broadcasting System, Inc. v. Democratic National Committee; Federal Communications Commission v. Business Executives' Move for Vietnam Peace; Post-Newsweek Stations, Capital Area, Inc., v. Business Executives' Move for Vietnam Peace; and American Broadcasting Companies v. Democratic National Committee, 41 LW 4688 (1973).

Condit, C. M., & Condit, D. M. (1992). Smoking OR health: Incremental erosion as a public interest group strategy. In E. L. Toth & R. L. Heath (Eds.), *Rhetorical and critical approaches to public relations* (pp. 241–256). Hillsdale, NJ: Lawrence Erlbaum.

Consolidated Edison Company of New York v. Public Service Commission, 447 U.S. 530 (1980).

Coombs, W. T. (1992). The failure of the Task Force on Food Assistance: A case study of the role of legitimacy in issue management. *Journal of Public Relations Research, 4,* 101–122.

Coombs, W. T. (1998). The Internet as potential equalizer: New leverage for confronting social irresponsibility. *Public Relations Review, 24,* 289–303.

Coombs, W. T. (1999). *Ongoing crisis communication: Planning, managing, and responding.* Thousand Oaks, CA: Sage.

Coombs, W. T. (2002). Assessing online issue threats: Issue contagions and their effect on issue prioritization. *Journal of Public Affairs, 2,* 215–229.

Coombs, W. T. (2007). *Ongoing crisis communication: Planning, managing, and responding* (2nd ed.). Thousand Oaks: Sage.

Coombs, W. T. (2008). The development of the situational crisis communication theory. In T. Hansen-Horn & B. D. Neff (Eds.), *Public relations: From theory to practice* (pp. 262–277). New York: Allyn & Bacon.

Coombs, W. T., & Holladay, S. J. (2007). *It's not just PR: Public relations in society.* Madison, MA: Blackwell.

Coors Boycott and Strike Support Coalition of Colorado Records Collection, 1974–1977 [bulk 1974–1977]. Denver, CO: Auraria Library Archives and Special Collections. Retrieved October 22, 2006, from http://carbon.cudenver.edu/public/library/archives/coors/main.htm

Cornwell, T. B., & Coote, L. V. (2005). Corporate sponsorship of a cause: The role of identification in purchase intent. *Journal of Business Research, 58,* 268–276.

Covello, V. T. (1992). Risk communication: An emerging area of health communication research. In S. A. Deetz (Ed.), *Communication yearbook* (Vol. 15, pp. 359–373). Thousand Oaks, CA: Sage.

Covello, V. T., & Mumpower, J. (1985). Risk analysis and risk management: An historical perspective. *Risk Analysis, 5*(2), 103–119.

Covello, V. T., Sandman, P. M., & Slovic, P. (1988). *Risk communication, risk statistics, and risk comparisons: A manual for plant managers.* Washington, DC: Chemical Manufacturers Association.

Cox, R. (2006). *Environmental communication and the public sphere.* Thousand Oaks, CA: Sage.

Crable, R. E., & Vibbert, S. L. (1985). Managing issues and influencing public policy. *Public Relations Review, 11*(2), 3–16.

Cronen, V. E., Pearce, W. B., & Harris, L. M. (1982). The coordinated management of meaning: A theory of communication. In F. E. X. Dance (Ed.), *Human communication theory: Comparative essays* (pp. 61–89). New York: Harper & Row.

Cummens, C. (2006, July 26). BP posts 30% jump in earnings, moves to improve safety in U.S. *The Wall Street Journal,* p. A2.

Cutler, B. D., & Muehling, D. D. (1989). Advocacy advertising and the boundaries of commercial speech. *Journal of Advertising, 18,* 40–50.

Cutler, B. D., & Muehling, D. D. (1991). Another look at advocacy advertising and the boundaries of commercial speech. *Journal of Advertising, 20*(4), 49–52.

Cutlip, S. M. (1994). *The unseen power: Public relations. A history.* Hillsdale, NJ: Lawrence Erlbaum.

Cutlip, S. M. (1995). *Public relations history: From the 17th to the 20th century.* Hillsdale, NJ: Lawrence Erlbaum.

Cutlip, S. M., & Center, A. H. (1982). *Effective public relations* (5th ed.). Englewood Cliffs, NJ: Prentice Hall.

Cutlip, S. M., Center, A. H., & Broom, G. M. (2006). *Effective public relations* (9th ed.). Upper Saddle River, NJ: Pearson.

Davies, J. C., Covello, V. T., & Allen, F. W. (Eds.). (1987). *Risk communication.* Washington, DC: Conservation Foundation.

Davis, G. F., & Thompson, T. A. (1994). A social movement perspective on corporate control. *Administrative Science Quarterly, 39,* 141–173.

Davison, W. P. (1972). Public opinion research as communication. *Public Opinion Quarterly, 36,* 311–322.

Delaney, K. J. (2007, November 15). Activists start Googling. *The Wall Street Journal,* p. B4.

Democratic National Committee v. FCC, 414 U.S. 94, 93 S.Ct. 2080 (1973).

Denbow, C. J., & Culbertson, H. M. (1985). Linkage beliefs and diagnosing an image. *Public Relations Review, 11*(1), 29–37.

Dillman, D. A., & Christenson, J. A. (1974). Toward the assessment of public values. *Public Opinion Quarterly, 38,* 206–221.

Dionisopoulos, G. N. (1986). Corporate advocacy advertising as political communication. In L. L. Kaid, D. Nimmo, & K. R. Sanders (Eds.), *New perspectives on political advertising* (pp. 2082–2106). Carbondale: Southern Illinois University Press.

Dionisopoulos, G. N., & Crable, R. E. (1988). Definitional hegemony as a public relations strategy: The rhetoric of the nuclear power industry after Three Mile Island. *Central States Speech Journal, 39,* 134–145.

Dionisopolous, G. N., & Vibbert, S. L. (1988). CBS vs Mobil Oil: Charges of creative bookkeeping. In H. R. Ryan (Ed.), *Oratorical encounters: Selected studies and sources of 20th century political accusation and apologies* (pp. 214–252). Westport, CT: Greenwood.

Divelbiss, R. I., & Cullen, M. R., Jr. (1981). Business, the media, and the American public. *Michigan State University Business Topics, 29*(1), 21–28.

Douglas, M. (1992). *Risk and blame.* London: Routledge.

Drake, B. H., & Drake, E. (1988). Ethical and legal aspects of managing corporate cultures. *California Management Review, 30,* 107–123.

Driskill, L. P., & Goldstein, J. R. (1986). Uncertainty: Theory and practice in organizational communication. *Journal of Business Communication, 23*(3), 41–57.

Druck, K. B. (1978). Dealing with exploding social and political forces. *Vital Speeches, 45*(4), 110–114.

DuBos, T. J. (1982, October 8). Letter to Jack Hart, School of Communication, University of Houston, Texas.

Dunham, L., Freeman, R. E., & Liedtka, J. (2006). Enhancing stakeholder practice: A particularized exploration of community. *Business Ethics Quarterly, 16,* 23–42.

Dunn, C. P. (1991). Are corporations inherently wicked? *Business Horizons, 34*(4), 3–8.

Dutton, J. E. (1993). Interpretations on automatic: A different view of strategic issue diagnosis. *Journal of Management Studies, 30,* 339–357.

Dutton, J. E., & Ashford, S. J. (1993). Selling issues to top management. *Academy of Management Review, 18,* 397–428.

Dutton, J. E., & Duncan, R. B. (1987). The creation of momentum for change through the process of strategic issue diagnosis. *Strategic Management Journal, 8,* 279–295.

Dutton, J. E., & Jackson, S. E. (1987). Categorizing strategic issues: Links to organizational action. *Academy of Management Review, 12*(1), 76–90.

Dutton, J. E., & Ottensmeyer, E. (1987). Strategic issue management systems: Forms, functions, and contexts. *Academy of Management Review, 12*(2), 355–365.

Edelman. (2006, January 23). *'A person like me' now most credible spokesperson for companies; trust in employees significantly higher than in CEOs, Edelman Trust Barometer finds.* Retrieved June 20, 2007, from http://www.edelman.com/news/ShowOne.asp?ID=102

Edelman Change and Employment Engagement Group. (2006). *Strategic intent: A leadership perspective on today's issues and tomorrow's trends for business success.* New York: Author.

Edelman, J. M. (1964). *The symbolic uses of politics.* Urbana: University of Illinois Press.

Edelman, J. M. (1977). *Political language: Words that succeed and policies that fail.* New York: Academic Press.

Edelman, M. (1988). *Constructing the political spectacle.* Chicago: University of Chicago Press.

Edge Broadcasting, 113 S. Ct., 2703 (1989).

Ehling, W. P., & Hesse, M. B. (1983). Use of "issue management" in public relations. *Public Relations Review, 9*(2), 18–35.

Einsiedel, E., & Thorne, B. (1999). Public response to uncertainty. In S. M. Friedman, S. Dunwoody, & C. L. Rogers (Eds.), *Communicating uncertainty: Media coverage of new and controversial science* (pp. 43–57). Mahwah, NJ: Lawrence Erlbaum.

Eisenberg, E. M. (1986). Meaning and interpretation in organizations. *Quarterly Journal of Speech, 72,* 88–113.

Elkington, J. (1994). Towards a sustainable corporation: Win-win-win business strategies for sustainable development. *California Management Review, 36*(2), 90–100.

Elmendorf, F. M. (1988). Generating grass-roots campaigns and public involvement. In R. L. Heath (Ed.), *Strategic issues management* (pp. 306–320). San Francisco: Jossey-Bass.

Elwood, W. N. (1995). Public relations is a rhetorical experience: The integral principle in case study analysis. In W. N. Elwood (Ed.), *Public relations inquiry as rhetorical criticism: Case studies of corporate discourse and social influence* (pp. 3–24). Westport, CT: Praeger.

Entman, R. (1993). Framing: Toward clarification of a fractured paradigm. *Journal of Communication, 43,* 51–58.

Entman, R. (2007). Framing bias: Media in the distribution of power. *Journal of Communication, 57,* 163–173.

Environmental Defense Fund. (2003). *Scorecard.* Retrieved March 26, 2003, from http://www.scorecard.org/community/index.tcl?zip_code=77547

Environmental Protection Agency (EPA). (1988, April). *Seven cardinal rules of risk communication.* Washington, DC: Author.

Environmental Protection Agency (EPA). (1997). *U.S. national profile on the management of chemicals: Executive summary.* Retrieved March 29, 2006, from http://www.epa.gov/oppfead1 /cb/csb_page

EPCRA, 42 U.S.C. 11001 et seq. (1986).

Epictetus. (1983). *Epictetus: The handbook* (N. P. White, Trans.). Indianapolis, IN: Hackett.

Epstein, E. M. (1987). The corporate social policy process: Beyond business ethics, corporate social responsibility, and corporate social responsiveness. *California Management Review, 29,* 99–114.

Erikson, K. (1994). *A new species of trouble: The human experience of modern disasters.* New York: W. W. Norton.

Ewing, R. P. (1979). The uses of futurist techniques in issues management. *Public Relations Quarterly, 24*(1), 15–18.

Ewing, R. P. (1980). Evaluating issues management. *Public Relations Journal, 36*(6), 14–16.

Ewing, R. P. (1987). *Managing the new bottom line: Issues management for senior executives.* Homewood, IL: Dow Jones-Irwin.

Fairness Doctrine, 30 RR 2d 1261 (1974).

Fairness Doctrine and the Public Interest Standards, 39 FR 26372 (1974).

Falkenberry, E. M. (1995). The Emergency Planning and Community Right-to-Know Act: A tool for toxic release reduction in the 90's. *Buffalo Environmental Law Journal, 3*(1), 1–36.

Farquhar, P. (1989, September). Managing brand equity. *Marketing Research,* pp. 24–34.

Fearn-Banks, K. (1996). *Crisis communications: A casebook approach.* Mahwah, NJ: Lawrence Erlbaum.

Fearn-Banks, K. (2001). Crisis communication: A review of some best practices. In R. L. Heath (Ed.), *Handbook of public relations* (pp. 479–486). Thousand Oaks, CA: Sage.

Federal Communications Commission (FCC). (n.d.). *About the FCC.* Retrieved November 6, 2007, from http://www.fcc.gov/aboutus.html

Federal Trade Commission (FTC). (n.d.). *Federal Trade Commission: A history.* Retrieved November 11, 2007, from http://www.ftc.gov/ftc/history/ftchistory.shtm

Fialka, J. J. (2006, September 19). Inside the failure of $8 billion effort to save prized fish. *The Wall Street Journal,* pp. A1, A12.

Fialka, J. J. (2007, April 27). Coalition ends ad campaign bashing coal. *The Wall Street Journal,* p. B4.

Fidler, L. A., & Johnson, J. D. (1984). Communication and innovation implementation. *Academy of Management Review, 9,* 704–711.

Finch, M. R., & Welker, L. S. (2004). Informed organization improvisation: A metaphor and method for understanding, anticipating, and performatively constructing the organizations' precrisis environment. In D. P. Millar & R. L. Heath (Eds.), *Responding to crisis: A rhetorical approach to crisis communication* (pp. 189–200). Mahwah, NJ: Lawrence Erlbaum.

Fine, M., Weiss, L., Pruitt, L. P., & Burns, A. (2004). *Off white: Readings on power, privilege, and resistance.* New York: Routledge.

Fink, S. (1986). *Crisis management: Planning for the inevitable.* New York: ANACOM.

First National Bank of Boston v. Bellotti, 435 U.S. 765 (1978).

Fischhoff, B. (1985). Managing risk perceptions. *Issues in Science and Technology, 2*(1), 83–96.

Fischhoff, B. (1990). *Risk issues in the news: Why experts and laymen disagree.* Washington, DC: Foundation for American Communities.

Fischhoff, B. (1995). Risk perception and communication unplugged: Twenty years of process. *Risk Analysis, 15,* 137–145.

Fischhoff, B., Slovic, P., Lichtenstein, S., Read, S., & Combs, B. (1978). How safe is safe enough? A psychometric study of attitudes towards technological risks and benefits. *Policy Sciences, 9,* 127–152.

Fishbein, M., & Ajzen, I. (1975). *Belief, attitude, intention, and behavior.* Reading, MA: Addison-Wesley.

Fisher, W. R. (1984). Narration as a human communication paradigm: The case of public moral argument. *Communication Monographs, 51*(1), 1–22.

Fisher, W. R. (1985a). The narrative paradigm: An elaboration. *Communication Monographs, 52,* 347–367.

Fisher, W. R. (1985b). The narrative paradigm: In the beginning. *Journal of Communication, 35*(4), 74–89.

Fisher, W. R. (1987). *Human communication as narration: Toward a philosophy of reason, value, and action.* Columbia: University of South Carolina Press.

Fisher, W. R. (1989). Clarifying the narrative paradigm. *Communication Monographs, 56,* 55–58.

Fishman, D. A. (1999). Valujet Flight 592: Crisis communication theory blended and extended. *Communication Quarterly, 47,* 345–375.

Fitzpatrick, K. (2006). Baselines for ethical advocacy in the "marketplace of ideas." In K. Fitzpatrick & C. Bronstein (Eds.), *Ethics in public relations: Responsible advocacy* (pp. 1–17). Thousand Oaks, CA: Sage.

Fitzpatrick, K., & Gauthier, C. (2001). Toward a professional responsibility theory of public relations ethics. *Journal of Mass Media Ethics, 16*(2/3), 193–212.

Fitzpatrick, K., & Palenchar, M. J. (2006). Disclosing special interests: Constitutional restrictions on front groups. *Journal of Public Relations Research, 18*(3), 203–224.

Fitzpatrick, K. R., & Rubin, M. S. (1995). Public relations vs. legal strategies in organizational crisis decision. *Public Relations Review, 21,* 21–33.

Fleisher, C. S. (2001). Emerging US public affairs practice: The 2000+ model. *Journal of Public Affairs, 1,* 44–52.

Fleisher, C. S. (2002). Analysis and analytical tools for managing corporate public affairs. *Journal of Public Affairs, 2,* 167–172.

Fleming, J. E. (1980). Linking public affairs with corporate planning. *California Management Review, 23*(2), 35–43.

Fombrun, C. J., & van Riel, C. B. M. (2004). *Fame & fortune.* Upper Saddle River, NJ: Prentice Hall.

Foundations test proxy power. (2007, January 19). *The Wall Street Journal,* p. W2.

Fowler, T. (2007, February 28). Power crisis tune changes quickly. *Houston Chronicle,* pp. D1, D5.

Fox, J. F. (1983). Communicating on issues: The CEO's changing role. *Public Relations Review, 9*(11), 11–23.

Fraser, E. A. (1982). Coalitions. In J. S. Nagelschmidt (Ed.), *The public affairs handbook* (pp. 192–199). New York: AMACOM.

Fraser, N. (2003). Rethinking recognition: Overcoming displacement and reification in cultural politics. In B. Hobson (Ed.), *Recognition struggles and social movements: Contested identities, agency and power* (pp. 21–32). Cambridge, UK: Cambridge University Press.

Frederick, W. C. (1986). Toward CSR3: Why ethical analysis is indispensable and unavoidable in corporate affairs. *California Management Review, 28*(4), 126–141.

Frederick, W. C., & Weber, J. (1990). The values of corporate managers and their critics: An empirical description and normative implications. In W. C. Frederick & L. E. Preston (Eds.), *Business ethics: Research issues and empirical studies* (pp. 123–144). Greenwich, CT: JAI.

Freeman, R. E. (1984). *Strategic management: A stakeholder approach.* Boston: Pitman.

Freudenberg, N. (1984). *Not in our backyards! Community action for health and the environment.* New York: Monthly Review Press.

Friendly, F. W. (1977). *The good guys, the bad guys and the First Amendment: Free speech vs. fairness in broadcasting.* New York: Vintage.

Frost, A. R., & Cooke, C. (1999). Brand vs. reputation: Managing an intangible asset. *Communication World, 16*(3), 22–29.

Galambos, L. (1975). *The public image of big business in America, 1880-1940: A quantitative study of social change.* Baltimore: Johns Hopkins University Press.

Galambos, L., & Pratt, J. (1988). *The rise of the corporate commonwealth.* New York: Basic Books.

Gamson, W. A. (1968). *Power and discontent.* Homewood, IL: Dorsey.

Gamson, W. A. (1975). *The strategy of social protest.* Homewood, IL: Dorsey.

Gandy, O. H., Jr. (1982). *Beyond agenda setting: Information subsidies and public policy.* Norwood, NJ: Ablex.

Gandy, O. H., Jr. (1992). Public relations and public policy: The structuration of dominance in the information age. In E. L. Toth & R. L. Heath (Eds.), *Rhetorical and critical approaches to public relations* (pp. 131–163). Hillsdale, NJ: Lawrence Erlbaum.

Garbett, T. (1981). *Corporate advertising: The what, the why, and the how.* New York: McGraw-Hill.

Gaudino, J. L., Fritsch, J., & Haynes, B. (1989). "If you knew what I knew, you'd make the same decision": A common misperception underlying public relations campaigns. In C. H. Botan & V. Hazleton Jr. (Eds.), *Public relations theory* (pp. 299–308). Hillsdale, NJ: Lawrence Erlbaum.

Gaunt, P., & Ollenburger, J. (1995). Issues management revisited: A tool that deserves another look. *Public Relations Review, 21,* 199–210.

Gay, C. D., & Heath, R. L. (1995). Working with experts in the risk communication infrastructure: Another challenge for public relations practitioners. *Public Relations Review, 21*(3), 211–224.

George R. Walker, 20 RR 2d 264 (1970).

Gerloff, E. A., Muir, N. K., & Bodensteiner, W. D. (1991). Three components of perceived environmental uncertainty: An exploratory analysis of the effects of aggregation. *Journal of Management, 17,* 749–768.

Geuter, G., & Stevens, A. L. (1983). *Mental modes.* Hillsdale, NJ: Lawrence Erlbaum.

Gildea, R. L. (1994–1995). Consumer survey confirms corporate social action affects buying decisions. *Public Relations Quarterly, 39*(4), 20–21.

Glasser, I. (1983). Introduction. In L. Siegel (Ed.), *Free speech, 1984: The rise of government controls on information, debate and communication* (pp. 1–2). New York: American Civil Liberties Union.

Goffman, E. (1974). *Frame analysis: An essay on the organization of experience.* Cambridge, MA: Harvard University Press.

Gold, R. L. (1982). Accommodation preempts confrontation. *Public Relations Quarterly, 27*(3), 23–28.

Goldstein, B. D. (2005). Advances in risk assessment and communication. *Annual Review of Public Health, 26,* 141–163.

Goodnight, G. T. (1982). The personal, technical, and public spheres of argument: A speculative inquiry into the art of public deliberation. *Journal of the American Forensic Association, 18,* 214–227.

Grier, P. (1984, December 26). Poisons in our midst are well-kept secret. *Rocky Mountain News,* p. 81.

Griese, N. L. (2001). *Arthur W. Page: Publisher, public relations pioneer, patriot.* Atlanta, GA: Anvil.

Griffin, L. M. (1952). The rhetoric of historical movements. *Quarterly Journal of Speech, 38,* 184–188.

Griffin, R. J., Dunwoody, S., & Neuwirth, K. (1999). Proposed model of the relationship of risk information seeking and processing to the development of preventive behaviors. *Environmental Research, 80*(2), 230–245.

Griffin, R. J., Neuwirth, K., & Dunwoody, S. (1995). Using the theory of reasoned action to examine the impact of health risk messages. In B. R. Burleson (Ed.), *Communication yearbook* (Vol. 18, pp. 201–228). Thousand Oaks, CA: Sage.

Grosjean v. American Press Co., 297 U.S. 233 (1936).

Grunig, J. E. (1978). Accuracy of communication from an external public to employees in a formal organization. *Human Communication Research, 5,* 40–53.

Grunig, J. E. (1980). Communication of scientific information to nonscientists. In B. Dervin & M. J. Voigt (Eds.), *Progress in communication sciences* (Vol. 2, pp. 167–214). Norwood, NJ: Ablex.

Grunig, J. E. (1989). Sierra club study shows who become activists. *Public Relations Review, 15,* 3–24.

Grunig, J. E. (1992). Communication, public relations, and effective organizations: An overview of the book. In J. E. Grunig (Ed.), *Excellence in public relations and communication management* (pp. 1–18). Hillsdale, NJ: Lawrence Erlbaum.

Grunig, J. E., & Grunig, L. S. (1989). Toward a theory of the public relations behavior of organizations: Review of a program of research. In J. E. Grunig & L. A. Grunig (Eds.), *Public relations research annual* (Vol. 1, pp. 27–63). Hillsdale, NJ: Lawrence Erlbaum.

Grunig, J. E., & Hunt, T. (1984). *Managing public relations.* New York: Holt, Rinehart and Winston.

Grunig, J. E., & Repper, F. C. (1992). Strategic management, publics, and issues. In J. E. Grunig (Ed.), *Excellence in public relations and communication management* (pp. 117–157). Hillsdale, NJ: Lawrence Erlbaum.

Grunig, L. A. (1992). Activism: How it limits the effectiveness of organizations and how excellent public relations departments respond. In J. E. Grunig (Ed.), *Excellence in public relations and communication management* (pp. 503–530). Hillsdale, NJ: Lawrence Erlbaum.

Grunig, L. A., Grunig, J. E., & Ehling, W. P. (1992). What is an effective organization? In J. E. Grunig (Ed.), *Excellence in public relations and communication management* (pp. 65–90). Hillsdale, NJ: Lawrence Erlbaum.

Guth, D. W. (1995). Organizational crisis and experience and public relations roles. *Public Relations Review, 21,* 123–136.

Hadden, S. (1989a). *A citizen's right to know: Risk communication and public policy.* Boulder, CO: Westview.

Hadden, S. (1989b). Institutional barriers to risk communication. *Risk Analysis, 9,* 301–308.

Haddock, T. (2000, November 21). Do corporate apologies really work? *Investor's Business Daily,* p. 1.

Hainsworth, B., & Meng, M. (1988). How corporations define issue management. *Public Relations Review, 14*(4), 18–30.

Hallahan, K. (1999). Seven models of framing: Implications for public relations. *Journal of Public Relations Research, 11,* 205–242.

Hallahan, K. (2001). The dynamics of issues activation and response: An issues process model. *Journal of Public Relations Research, 13,* 27–59.

Hallahan, K. (2004). "Community" as a foundation for public relations theory and practice. In P. J. Kalbfleisch (Ed.), *Communication yearbook* (Vol. 28, pp. 232–279). Mahwah, NJ: Lawrence Erlbaum.

Hallahan, K. (2009). Crises and risks in cyberspace. In R. L. Heath & H. D. O'Hair, (Eds.), *Handbook of crisis and risk communication* (pp. 415–448). New York: Routledge.

Hansson, S. O. (1989). Dimensions of risk. *Risk Analysis, 9,* 107–112.

Hauser, G. A. (1986). *Introduction to rhetorical theory.* Prospect Heights, IL: Waveland.

Hax, A. C., & Majluf, N. S. (1991). *The strategy concept and process: A pragmatic approach.* Englewood Cliffs, NJ: Prentice Hall.

Hays, K. (2007a, December 12). BP engineer: Facts hedged to make unit appear safer. *Houston Chronicle*, pp. A1, A7.

Hays, K. (2007b, June 15). It's all about safety, new BP chief says. *Houston Chronicle*, pp. A1, A8.

Hazlett, T. W. (1989). The fairness doctrine and the First Amendment. *Public Interest*, *96*, 103–116.

Hearit, K. M. (1994). Apologies and public relations crises at Chrysler, Toshiba, and Volvo. *Public Relations Review, 20*, 113–126.

Hearit, K. M. (1996). The use of counter-attack in apologetic public relations crises: The case of General Motors vs. Dateline NBC. *Public Relations Review, 22*, 233–248.

Hearit, K. M. (2006). *Crisis management by apology: Corporate response to allegations of wrongdoing.* Mahwah, NJ: Lawrence Erlbaum.

Hearne, S. A. (1996). Tracking toxics: Chemical use and the public's "right-to-know." *Environment, 38*(6), 1–11.

Heath, R. L. (1987–1988). Are focus groups a viable tool for PR practitioners to help their companies establish corporate responsibility? *Public Relations Quarterly, 32*(4), 24–28.

Heath, R. L. (Ed.). (1988). *Strategic issues management: How organizations influence and respond to public interests and policies.* San Francisco: Jossey-Bass.

Heath, R. L. (1990). Corporate issues management: Theoretical underpinnings and research foundations. In J. E. Grunig & L. A. Grunig (Eds.), *Public relations research annual* (Vol. 2, pp. 29–65). Hillsdale, NJ: Lawrence Erlbaum.

Heath, R. L. (1991a). Effects of internal rhetoric on management response to external issues: How corporate culture failed the asbestos industry. *Journal of Applied Communication, 18*(2), 153–167.

Heath, R. L. (1991b). Public relations research and education: Agendas for the 1990s. *Public Relations Review, 17*(2), 185–194.

Heath, R. L. (1992). The wrangle in the marketplace: A rhetorical perspective of public relations. In E. L. Toth & R. L. Heath (Eds.), *Rhetorical and critical approaches to public relations* (pp. 17–36). Hillsdale, NJ: Lawrence Erlbaum.

Heath, R. L. (1993). Toward a paradigm for the study and practice of public relations: A rhetorical approach to zones of meaning and organizational prerogatives. *Public Relations Review, 19*(2), 141–155.

Heath, R. L. (1994). *Management of corporate communication: From interpersonal contacts to external affairs.* Hillsdale, NJ: Lawrence Erlbaum.

Heath, R. L. (1995). Corporate environmental risk communication: Cases and practices along the Texas Gulf Coast. In B. R. Burleson (Ed.), *Communication yearbook* (Vol. 18, pp. 63–99). Thousand Oaks, CA: Sage.

Heath, R. L. (1998). New communication technologies: An issues management point of view. *Public Relations Review, 24*, 273–288.

Heath, R. L. (2000). A rhetorical perspective on the values of public relations research: Crossroads and pathways toward concurrence. *Journal of Public Relations Research, 12*(1), 69–91.

Heath, R. L. (2001). A rhetorical enactment rationale for public relations: The good organization communicating well. In R. L. Heath (Ed.), *Handbook of public relations* (pp. 31–50). Thousand Oaks, CA: Sage.

Heath, R. L. (2006a). A rhetorical theory approach to issues management. In C. H. Botan & V. Hazleton (Eds.), *Public relations theory II* (pp. 63–99). Mahwah, NJ: Lawrence Erlbaum.

Heath, R. L. (2006b). Onward into more fog: Thoughts on public relations research directions. *Journal of Public Relations Research, 18,* 93–114.

Heath, R. L. (2007a). Management through advocacy. In E. L. Toth (Ed.), *The future of excellence in public relations and communication management: Challenges for the next generation* (pp. 41–65). Mahwah, NJ: Lawrence Erlbaum.

Heath, R. L. (2007b). Power resource management: Pushing buttons and building cases. In T. Hansen-Horn & B. D. Neff (Eds.), *Public relations: From theory to practice* (pp. 2–19). New York: Allyn & Bacon.

Heath, R. L., & Abel, D. D. (1996a). Proactive response to citizen risk concerns: Increasing citizens' knowledge of emergency response practices. *Journal of Public Relations Research, 8,* 151–171.

Heath, R. L., & Abel, D. D. (1996b). Types of knowledge as predictors of company support: The role of information in risk communication. *Journal of Public Relations Research, 8,* 35–55.

Heath, R. L., Bradshaw, J., & Lee, J. (2002). Community relationship building: Local leadership in the risk communication infrastructure. *Journal of Public Relations Research, 14,* 317–353.

Heath, R. L., & Coombs, W. T. (2006). *Today's public relations: An introduction.* Thousand Oaks, CA: Sage.

Heath, R. L., & Cousino, K. R. (1990). Issues management: End of first decade progress report. *Public Relations Review, 17*(1), 6–18.

Heath, R. L., & Douglas, W. (1990). Involvement: A key variable in people's reaction to public policy issues. In J. E. Grunig & L. A. Grunig (Eds.), *Public relations research annual* (Vol. 2, pp. 93–204). Hillsdale, NJ: Lawrence Erlbaum.

Heath, R. L., & Douglas, W. (1991). Effects of involvement on reactions to sources of messages and to message clusters. In L. A. Grunig & J. E. Grunig (Eds.), *Public relations research annual* (Vol. 3, pp. 179–193). Hillsdale, NJ: Lawrence Erlbaum.

Heath, R. L., Douglas, W., & Russell, M. (1995). Constituency building: Determining employees' willingness to participate in corporate political activities. *Journal of Public Relations Research, 7,* 273–288.

Heath, R. L., Lee, J., & Jares, S. M. (1999). Decision making encroachment and cooperative relationships between public relations and legal counselors in the management of organizational crisis. *Journal of Public Relations Research, 11,* 243–270.

Heath, R. L., Liao, S., & Douglas, W. (1995). Effects of perceived economic harms and benefits on issue involvement, information use, and action: A study in risk communication. *Journal of Public Relations Research, 7,* 89–109.

Heath, R. L., & Nathan, K. (1991). Public relations' role in risk communication: Information, rhetoric and power. *Public Relations Quarterly, 35*(4), 15–22.

Heath, R. L., & Nelson, R. A. (1986). *Issues management: Corporate public policymaking in an information society.* Beverly Hills, CA: Sage.

Heath, R. L., & Palenchar, M. J. (2000). Community relations and risk communications: A longitudinal study of the impact of emergency response messages. *Journal of Public Relations Research, 12*(2), 131–161.

Heath, R. L., & Ryan, M. (1989). Public relations' role in defining corporate social responsibility. *Journal of Mass Media Ethics, 4*(1), 21–28.

Heerema, D. L., & Giannini, R. (1991). Business organizations and the sense of community. *Business Horizons, 34*(4), 87–93.

Heineman, B. W., Jr. (2005, June 28). Are you a good corporate citizen? *The Wall Street Journal,* p. B2.

Helfand, G. E., & Peyton, L. J. (1999). A conceptual model for environmental justice. *Social Science Quarterly, 80*(1), 68–83.

Herremans, I. M., Akathaporn, P., & McInnes, M. (1993). An investigation of corporate social responsibility reputation and economic performance. *Accounting, Organizations, & Society, 18,* 587–604.

Heugens, P. P. M. A. R., & van Oosterhout, H. J.. (2002). The confines of stakeholder management: Evidence from the Dutch manufacturing sector. *Journal of Business Ethics, 40,* 387–403.

Hiebert, R. E. (1991). Public relations as a weapon of modern warfare. *Public Relations Review, 17,* 107–116.

Hill, J. W. (1958). *Corporate public relations: Arm of modern management.* New York: Harper & Brothers.

Hill, J. W. (1963). *The making of a public relations man.* New York: David McKay Company.

Hillman, A. J. (2001). Public affairs, issues management and political strategy: Methodological issues that count—A different view. *Journal of Public Affairs, 1/2,* 356–361.

Hoeffler, S., & Keller, K. L. (2003). The marketing advantages of strong brands. *Journal of Brand Management, 10,* 421–445.

Hobbs, J. D. (1991, November). *"Treachery by any other name": A case study of the Toshiba public relations crisis.* Paper presented at the meeting of the Speech Communication Association, Atlanta, GA.

Hoffman, A. J., & Ocasio, W. (2001). Not all events are attended equally: Toward a middle-range theory of industry attention to external events. *Organization Science, 12,* 414–434.

Holman, J. M. (1998). *An information commons: Protection for free expression in the new information environment.* Unpublished doctoral dissertation, Indiana University, Bloomington.

Holsinger, R. L., & Dilts, J. P. (1997). *Media law* (4th ed.). New York: McGraw-Hill.

Hosmer, L. T. (1991). Managerial responsibilities on the micro level. *Business Horizons, 34*(4), 49–55.

Hsu, J. L., & Liu, G. S. (2000). Consumer perceptions of fluid milk advertising in Taiwan. *International Journal of Advertising, 19,* 471–486.

Huber, G. P., & Daft, R. L. (1987). The information environments of organizations. In F. M. Jablin, L. L. Putnam, K. H. Roberts, & L. W. Porter (Eds.), *Handbook of organizational communication: An interdisciplinary perspective* (pp. 130–164). Newbury Park, CA: Sage.

Hudson, K. (2007, February 2). Wal-Mart wants suppliers, workers to join green effort. *The Wall Street Journal,* p. A14.

Hunger, J. D., & Wheelen, T. L. (1993). *Strategic management* (4th ed.). Reading, MA: Addison-Wesley.

Ihlen, O. (2005). The power of social capital: Adapting Bourdieu to the study of public relations. *Public Relations Review, 31,* 492–496.

Ingersoll, B. (1985, April 24). Annual meetings are much calmer affairs under changed SEC shareholder rules. *The Wall Street Journal,* p. 35.

Isaac, R. J., & Isaac, E. (1984, September 6). Subsidizing political hidden agendas. *The Wall Street Journal,* p. 28.

Ivanovich, D., & Clanton, B. (2007, June 12). OSHA steps up refinery oversight. *Houston Chronicle,* pp. D1, D5.

Iverson, A. C. (1982, April). *Advertising in a hostile environment.* Paper presented to The Popular Culture Association, Louisville, KY.

Jackson, P. (1982). Tactics of confrontation. In J. S. Nagelschmidt (Ed.), *The public affairs handbook* (pp. 211–220). New York: AMACOM.

Jacobson, J. D. (2003). Safeguarding national security through public release of environmental information: Moving the debate to the next level. *Environmental Law, 9,* 327–397.

James, D. O., Lyman, M., & Foreman, S. K. (2006). Does the tail wag the dog? Brand personality in brand alliance evaluation. *Journal of Product & Brand Management, 15*(3), 173–183.

Jaques, A. (2000). *Don't just stand there: The Do-it Plan for effective issue management.* Victoria, Australia: Issue Outcomes.

Jevons, C. (2005). Beyond products brand management: Names, brands, branding: Beyond the signs, symbols, products and services. *Journal of Product & Brand Management, 14*(2), 117–188.

Johannsen, R. L., Strickland, R., & Eubanks, R. T. (Eds.). (1970). *Language is sermonic: Richard M. Weaver on the nature of rhetoric.* Baton Rouge: Louisiana State University Press.

Johnson, J. (1983). Issues management: What are the issues? An introduction to issues management. *Business Quarterly, 48*(3), 22–31.

Johnson, S. M. (2005). Terrorism, security, and environmental protection. *William & Mary Environmental Law & Policy Review, 29*(1), 107–158.

Jones, B. L., & Chase, W. H. (1979). Managing public issues. *Public Relations Review, 5*(2), 3–23.

Jones, R. (2002). Challenges to the notion of publics in public relations: Implications of the risk society for the discipline. *Public Relations Review, 28*(1), 49–62.

Juanillo, N. K., Jr., & Scherer, C. W. (1995). Attaining a state of informed judgments: Toward a dialectical discourse on risk. In B. R. Burleson (Ed.), *Communication yearbook* (Vol. 18, pp. 278–299). Thousand Oaks, CA: Sage.

Kaiser Aluminum & Chemical Corporation. (1980, August). *At issue: Access to television.* Oakland, CA: Author.

Kamm, T. (1984, December 26). French town with Union Carbide Corp. plant has dual concerns: Safety and unemployment. *The Wall Street Journal,* p. 15.

Kanetkar, V., Weinberg, C. B., & Weiss, D. L. (1992, Fall). Price sensitivity and television advertising exposures: Some empirical findings. *Marketing Science, 11,* 359–371.

Kapferer, J. (1997). *Strategic brand management.* London. Kogan Page Limited.

Kasky v. Nike Inc., et al., 45 P.3d 243 (Calif. 2002).

Kasperson, R. E. (1992). The social amplification of risk: Progress in developing an integrative framework. In S. Krimsky & D. Golding (Eds.), *Social theories of risk* (pp. 153–178). Westport, CT: Praeger.

Kasperson, R. E., Renn, O., Slovic, P., Brown, H. S., Emel, J., Goble, R., et al. (1988). The social amplification of risk: A conceptual framework. *Risk Analysis, 8*(2), 177–187.

Kates, R. W., & Kasperson, J. X. (1983). Comparative risk analysis of technological hazards [Review]. *Proceedings of National Academy of Sciences, 80,* 7027–7038.

Keller, K. L. (1993, January). Conceptualizing, measuring, and managing customer-based brand equity. *Journal of Marketing, 57,* 1–22.

Keller, K. L. (1998). Measuring customer-based brand equity. In F. R. Esch (Ed.), *Perspectives of modern brand management* (pp. 989–1010). Wiesbaden, Germany: Gabler.

Keller, K. L., & Lehmann, D. R. (2006). Brands and branding: Research findings and future priorities. *Marketing Science, 25,* 740–759.

Kelly, O. (1982, September 6). Corporate crime: The untold story. *U.S. News & World Report,* pp. 25–29.

Kelsey, J. (2007, February 13). *Americans not ready for digital TV* [Radio interview]. Washington, DC: National Public Radio.

Kerr, R. L. (2007). Justifying corporate speech regulation through a town-meeting understanding of the marketplace of ideas. *Journalism Communication Monographs, 9*(2), 57–113.

Kim, Y. (1998). Advertising expenditure, brand equity and returns: The integration between psychological effectiveness and economic efficiency. In D. Muehling (Ed.), *Proceeding of the American Academy of Advertising* (pp. 241–248). Athens, GA: American Academy of Advertising.

Kim, Y. (2001). Measuring the economic value of public relations. *Journal of Public Relations Research, 13*(1), 3–26.

Kluger, R. (1996). *Ashes to ashes: America's hundred-year cigarette war, the public health, and the unabashed triumph of Philip Morris.* New York: Knopf.

Knight, G., & Greenberg, J. (2002). Promotionalism and subpolitics: Nike and its labor critics. *Management Communication Quarterly, 15,* 541–570.

Knox, S., & Bickerton, D. (2003). The six conventions of corporate branding. *European Journal of Marketing, 37,* 998–1016.

Kolko, G. (1967). *The triumph of conservatism: A reinterpretation of American history, 1900–1916.* Chicago: Quadrangle.

Krimsky, S. (1992). The role of theory in risk studies. In S. Krimsky & D. Golding (Eds.), *Social theories of risk* (pp. 3–22). Westport, CT: Praeger.

Krimsky, S. (2007). Risk communication in the Internet age: The rise of disorganized skepticism. *Environmental Hazards, 7,* 157–164.

Krimsky, S., & Golding, D. (1992). Preface. In S. Krimsky & D. Golding (Eds.), *Social theories of risk* (pp. xiii–xvii). Westport, CT: Praeger.

Krimsky, S., & Plough, A. (1988). *Environmental hazards: Communicating risks as a social process.* Dover, MA: Auburn House.

Krippendorff, K., & Eleey, M. F. (1986). Monitoring a group's symbolic environment. *Public Relations Review, 12*(1), 13–36.

Kruckeberg, D., & Starck, K. (1988). *Public relations and community: A reconstructed theory.* New York: Praeger.

Krugman, P. (2006, April 18). He made Exxon Mobil an enemy of the planet. *Houston Chronicle,* p. B9.

Kuntz, P. (1994, January 22). Lobby bill would plug holes but depends on good will. *Congressional Quarterly, 52*(3), 103–105.

LaDou, J. (2004, March). The asbestos cancer epidemic: Commentary. *Environmental Health Perspectives.* Retrieved February 2, 2008, from http://findarticles.com/p/articles/mi_m 0CYP/is _3_112/ai_115034515

Laird, F. N. (1989). The decline of deference: The political context of risk communication. *Risk Analysis, 9,* 543–550.

Lauzen, M. M. (1994). Public relations practitioner role enactment in issues management. *Journalism Quarterly, 71,* 356–369.

Lauzen, M. M. (1995). Toward a model of environmental scanning. *Journal of Public Relations Research, 7,* 187–203.

Lauzen, M. M., & Dozier, D. M. (1994). Issues management mediation of linkages between environmental complexity and management of public relations function. *Journal of Public Relations Research, 6,* 163–184.

Leading 100 business/industrial advertisers spend $420 million. (1985). *Business Marketing, 70*(4), 60–163.

LeBon, G. (1925). *The crowd: A study of the popular mind.* New York: Macmillan.

Leeper, R. V. (2001). In search of a metatheory for public relations: An argument for communitarianism. In R. L. Heath (Ed.), *Handbook of public relations* (pp. 93–104). Thousand Oaks, CA: Sage.

Leeper, R. V. (2005). Communitarianism. In R. L. Heath (Ed.), *Encyclopedia of public relations* (pp. 168–171). Thousand Oaks, CA: Sage.

Leichty, G., & Warner, E. (2001). Cultural topoi: Implications for public relations. In R. L. Heath (Ed.), *Handbook of public relations* (pp. 61–74). Thousand Oaks, CA: Sage.

Leiss, W. (1996). Three phases in the evolution of risk communication practice. *Annals of the American Academy of Political and Social Science, 545,* 85–94.

Leitch, S., & Neilson, D. (2001). Bringing publics into public relations: New theoretical frameworks for practice. In R. L. Heath (Ed.), *Handbook of public relations* (pp. 127–138). Thousand Oaks, CA: Sage.

Lentz, C. S. (1996). The fairness in broadcasting doctrine and the Constitution: Forced one-stop shopping in the "marketplace of ideas." *University of Illinois Law Review, 271,* 1–39.

Lerbinger, O. (1997). *The crisis manager: Facing risk and responsibility.* Mahwah, NJ: Lawrence Erlbaum.

Lesly, P. (1983). Policy, issues, and opportunities. In P. Lesly (Ed.), *Lesly's public relations handbook* (3rd ed., pp. 14–21). Englewood Cliffs, NJ: Prentice Hall.

Lesly, P. (1984). *Overcoming opposition: A survival manual for executives.* Englewood Cliffs, NJ: Prentice Hall.

Lesly, P. (1992). Coping with opposition groups. *Public Relations Review, 18,* 325–334.

Lewis, B. C. (2005). What you don't know can hurt you: The importance of information in the battle against environmental class and racial discrimination. *William & Mary Environmental Law & Policy Review, 29,* 267–326.

Liebhold, P., & Rubenstein, H. (1998). *Between a rock and a hard place: A history of American sweatshops, 1820–Present.* Retrieved February 8, 2008, from http://history matters.gmu.edu/d/145

Lindell, M. K., & Perry, R. W. (2004). *Communicating environmental risk in multiethnic communities.* Thousand Oaks, CA: Sage.

Lippmann, W. (1961). *Drift and mastery: An attempt to diagnose the current unrest.* Englewood Cliffs, NJ: Prentice Hall. (Original work published 1918)

Littlejohn, S. E. (1986). Competition and cooperation: New trends in corporate public issue identification and resolution. *California Management Review, 29*(1), 109–123.

Liu, J. T., & Smith, V. K. (1990). Risk communication and attitude change: Taiwan's national debate over nuclear power. *Journal of Risk and Uncertainty, 3,* 331–349.

Loddeke, L. (1984, December 16). Legislative work under way in aftermath of India tragedy. *Houston Post,* p. 8B.

Lucaites, J. L., & Condit, C. M. (1985). Re-constructing narrative theory: A functional perspective. *Journal of Communication, 35*(4), 90–108.

Lukasik, S. J. (1981). Information for decision making. *Public Relations Quarterly, 26*(3), 19–22.

Macauley, M. K. (2006, January). *Issues at the forefront of public policy for environmental risk.* Paper presented at the American Meteorological Society's Annual Policy Colloquium, Washington, DC.

MacNaughton, D. S. (1976, December). Managing social responsiveness. *Business Horizons, 19,* 19–24.

Maguire, S., & Ellis, J. (2009). The precautionary principle and risk communication. In R. L. Heath & H. D. O'Hair (Eds.), *Handbook of crisis and risk communication* (pp. 120–140). New York: Routledge.

Mahon, J. F., & McGowan, R. A. (1991). Searching for common good: A process-oriented approach. *Business Horizons, 34*(4), 79–86.

Makeover, J. (1994). *Beyond the bottom line: Putting social responsibility to work for your business and the world.* New York: Simon & Schuster.

Marbach, W. D., Gibney, F., Gander, M., Tsuruoka, D., & Greenburg, N. F. (1984, December 17). A company in shock. *Newsweek,* p. 37.

Marconi, J. (1992). *Crisis marketing: When bad things happen to good companies.* Chicago: Probus.

Marra, F. J. (2004). Excellent crisis communication: Beyond crisis plans. In D. P. Millar & R. L. Heath (Eds.), *Responding to crisis: A rhetorical approach to crisis communication* (pp. 311–325). Mahwah, NJ: Lawrence Erlbaum.

Martin, R. H., & Boynton, L. A. (2005). From liftoff to landing: NASA's crisis communication and resulting media coverage following the *Challenger* and *Columbia* tragedies. *Public Relations Review, 31,* 253–261.

Marx, T. G. (1986). Integrating public affairs and strategic planning. *California Management Review, 29*(1), 141–147.

McComas, K. A. (2003). Citizen satisfaction with public meetings used for risk communication. *Journal of Applied Communication Research, 31,* 164–184.

McComas, K. A. (2006). Defining moments in risk communication research: 1995–2005. *Journal of Health Communication, 11,* 75–91.

McComas, K. A., Arvai, J., & Besley, J. C. (2009). Linking public participation and decision making through risk communication. In R. L. Heath & H. D. O'Hair (Eds.), *Handbook of crisis and risk communication* (pp. 367–388). New York: Routledge.

McCombs, M. E. (1977). Agenda setting function of mass media. *Public Relations Review, 3*(4), 89–95.

McCombs, M. E. (1992). Explorers and surveyors: Expanding strategies for agenda-setting research. *Journalism Quarterly, 69,* 813–824.

McCombs, M. E., Einsiedel, E., & Weaver, D. (1991). *Contemporary public opinion: Issues and the news.* Hillsdale, NJ: Lawrence Erlbaum.

McCombs, M. E., Llamas, J. P., Lopez-Escobar, E., & Rey, F. (1997). Setting the agenda of attributes in the 1996 Spanish general election. *Journal of Communication, 50,* 77–92.

McCombs, M. E., & Shaw, D. L. (1972). The agenda-setting function of the mass media. *Public Opinion Quarterly, 36*(2), 176–187.

McCoy, T. S. (1989). Revoking the fairness doctrine: The year of the contra. *Communications and the Law, 11*(3), 67–83.

McElreath, M. P. (1980). *Priority research questions in public relations for the 1980s*. New York: Foundation for Public Relations Research and Education.

McGinnis, M. A. (1984). The key to strategic planning: Integrating analysis and intuition. *Sloan Management Review, 26*(3), 45–52.

McGuire, J. W. (1990). Managerial motivation and ideology. In W. C. Frederick & L. E. Preston (Eds.), *Business ethics: Research issues and empirical studies* (pp. 51–75). Greenwich, CT: JAI.

McKie, D., & Munshi, D. (2007). *Reconfiguring public relations: Ecology, equity, and enterprise*. Abindgon, UK: Routledge.

McLaughlin, B. (Ed.). (1969). *Studies in social movements: A social psychological perspective*. New York: Free Press.

McLeod, J. M., & Chaffee, S. H. (1973). Interpersonal approaches to communication research. *American Behavioral Scientist, 16*, 469–500.

McLuhan, M. (1969). *The Gutenberg galaxy*. New York: Signet.

Mead, G. H. (1934). *Mind, self, and society*. Chicago: University of Chicago Press.

Meadow, R. G. (1981). The political dimensions of nonproduct advertising. *Journal of Communication, 31*(3), 69–82.

Meier, B. (1985, February 8). Study by EPA finds laws may be insufficient to protect the public against toxic chemicals. *The Wall Street Journal*, p. 4.

Meijer, M.-M., & Kleinnijenhuis, J. (2006). Issue news and corporate reputation: Applying the theories of agenda setting and issue ownership in the field of business communication. *Journal of Communication, 56*, 543–559.

Mendelsohn, H. (1973). Some reasons why information campaigns can succeed. *Public Opinion Quarterly, 37*, 50–61.

Metzler, M. S. (2001). The centrality of organizational legitimacy to public relations practice. In R. L. Heath (Ed.), *Handbook of public relations* (pp. 321–333). Thousand Oaks, CA: Sage.

Meyers, R. A., Newhouse, T. L., & Garrett, D. E. (1978). Political momentum: Television news treatment. *Communication Monographs, 45*, 382–388.

The Miami Herald Publishing Company v. Pat L. Tornillo, 418 U.S. 241-62 (1974).

Millar, D. P., & Heath, R. L. (Eds.). (2004). *Responding to crisis: A rhetorical approach to crisis communication*. Mahwah, NJ: Lawrence Erlbaum.

Miller, W. H. (1987, November 2). Issue management: "No longer a sideshow." *Industry Week*, pp. 125–129.

Misol, L. (2006). *Private companies and public interest: Why corporations should welcome global human rights rules*. Human Rights Watch. Retrieved February 4, 2008, from http://www.business-humanrights.org/Categories/Principles/UNGlobalCompact?batch_start=241

Mitroff, I. I. (1983). *Stakeholders of the organizational mind: Toward a new view of organizational policy making*. San Francisco: Jossey-Bass.

Mitroff, I. I. (1994). Crisis management and environmentalism: A natural fit. *California Management Board, 36*(2), 101–113.

Moore, M. (Ed.). (1989). *Health risks and the press: Perspectives on media coverage of risk assessment and health*. Washington, DC: Media Institute.

Moore, R. H. (1979). Research by the Conference Board sheds light on problems of semantics, issue identification and classification—And some likely issues for the '80s. *Public Relations Journal, 35*(11), 43–46.

Moore, R. H. (1982). The evolution of public affairs. In J. S. Nagelschmidt (Ed.), *The public affairs handbook* (pp. xiii–xv). New York: AMACOM.

Morgan, G. (1982). Cybernetics and organization theory: Epistemology or technique? *Human Relations, 35,* 521–537.

Morgan, G. (1986). *Images of organization.* Beverly Hills, CA: Sage.

Morgan, M. G., Fischhoff, B., Bostrom, A., & Atman, C. J. (2002). *Risk communication: A mental models approach.* Cambridge, UK: Cambridge University Press.

Morris, C. R. (2005). *The tycoons: How Andrew Carnegie, John D. Rockefeller, Jay Gould, and J. P. Morgan invented the American super economy.* New York: Holt.

Motion, J., & Leitch, S. (2007). A toolbox for public relations: The *oeuvre* of Michel Foucault. *Public Relations Review, 33,* 263–268.

Muller v. Oregon, 208 U.S. 412 (1908).

Munoz, S. S. (2006, December 13). U.S. moves to tighten rules on lead in children's jewelry. *The Wall Street Journal,* p. D9.

Murphy, P. (1992). The limits of symmetry: A game theory approach to symmetric and asymmetric public relations. In L. A. Grunig & J. E. Grunig (Eds.), *Public relations research annual* (Vol. 3, pp. 115–131). Hillsdale, NJ: Lawrence Erlbaum.

Murphy, P., & Dee, J. (1996). Reconciling the preferences of environmental activists and corporate policymakers. *Journal of Public Relations Research, 8,* 1–33.

Myers, K. N. (1993). *Total contingency planning for disasters: Managing risk, minimizing loss, and ensuring business continuity.* New York: John Wiley.

Naisbitt, J. (1982). *Megatrends: Ten new directions transforming our lives.* New York: Warner.

Nathan, K., & Heath, R. L. (1992, August). *Demographic factors and risk communication variables: Knowledge, benefits, control, involvement and uncertainty.* Paper presented at the Association of Educational Journalism and Mass Communication Convention, Montreal, Canada.

Nathan, K., Heath, R. L., & Douglas, W. (1992). Tolerance for potential environmental health risks: The influence of knowledge, benefits, control, involvement and uncertainty. *Journal of Public Relations Research, 4,* 235–258.

National Commission on Egg Nutrition v. FTC, 570 F. 2d. (1978).

National Football League Players Association, 27 RR 2d 179 (1973).

National Research Council (NRC). (1989). *Improving risk communication.* Washington, DC: National Academy Press.

Nelkin, D. (1989). Communicating technological risk: The social construction of risk perception. *Annual Review of Public Health, 10,* 95–113.

Nelson, R. A., & Heath, R. L. (1986). A systems model for corporate issues management. *Public Relations Quarterly, 31*(3), 20–24.

Nelson, T. E., & Oxley, Z. M. (1999). Issue framing effects on belief importance and opinion. *Journal of Politics, 61,* 1040–1067.

Nelson, T. E., Oxley, Z. M., & Clawson, R. A. (1997). Toward a psychology of framing effects. *Political Behavior, 19*(3), 221–246.

New York Times Co. v. Sullivan, 376 U.S. 254 (1964).

Newman, K. M. (1988). *Toxic chemical disclosures: An overview of new problems, new opportunities for the professional communicator.* New York: Public Relations Society of America.

Nike. (2007). *Innovate for a better world: Nike FY05-06 corporate responsibility report.* Beaverton, OR: Author.

Nike, Inc. et al., v. Marc Kasky, 539 U.S. (2003).

Nimmo, D. D., & Combs, J. E. (1982). Fantasies and melodramas in television network news: The case of Three Mile Island. *Western Journal of Speech Communication, 47,* 45–55.

Noah, T. (1993, December 29). Ethanol boon shows how Archer-Daniels gets its way in Washington with low-key lobbying. *The Wall Street Journal,* p. A10.

Noelle-Neumann, E. (1983). The effect of media on media effects research. *Journal of Communication, 33*(3), 157–165.

Noelle-Neumann, E. (1984). *The spiral of silence: Public opinion—Our public skin.* Chicago: University of Chicago Press.

Norris, F. (1903). *The pit: A story of Chicago.* New York: Doubleday, Page.

Oberschall, A. (1973). *Social conflict and social movements.* Englewood Cliffs, NJ: Prentice Hall.

Oberschall, A. (1978). The decline of the 1960s social movements. In L. Kriegsberg (Ed.), *Research in social movements, conflict, and change: An annual compilation of research* (Vol. 1, pp. 257–289). Greenwich, CT: JAI.

Oepen, M. (2000). Environmental communication in a context. In M. Oepen & W. Hamacher (Eds.), *Communicating the environment: Environmental communication for sustainable development* (pp. 41–61). New York: Peter Lang.

Olasky, M. N. (1987). *Corporate public relations: A new historical perspective.* Hillsdale, NJ: Lawrence Erlbaum.

Opinion Research Corporation. (1981, June). Priority analysis of 45 national issues. *Public Opinion Index,* p. 39.

O'Rourke, D., & Macey, G. P. (2003). Community environmental policing: Assessing new strategies of public participation in environmental regulation. *Journal of Policy Analysis and Management, 22,* 383–414.

Oster, S., & Spencer, K. (2006, September 30). A poison spreads amid China's boom. *The Wall Street Journal,* pp. A1, A6.

Ostrow, S. D. (1991). It will happen here. *Bank Marketing, 23*(7), 24–27.

O'Toole, J. E. (1975a). Advocacy advertising act II. *Cross Currents in Corporate Communications, 2,* 33–37.

O'Toole, J. E. (1975b). Advocacy advertising shows the flag. *Public Relations Journal, 31*(11), 14–16.

Otten, A. L. (1984, December 31). States begin to protect employees who blow whistle on their firms. *The Wall Street Journal,* p. 11.

Otway, H. (1992). Public wisdom, expert fallibility: Toward a contextual theory of risk. In S. Krimsky & D. Golding (Eds.), *Social theories of risk* (pp. 215–228). Westport, CT: Praeger.

Owen, C., & Scherer, R. (1993). Social responsibility and market share. *Review of Business, 15*(1), 11–16.

Palenchar, M. J. (2008). Risk communication and community right to know: A public relations obligation to inform [Electronic version]. *Public Relations Journal, 2*(1), 1–26.

Palenchar, M. J. (2009). Historical trends in risk and crisis communication. In R. L. Heath & H. D. O'Hair (Eds.), *Handbook of crisis and risk communication* (pp. 31–53). New York: Routledge.

Palenchar, M. J., & Heath, R. L. (2002). Another part of the risk communication model: Analysis of communication processes and message content. *Journal of Public Relations Research, 13,* 127–158.

Palenchar, M. J., & Heath, R. L. (2006). Responsible advocacy through strategic risk communication. In K. Fitzpatrick & C. Bronstein (Eds.), *Ethics in public relations: What is responsible advocacy?* (pp. 131–153). Thousand Oaks, CA: Sage.

Palenchar, M. J., & Heath, R. L. (2007). Strategic risk communication: Adding value to society. *Public Relations Review, 33,* 120–129.

Palenchar, M. J., Heath, R. L., & Dunn, E. (2005). Terrorism and industrial chemical production: A new era of risk communication. *Communication Research Reports, 22*(1), 59–67.

Palese, M., & Crane, T. Y. (2002). Building an integrated issue management process as a source of sustainable competitive advantage. *Journal of Public Affairs, 2,* 284–293.

Paluszek, J. (1995). The rebirth of corporate social responsibility. *Public Relations Strategist, 1*(4), 48–51.

Parenti, M. (1986). *Inventing reality: The politics of the mass media.* New York: St. Martin's.

Patel, P. (2007, July 21). Conditions at BP similar to '05, OSHA says in fine. *Houston Chronicle,* pp. A1, A10.

Pauchant, T. C., & Mitroff, I. I. (1992). *Transforming the crisis-prone organization.* San Francisco: Jossey-Bass.

Pearce, W. B., & Cronen, V. E. (1980). *Communication, action, and meaning.* New York: Praeger.

Pearson, C. M., Clair, J. A., Misra, S. K., & Mitroff, I. I. (1997). Managing the unthinkable. *Organizational Dynamics, 26*(2), 51–64.

Pearson, R. (1989a). Beyond ethical relativism in public relations: Co-orientation, rules, and the idea of communication symmetry. In J. E. Grunig & L. A. Grunig (Eds.), *Public relations research annual* (Vol. 1, pp. 67–86). Hillsdale, NJ: Lawrence Erlbaum.

Pearson, R. (1989b). Business ethics as communication ethics: Public relations practice and the idea of dialogue. In C. H. Botan & V. Hazleton Jr. (Eds.), *Public relations theory* (pp. 111–131). Hillsdale, NJ: Lawrence Erlbaum.

Pearson, R. (1990). Ethical systems or strategic values? Two faces of systems theory in public relations. In L. A. Grunig & J. E. Grunig (Eds.), *Public relations research annual* (Vol. 2, pp. 219–234). Hillsdale, NJ: Lawrence Erlbaum.

Penrose, J. M. (2000). The role of perception in crisis planning. *Public Relations Review, 26*(2), 155–171.

Perspectives on current developments: Truth vs. provability at the FTC. (1983). *Regulation: AEI Journal of Government and Society, 7*(2), 4–6.

Peters, R. G., Covello, V. T., & McCallum, D. B. (1997). The determinants of trust and credibility in environmental risk communication: An empirical study. *Risk Analysis, 17*(1), 43–54.

Petersen, B. K., & Lang, A. R. (2000). *A 200-year analysis of U.S. Supreme Court interpretations of public relations.* Paper presented at the Association for Education in Journalism and Mass Communications Southeast Colloquium, Chapel Hill, NC.

Petrocik, J. R., Benoit, W. L., & Hansen, G. J. (2003). Issue ownership and presidential campaigning, 1952–2000. *Political Science Quarterly, 118,* 599–626.

Petty, R. E., & Cacioppo, J. T. (1986). *Communication and persuasion: Central and peripheral routes to attitude change.* New York: Springer-Verlag.

Petzinger, T., Jr., & Burrough, B. (1984, December 14). U.S. cities and towns ponder the potential for chemical calamity. *The Wall Street Journal,* pp. 1, 6.

Pfeffer, J. (1981). *Power in organizations.* Boston: Pitman.

Pfeffer, J. (1992). *Managing with power: Politics and influence in organizations.* Boston: Harvard Business School Press.

Phillips, K. (1981). Business and the media. *Public Affairs Review, 2,* 53–60.

Pidgeon, N., Kasperson, R. E., & Slovic, P. (2003). Introduction. In N. Pidgeon, R. E. Kasperson, & P. Slovic (Eds.), *The social amplification of risk* (pp. 1–11). Cambridge, UK: Cambridge University Press.

Pinkham, D. (2003). *Issues management.* Retrieved October 12, 2006, from http://www.pac.org/public/issues_management.shtml

Pinsdorf, M. K. (1991). Flying different skies: How cultures respond to airline disasters. *Public Relations Review, 17*(1), 37–56.

Pires, M. A. (1988). Building coalitions with external constituencies. In R. L. Heath (Ed.), *Strategic issues management: How organizations influence and respond to public interests and policies* (pp. 185–198). San Francisco: Jossey-Bass.

Pitta, D. A., & Katsanis, L. P. (1995). Understanding brand equity for successful brand extension. *Journal of Consumer Marketing, 12*(4), 51–64.

Plessy v. Ferguson, 163 U.S. 537 (1896).

Plough, A., & Krimsky, S. (1987). The emergence of risk communication studies: Social and political context. *Science, Technology, & Human Values, 12*(3–4), 4–10.

Post, J. E. (1978). *Corporate behavior and social change.* Reston, VA: Reston.

Post, J. E. (1979). Corporate response models and public affairs management. *Public Relations Quarterly, 24*(4), 27–32.

Post, J. E., Murray, E. A., Jr., Dickie, R. B., & Mahon, J. F. (1982). The public affairs function in American corporations: Development and relations with corporate planning. *Long Range Planning, 15*(2), 12–21.

Post, J. E., Murray, E. A., Jr., Dickie, R. B., & Mahon, J. F. (1983). Managing public affairs: The public affairs function. *California Management Review, 26,* 135–150.

Premeaux, S. R., & Mondy, R. W. (1993). Linking management behavior to ethical philosophy. *Journal of Business Ethics, 12,* 349–357.

Prior-Miller, M. (1989). Four major social scientific theories and their value to the public relations researcher. In C. H. Botan & V. Hazleton Jr. (Eds.), *Public relations theory* (pp. 67–81). Hillsdale, NJ: Lawrence Erlbaum.

Public Affairs Council. (1978). *The fundamentals of issue management.* Washington, DC: Author.

Public Relations Society of America (PRSA). (1987). Report of Special Committee on Terminology. *International Public Relations Review, 11*(2), 6–11.

Quarantelli, E. L. (1988). Disaster crisis management: A summary of research findings. *Journal of Management Studies, 25*(4), 373–385.

Quintilian. (1920–1922). *The institutio oratorio* (H. E. Butler, Trans., Vols. 1–4). Cambridge, MA: Harvard University Press.

Quintilian. (1966). *Quintilian on education* (W. Smail, Trans.). New York: Teachers College Press.

Radio Station KKHI, 47 RR 2d 839 (1980).

Raj, S. P. (1982, June). The effects of advertising on high and low loyalty consumer segments. *Journal of Consumer Research, 9,* 77–89.

Raucher, A. R. (1968). *Public relations and business: 1900–1929.* Baltimore: Johns Hopkins University Press.

Rawlins, B. L., & Bowen, S. A. (2004). Publics. In R. L. Heath (Ed.), *Encyclopedia of public relations* (pp. 718–721). Thousand Oaks, CA: Sage.

Rayner, S. (1992). Cultural theory and risk analysis. In S. Krimsky & D. Golding (Eds.), *Social theories of risk* (pp. 83–115). Westport, CT: Praeger.

Reber, B. H., & Berger, B. K. (2005). Framing analysis of activist rhetoric: How the Sierra Club succeeds or fails at creating salient messages. *Public Relations Review, 31,* 185–195.

Reber, B. H., & Kim, J. K. (2006). How activist groups use websites in media relations: Evaluating online press rooms. *Journal of Public Relations Research, 18,* 313–333.

Red Lion Broadcasting Co. v. FCC, 395 U.S. 367 (1969).

Reeves, P. N. (1993). Issues management: The other side of strategic planning. *Hospital & Health Services Administration, 38*(2), 229–241.

Renfro, W. L. (1982). Managing the issues of the 1980s. *The Futurist, 16*(8), 61–66.

Renfro, W. L. (1993). *Issues management in strategic planning.* Westport, CT: Quorum.

Renn, O. (1992a). Concepts of risk: A classification. In S. Krimsky & D. Golding (Eds.), *Social theories of risk* (pp. 53–79). Westport, CT: Praeger.

Renn, O. (1992b). The social arena concept of risk debates. In S. Krimsky & D. Golding (Eds.), *Social theories of risk* (pp. 179–196). Westport, CT: Praeger.

Renn, O. (2009). Communication: Insights and requirements for designing successful communication programs on health and environmental hazards. In R. L. Heath & H. D. O'Hair (Eds.), *Handbook of crisis and risk communication* (pp. 81–99). New York: Routledge.

Reno v. American Civil Liberties Union, 521 U.S. 844, 117 S.Ct. 2329 (1997).

Report on the Handling of Public Issues Under the Fairness Doctrine and the Public Interest Standards of the Communications Act, 48 FCC 2d a (1974).

Reynolds, B. (2002, October). *Crisis and emergency risk communication.* Atlanta, GA: Centers for Disease Control and Prevention.

Rhody, R. (1983). The public's right to know. *IPRA Review, 7*(11), 46–47.

Richards, J. I. (1990). *Deceptive advertising: Behavioral study of a legal concept.* Hillsdale, NJ: Lawrence Erlbaum.

Rohrmann, B., Wiedemann, P. M., & Stegelmann, H. U. (Eds.). (1990). *Risk communication: An interdisciplinary bibliography* (4th ed.). Jülich, Germany: Research Center.

Ronick, H. R. (1983). The F.T.C.: An overview. *Cases & Comment, 88*(4), 35–38.

Roper, J. (2002). Government, corporate or social power? The Internet as a tool in the struggle for dominance in public policy. *Journal of Public Affairs, 2,* 113–124.

Roper, J. (2005). Symmetrical communication: Excellent public relations or a strategy of hegemony? *Journal of Public Relations Review, 17,* 69–86.

Rosenblatt, R. (1984, December 17). All the world gasped. *Time,* p. 20.

Ross, I. (1976). Public relations isn't kid glove stuff at Mobil. *Fortune, 94*(9), 106–111, 196–202.

Rowan, K. (1994). What risk communicators need to know: An agenda for research. In B. R. Burleson (Ed.), *Communication yearbook* (Vol. 18, pp. 300–319). Thousand Oaks, CA: Sage.

Rowan, K., Botan, C., Kreps, G., Samoilenko, S., & Farnsworth, K. (2009). Risk communication education for local emergency managers: Using the CAUSE model for research, education, and outreach. In R. L. Heath & H. D. O'Hair (Eds.), *Handbook of crisis and risk communication* (pp. 170–193). New York: Routledge.

Ryan, M. (1986). Public relations practitioners' views of corporate social responsibility. *Journalism Quarterly, 63,* 740–747.

Ryan, M., & Martinson, D. L. (1983). The PR officer as corporate conscience. *Public Relations Quarterly, 28*(2), 20–23.

Ryan, M., & Martinson, D. L. (1984). Ethical values, the flow of journalistic information and public relations persons. *Journalism Quarterly, 61*, 27–34.

Ryan, M., & Martinson, D. L. (1985). Public relations practitioners, public interest and management. *Journalism Quarterly, 62*, 111–115.

Sandman, P. M. (1993). *Responding to community outrage: Strategies for effective risk communication.* Fairfax, VA: American Industrial Hygiene Association.

SARA: Superfund Amendments and Reauthorization Act of 1986 (SARA), U.S. Code, vol. 42, sec. 9601, et seq. (1995).

Sawaya, R. N., & Arrington, C. B. (1988). Linking corporate planning with strategic issues. In R. L. Heath (Ed.), *Strategic issues management: How organizations influence and respond to public interests and policies* (pp. 73–86). San Francisco: Jossey-Bass.

Scherer, C. W., & Cho, H. (2003). A social network contagion theory of risk perception. *Risk Analysis, 23*, 261–267.

Scheufele, D. A., & Tewksbury, D. (2007). Framing, agenda setting, and priming: The evolution of three media effects models. *Journal of Communication, 57*(1), 9–20.

Schlosser, E. (2006). *Chew on this.* Boston: Houghton Mifflin.

Schmertz, H. (1986). *Good-bye to the low profile: The art of creative confrontation.* Boston: Little, Brown.

Schneider, M. D. (1996). Telecom act throws open competition in electronic mass media and telecommunications. *Communications Lawyer, 14*(2), 9–10.

Schuler, D. A. (2001). Public affairs, issues management and political strategy: Methodological approaches that count. *Journal of Public Affairs, 1/2*, 336–355.

Schultze, Q. J. (1981). Advertising and public utilities: 1900–1917. *Journal of Advertising, 10*(4), 41–44, 48.

Schwenk, C. R. (1984). Cognitive simplification processes in strategic decision making. *Strategic Management Journal, 5*, 111–128.

Scott, R. L., & Smith D. K. (1969). The rhetoric of confrontation. *Quarterly Journal of Speech, 55*, 1–8.

Seeger, M. W., Sellnow, T. L., & Ulmer, R. R. (2003). *Communication and organizational crisis.* Westport, CT: Praeger.

Selikoff, I. J., Churg, J., & Hammond, E. C. (1964). Asbestos exposure and neoplasia. *Journal of American Medical Association, 188*, 22–26.

Sellnow, T. L., Seeger, M. W., & Ulmer, R. R. (2002). Chaos theory, informational needs, and natural disasters. *Journal of Applied Communication Research, 30*, 269–292.

Sellnow, T. L., Ulmer, R. R., & Seeger, M. W. (2004). Stakes. In R. L. Heath (Ed.), *Encyclopedia of public relations* (pp. 811–813). Thousand Oaks, CA: Sage.

Sethi, S. P. (1976a). Dangers of advocacy advertising. *Public Relations Journal, 32*(11), 42–47.

Sethi, S. P. (1976b, Summer). Management fiddles while public affairs flops. *Business and Society Review, 18*, 9–11.

Sethi, S. P. (1977). *Advocacy advertising and large corporations: Social conflict, big business image, the news media, and public policy.* Lexington, MA: D. C. Heath.

Sethi, S. P. (1981, November). *Advocacy advertising in America.* Keynote address given to the Advocacy Advertising Conference, sponsored by the Conference Board of Canada, Toronto, Ontario.

Sethi, S. P. (1987). A novel communications approach to building effective relations with external constituencies. *International Journal of Advertising, 6,* 279–298.

Shants, F. B. (1978). Countering the anti-nuclear activists. *Public Relations Journal, 34*(10), 10.

Shapiro, M. D. (2005). Equity and information: Information regulation, environmental justice, and risks from toxic chemicals. *Journal of Policy Analysis and Management, 24,* 373–398.

Sherif, C., Sherif, M., & Nebergall, R. (1965). *Attitude and attitude change: The social judgment-involvement approach.* Philadelphia: W. B. Saunders.

Shrivastava, P. (1987). *Bhopal: Anatomy of a crisis.* Cambridge, MA: Ballinger.

Simms, M. (1994). Defining privacy in employee health screening cases: Ethical ramifications concerning the employee/employer relationship. *Journal of Business Ethics, 13,* 315–325.

Simons, H. W. (1970). Requirements, problems, and strategies: A theory of persuasion for social movements. *Quarterly Journal of Speech, 56,* 1–11.

Simons, H. W. (1972). Persuasion in social conflicts: A critique of prevailing conceptions and a framework for future research. *Speech Monographs, 39,* 229–247.

Simons, H. W. (1974). The carrot and stick as handmaidens of persuasion in conflict situations. In G. R. Miller & H. W. Simons (Eds.), *Perspectives on communication in social conflict* (pp. 172–205). Englewood Cliffs, NJ: Prentice Hall.

Simons, H. W. (1976). Changing notions about social movements. *Quarterly Journal of Speech, 62,* 425–430.

Sims, R. R. (1992). The challenge of ethical behavior in organizations. *Journal of Business Ethics, 11,* 505–513.

Sinclair, U. (1906). *The jungle.* New York: Doubleday, Page.

Sjoberg, L. (2000). Factors in risk perception. *Risk Analysis, 20,* 1–11.

Slovic, P. (1979). Rating the risks. *Environment, 21*(3), 14–39.

Slovic, P. (1987). Perception of risk. *Science, 230,* 280–285.

Slovic, P. (1992). Perception of risk: Reflections on the psychometric paradigm. In S. Krimsky & D. Golding (Eds.), *Social theories of risk* (pp. 117–152). Westport, CT: Praeger.

Slovic, P., Fischhoff, B., & Lichtenstein, S. (1987). Behavioral decision theory perspectives on protective behavior. In N. D. Weinstein (Ed.), *Taking care: Understanding and encouraging self-protected behavior* (pp. 14–41). Cambridge, UK: Cambridge University Press.

Small, W. J. (1991). Exxon *Valdez:* How to spend billions and still get a black eye. *Public Relations Review, 17*(1), 9–25.

Smelser, N. J. (1963). *Theory of collective behavior.* New York: Free Press.

Smith, J. W. (1991). Thinking about brand equity and the analysis of customer transactions. In K. L. Keller (Ed.), *Strategic brand management: Building, measuring, and managing brand equity* (pp. 13–48). Upper Saddle River, NJ: Prentice Hall.

Smith, M. B. (2001). 'Silence, Miss Carson!' Science, gender, and the reception of Silent Spring. *Feminist Studies, 27,* 733–752.

Smith, M. E., & Ferguson, D. P. (2001). Activism. In R. L. Heath (Ed.), *Handbook of public relations* (pp. 291–300). Thousand Oaks, CA: Sage.

Smith, M. F. (2005). Activism. In R. L. Heath (Ed.), *Encyclopedia of public relations* (pp. 5–9). Thousand Oaks, CA: Sage.

Smith, N. C. (1995). Marketing strategies for the ethics era. *Sloan Management Review,* *36*(4), 85–97.

Smith, R., & Carlton, J. (2007, March 3–4). Environmentalist groups feud over terms of the TXU buyout. *The Wall Street Journal,* pp. A1, A6.

Solomon, C. (1993, April 15). Exxon attacks scientific views of *Valdez* spill. *The Wall Street Journal,* pp. B1, B5.

Solomon, J. B., & Russell, M. (1984, December 14). U.S. chemical disclosure-law efforts getting boost from tragedy in Bhopal. *The Wall Street Journal,* p. 18.

Sowa, B. C. (2005). Brand equity and branding. In R. L. Heath (Ed.), *Encyclopedia of public relations* (pp. 95–98). Thousand Oaks, CA: Sage.

Spencer, T. (2004). Of legitimacy, legality and public affairs. *Journal of Public Affairs, 4,* 205–209.

Spicer, C. H. (2007). Collaborative advocacy and the creation of trust: Toward an understanding of stakeholder claims and risks. In E. L. Toth (Ed.), *The future of excellence in public relations and communication management* (pp. 27–40). Mahwah, NJ: Lawrence Erlbaum.

Spickett-Jones, J. G., Kitchen, P. J., & Reast, J. D. (2003). Social facts and ethical hardware: Ethics in the value proposition. *Journal of Communication Management, 8*(1), 68–82.

Springston, J. K., & Keyton, J. (2001). Public relations field dynamics. In R. L. Heath (Ed.), *Handbook of public relations* (pp. 115–126). Thousand Oaks, CA: Sage.

Sproule, J. M. (1989). Organizational rhetoric and the public sphere. *Communication Studies, 40,* 258–265.

Starr, C. (1969). Social benefit versus technological risk. *Science, 165,* 1232–1238.

Steckmest, F. W. (with the Resource and Review Committee for the Business Roundtable). (1982). *Corporate performance: The key to public trust.* New York: McGraw-Hill.

Steffens, L. (1904). *The shame of the cities.* New York: McClure, Phillips.

Steffy, L. (2007a). New boss knows he has plenty to do to repair BP's tattered image. *Houston Chronicle,* pp. A1, A8.

Steffy, L. (2007b, February 28). Welcome to state's Wild West utility deregulation. *Houston Chronicle,* pp. D1, D5.

Stephenson, D. R. (1982). How to turn pitfalls into opportunities in crisis situations. *Public Relations Quarterly, 27*(3), 11–15.

Stewart, C., Smith, C., & Denton, R. E., Jr. (1984). *Persuasion and social movements.* Prospect Heights, IL: Waveland.

Stridsberg, A. B. (1977). *Corporate advertising: How advertisers present points of view in public affairs.* New York: Hastings House.

Stroup, M. A. (1988). Identifying critical issues for better corporate planning. In R. L. Heath (Ed.), *Strategic issues management: How organizations influence and respond to public interests and policies* (pp. 87–97). San Francisco: Jossey-Bass.

Stryker, S., Owens, T. J., & White, R. W. (Eds.). (2000). *Self, identity, and social movements.* Minneapolis: University of Minnesota Press.

Sullivan, A. (1993, August 31). Oil industry projects a surge in outlays to meet U.S. environmental standards. *The Wall Street Journal,* p. A2.

Szasz, A. (1994). *Ecopopulism.* Minneapolis: University of Minnesota Press.

Tansey, J., & Rayner, S. (2009). Cultural theory and risk. In R. L. Heath & H. D. O'Hair (Eds.), *Handbook of crisis and risk communication* (pp. 53–80). New York: Routledge.

Tarbell, I. (1904). *The history of the Standard Oil Company*. New York: McClure, Phillips.

Tarde, G. (1922). *L'opinion et la foule* [Opinion and the crowd]. Paris: Alcan.

Tedlow, R. S. (1979). *Keeping the corporate image: Public relations and business: 1900–1950*. Greenwich, CT: JAI.

Thomas, J. B., Clark, S. M., & Giola, D. A. (1993). Strategic sensemaking and organizational performance: Linkages among scanning, interpretation, action, and outcomes. *Academy of Management Journal, 36,* 239–270.

Thomas, K., Swaton, E., Fishbein, M., & Otway, H. J. (1980). Nuclear energy: The accuracy of policy makers' perceptions of public beliefs. *Behavioral Science, 25,* 332–344.

Tichenor, P. J., Donohue, G. A., & Olien, C. H. (1977). Community research and evaluating community relations. *Public Relations Review, 3*(4), 96–109.

Toch, H. (1965). *The social psychology of social movements*. Indianapolis, IN: Bobbs-Merrill.

Toth, E. L. (2006). Building public affairs. In C. Botan & V. Hazleton (Eds.), *Public relations theory II* (pp. 499–522). Mahwah, NJ: Lawrence Erlbaum.

Toulmin, S. E. (1964). *The uses of argument*. Cambridge, UK: Cambridge University Press.

Trans-fat content in fast foods varies widely by country, city. (2006, April 13). *The Wall Street Journal*, p. D3.

Trost, C. (1985, January 7). Bhopal disaster spurs debate over usefulness of criminal sanctions in industrial accidents. *The Wall Street Journal*, p. 14.

Tucker, K., Broom, G., & Caywood, C. (1993). Managing issues acts as bridge to strategic planning. *Public Relations Journal, 49*(11), 38–40.

Tucker, K., & McNerney, S. L. (1992). Building coalitions to initiate change. *Public Relations Journal, 48*(1), 28–30.

Tucker, K., & Trumpfheller, B. (1993). Building an issues management system. *Public Relations Journal, 49*(11), 36–37.

Tversky, A., & Kahneman, D. (1986). Judgment under uncertainty: Heuristics and biases. In H. R. Arkes & K. R. Hammond (Eds.), *Judgment and decision making* (pp. 38–55). Cambridge, UK: Cambridge University Press.

Tyler, L. (2005). Towards a postmodern understanding of crisis communication. *Public Relations Review, 31,* 566–571.

Ulmer, R. R., Seeger, M. W., & Sellnow, T. L. (2004). Stakeholder theory. In R. L. Heath (Ed.), *Encyclopedia of public relations* (pp. 808–811). Thousand Oaks, CA: Sage.

Ulmer, R. R., Sellnow, T. L., & Seeger, M. W. (2007). *Effective crisis communication: Moving from crisis to opportunity*. Thousand Oaks, CA: Sage.

Union Carbide. (2004, October). *Chronology of key events related to the Bhopal Incident*. Retrieved February 28, 2007, from http://bhopal.net/bhopal.con/chronology

U.S. Chemical Safety and Hazard Investigation Board. (2007). *BP America refinery explosion*. Retrieved December 17, 2007, from http://www.chemsafety.gov/index.cfm?folder=current_investigations&page=info&INV_ID=52

U.S. Congress. (1978a). *House of Representatives, Committee on Government Operations, IRS administration of tax laws relating to lobbying* (95th Cong., 2nd sess.). Washington, DC: Government Printing Office.

U.S. Congress. (1978b). *Senate, Committee on the Judiciary, Subcommittee on Administrative Practice and Procedure, sourcebook on corporate image and corporate advocacy advertising* (95th Cong., 2nd sess.). Washington, DC: Government Printing Office.

U.S. Consumer Product Safety Commission. (2006, March 23). *Reebok recalls bracelet linked to child's lead poisoning death.* Retrieved February 14, 2008, from http://www.cpsc.gov/cpscpub/prerel/prhtml06/06119.html

Vaara, E., Tienari, J., & Laurila, J. (2006). Pulp and paper fiction: On the discursive legitimation of global industrial restructuring. *Organization Studies, 27,* 789–810.

Valente, T. W., Paredes, P., & Poppe, P. R. (1998). Matching the message to the process: The relative ordering of knowledge, attitudes, and practices in behavior change research. *Human Communication Research, 24,* 366–385.

Van Ruler, B., & Vercic, D. (2005). Reflective communication management: Future ways for public relations research. In P. J. Kalbfleisch (Ed.), *Communication yearbook* (Vol. 29, pp. 239–273). Mahwah, NJ: Lawrence Erlbaum.

Viosca, C. R., Jr., Bergiel, B. J., & Balsmeier, P. (2005). Country equity: South Africa, a case in point. *Journal of Promotion Management, 12*(1), 85–95.

Virginia State Board of Pharmacy v. Virginia Citizens Consumer Council, 425 U.S. 748 (1976).

Wallace, K. R. (1963). The substance of rhetoric: Good reasons. *Quarterly Journal of Speech, 49,* 239–249.

Wallack, L., Dorfman, L., Jernigan, D., & Themba, M. (1993). *Media advocacy and public health.* Newbury Park, CA: Sage.

Walgrave, S., & Van Aeist, P. (2006). The contingency of the mass media's political agenda setting power: Toward a preliminary theory. *Journal of Communication, 56,* 88–109.

Wan, H., & Pfau, M. (2004). The relative effectiveness of inoculation, bolstering, and combined approaches in crisis communication. *Journal of Public Relations Research,* 16(3), 301–328.

Ware, B. L., & Linkugel, W. A. (1973). They spoke in defense of themselves: On the generic criticism of apologia. *Quarterly Journal of Speech, 59,* 273–283.

Wartick, S. L., & Cochran, P. L. (1985). The evolution of corporate responsibility model. *Academy of Management Review, 10,* 759–769.

Wartick, S. L., & Mahon, J. F. (1994). Toward a substantive definition of the corporate issue construct. *Business & Society, 33,* 293–311.

Wartick, S. L., & Rude, R. E. (1986). Issues management: Corporate fad or corporate function? *California Management Review, 29*(1), 124–140.

Waymer, D., & Heath, R. L. (2007). Emergent agents: The forgotten publics in crisis communication and issues management research. *Journal of Applied Communication Research, 35,* 88–108.

Waz, J. (1983). Fighting the fair fight. *Channels, 2*(2), 66–69.

WCMP Broadcasting Co., 27 RR 2d 1000 (1973).

Weaver, D. H. (2007). Thoughts on agenda setting, framing, and priming. *Journal of Communication, 57,* 142–147.

Weaver, P. H. (1988). The self-destructive corporation. *California Management Review, 30*(3), 128–143.

Webler, T., & Tuler, S. (2006). Four perspectives on public participation process in environmental assessment and decision making: Combined results from 10 case studies. *Policy Studies Journal, 34,* 699–722.

Weick, K. E. (1988). Enacted sensemaking in crisis situations. *Journal of Management Studies, 25,* 305–317.

Weinstein, A. K. (1979). Management issues for the coming decade. *University of Michigan Business Review, 31*(9), 29–32.

Weissman, G. (1984). Social responsibility and corporate success. *Business and Society Review, 51,* 67–68.

Werder, K. P. (2006). Responding to activism: An experimental analysis of public relations strategy influence on attributes of publics. *Journal of Public Relations Research, 18,* 335–356.

Whitaker, M., Mazumdar, S., Gibney, F., Jr., & Behr, E. (1984, December 17). It was like breathing fire. *Newsweek,* pp. 26–32.

White, H. (1981). The value of narrative in the representation of reality. In W. J. T. Mitchell (Ed.), *On narrative* (pp. 1–23). Chicago: University of Chicago Press.

Widmer, L. (2000, Nov.). When your name is at risk. *Risk and Insurance.* Retrieved March 3, 2007, from: http://findarticles.com/p/articles/mi_m0BJK/is_14_11/ai_67315650/pg_2

Wiebe, R. H. (1967). *The search for order: 1877–1920.* New York: Hill & Wang.

Wiebe, R. H. (1968). *Businessmen and reform: A study of the progressive movement.* Chicago: Quadrangle.

William F. Bolger et al. v. Young Drug Products Corp., USDC Dist Col, 526 FSupp, 823 (1981).

Williams, P. R. (1982). The new technology and its implications for organizational communicators. *Public Relations Quarterly, 27*(1), 15–16.

Winslow, R. (1985a, January 28). Union Carbide moved to bar accident at U.S. plant before Bhopal tragedy. *The Wall Street Journal,* p. 6.

Winslow, R. (1985b, February 13). Union Carbide plans to resume making methyl isocyanate at its U.S. facility. *The Wall Street Journal,* p. 2.

Winters, L. C. (1988). Does it pay to advertise to hostile audiences with corporate advertising? *Journal of Advertising Research, 28*(3), 11–18.

Witte, K., Meyer, G., & Martel, D. (2000). *Effective health risk messages.* Thousand Oaks, CA: Sage.

Wood, L. (2000). Brands and brand equity: Definition and management. *Management Decision, 38,* 662–669.

Wynder, E. L., Graham, E. A., & Croninger, A. B. (1953). Experimental production of carcinoma with cigarette tar. *Cancer Research, 13,* 855–864.

Wynne, B. (1992). Risk and social learning: Refinement to engagement. In S. Krimsky & D. Golding (Eds.), *Social theories of risk* (pp. 275–300). Westport, CT: Praeger.

Wynne, B. (1996). May the sheep safely graze? A reflexive view of the expert-lay knowledge divide. In S. Lash, B. Szerszynski, & B. Wynne (Eds.), *Risk, environment and modernity: Towards a new ecology* (pp. 44–83). London: Sage.

Zachary, G. P. (1992, February 6). All the news? *The Wall Street Journal,* pp. A1, A8.

Zamiska, N., Leow, J., & Oster, S. (2007, May 30). China confronts crisis over food safety. *Wall Street Journal,* p. A3.

Zhu, J., Watt, J. H., Snyder, L. B., Yan, J., & Jiang, Y. (1993). Public issue priority formation: Media agenda setting and social interaction. *Journal of Communication, 43*(1), 8–29.

Index

About the Authors

Robert L. Heath is Professor Emeritus at the School of Communication, University of Houston, and Academic Consultant in the College of Commerce, Faculty of Management and Marketing at the University of Wollongong in Australia. He is one of the academic pioneers in examining the history and theoretical foundations of strategic issues management. He is author or editor of 12 books (and 2 second editions) and 100 articles in major journals and leading edited books. In addition to strategic issues management, he has written on rhetorical theory, social movements, communication theory, public relations, organizational communication, crisis communication, risk communication, terrorism, and reputation management. He edited the *Encyclopedia of Public Relations* and the *Handbook of Public Relations*. He has lectured in many countries, to business and nonprofit groups, and for various professional organizations. In May 2007, he was saluted by the Issue Management Council for his leadership over 3 decades to foster mutual interests between the corporation and all stakeholders and stakeseekers.

Michael J. Palenchar is an Assistant Professor in Public Relations at the University of Tennessee's School of Advertising and Public Relations, College of Communication and Information (PhD, University of Florida; MA, University of Houston). Research interests include risk communication and issues management related to manufacturing, community relations and community awareness of emergency response protocols and manufacturing risks, community right-to-know issues, crisis communication, front groups, and general public relations. He has more than a decade of professional experience working in corporate, nonprofit, and agency environments, and he is also a risk communication and issues management research consultant for clients ranging from *Fortune* 500 companies to local government and nongovernmental agencies. His research has been published in the *Journal of Public Relations Research, Public Relations Review, Public Relations Journal, Environmental Communication,* and *Communication Research Reports*. He has 5 book chapters on risk, terrorism, and professional ethics and more than 40 regional, national, or international communication conference papers, winning 12 national or international top paper awards. With coauthor Robert L. Heath in 2000 and Kathy Fitzpatrick in 2007, he won the Pride Award from the Public Relations Division, National Communication Association, for top published article in the field of public relations. He is an active member of Association for Education in Journalism and Mass Communication, National Communication Association, Public Relations Society of America, and International Communication Association.